A Comprehensive Manual of Abhidhamma

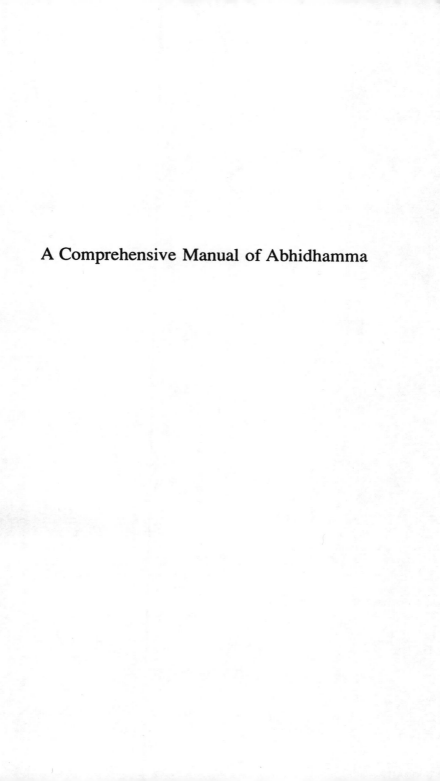

A Comprehensive Manual of Abhidhamma

The Abhidhammattha Sangaha of Ācariya Anuruddha

Bhikkhu Bodhi, General Editor

Pali text originally edited and translated by
Mahāthera Nārada

Translation revised by
Bhikkhu Bodhi

Introduction and explanatory guide by
U Rewata Dhamma & Bhikkhu Bodhi

Abhidhamma tables by
U Sīlānanda

BUDDHIST PUBLICATION SOCIETY
KANDY SRI LANKA

Published in 1993

Buddhist Publication Society
P.O. Box 61
54, Sangharaja Mawatha
Kandy, Sri Lanka

Grateful acknowledgement is made to the Pali Text Society and to Ven. U Sīlānanda for permission to use the Abhidhamma tables indicated in "A Note on the Tables" following the Preface.

ISBN 955-24-0103-8

Typeset at the BPS
Text set in Times with Helvetica headings
Tables typeset by Karunaratne & Sons Ltd.

Printed in Sri Lanka by
Karunaratne & Sons Ltd.
647, Kularatne Mawatha
Colombo 10.

ABOUT THE CONTRIBUTORS

MAHĀTHERA NĀRADA was born in Colombo in 1898. At the age of 18 he was ordained as a novice under the revered teacher, Ven. Pelene Vajirañāṇa Mahānāyaka Thera, and at the age of 20 he received the higher ordination. During his 65 years in the Sangha, Ven. Nārada distinguished himself by his piety, his disciplined conduct, and his work in propagating the Buddha Dhamma both in Sri Lanka and abroad. He passed away in Colombo in 1983. Ven. Nārada is best known for his book *The Buddha and His Teachings*, widely regarded as one of the clearest and most detailed introductions to Theravada Buddhism in English.

BHIKKHU BODHI is a Buddhist monk of American nationality, born in New York City in 1944. After completing a doctorate in philosophy at the Claremont Graduate School, he came to Sri Lanka for the purpose of entering the Sangha. He received novice ordination in 1972 and higher ordination in 1973, both under the eminent scholar-monk, Ven. Balangoda Ananda Maitreya, with whom he studied Pali and Dhamma. He is the author of several works on Theravada Buddhism, including four translations of major Pali suttas along with their commentaries. Since 1984 he has been the Editor for the Buddhist Publication Society, and since 1988 its President.

U REWATA DHAMMA was born in Burma and entered the monastery at an early age. He studied Pali and Theravada Buddhism under various eminent scholar- monks in Burma and passed the highest examination in scriptural studies at the age of 23. In 1953 the then president of Burma awarded him the prestigious title of *Sāsanadhaja-siripavara-dhammācariya*. He studied in India from 1956 to 1967, obtaining a doctorate from the Benares Hindu University. In 1975 he moved to England, where he established a Buddhist centre in Birmingham as his base, and he now teaches meditation and Buddhism at various centres in Europe and the United States. Ven. Rewata Dhamma edited and published the *Abhidhammattha Sangaha* with the *Vibhāvinī-Ṭīkā* in 1965 and the *Visuddhimagga* with its *Mahā-Ṭīkā* in 1970, both in Varanasi. His translation of the *Abhidhammattha Sangaha* into Hindi, with his own commentary written in Hindi, was published in 1967 and was awarded the Kalidasa Prize by the Hindi Academy as one of the outstanding books of the year. It is used as a textbook in Buddhist studies in many universities in India.

U SILĀNANDA was born in Burma and has been a Buddhist monk since 1947. He holds two degrees of *Dhammācariya* (Master of Dhamma) and was a university lecturer in Pali and Buddhist studies in Sagaing and Mandalay. He held a prominent position in the Sixth Buddhist Council, convened in Rangoon in 1954, as the chief compiler of the comprehensive Pali-Burmese Dictionary and as one of the final editors of the Pali Canon and Commentaries. Since 1979 he has been living in the United States, where he teaches Vipassana meditation, Abhidhamma, and various other aspects of Theravada Buddhism. Ven. Sīlānanda is the Founder-abbot of the Dhammānanda Vihara and the Spiritual Director of the Theravada Buddhist Society of America and the Dhammachakka Meditation Center in California. His book *The Four Foundations of Mindfulness* is published by Wisdom Publications.

GENERAL CONTENTS

DETAILED CONTENTS

CHAPTER I
COMPENDIUM OF CONSCIOUSNESS

CHAPTER II
COMPENDIUM OF MENTAL FACTORS

CHAPTER III
COMPENDIUM OF THE MISCELLANEOUS

CHAPTER IV
COMPENDIUM OF THE COGNITIVE PROCESS

CHAPTER V

COMPENDIUM OF THE PROCESS-FREED

CHAPTER VI
COMPENDIUM OF MATTER

CHAPTER VII
COMPENDIUM OF CATEGORIES

CHAPTER IX

COMPENDIUM OF MEDITATION SUBJECTS

LIST OF TABLES

CHAPTER I

CHAPTER II

CHAPTER III

CHAPTER IV

CHAPTER V

CHAPTER VI

CHAPTER VII

CHAPTER VIII

CHAPTER IX

ABBREVIATIONS

Names of Texts

A.	Anguttara Nikāya
Asl.	Atthasālinī (commentary to Dhs.)
D.	Dīgha Nikāya
Dhs.	Dhammasanganī
Expos.	*The Expositor* (trans. of Asl.)
M.	Majjhima Nikāya
Pṭs.	Paṭisambhidāmagga
S.	Saṁyutta Nikāya
Smv.	Sammohavinodanī (commentary to Vibhanga)
Vibhv.	Vibhāvinī-Ṭīkā
Vism.	Visuddhimagga

In references to Pali texts separated by a slash, the figure to the left of the slash indicates the number of the text, the figure to the right the volume and page number of the Pali Text Society edition. References to Vism. are to chapter and section number of Bhikkhu Ñāṇamoli's translation, *The Path of Purification*.

Terms used in Tables

Advt.	adverting
aggr.	aggregate
Arh.	Arahant, Arahantship
assoc.	associated (with)
bhv.	bhavanga
btf.	beautiful
cetas.	cetasika
comp.	compassion
conas.	conascent
cons.	consciousness
consness.	consciousness
delus.	delusion
dissoc.	dissociated (from)
eqn.	equanimity
exc.	except
exs.	course of existence
FMS	fine-material sphere
fnc.	functional

frt.	fruition
gt.	great
gt. ess.	great essential
in. applic.	initial application
infr.	inferior
IS	immaterial sphere
invs.	investigating
jav.	javana
knwl.	knowledge
mat.	material, matter
m-d-advt.	mind-door adverting
med.	medium
mun.	mundane
n.p. nor n-p.	neither perception nor non-perception
N.R.	non-returner, non-returning
one-ptns.	one-pointedness
O.R.	once-returner, once-returning
reb.	rebirth-linking
recv.	receiving
rst.	resultant
rtd.	rooted
rtls.	rootless
sbl.	sublime
S.E.	stream-enterer, stream-entry
spm.	supramundane
SS	sense sphere
supr.	superior
sus. applic.	sustained application
univ.	universal
unwh.	unwholesome
w.	with
wh.	wholesome
wo.	without

PREFACE

The present volume contains the Pali text, an English translation, and a detailed exposition of Ācariya Anuruddha's *Abhidhammattha Sangaha*, the main primer for the study of Abhidhamma used throughout the Theravada Buddhist world. This volume began almost four years ago as a revised version of Ven. Mahāthera Nārada's long-standing edition and annotated translation of the *Sangaha, A Manual of Abhidhamma*. Now, as the time approaches for it to go to press, it has evolved into what is virtually an entirely new book published under essentially the same title. That title has been retained partly to preserve its continuity with its predecessor, and partly because the name "Manual of Abhidhamma" is simply the most satisfactory English rendering of the Pali title of the root text, which literally means "a compendium of the things contained in the Abhidhamma." To the original title the qualification "comprehensive" has been added to underscore its more extensive scope.

A brief account seems to be called for of the evolution through which this book has gone. Although Ven. Nārada's *Manual*, in the four editions through which it passed, had served admirably well for decades as a beginner's guide to the Abhidhamma, the work obviously required upgrading both in technical exposition and in arrangement. Thus when the need for a reprint of the *Manual* became imminent in late 1988, I contacted Ven. U Rewata Dhamma of the Buddhist Vihara, Birmingham, requesting him to prepare a set of corrections to the explanatory notes in the Fourth Edition. I also suggested that he should add any further information he thought would be useful to the serious student of Abhidhamma. I particularly wanted the assistance of Ven. U Rewata Dhamma in this task because he sustains a rare combination of qualifications: he is a traditionally trained bhikkhu from Burma, the heartland of Theravada Abhidhamma studies; he has himself edited the *Abhidhammattha Sangaha* and its classical commentary, the *Vibhāvinī-Ṭīkā*; he has written his own commentary on the work (in Hindi); and he is fluent in English.

While Ven. Rewata Dhamma in England was compiling his revisions to the notes, in Sri Lanka I set about reviewing Ven. Nārada's English translation of the *Sangaha*. A close comparison with the Pali text in several editions, and with the commentarial gloss, led to a number of changes both in the translation and in Ven. Nārada's Pali edition of the root text. In revising the translation my objective was not merely to correct minor errors but also to achieve a high degree of consistency and adequacy in the rendering of Pali technical terms. To facilitate cross-references to *The Path of Purification*, Bhikkhu Ñāṇamoli's masterly translation of the *Visuddhimagga,* I adopted much of the terminology used in the latter work, though in some instances I have allowed Ven. Nārada's choices to stand while in others I have opted for still different alternatives. Towards the very close of my editorial work on the *Manual* I came upon the Pali Text Society's recent edition of the *Abhidhammattha Sangaha*, edited by Ven. Hammalawa Saddhātissa. This enabled me to make a few additional corrections of the Pali text, but unfortunately I encountered this edition too late to utilize its scheme for numbering the paragraphs of the *Sangaha.*

The major challenge in preparing this new edition was the composing of the explanatory guide. At first, when we started work, our intention was to retain as much as we could of Ven. Nārada's original annotations, making alterations in them and introducing new material only when we thought this would be necessary or especially desirable. However, as we proceeded, it soon became clear that far more sweeping changes were required. The wish to provide precise and detailed explanations of all the essential principles comprised in the *Abhidhammattha Sangaha* sent both Ven. Rewata Dhamma and myself for frequent consultations to the *Sangaha's* two principal commentaries, the *Abhidhammattha-vibhāvinī-Ṭīkā* by Ācariya Sumangalasāmi (Sri Lanka, late twelfth century) and the *Paramatthadīpanī-Ṭīkā* by Ledi Sayadaw (Burma, first published in 1897). It is from these two commentaries that much of the explanatory material in the guide has been extracted.

These two commentaries, as is well known among Abhidhamma scholars, often take opposite stands in their handling of technical questions, the Ledi Sayadaw commentary launching a sustained critique of the older work. Since our purpose here has been to elucidate the fundamental tenets of the Abhidhamma rather than to enter into the fray of controversy, we have focused on the convergences between the two commentaries or their complementary contributions. Generally we have avoided the contentions that divide them, though on occasion, when their differences seemed intrinsically interesting, we have cited their mutually opposed opinions. A great amount of information has also been drawn from the *Visuddhimagga*, which includes a lengthy Abhidhamma-style tract in its chapters on "the soil of understanding" (*paññābhūmi,* XIV-XVII).

From the mass of explanatory material thus collected, we have tried to compose a detailed guide to the *Abhidhammattha Sangaha* that will at once be capable of steering the newcomer through the intricacies of the Abhidhamma yet will also prove stimulating and illuminating to the veteran student. The explanatory guide follows strictly the traditional methods of exposition as maintained in the Theravadin monastic community. Thus it deliberately avoids ventures into personal interpretation as well as sidelong comparisons with modern philosophy and psychology. While such comparative studies have their indubitable value, we felt that they should be excluded from an "inside" presentation of the Abhidhamma teaching as upheld by Theravada orthodoxy.

The entire work has been structured somewhat in the manner of a classical commentary. Each section contains a passage from the Pali text of the *Abhidhammattha Sangaha*, followed by an exact translation and then by an explanation of the important terms and ideas occurring in the passage cited. Such an approach is necessary because the *Sangaha* was composed as a concise, highly terse synopsis of the Abhidhamma, an instruction manual which assumes that a living teacher would flesh out the outline for his students with instruction. Read by itself the *Sangaha* hovers at the edge of the arcane.

The Introduction, which is again the joint composition of Ven. Rewata Dhamma and myself, is intended to introduce the reader not only to the *Abhidhammattha Sangaha* but to the entire Abhidhamma philosophy in its broader perspectives and aims as well as to the body of Abhidhamma literature from which the philosophy derives. In the final stage of the preparation of this volume we were fortunate to receive permission from another Burmese Abhidhamma scholar, Ven. U Sīlānanda, to make use of a large number of Abhidhamma tables that he had prepared for his students in the United States. These tables, compressing a vast amount of information into a concise schematic arrangement, will no doubt prove highly effective study aids in grasping the details of the Abhidhamma. To Ven. Sīlānanda also belongs credit for the lists of textual sources for the states of consciousness and the mental factors, included here as appendices.

To conclude this Preface there remains only the pleasant task of acknowledging the generous help which others have extended towards the completion of this book.

Ven. U Rewata Dhamma wishes to express his gratitude to those who helped him with his share of the work: Mirko Fryba, Mar Mar Lwin, Peter Kelly, Jill Robinson, Upasaka Karuna Bodhi, and Dhamma Tilak.

I myself wish to thank Ven. U Rewata Dhamma for taking out time from a tight schedule to compile the material that was incorporated into this book; I also express appreciation to the team of helpers who made his work easier. Closer to home, I thank Ayyā Nyanasirī for entering onto disk, with remarkable accuracy, the Pali text and revised English translation of the *Abhidhammattha Sangaha*; Savithri Chandraratne for endisking the handwritten manuscript of the expository guide, also with remarkable accuracy; and Ayyā Vimalā for her perceptive comments on a draft version of the guide, which led to significant improvements in the text. Finally I extend thanks to Ven. U Sīlānanda for kindly permitting us to use his valuable tables for this edition.

BHIKKHU BODHI

Kandy, Sri Lanka
August 1992

A NOTE ON THE TABLES

The following tables were provided by Ven. U Sīlānanda, and were originally intended by him for private instruction: 1.1, 2.2, 2.3, 2.4, 3.1, 3.2, 3.3, 3.4, 3.5, 3.6, 3.8, 4.2, 4.3, 4.4, 4.5, 5.5, 5.6, 5.7, 6.2, 6.3, 8.2, 8.3, 9.1.

The following tables appeared in Ven. Mahāthera Nārada's *Manual of Abhidhamma*: 1.11, 4.1, 5.1, 7.1, 7.3.

Table 5.4 is based on U Nārada, *Guide to Conditional Relations*, Part 1, Chart 7 (pp. 198-99); Table 7.4 is based on U Nārada, trans., *Discourse on Elements*, Method of Chapter I Chart (facing p. 26). Both are used with the kind permission of the Pali Text Society.

The originals of the above tables have been modified in some respects for the purposes of this edition. The other tables appearing in this book have either been newly created or are in general use in the study of Abhidhamma. They are used with his kind permission.

INTRODUCTION

The nucleus of the present book is a medieval compendium of Buddhist philosophy entitled the *Abhidhammattha Sangaha*. This work is ascribed to Ācariya Anuruddha, a Buddhist savant about whom so little is known that even his country of origin and the exact century in which he lived remain in question. Nevertheless, despite the personal obscurity that surrounds the author, his little manual has become one of the most important and influential textbooks of Theravada Buddhism. In nine short chapters occupying about fifty pages in print, the author provides a masterly summary of that abstruse body of Buddhist doctrine called the Abhidhamma. Such is his skill in capturing the essentials of that system, and in arranging them in a format suitable for easy comprehension, that his work has become the standard primer for Abhidhamma studies throughout the Theravada Buddhist countries of South and Southeast Asia. In these countries, particularly in Burma where the study of Abhidhamma is pursued most assiduously, the *Abhidhammattha Sangaha* is regarded as the indispensable key to unlock this great treasure-store of Buddhist wisdom.

The Abhidhamma

At the heart of the Abhidhamma philosophy is the Abhidhamma Piṭaka, one of the divisions of the Pali Canon recognized by Theravada Buddhism as the authoritative recension of the Buddha's teachings. This canon was compiled at the three great Buddhist councils held in India in the early centuries following the Buddha's demise: the first, at Rājagaha, convened three months after the Buddha's Parinibbāna by five hundred senior monks under the leadership of the Elder Mahākassapa; the second, at Vesālī, a hundred years later; and the third, at Pāṭaliputta, two hundred years later. The canon that emerged from these councils, preserved in the Middle Indian language now called Pali, is known as the Tipiṭaka, the three "baskets" or collections of the teachings. The first collection, the Vinaya Piṭaka, is the book of discipline, containing the rules of conduct for the bhikkhus and bhikkhunis—the monks and nuns—and the regulations governing the Sangha, the monastic order. The Sutta Piṭaka, the second collection, brings together the Buddha's discourses spoken by him on various occasions during his active ministry of forty-five years. And the third collection is the Abhidhamma Piṭaka, the "basket" of the Buddha's "higher" or "special" doctrine.

This third great division of the Pali Canon bears a distinctly different character from the other two divisions. Whereas the Suttas and Vinaya serve an obvious practical purpose, namely, to proclaim a clear-cut message of deliverance and to lay down a method of personal training, the Abhidhamma Piṭaka presents the appearance of an abstract and highly technical systemization of the doctrine. The collection consists of seven books: the *Dhammasaṅgaṇī*, the *Vibhaṅga*, the *Dhātukathā*, the *Puggalapaññatti*, the *Kathāvatthu*, the *Yamaka*, and the *Paṭṭhāna*. Unlike the Suttas, these are not records of discourses and discussions occurring in real-life settings; they are, rather, full-blown treatises in which the principles of the doctrine have been methodically organized, minutely defined, and meticulously tabulated and classified. Though they were no doubt originally composed and transmitted orally and only written down later, with the rest of the canon in the first century B.C., they exhibit the qualities of structured thought and rigorous consistency more typical of written documents.

In the Theravada tradition the Abhidhamma Piṭaka is held in the highest esteem, revered as the crown jewel of the Buddhist scriptures. As examples of this high regard, in Sri Lanka King Kassapa V (tenth century A.C.) had the whole Abhidhamma Piṭaka inscribed on gold plates and the first book set in gems, while another king, Vijayabāhu (eleventh century) used to study the *Dhammasaṅgaṇī* each morning before taking up his royal duties and composed a translation of it into Sinhala. On a cursory reading, however, this veneration given to the Abhidhamma seems difficult to understand. The texts appear to be merely a scholastic exercise in manipulating sets of doctrinal terms, ponderous and tediously repetitive.

The reason the Abhidhamma Piṭaka is so deeply revered only becomes clear as a result of thorough study and profound reflection, undertaken in the conviction that these ancient books have something significant to communicate. When one approaches the Abhidhamma treatises in such a spirit and gains some insight into their wide implications and organic unity, one will find that they are attempting nothing less than to articulate a comprehensive vision of the totality of experienced reality, a vision marked by extensiveness of range, systematic completeness, and analytical precision. From the standpoint of Theravada orthodoxy the system that they expound is not a figment of speculative thought, not a mosaic put together out of metaphysical hypotheses, but a disclosure of the true nature of existence as apprehended by a mind that has penetrated the totality of things both in depth and in the finest detail. Because it bears this character, the Theravada tradition regards the Abhidhamma as the most perfect expression possible of the Buddha's unimpeded omniscient knowledge (*sabbaññutā-ñāṇa*). It is his statement of the way things appear to the mind of a Fully Enlightened One, ordered in accordance with the two poles of his teaching: suffering and the cessation of suffering.

The system that the Abhidhamma Piṭaka articulates is simultaneously a philosophy, a psychology, and an ethics, all integrated into the framework of a program for liberation. The Abhidhamma may be described as a philosophy because it proposes an ontology, a perspective on the nature of the real. This perspective has been designated the "dhamma theory" (*dhammavāda*). Briefly, the dhamma theory maintains that ultimate reality consists of a multiplicity of elementary constituents called *dhammas*. The dhammas are not noumena hidden behind phenomena, not "things in themselves" as opposed to "mere appearances," but the fundamental components of actuality. The dhammas fall into two broad classes: the unconditioned dhamma, which is solely Nibbāna, and the conditioned dhammas, which are the momentary mental and material phenomena that constitute the process of experience. The familiar world of substantial objects and enduring persons is, according to the dhamma theory, a conceptual construct fashioned by the mind out of the raw data provided by the dhammas. The entities of our everyday frame of reference possess merely a consensual reality derivative upon the foundational stratum of the dhammas. It is the dhammas alone that possess ultimate reality: determinate existence "from their own side" (*sarūpato*) independent of the mind's conceptual processing of the data.

Such a conception of the nature of the real seems to be already implicit in the Sutta Piṭaka, particularly in the Buddha's disquisitions on the aggregates, sense bases, elements, dependent arising, etc., but it remains there tacitly in the background as the underpinning to the more pragmatically formulated teachings of the Suttas. Even in the Abhidhamma Piṭaka itself the dhamma theory is not yet expressed as an explicit philosophical tenet; this comes only later, in the Commentaries. Nevertheless, though as yet implicit, the theory still comes into focus in its role as the regulating principle behind the Abhidhamma's more evident task, the project of systemization.

This project starts from the premise that to attain the wisdom that knows things "as they really are," a sharp wedge must be driven between those types of entities that possess ontological ultimacy, that is, the dhammas, and those types of entities that exist only as conceptual constructs but are mistakenly grasped as ultimately real. Proceeding from this distinction, the Abhidhamma posits a fixed number of dhammas as the building blocks of actuality, most of which are drawn from the Suttas. It then sets out to define all the doctrinal terms used in the Suttas in ways that reveal their identity with the ontological ultimates recognized by the system. On the basis of these definitions, it exhaustively classifies the dhammas into a net of pre-determined categories and modes of relatedness which highlight their place within the system's structure. And since the system is held to be a true reflection of actuality, this means that the classification pinpoints the place of each dhamma within the overall structure of actuality.

The Abhidhamma's attempt to comprehend the nature of reality, contrary to that of classical science in the West, does not proceed from the standpoint of a neutral observer looking outwards towards the external world. The primary concern of the Abhidhamma is to understand the nature of experience, and thus the reality on which it focuses is conscious reality, the world as given in experience, comprising both knowledge and the known in the widest sense. For this reason the philosophical enterprise of the Abhidhamma shades off into a phenomenological psychology. To facilitate the understanding of experienced reality, the Abhidhamma embarks upon an elaborate analysis of the mind as it presents itself to introspective meditation. It classifies consciousness into a variety of types, specifies the factors and functions of each type, correlates them with their objects and physiological bases, and shows how the different types of consciousness link up with each other and with material phenomena to constitute the ongoing process of experience.

This analysis of mind is not motivated by theoretical curiosity but by the overriding practical aim of the Buddha's teaching, the attainment of deliverance from suffering. Since the Buddha traces suffering to our tainted attitudes—a mental orientation rooted in greed, hatred, and delusion—the Abhidhamma's phenomenological psychology also takes on the character of a psychological ethics, understanding the term "ethics" not in the narrow sense of a code of morality but as a complete guide to noble living and mental purification. Accordingly we find that the Abhidhamma distinguishes states of mind principally on the basis of ethical criteria: the wholesome and the unwholesome, the beautiful factors and the defilements. Its schematization of consciousness follows a hierarchical plan that corresponds to the successive stages of purity to which the Buddhist disciple attains by practice of the Buddha's path. This plan traces the refinement of the mind through the progression of meditative absorptions, the fine-material-sphere and immaterial-sphere jhānas, then through the stages of insight and the wisdom of the supramundane paths and fruits. Finally, it shows the whole scale of ethical development to culminate in the perfection of purity attained with the mind's irreversible emancipation from all defilements.

All three dimensions of the Abhidhamma—the philosophical, the psychological, and the ethical—derive their final justification from the cornerstone of the Buddha's teaching, the program of liberation announced by the Four Noble Truths. The ontological survey of dhammas stems from the Buddha's injunction that the noble truth of suffering, identified with the world of conditioned phenomena as a whole, must be fully understood (*pariññeyya*). The prominence of mental defilements and requisites of enlightenment in its schemes of categories, indicative of its psychological and ethical concerns, connects the Abhidhamma to the second and fourth noble truths, the origin of suffering and the way leading to its end. And the entire taxonomy of dhammas elaborated by the system reaches its consummation in the "unconditioned element" (*asankhatā dhātu*), which is Nibbāna, the third noble truth, that of the cessation of suffering.

The Twofold Method

The great Buddhist commentator, Ācariya Buddhaghosa, explains the word "Abhidhamma" as meaning "that which exceeds and is distinguished from the Dhamma" (*dhammātireka-dhammavisesa*), the prefix *abhi* having the sense of preponderance and distinction, and *dhamma* here signifying the teaching of the Sutta Piṭaka.[1] When the Abhidhamma is said to surpass the teaching of the Suttas, this is not intended to suggest that the Suttanta teaching is defective in any degree or that the Abhidhamma proclaims some new revelation of esoteric doctrine unknown to the Suttas. Both the Suttas and the Abhidhamma are grounded upon the Buddha's unique doctrine of the Four Noble Truths, and all the principles essential to the attainment of enlightenment are already expounded in the Sutta Piṭaka. The difference between the two in no way concerns fundamentals but is, rather, partly a matter of scope and partly a matter of method.

As to scope, the Abhidhamma offers a thoroughness and completeness of treatment that cannot be found in the Sutta Piṭaka. Ācariya Buddhaghosa explains that in the Suttas such doctrinal categories as the five aggregates, the twelve sense bases, the eighteen elements, and so forth, are classified only partly, while in the Abhidhamma Piṭaka they are classified fully according to different schemes of classification, some common to the Suttas, others unique to the Abhidhamma.[2] Thus the Abhidhamma has a scope and an intricacy of detail that set it apart from the Sutta Piṭaka.

The other major area of difference concerns method. The discourses contained in the Sutta Piṭaka were expounded by the Buddha under diverse circumstances to listeners with very different capacities for comprehension. They are primarily pedagogical in intent, set forth in the way that will be most effective in guiding the listener in the practice of the teaching and in arriving at a penetration of its truth. To achieve this end the Buddha freely employs the didactic means required to make the doctrine intelligible to his listeners. He uses simile and metaphor; he exhorts, advises, and inspires; he sizes up the inclinations and aptitudes of his audience and adjusts the presentation of the teaching so that it will awaken a positive response. For this reason the Suttanta method of teaching is described as *pariyāya-dhammadesanā*, the figurative or embellished discourse on the Dhamma.

In contrast to the Suttas, the Abhidhamma Piṭaka is intended to divulge as starkly and directly as possible the totalistic system that underlies the Suttanta expositions and upon which the individual discourses draw. The Abhidhamma takes no account of the personal inclinations and cognitive capacities of the listeners; it makes no concessions to particular pragmatic requirements. It reveals the architectonics of actuality in an abstract, formalistic manner utterly devoid of literary embellishments and pedagogical expedients. Thus the Abhidhamma method is described as the *nippariyāya-dhammadesanā*, the literal or unembellished discourse on the Dhamma.

This difference in technique between the two methods also influences their respective terminologies. In the Suttas the Buddha regularly makes use of conventional language (*vohāravacana*) and accepts conventional truth (*sammutisacca*), truth expressed in terms of entities that do not possess ontological ultimacy but can still be legitimately referred to them. Thus in the Suttas the Buddha speaks of "I" and "you," of "man" and "woman," of living beings, persons, and even self as though they were concrete realities. The Abhidhamma method of exposition, however, rigorously restricts itself to terms that are valid from the standpoint of ultimate truth (*paramatthasacca*): dhammas, their characteristics, their functions, and their relations. Thus in the Abhidhamma all such conceptual entities provisionally accepted in the Suttas for purposes of meaningful communication are resolved into their ontological ultimates, into bare mental and material phenomena that are impermanent, conditioned, and dependently arisen, empty of any abiding self or substance.

But a qualification is necessary. When a distinction is drawn between the two methods, this should be understood to be based on what is most characteristic of each Piṭaka and should not be interpreted as an absolute dichotomy. To some degree the two methods overlap and interpenetrate. Thus in the Sutta Piṭaka we find discourses that employ the strictly philosophical terminology of aggregates, sense bases, elements, etc., and thus come within the bounds of the Abhidhamma method. Again, within the Abhidhamma Piṭaka we find sections, even a whole book (the *Puggalapaññatti*), that depart from the rigorous manner of expression and employ conventional terminology, thus coming within the range of the Suttanta method.

Distinctive Features of the Abhidhamma

Apart from its strict adherence to the philosophical method of exposition, the Abhidhamma makes a number of other noteworthy contributions integral to its task of systemization. One is the employment, in the main books of the Abhidhamma Piṭaka, of a *mātikā*—a matrix or schedule of categories—as the blueprint for the entire edifice. This matrix, which comes at the very beginning of the *Dhammasaṅgaṇī* as a preface to the Abhidhamma Piṭaka proper, consists of 122 modes of classification special to the Abhidhamma method. Of these, twenty-two are triads (*tika*), sets of three terms into which the fundamental dhammas are to be distributed; the remaining hundred are dyads (*duka*), sets of two terms used as a basis for classification.[3] The matrix serves as a kind of grid for sorting out the complex manifold of experience in accordance with principles determined by the purposes of the Dhamma. For example, the triads include such sets as states that are wholesome, unwholesome, indeterminate; states associated with pleasant feeling, painful feeling, neutral feeling; states that are kamma results, productive of kamma results, neither; and so forth. The dyads include such sets as states that are roots, not roots; states concomitant with roots, not so concomitant; states that are conditioned, unconditioned; states that are mundane, supramundane; and so forth. By means of its selection of categories, the matrix embraces the totality of phenomena, illuminating it from a variety of angles philosophical, psychological, and ethical in nature.

A second distinguishing feature of the Abhidhamma is the dissection of the apparently continuous stream of consciousness into a succession of discrete evanescent cognitive events called *cittas*, each a complex unity involving consciousness itself, as the basic awareness of an object, and a constellation of mental factors (*cetasika*) exercising more specialized tasks in the act of cognition. Such a view of consciousness, at least in outline, can readily be derived from the Sutta Piṭaka's analysis of experience into the five aggregates, among which the four mental aggregates are always inseparably conjoined, but the conception remains there merely suggestive. In the Abhidhamma Piṭaka the suggestion is not simply picked up, but is expanded into an extraordinarily detailed and coherent picture of the functioning of consciousness both in its microscopic immediacy and in its extended continuity from life to life.

A third contribution arises from the urge to establish order among the welter of technical terms making up the currency of Buddhist discourse. In defining each of the dhammas, the Abhidhamma texts collate long lists of synonyms drawn mostly from the Suttas. This method of definition shows how a single dhamma may enter under different names into different sets of categories. For example, among the defilements, the mental factor of greed (*lobha*) may be found as the taint of sensual desire, the taint of (attachment to) existence, the bodily knot of covetousness, clinging to sensual pleasures, the hindrance of sensual desire, etc.; among the requisites of enlightenment, the mental factor of wisdom (*paññā*) may be found as the faculty and power of wisdom, the enlightenment factor of investigation of states, the path factor of right view, etc. In establishing these correspondences, the Abhidhamma helps to exhibit the interconnections between doctrinal terms that might not be apparent from the Suttas themselves. In the process it also provides a precision-made tool for interpreting the Buddha's discourses.

The Abhidhamma conception of consciousness further results in a new primary scheme for classifying the ultimate constituents of existence, a scheme which eventually, in the later Abhidhamma literature, takes precedence over the schemes inherited from the Suttas such as the aggregates, sense bases, and elements. In the Abhidhamma Piṭaka the latter categories still loom large, but the view of mind as consisting of momentary concurrences of consciousness and its concomitants leads to a fourfold method of classification more congenial to the system. This is the division of actuality into the four ultimate realities (*paramattha*): consciousness, mental factors, material phenomena, and Nibbāna (*citta, cetasika, rūpa, nibbāna*), the first three comprising conditioned reality and the last the unconditioned element.

The last novel feature of the Abhidhamma method to be noted here—contributed by the final book of the Piṭaka, the *Paṭṭhāna*—is a set of twenty-four conditional relations laid down for the purpose of showing how the ultimate realities are welded into orderly processes. This scheme of conditions supplies the necessary complement to the analytical approach that dominates the earlier books of the Abhidhamma. The method of analysis proceeds by dissecting apparent wholes into their component parts, thereby exposing their voidness of any indivisible core that might qualify as self or substance. The synthetic method plots the conditional relations of the bare phenomena obtained by analysis to show that they are not isolated self-contained units but nodes in a vast multi-layered web of inter-related, inter-dependent events. Taken in conjunction, the analytical method of the earlier treatises of the Abhidhamma Piṭaka and the synthetic method of the *Paṭṭhāna* establish the essential unity of the twin philosophical principles of Buddhism, non-self or egolessness (*anattā*) and dependent arising or conditionality (*paṭicca samuppāda*). Thus the foundation of the Abhidhamma methodology remains in perfect harmony with the insights that lie at the heart of the entire Dhamma.

The Origins of the Abhidhamma

Although modern critical scholarship attempts to explain the formation of the Abhidhamma by a gradual evolutionary process,[4] Theravada orthodoxy assigns its genesis to the Buddha himself. According to the Great Commentary (*mahā-aṭṭhakathā*) quoted by Ācariya Buddhaghosa, "What is known as Abhidhamma is not the province nor the sphere of a disciple; it is the province, the sphere of the Buddhas."[5] The commentarial tradition holds, moreover, that it was not merely the spirit of the Abhidhamma, but the letter as well, that was already realized and expounded by the Buddha during his lifetime.

The *Atthasālinī* relates that in the fourth week after the Enlightenment, while the Blessed One was still dwelling in the vicinity of the Bodhi Tree, he sat in a jewel house (*ratanaghara*) in the northwest direction. This jewel house was not literally a house made of precious stones, but was the place where he contemplated the seven books of the Abhidhamma Piṭaka. He contemplated their contents in turn, beginning with the *Dhammasanganī*, but while investigating the first six books his body did not emit rays. However, upon coming to the *Paṭṭhāna*, when "he began to contemplate the twenty-four universal conditional relations of root, object, and so on, his omniscience certainly found its opportunity therein. For as the great fish Timiratipingala finds room only in the great ocean 84,000 yojanas in depth, so his omniscience truly finds room only in the Great Book. Rays of six colours—indigo, golden, red, white, tawny, and dazzling—issued from the Teacher's body, as he was contemplating the subtle and abstruse Dhamma by his omniscience which had found such opportunity."[6]

Theravada orthodoxy thus maintains that the Abhidhamma Piṭaka is authentic Word of the Buddha, in this respect differing from an early rival school, the Sarvāstivādins. This school also had an Abhidhamma Piṭaka consisting of seven books, considerably different in detail from the Theravada treatises. According to the Sarvāstivādins, the books of the Abhidhamma Piṭaka were composed by Buddhist disciples, several being attributed to authors who appeared generations after the Buddha. The Theravada school, however, holds that the Blessed One himself expounded the books of the Abhidhamma, except for the detailed refutation of deviant views in the *Kathāvatthu*, which was the work of the Elder Moggaliputta Tissa during the reign of Emperor Asoka.

The Pali Commentaries, apparently drawing upon an old oral tradition, maintain that the Buddha expounded the Abhidhamma, not in the human world to his human disciples, but to the assembly of devas or gods in the Tāvatiṁsa heaven. According to this tradition, just prior to his seventh annual rains retreat the Blessed One ascended to the Tāvatiṁsa heaven and there, seated on the Paṇḍukambala stone at the foot of the Pāricchattaka tree, for the three months of the rains he taught the Abhidhamma to the devas who had assembled from the ten thousand world-systems. He made the chief recipient of the teaching his mother, Mahāmāyā-devī, who had been reborn as a deva. The reason the Buddha taught the Abhidhamma in the deva world rather than in the human realm, it is said, is because in order to give a complete picture of the Abhidhamma it has to be expounded from the beginning to the end to the same audience in a single session. Since the full exposition of the Abhidhamma requires three months, only devas and Brahmās could receive it in unbroken continuity, for they alone are capable of remaining in one posture for such a length of time.

However, each day, to sustain his body, the Buddha would descend to the human world to go on almsround in the northern region of Uttarakuru. After collecting almsfood he went to the shore of Anotatta Lake to partake of his meal. The Elder Sāriputta, the General of the Dhamma, would meet the Buddha there and receive a synopsis of the teaching given that day in the deva world: "Then to him the Teacher gave the method, saying, 'Sāriputta, so much doctrine has been shown.' Thus the giving of the method was to the chief disciple, who was endowed with analytical knowledge, as though the Buddha stood on the edge of the shore and pointed out the ocean with his open hand. To the Elder also the doctrine taught by the Blessed One in hundreds and thousands of methods became very clear."[7]

Having learnt the Dhamma taught him by the Blessed One, Sāriputta in turn taught it to his own circle of 500 pupils, and thus the textual recension of the Abhidhamma Piṭaka was established. To the Venerable Sāriputta is ascribed the textual order of the Abhidhamma treatises as well as the numerical series in the *Paṭṭhāna*. Perhaps we should see in these admissions of the *Atthasālinī* an implicit acknowledgement that while the philosophical vision of the Abhidhamma and its basic architecture originate from the Buddha, the actual working out of the details, and perhaps even the prototypes of the texts themselves, are to be ascribed to the illustrious Chief Disciple and his entourage of students. In other early Buddhist schools, too, the Abhidhamma is closely connected with the Venerable Sāriputta, who in some traditions is regarded as the literal author of Abhidhamma treatises.[8]

The Seven Books

A brief outline of the contents of the seven canonical Abhidhamma books will provide some insight into the plethora of textual material to be condensed and summarized by the *Abhidhammattha Sangaha*. The first book, the *Dhammasanganī*, is the fountainhead of the entire system. The title may be translated "Enumeration of Phenomena," and the work does in fact undertake to compile an exhaustive catalogue of the ultimate constituents of existence.

Opening with the *mātikā*, the schedule of categories which serves as the framework for the whole Abhidhamma, the text proper is divided into four chapters. The first, "States of Consciousness," takes up about half of the book and unfolds as an analysis of the first triad in the *mātikā*, that of the wholesome, the unwholesome, and the indeterminate. To supply that analysis, the text enumerates 121 types of consciousness classified by way of their ethical quality.[9] Each type of consciousness is in turn dissected into its concomitant mental factors, which are individually defined in full. The second chapter, "On Matter," continues the inquiry into the ethically indeterminate by enumerating and classifying the different types of material phenomena. The third chapter, called "The Summary," offers concise explanations of all the terms in the Abhidhamma matrix and the Suttanta matrix as well. Finally, a concluding "Synopsis" provides a more condensed explanation of the Abhidhamma matrix but omits the Suttanta matrix.

The *Vibhanga*, the "Book of Analysis," consists of eighteen chapters, each a self-contained dissertation, dealing in turn with the following: aggregates, sense bases, elements, truths, faculties, dependent arising, foundations of mindfulness, supreme efforts, means to accomplishment, factors of enlightenment, the eightfold path, jhānas, illimitables, training rules, analytical knowledges, kinds of knowledge, minor points (a numerical inventory of defilements), and "the heart of the doctrine" (*dhammahadaya*), a psycho-cosmic topography of the Buddhist universe. Most of the chapters in the *Vibhanga*, though not all, involve three subsections: an analysis according to the methodology of the Suttas; an analysis according to the methodology of the Abhidhamma proper; and an interrogation section, which applies the categories of the matrix to the subject under investigation.

The *Dhātukathā*, the "Discourse on Elements," is written entirely in catechism form. It discusses all phenomena with reference to the three schemata of aggregates, sense bases, and elements, seeking to determine whether, and to what extent, they are included or not included in them, and whether they are associated with them or dissociated from them.

The *Puggalapaññatti*, "Concepts of Individuals," is the one book of the Abhidhamma Piṭaka that is more akin to the method of the Suttas than to the Abhidhamma proper. The work begins with a general enumeration of types of concepts, and this suggests that it was originally intended as a supplement to the other books in order to take account of the conceptual realities excluded by the strict application of the Abhidhamma method. The bulk of the work provides formal definitions of different types of individuals. It has ten chapters: the first deals with single types of individuals; the second with pairs; the third with groups of three, etc.

The *Kathāvatthu*, "Points of Controversy," is a polemical treatise ascribed to the Elder Moggaliputta Tissa. He is said to have compiled it during the time of Emperor Asoka, 218 years after the Buddha's Parinibbāna, in order to refute the heterodox opinions of the Buddhist schools outside the Theravadin fold. The Commentaries defend its inclusion in the Canon by holding that the Buddha himself, foreseeing the errors that would arise, laid down the outline of rebuttal, which Moggaliputta Tissa merely filled in according to the Master's intention.

The *Yamaka*, the "Book of Pairs," has the purpose of resolving ambiguities and defining the precise usage of technical terms. It is so called owing to its method of treatment, which throughout employs the dual grouping of a question and its converse formulation. For instance, the first pair of questions in the first chapter runs thus: "Are all wholesome phenomena wholesome roots? And are all wholesome roots wholesome phenomena?" The book contains ten chapters: roots, aggregates, sense bases, elements, truths, formations, latent dispositions, consciousness, phenomena, and faculties.

The *Paṭṭhāna*, the "Book of Conditional Relations," is probably the most important work of the Abhidhamma Piṭaka and thus is traditionally designated the "Great Treatise" (*mahāpakaraṇa*). Gigantic in extent as well as in substance, the book comprises five volumes totalling 2500 pages in the Burmese-script Sixth Council edition. The purpose of the *Paṭṭhāna* is to apply its scheme of twenty-four conditional relations to all the phenomena incorporated in the Abhidhamma matrix. The main body of the work has four great divisions: origination according to the positive method, according to the negative method, according to the positive-negative method, and according to the negative-positive method. Each of these in turn has six sub-divisions: origination of triads, of dyads, of dyads and triads combined, of triads and dyads combined, of triads and triads combined, and of dyads and dyads combined. Within this pattern of twenty-four sections, the twenty-four modes of conditionality are applied in due order to all the phenomena of existence in all their conceivable permutations. Despite its dry and tabular format, even from a "profane" humanistic viewpoint the *Paṭṭhāna* can easily qualify as one of the truly monumental products of the human mind, astounding in its breadth of vision, its rigorous consistency, and its painstaking attention to detail. To Theravada orthodoxy, it is the most eloquent testimony to the Buddha's unimpeded knowledge of omniscience.

The Commentaries

The books of the Abhidhamma Piṭaka have inspired a voluminous mass of exegetical literature composed in order to fill out, by way of explanation and exemplification, the scaffoldings erected by the canonical texts. The most important works of this class are the authorized commentaries of Ācariya Buddhaghosa. These are three in number: the *Atthasālinī*, "The Expositor," the commentary to the *Dhammasaṅgaṇī*; the *Sammohavinodanī* , "The Dispeller of Delusion," the commentary to the *Vibhaṅga*; and the *Pañcappakaraṇa Aṭṭhakathā*, the combined commentary to the other five treatises. To this same stratum of literature also belongs the *Visuddhimagga*, "The Path of Purification," also composed by Buddhaghosa. Although this last work is primarily an encyclopaedic guide to meditation, its chapters on "the soil of understanding" (XIV-XVII) lay out the theory to be mastered prior to developing insight and thus constitute in effect a compact dissertation on Abhidhamma. Each of the commentaries in turn has its subcommentary (*mūlaṭīkā*), by an elder of Sri Lanka named Ācariya Ānanda, and these in turn each have a sub-subcommentary (*anuṭīkā*), by Ānanda's pupil Dhammapāla (who is to be distinguished from the great Ācariya Dhammapāla, author of the *ṭīkās* to Buddhaghosa's works).

When the authorship of the Commentaries is ascribed to Ācariya Buddhaghosa, it should not be supposed that they are in any way original compositions, or even original attempts to interpret traditional material. They are, rather, carefully edited versions of the vast body of accumulated exegetical material that Buddhaghosa found at the Mahāvihāra in Anurādhapura. This material must have preceded the great commentator by centuries, representing the collective efforts of generations of erudite Buddhist teachers to elucidate the meaning of the canonical Abhidhamma. While it is tempting to try to discern evidence of historical development in the Commentaries over and beyond the ideas embedded in the Abhidhamma Piṭaka, it is risky to push this line too far, for a great deal of the canonical Abhidhamma seems to require the Commentaries to contribute the unifying context in which the individual elements hang together as parts of a systematic whole and without which they lose important dimensions of meaning. It is thus not unreasonable to assume that a substantial portion of the commentarial apparatus originated in close proximity to the canonical Abhidhamma and was transmitted concurrently with the latter, though lacking the stamp of finality it was open to modification and amplification in a way that the canonical texts were not.

Bearing this in mind, we might briefly note a few of the Abhidhammic conceptions that are characteristic of the Commentaries but either unknown or recessive in the Abhidhamma Piṭaka itself. One is the detailed account of the cognitive process (*cittavīthi*). While this conception seems to be tacitly recognized in the canonical books, it now comes to be drawn out for use as an explanatory tool in its own right. The functions of the *cittas*, the different types of consciousness, are specified, and in time the *cittas* themselves come to be designated by way of their functions. The term *khaṇa*, "moment," replaces the canonical *samaya*, "occasion," as the basic unit for delimiting the occurrence of events, and the duration of a material phenomenon is determined to be seventeen moments of mental phenomena. The division of a moment into three sub-moments—arising, presence, and dissolution—also seems to be new to the Commentaries.[10] The organization of material phenomena into groups (*kalāpa*), though implied by the distinction between the primary elements of matter and derived matter, is first spelled out in the Commentaries, as is the specification of the heart-base (*hadayavatthu*) as the material basis for mind element and mind-consciousness element.

The Commentaries introduce many (though not all) of the categories for classifying kamma, and work out the detailed correlations between kamma and its results. They also close off the total number of mental factors (*cetasika*). The phrase in the *Dhammasaṅgaṇī*, "or whatever other (unmentioned) conditionally arisen immaterial phenomena there are on that occasion," apparently envisages an open-ended universe of mental factors, which the Commentaries delimit by specifying the "or-whatever states" (*yevāpanakā dhammā*). Again, the Commentaries consummate the dhamma theory by supplying the formal definition of dhammas as "things which bear their own intrinsic nature" (*attano sabhāvaṁ dhārentī ti dhammā*). The task of defining specific dhammas is finally rounded off by the extensive employment of the fourfold defining device of characteristic, function, manifestation, and proximate cause, a device derived from a pair of old exegetical texts, the *Peṭakopadesa* and the *Nettipakaraṇa*.

The Abhidhammattha Sangaha

As the Abhidhamma system, already massive in its canonical version, grew in volume and complexity, it must have become increasingly unwieldy for purposes of study and comprehension. Thus at a certain stage in the evolution of Theravada Buddhist thought the need must have become felt for concise summaries of the Abhidhamma as a whole in order to provide the novice student of the subject with a clear picture of its main outlines—faithfully and thoroughly, yet without an unmanageable mass of detail.

To meet this need there began to appear, perhaps as early as the fifth century and continuing well through the twelfth, short manuals or compendia of the Abhidhamma. In Burma these are called *let-than* or "little-finger manuals," of which there are nine:

1. *Abhidhammattha Sangaha*, by Ācariya Anuruddha;
2. *Nāmarūpa-pariccheda*, by the same;
3. *Paramattha-vinicchaya*, by the same (?);
4. *Abhidhammāvatāra*, by Ācariya Buddhadatta (a senior contemporary of Buddhaghosa);
5. *Rūpārupa-vibhāga*, by the same;
6. *Sacca-sankhepa*, by Bhadanta Dhammapāla (probably Sri Lankan; different from the great subcommentator);
7. *Moha-vicchedanī*, by Bhadanta Kassapa (South Indian or Sri Lankan);
8. *Khemạ-pakaraṇa*, by Bhadanta Khema (Sri Lankan);
9. *Nāmacāra-dīpaka*, by Bhadanta Saddhamma Jotipāla (Burman).

Among these, the work that has dominated Abhidhamma studies from about the twelfth century to the present day is the first mentioned, the *Abhidhammattha Sangaha*, "The Compendium of Things contained in the Abhidhamma." Its popularity may be accounted for by its remarkable balance between concision and comprehensiveness. Within its short scope all the essentials of the Abhidhamma are briefly and carefully summarized. Although the book's manner of treatment is extremely terse even to the point of obscurity when read alone, when studied under a qualified teacher or with the aid of an explanatory guide, it leads the student confidently through the winding maze of the system to a clear perception of its entire structure. For this reason throughout the Theravada Buddhist world the *Abhidhammattha Sangaha* is always used as the first textbook in Abhidhamma studies. In Buddhist monasteries, especially in Burma, novices and young bhikkhus are required to learn the *Sangaha* by heart before they are permitted to study the books of the Abhidhamma Piṭaka and its Commentaries.

Detailed information about the author of the manual, Ācariya Anuruddha, is virtually non-existent. He is regarded as the author of two other manuals, cited above, and it is believed in Buddhist countries that he wrote altogether nine compendia, of which only these three have survived. The *Paramattha-vinicchaya* is written in an elegant style of Pali and attains a high standard of literary excellence. According to the colophon, its author was born in Kāveri in the state of Kāñcipura (Conjeevaram) in South India. Ācariya Buddhadatta and Ācariya Buddhaghosa are also said to have resided in the same area, and the subcommentator Ācariya Dhammapāla was probably a native of the region. There is evidence that for several centuries Kāñcipura had been an important centre of Theravada Buddhism from which learned bhikkhus went to Sri Lanka for further study.

It is not known exactly when Ācariya Anuruddha lived and wrote his manuals. An old monastic tradition regards him as having been a fellow student of Ācariya Buddhadatta under the same teacher, which would place him in the fifth century. According to this tradition, the two elders wrote their respective books, the *Abhidhammattha Sangaha* and the *Abhidhammāvatāra*, as gifts of gratitude to their teacher, who remarked: "Buddhadatta has filled a room with all kinds of treasure and locked the door, while Anuruddha has also filled a room with treasure but left the door open."[11] Modern scholars, however, do not endorse this tradition, maintaining on the basis of the style and content of Anuruddha's work that he could not have lived earlier than the eighth century, more probably between the tenth and early twelfth centuries.[12]

In the colophon to the *Abhidhammattha Sangaha* Ācariya Anuruddha states that he wrote the manual at the Mūlasoma Monastery, which all exegetical traditions place in Sri Lanka. There are several ways to reconcile this fact with the concluding stanzas of the *Paramattha-vinicchaya*, which state that he was born in Kañcipura. One hypothesis is that he was of South Indian descent but came to Sri Lanka, where he wrote the *Sangaha*. Another, advanced by G.P. Malalasekera, holds that he was a native of Sri Lanka who spent time at Kañcipura (which, however, passes over his statement that he was *born* in Kañcipura). Still a third hypothesis, proposed by Ven. A.P. Buddhadatta Mahāthera, asserts that there were two different monks named Anuruddha, one in Sri Lanka who was the author of the *Abhidhammattha Sangaha*, another in Kāñcipura who wrote the *Paramattha-vinicchaya*.[13]

Commentaries on the Sangaha

Owing to its extreme concision, the *Abhidhammattha Sangaha* cannot be easily understood without explanation. Therefore to elucidate its terse and pithy synopsis of the Abhidhamma philosophy, a great number of *ṭīkās* or commentaries have been written upon it. In fact, this work has probably stimulated more commentaries than any other Pali text, written not only in the Pali language but also in Burmese, Sinhala, Thai, etc. Since the fifteenth century Burma has been the international centre of Abhidhamma studies, and therefore we find many commentaries written on it by Burmese scholars both in Pali and in Burmese. Commentaries on the *Sangaha* in Pali alone number nineteen, of which the following are the most important:

1. *Abhidhammatthasangaha-Ṭīkā*, also known as the *Porāṇa-Ṭīkā*, "the Old Commentary." This is a very small *ṭīkā* written in Sri Lanka in the twelfth century by an elder named Ācariya Navavimalabuddhi.

2. *Abhidhammatthavibhāvinī-Ṭīkā*, or in brief, the *Vibhāvinī*, written by Ācariya Sumangalasāmi, pupil of the eminent Sri Lankan elder Sāriputta Mahāsāmi, also in the twelfth century. This *ṭīkā* quickly superceded the Old Commentary and is generally considered the most profound and reliable exegetical work on the *Sangaha*. In Burma this work is known as *ṭīkā-gyaw*, "the Famous Commentary." The author is greatly respected for his erudition and mastery of the Abhidhamma. He relies heavily on older authorities such as the *Abhidhamma-Anuṭīkā* and the *Visuddhimagga-Mahāṭīkā* (also known as the *Paramatthamañjūsā*). Although Ledi Sayadaw (see below) criticized the *Vibhāvinī* extensively in his own commentary on the *Sangaha*, its popularity has not diminished but indeed has even increased, and several Burmese scholars have risen to defend it against Ledi Sayadaw's criticisms.

3. *Sankhepa-vaṇṇanā*, written in the sixteenth century by Bhadanta Saddhamma Jotipāla, also known as Chapada Mahāthera, a Burmese monk who visited Sri Lanka during the reign of Parākramabāhu VI of Kotte (fifteenth century).[14]

4. *Paramatthadīpanī-Ṭīkā*, "The Elucidation of the Ultimate Meaning," by Ledi Sayadaw. Ledi Sayadaw of Burma (1846-1923) was one of the greatest scholar-monks and meditation masters of the Theravada tradition in recent times. He was the author of over seventy manuals on different aspects of Theravada Buddhism, including philosophy, ethics,

meditation practice, and Pali grammar. His *ṭīkā* created a sensation in the field of Abhidhamma studies because he pointed out 325 places in the esteemed *Vibhāvinī-ṭīkā* where he alleged that errors and misinterpretations had occurred, though his criticisms also set off a reaction in defense of the older work.

5. *Ankura-Ṭīkā*, by Vimala Sayadaw. This *ṭīkā* was written fifteen years after the publication of the *Paramatthadīpanī* and supports the commonly accepted opinions of the *Vibhāvinī* against Ledi Sayadaw's criticisms.

6. *Navanīta-Ṭīkā*, by the Indian scholar Dhammānanda Kosambi, published originally in *devanāgarī* script in 1933. The title of this work means literally "The Butter Commentary," and it is so called probably because it explains the *Sangaha* in a smooth and simple manner, avoiding philosophical controversy.

Outline of the Sangaha

The *Abhidhammattha Sangaha* contains nine chapters. It opens by enumerating the four ultimate realities—consciousness, mental factors, matter, and Nibbāna. The detailed analysis of these is the project set for its first six chapters. Chapter I is the Compendium of Consciousness, which defines and classifies the 89 and 121 *cittas* or types of consciousness. In scope this first chapter covers the same territory as the States of Consciousness chapter of the *Dhammasaṅgaṇī*, but it differs in approach. The canonical work begins with an analysis of the first triad in the *mātikā*, and therefore initially classifies consciousness on the basis of the three ethical qualities of wholesome, unwholesome, and indeterminate; then within those categories it subdivides consciousness on the basis of plane into the categories of sense sphere, fine-material sphere, immaterial sphere, and supramundane. The *Sangaha*, on the other hand, not being bound to the *mātikā*, first divides consciousness on the basis of plane, and then subdivides it on the basis of ethical quality.

The second chapter, the Compendium of Mental Factors, first enumerates the fifty-two *cetasikas* or concomitants of consciousness, divided into four classes: universals, occasionals, unwholesome factors, and beautiful factors. Thereafter the factors are investigated by two complimentary methods: first, the method of association (*sampayoganaya*), which takes the mental factors as the unit of inquiry and elicits the types of consciousness with which they are individually associated; and second, the method of inclusion or combination (*sangahanaya*), which takes the types of consciousness as the unit of inquiry and elicits the mental factors that enter into the constitution of each. This chapter again draws principally upon the first chapter of the *Dhammasaṅgaṇī*.

The third chapter, entitled Compendium of the Miscellaneous, classifies the types of consciousness along with their factors with respect to six categories: root (*hetu*), feeling (*vedanā*), function (*kicca*), door (*dvāra*), object (*ārammaṇa*), and base (*vatthu*).

The first three chapters are concerned principally with the structure of consciousness, both internally and in relation to external variables. In contrast, the next two chapters deal with the dynamics of consciousness, that is, with its modes of occurrence. According to the Abhidhamma, consciousness occurs in two distinct but intertwining modes—as active process and as passive flow. Chapter IV explores the nature of the "cognitive process," Chapter V the passive "process-freed" flow, which it prefaces with a survey of the traditional Buddhist cosmology. The exposition here is largely based upon the Abhidhamma Commentaries. Chapter VI, Compendium of Matter, turns from the mental realm to the material world. Based primarily on the second chapter of the *Dhammasaṅgaṇī*, it enumerates the types of material phenomena, classifies them in various ways, and explains their modes of origination. It also introduces the commentarial notion of material groups, which it treats in detail, and describes the occurrence of material processes in the different realms of existence. This chapter concludes with a short section on the fourth ultimate reality, Nibbāna, the only unconditioned element in the system.

With the sixth chapter, Ācariya Anuruddha has completed his analytical exposition of the four ultimate realities, but there remain several important subjects which must be explained to give a complete picture of the Abhidhamma. These are taken up in the last three chapters. Chapter VII, the Compendium of Categories, arranges the ultimate realities into a variety of categorical schemes that fall under four broad headings: a compendium of defilements; a compendium of mixed categories, which include items of different ethical qualities; a compendium of the requisites of enlightenment; and a compendium of the whole, an all-inclusive survey of the Abhidhamma ontology. This chapter leans heavily upon the *Vibhaṅga*, and to some extent upon the *Dhammasaṅgaṇī*.

Chapter VIII, the Compendium of Conditionality, is introduced to include the Abhidhamma teaching on the inter-relatedness of physical and mental phenomena, thereby complementing the analytical treatment of the ultimate realities with a synthetical treatment laying bare their functional correlations. The exposition summarily presents two alternative approaches to conditionality found in the Pali Canon. One is the method of dependent arising, prominent in the Suttas and analyzed from both Suttanta and Abhidhamma angles in the *Vibhanga* (VI). This method examines conditionality in terms of the cause-and-result pattern that maintains bondage to *saṁsāra*, the cycle of birth and death. The other is the method of the *Paṭṭhāna*, with its twenty-four conditional relations. This chapter concludes with a brief account of concepts (*paññatti*), thereby drawing in the *Puggalapaññatti*, at least by implication.

The ninth and final chapter of the *Sangaha* is concerned, not with theory, but with practice. This is the Compendium of Meditation Subjects. This chapter functions as a kind of summary of the *Visuddhimagga*. It concisely surveys all the methods of meditation exhaustively explained in the latter work, and it sets forth condensed accounts of the stages of progress in both systems of meditation, concentration and insight. Like the masterwork it summarizes, it concludes with an account of the four types of enlightened individuals and the attainments of fruition and cessation. This arrangement of the *Abhidhammattha Sangaha* perhaps serves to underscore the ultimate soteriological intent of the Abhidhamma. All the theoretical analysis of mind and matter finally converges upon the practice of meditation, and the practice culminates in the attainment of the supreme goal of Buddhism, the liberation of the mind by non-clinging.

A Manual of Abhidhamma
(*Abhidhammattha Sangaha*)

Namo tassa Bhagavato Arahato
Sammāsambuddhassa

CHAPTER I
COMPENDIUM OF CONSCIOUSNESS
(*Cittasangahavibhāga*)

§1 Words of Praise
(*thutivacana*)

Sammāsambuddham atulaṁ
Sasaddhammagaṇuttamaṁ
Abhivādiya bhāsissaṁ
Abhidhammatthasangahaṁ.

Having respectfully saluted the Fully Enlightened One, the Peerless One, along with the Sublime Teaching and the Noble Order, I will speak the Manual of Abhidhamma—a compendium of the things contained in the Abhidhamma.

Guide to §1

Having respectfully saluted (*abhivādiya*): It is an established practice in the Pali Buddhist tradition for expositors of the Dhamma to begin their expositions with a verse of homage to the Triple Gem—the Buddha, the Dhamma, and the Sangha—the ultimate refuge for all who seek the undistorted comprehension of actuality. Thus, following this custom, with deep devotion the author, Ācariya Anuruddha, opens his treatise with a verse of praise in which he expresses his veneration for the Triple Gem. A thought of veneration directed towards a worthy object is a wholesome kamma that generates merit in the mental continuum of the person who gives rise to such a thought. When this veneration is directed towards the most worthy objects of homage—the Triple Gem—the merit generated is vast and powerful. Such merit, accumulated in the mind, has the capacity to ward off obstructions to the fulfilment of one's virtuous undertakings and to support their successful completion. Moreover, for a follower of the Buddha the writing of a book on the Dhamma is a valuable opportunity to develop the perfection of wisdom (*paññāpāramī*). Therefore, when beginning his work, the author expresses, with blissful words of praise, his joy at gaining such an opportunity.

The Fully Enlightened One (*sammāsambuddha*): The Buddha is called the Fully Enlightened One because he is the one who has fully understood by himself the ultimate nature of all phenomena both in their particular and universal characteristics. The term implies the direct knowledge of all realities gained without help from a teacher. The Buddha is also called the Peerless One (*atula*) because his qualities and attributes cannot be matched by any other being. Though all Arahants possess the distinguished qualities of morality, concentration, and wisdom sufficient to result in liberation, none possess the innumerable and immeasurable virtues with which a supreme Buddha is fully endowed—the ten Tathāgata's powers of knowledge (M.12), the four grounds of self-confidence (M.12), the attainment of great compassion (Pṭs.i,126), and the unobstructed knowledge of omniscience (Pṭs.i,131). Hence the Buddha is without a peer among all sentient beings. As it is said: "There is one person, bhikkhus, who is unique, without a peer, without counterpart, incomparable, unequalled, matchless, unrivalled, the best of humans—the Tathāgata, the Arahant, the Fully Enlightened One" (A.1:13/i,22).

The Sublime Teaching (*saddhamma*): The Teaching, or Dhamma, signifies the three aspects of study (*pariyatti*), practice (*paṭipatti*), and realization (*paṭivedha*). "Study" is the study of the Tipiṭaka, the scriptures which record the teachings of the Buddha, comprising the three collections of the Vinaya, the Suttas, and the Abhidhamma. "Practice" is the threefold training in virtue, concentration, and wisdom. "Realization" is the penetration of the supramundane paths and attainment of the noble fruits. Each of these is the foundation for the next, since study provides the guidelines to practice and practice brings the breakthrough to realization. The Teaching is called "sublime" in the sense of true and good, because when it is applied in accordance with the Buddha's instructions it definitely leads to the attainment of Nibbāna, the supreme truth and highest good.

And the Noble Order (*gaṇuttama*): The word *gaṇa*, meaning company or group, is used here as a synonym of *sangha*, the community or order. There are two kinds of Sangha: the conventional Sangha (*sammutisangha*), the order of bhikkhus and bhikkhunis, fully ordained monks and nuns; and the Sangha of noble ones (*ariyasangha*), referred to in the verse of homage as "the Noble Order." The Noble Order is the noble or holy community of the accomplished followers of the Buddha—that is, the four pairs of persons who have arrived at the planes of the noble ones, distinguished as eightfold according to whether they have reached the paths or the fruits of stream-entry, once-returning, non-returning, and Arahantship.

I will speak the Manual of Abhidhamma: The title of the work, *Abhidhammattha Sangaha*, literally means "a compendium of the things contained in the Abhidhamma," that is, in the Buddha's special or "distinguished" (*abhi*) teaching (*dhamma*) handed down in the Abhidhamma Piṭaka. The author's statement, "I will speak" (*bhāsissaṁ*) reminds us that our text is meant to be recited and learnt by heart so that it will always be available to us as an instrument for analyzing reality.

§2 The Fourfold Ultimate Reality (*catudhā paramattha*)

Tattha vutt'ābhidhammatthā
Catudhā paramatthato
Cittaṁ cetasikaṁ rūpaṁ
Nibbānam iti sabbathā.

The things contained in the Abhidhamma, spoken of therein, are altogether fourfold from the standpoint of ultimate reality: consciousness, mental factors, matter, and Nibbāna.

Guide to §2

From the standpoint of ultimate reality (*paramatthato*): According to the Abhidhamma philosophy, there are two kinds of realities—the conventional (*sammuti*) and the ultimate (*paramattha*). Conventional realities are the referents of ordinary conceptual thought (*paññatti*) and conventional modes of expression (*vohāra*). They include such entities as living beings, persons, men, women, animals, and the apparently stable persisting objects that constitute our unanalyzed picture of the world. The Abhidhamma philosophy maintains that these notions do not possess ultimate validity, for the objects which they signify do not exist in their own right as irreducible realities. Their mode of being is conceptual, not actual. They are products of mental construction (*parikappanā*), not realities existing by reason of their own nature.

Ultimate realities, in contrast, are things that exist by reason of their own intrinsic nature (*sabhāva*). These are the dhammas: the final, irreducible components of existence, the ultimate entities which result from a correctly performed analysis of experience. Such existents admit of no further reduction, but are themselves the final terms of analysis, the true constituents of the complex manifold of experience. Hence the word *paramattha* is applied to them, which is derived from *parama* = ultimate, highest, final, and *attha* = reality, thing.

The ultimate realities are characterized not only from the ontological angle as the ultimate existents, but also from the epistemological angle as the ultimate objects of right knowledge. As one extracts oil from sesame seed, so one can extract the ultimate realities from the conventional realities. For example "being," and "man," and "woman" are concepts suggesting that the things they signify possess irreducible ultimate unity. However, when we wisely investigate these things with the analytical tools of the Abhidhamma, we find that they do not possess the ultimacy implied by the concepts, but only a conventional reality as an assemblage of impermanent factors, of mental and physical processes. Thus by examining the conventional realities with wisdom, we eventually arrive at the objective actualities that lie behind our conceptual constructs. It is these objective actualities—the dhammas, which maintain their intrinsic natures independently of the mind's constructive functions—that form the ultimate realities of the Abhidhamma.

Although ultimate realities exist as the concrete essences of things, they are so subtle and profound that an ordinary person who lacks training cannot perceive them. Such a person cannot see the ultimate realities because his mind is obscured by concepts, which shape reality into conventionally defined appearances. Only by means of wise or thorough attention to things (*yoniso manasikāra*) can one see beyond the concepts and take the ultimate realities as one's object of knowledge. Thus *paramattha* is described as that which belongs to the domain of ultimate or supreme knowledge.[1]

Altogether fourfold: In the Suttas the Buddha usually analyzes a being or individual into five types of ultimate realities, the five aggregates (*pañcakkhandha*): matter, feeling, perception, mental formations, and consciousness. In the Abhidhamma teaching the ultimates are grouped into the four categories enumerated in the text. The first three—consciousness, mental factors, and matter—comprise all conditioned realities. The five aggregates of the Suttanta teaching fit within these three categories. The aggregate of consciousness (*viññāṇakkhandha*) is here comprised by consciousness (*citta*), the word *citta* generally being employed to refer to different classes of consciousness distinguished by their concomitants. The middle three aggregates are, in the Abhidhamma, all included within the category of mental factors (*cetasikas*), the mental states that arise along with consciousness performing diverse functions. The Abhidhamma philosophy enumerates fifty-two mental factors: the aggregates of feeling and perception are each counted as one factor; the aggregate of mental formations (*sankhārakkhandha*) of the Suttas is finely subdivided into fifty mental factors. The aggregate of matter is, of course, identical with the Abhidhamma category of matter, which will later be divided into twenty-eight types of material phenomena.

To these three types of reality, which are conditioned, is added a fourth reality, which is unconditioned. That reality, which is not included in the five aggregates, is Nibbāna, the state of final deliverance from the suffering inherent in conditioned existence. Thus in the Abhidhamma philosophy there are altogether these four ultimate realities: consciousness, mental factors, matter, and Nibbāna.

§3 Four Classes of Consciousness (*catubbidha citta*)

Tattha cittaṁ tāva catubbidhaṁ hoti: (i) kāmāvacaraṁ; (ii) rūpāvacaraṁ; (iii) arūpāvacaraṁ; (iv) lokuttarañ cā ti.

Of them, consciousness, firstly, is fourfold: (i) sense-sphere consciousness; (ii) fine-material-sphere consciousness; (iii) immaterial-sphere consciousness; (iv) supramundane consciousness.

Guide to §3

Consciousness: The first chapter of the *Abhidhammattha Sangaha* is devoted to an examination of *citta*, consciousness or mind, the first of the four ultimate realities. Consciousness is taken up for study first because the focus of the Buddhist analysis of reality is experience, and consciousness is the principal element in experience, that which constitutes the knowing or awareness of an object.

The Pali word *citta* is derived from the verbal root *citi*, to cognize, to know. The commentators define *citta* in three ways: as agent, as instrument, and as activity. As the agent, citta is that which cognizes an object (*ārammaṇaṁ cintetī ti cittaṁ*). As the instrument, citta is that by means of which the accompanying mental factors cognize the object (*etena cintentī ti cittaṁ*). As an activity, citta is itself nothing other than the process of cognizing the object (*cintanamattaṁ cittaṁ*).

The third definition, in terms of sheer activity, is regarded as the most adequate of the three: that is, citta is fundamentally an activity or process of cognizing or knowing an object. It is not an agent or instrument possessing actual being in itself apart from the activity of cognizing. The definitions in terms of agent and instrument are proposed to refute the wrong view of those who hold that a permanent self or ego is the agent and instrument of cognition. The Buddhist thinkers point out, by means of these definitions, that it is not a self that performs the act of cognition, but citta or consciousness. This citta is nothing other than the act

TABLE 1.1 :
THE 89 AND 121 CITTAS AT A GLANCE

MUNDANE CITTAS 81

Sense–sphere cittas 54

Unwholesome cittas 12

(1) – (8)	Greed–rooted cittas	8
(9) – (10)	Hatred–rooted cittas	2
(11) – (12)	Delusion–rooted cittas	2

Rootless cittas 18

(13) – (19)	Unwholesome–resultant	7
(20) – (27)	Wholesome–resultant	8
(28) – (30)	Rootless functional	3

Sense–sphere beautiful cittas 24

(31) – (38)	Sense–sphere wholesome	8
(39) – (46)	Sense–sphere resultant	8
(47) – (54)	Sense–sphere functional	8

Fine–material–sphere cittas 15

(55) – (59)	Fine–material–sphere wholesome	5
(60) – (64)	Fine–material–sphere resultant	5
(65) – (69)	Fine–material–sphere functional	5

Immaterial–sphere cittas 12

(70) – (73)	Immaterial–sphere wholesome	4
(74) – (77)	Immaterial–sphere resultant	4
(78) – (81)	Immaterial–sphere functional	4

SUPRAMUNDANE CITTAS 8 or 40

Supramundane wholesome cittas 4 or 20

(82) or (82) – (86)	Path of stream–entry	1 or 5
(83) or (87) – (91)	Path of once–returning	1 or 5
(84) or (92) – (96)	Path of non–returning	1 or 5
(85) or (97) – (101)	Path of Arahantship	1 or 5

Supramundane resultant cittas 4 or 20

(86) or (102) – (106)	Fruit of stream–entry	1 or 5
(87) or (107) – (111)	Fruit of once–returning	1 or 5
(88) or (112) – (116)	Fruit of non–returning	1 or 5
(89) or (117) – (121)	Fruit of Arahantship	1 or 5

of cognizing, and that act is necessarily impermanent, marked by rise and fall.

To elucidate the nature of any ultimate reality, the Pali commentators propose four defining devices by means of which it can be delimited. These four devices are: (1) its characteristic (*lakkhaṇa*), i.e. the salient quality of the phenomenon; (2) its function (*rasa*), its performance of a concrete task (*kicca*) or achievement of a goal (*sampatti*); (3) its manifestation (*paccupaṭṭhāna*), the way it presents itself within experience; and (4) its proximate cause (*padaṭṭhāna*), the principal condition upon which it depends.

In the case of citta, its characteristic is the knowing of an object (*vijānana*). Its function is to be a "forerunner" (*pubbangama*) of the mental factors in that it presides over them and is always accompanied by them. Its manifestation—the way it appears in the meditator's experience—is as a continuity of processes (*sandhāna*). Its proximate cause is mind-and-matter (*nāmarūpa*), because consciousness cannot arise alone, in the complete absence of mental factors and material phenomena.

While citta has a single characteristic as the cognizing of an object, a characteristic that remains the same in all its diverse manifestations, the Abhidhamma distinguishes citta into a variety of types. These types, also called cittas, are reckoned as 89 or, by a finer method of differentiation, as 121. (See Table 1.1.) What we ordinarily think of as consciousness is really a series of cittas, momentary acts of consciousness, occurring in such rapid succession that we cannot detect the discrete occasions, which are of diverse types. The Abhidhamma not only distinguishes the types of consciousness, but more importantly, it also exhibits them as ordered into a *cosmos*, a unified and closely interwoven whole.

To do so it employs several overlapping principles of classification. The first of these, introduced in the present section of the *Sangaha*, is the plane (*bhūmi*) of consciousness. There are four planes of consciousness. Three are mundane: the sense sphere, the fine-material sphere, and the immaterial sphere; the fourth plane is the supramundane. The word *avacara*, "sphere," which qualifies the first three planes, means "that which moves about in, or frequents, a particular locality." The locality frequented is the plane of existence (also *bhūmi*) designated by the name of the sphere, that is, the sensuous, the fine-material, and the immaterial planes of existence. However, though the three spheres of consciousness have a particularly close connection with the corresponding planes of existence, they are not identical. The spheres of consciousness are categories for classifying types of cittas, the planes of existence are realms or worlds into which beings are reborn and in which they pass their lives.

A definite relation nevertheless exists between the spheres of consciousness and the planes of existence: a particular sphere of consciousness comprises those types of consciousness which are typical of the corresponding plane of existence and which *frequent* that plane by tending to arise most often there. Consciousness of a particular sphere is not tied to the corresponding plane, but may arise in other planes of existence as well; for instance, fine-material and immaterial-sphere cittas can arise in the sensuous plane, and sense-sphere cittas can arise in the fine-material and immaterial planes. But still a connection is found, in that a sphere of consciousness is *typical* for the plane that shares its name. Moreover, the kammically active cittas of any particular sphere, the cittas that generate kamma, tend to produce rebirth into the corresponding plane of existence, and if they succeed in gaining the opportunity to generate rebirth, they will do so only in that plane, not in any other plane. Hence the tie between the spheres of consciousness and the corresponding planes of existence is extremely close.

Sense-sphere consciousness (***kāmāvacaracitta***): The word *kāma* means both subjective sensuality, i.e. craving for sense pleasures, and objective sensuousness, i.e. the five external sense-objects—visible forms, sounds, smells, tastes, and tangibles. The *kāmabhūmi* is the sensuous plane of existence, which comprises eleven realms—the four woeful states, the human realm, and the six sensuous heavens. Sense-sphere consciousness includes all those cittas that have their proper domain in the sensuous plane of existence, though they may arise in other planes as well.

Fine-material-sphere consciousness (***rūpāvacaracitta***): The fine-material sphere is the plane of consciousness corresponding to the fine-material plane of existence (*rūpabhūmi*), or the plane of consciousness pertaining to the states of meditative absorption called the *rūpajjhānas*. Any consciousness which mostly moves about in this realm is understood to belong to the fine-material sphere. The *rūpajjhānas* are so called because they are usually attained in meditation by concentrating on a material object (*rūpa*), which may be a device such as the earth-kasina, etc. (see IX, §6) or the parts of one's own body, etc. Such an object becomes the basis on which the jhānas are developed. The exalted states of consciousness attained on the basis of such objects are called *rūpāvacaracitta*, consciousness of the fine-material sphere.

Immaterial-sphere consciousness (***arūpāvacaracitta***): The immaterial sphere is the plane of consciousness corresponding to the immaterial plane of existence (*arūpabhūmi*), or the plane of consciousness pertaining to the immaterial absorptions—the *arūpajjhānas*. Any consciousness which mostly moves about in this realm is understood to belong to the immaterial sphere. When one meditates to attain the formless meditative states beyond the *rūpajjhānas*, one must discard all objects connected with material form and focus upon some non-material object, such as the infinity of space, etc. The exalted states of consciousness attained on the basis of such objects are called *arūpāvacaracitta*, consciousness of the immaterial sphere.

Supramundane consciousness (*lokuttaracitta*): The word *lokuttara*, supramundane, is derived from *loka* = world, and *uttara* = beyond, transcendent to. The concept of "world" is threefold: the world of living beings (*sattaloka*), the physical universe (*okāsaloka*), and the world of formations (*sankhāraloka*), that is, the totality of conditioned phenomena, physical and mental. The notion of world relevant here is the world of formations, that is, all mundane phenomena included within the five aggregates of clinging. That which transcends the world of conditioned things is the unconditioned element, Nibbāna, and the types of consciousness that directly accomplish the realization of Nibbāna are called *lokuttaracitta*, supramundane consciousness. The other three types are called, in distinction, *lokiyacitta*, mundane consciousness.

* * *

We thus see that consciousness can be classified by way of plane into four broad divisions: sense-sphere consciousness, fine-material-sphere consciousness, immaterial-sphere consciousness, and supramundane consciousness. Consciousness can also be classified on the basis of other principles besides plane. One principle of classification that plays an important role in the Abhidhamma philosophy is kind or nature (*jāti*).

With respect to its nature, consciousness divides into four classes: unwholesome, wholesome, resultant, and functional. Unwholesome consciousness (*akusalacitta*) is consciousness that is accompanied by one or another of the three unwholesome roots—greed, hatred, and delusion. Such consciousness is called unwholesome because it is mentally unhealthy, morally blameworthy, and productive of painful results. Wholesome consciousness (*kusalacitta*) is consciousness that is accompanied by the wholesome roots—non-greed or generosity, non-hatred or loving-kindness, and non-delusion or wisdom. Such consciousness is mentally healthy, morally blameless, and productive of pleasant results.

Both wholesome and unwholesome consciousness constitute *kamma*, volitional action. Those cittas or states of consciousness that arise through the ripening of kamma are called resultants (*vipāka*). These constitute a third class of citta distinct from the former two, a class that comprises both the results of wholesome kamma and the results of unwholesome kamma. It should be understood that both kamma and its results are purely mental. Kamma is volitional activity associated with wholesome or unwholesome cittas; its results are other cittas which experience the maturation of kamma.

The fourth class of consciousness, according to the division by way of nature, is called in Pali *kiriya* or *kriyā*, rendered here as "functional." This type of consciousness is neither kamma nor kamma resultant. It involves activity, yet this activity is not kammically determinate and thus is not capable of producing kammic results.

Resultant consciousness and functional consciousness are neither wholesome nor unwholesome. Instead, they are classified as indeterminate (*abyākata*), that is, consciousness which cannot be determined in terms of the dichotomy of wholesome and unwholesome.

Sense-Sphere Consciousness—54
(*kāmāvacaracittāni*)

Unwholesome Consciousness—12
(*akusalacittāni*)

§4 Consciousness Rooted in Greed (*lobhamūlacittāni*)—8

Tattha katamaṁ kāmāvacaraṁ?

1. Somanassasahagataṁ diṭṭhigatasampayuttaṁ asankhārikam ekaṁ.

2. Somanassasahagataṁ diṭṭhigatasampayuttaṁ sasankhārikam ekaṁ.

3. Somanassasahagataṁ diṭṭhigatavippayuttaṁ asankhārikam ekaṁ.

4. Somanassasahagataṁ diṭṭhigatavippayuttaṁ sasankhārikam ekaṁ.

5. Upekkhāsahagataṁ diṭṭhigatasampayuttaṁ asankhārikam ekaṁ.

6. Upekkhāsahagataṁ diṭṭhigatasampayuttaṁ sasankhārikam ekaṁ.

7. Upekkhāsahagataṁ diṭṭhigatavippayuttaṁ asankhārikam ekaṁ.

8. Upekkhāsahagataṁ diṭṭhigatavippayuttaṁ sasankhārikam ekan ti.

Imānī aṭṭha pi lobhasahagatacittāni nāma.

Amongst them what pertains to the sense sphere?

1. One consciousness, accompanied by joy, associated with wrong view, unprompted.

2. One consciousness, accompanied by joy, associated with wrong view, prompted.

3. One consciousness, accompanied by joy, dissociated from wrong view, unprompted.

4. One consciousness, accompanied by joy, dissociated from wrong view, prompted.

5. One consciousness, accompanied by equanimity, associated with wrong view, unprompted.

6. One consciousness, accompanied by equanimity, associated with wrong view, prompted.

7. One consciousness, accompanied by equanimity, dissociated from wrong view, unprompted.

8. One consciousness, accompanied by equanimity, dissociated from wrong view, prompted.

These eight types of consciousness are accompanied by greed.

Guide to §4

Unwholesome consciousness: In analyzing unwholesome consciousness, the Abhidhamma first classifies it by way of its most prominent root (*mūla, hetu*), whether greed (*lobha*), hatred (*dosa*), or delusion (*moha*). Greed and hatred, according to the Abhidhamma, are mutually exclusive: they cannot coexist within the same citta. Thus those states of consciousness in which greed is the principal root are termed "cittas rooted in greed," of which eight are enumerated. Those states in which hatred is the principal root are termed "cittas rooted in hatred," of which two are enumerated. The third unwholesome root, delusion, is present in every state of unwholesome consciousness. Thus, in those cittas rooted in greed and in those rooted in hatred, delusion is also found as an underlying root. Nevertheless, there are types of consciousness in which delusion arises without the accompaniment of greed or hatred. These cittas— two in number—are called consciousness involving sheer delusion or "cittas rooted in delusion." (See Table 1.2.)

Consciousness rooted in greed (***lobhamūlacittāni***): The Abhidhamma begins its analysis of the three classes of unwholesome consciousness by distinguishing the different cittas rooted in greed, as greed is always mentioned first among the unwholesome roots. The Pali word *lobha* includes all varieties of greed ranging from intense passion or cupidity to subtle liking and attachment. Consciousness rooted in greed is divided into eight types on the basis of three principles of dichotomization. One is the concomitant feeling (*vedanā*), whether a feeling of joy or equanimity; the second is the presence or absence of wrong view; the third is the consideration whether the citta is prompted or unprompted. From the permutations of these three distinctions, eight types of consciousness are obtained.

Accompanied by joy (*somanassasahagata*): The word *somanassa*, joy, is derived from *su* = pleasant + *manas* = mind; thus it means literally a pleasant mental state. *Somanassa* is a type of feeling, specifically, pleasant mental feeling. All consciousness is accompanied by some feeling, which may be bodily or mental, pleasant, painful, or neutral. *Somanassa* is a feeling which is mental rather than bodily, and pleasant rather than painful or neutral. This feeling "accompanies" (*sahagata*) this type of consciousness in that it is inextricably blended with it, just as when the waters of two rivers meet, they blend together and cannot be distinguished.

The Abhidhamma describes four cittas rooted in greed that are accompanied by joy. The other four cittas in this class are *accompanied by equanimity (upekkhāsahagata)*. The word *upekkhā* is often used in the Pali texts to signify the lofty spiritual quality of equanimity or impartiality, the state of mind which cannot be swayed by biases and preferences. Here, however, the word is used simply to mean neutral feeling, a mental feeling which leans neither towards gladness nor dejection. In contrast to pleasant and painful feelings, which experience the object in diametrically opposed ways, *upekkhā* experiences the object in a neutral manner. Thus *upekkhā* or equanimous feeling is also called *adukkhamasukhā vedanā*, neither-painful-nor-pleasant feeling.

Associated with wrong view (*diṭṭhigatasampayutta*): Having divided the greed-rooted consciousness into two classes on the basis of feeling—as accompanied by joy or by equanimity—the same consciousness is again divided on the basis of its relationship to wrong view. The word *diṭṭhi* means view, and unless it is specified by the prefix *sammā*, "right," it generally refers to wrong view (*micchā diṭṭhi*).[2] Wrong view accompanies the consciousness rooted in greed as a conviction, belief, opinion or rationalization. The view may either reinforce the attachment from which the consciousness springs by providing it with a rational justification, or the view itself may be an object of attachment in its own right. Wrong view is associated with four types of consciousness in all—two accompanied by joy and two accompanied by equanimity. The other four are *dissociated from wrong view* (*diṭṭhigatavippayutta*), in that greed operates in them without any accompanying justification provided by a view.

Unprompted (*asankhārika*): The third differentiating principle of consciousness rooted in greed is the presence or absence of prompting.

TABLE 1.2: THE UNWHOLESOME CITTAS

	Root	Feeling	Assoc. with	Dissoc. from	Prompted	No.
1	Greed	Joy	Wrong view	...	No	(1)
2	"	"	Wrong view	...	Yes	(2)
3	"	"	...	Wrong view	No	(3)
4	"	"	...	Wrong view	Yes	(4)
5	"	Equanimity	Wrong view	...	No	(5)
6	"	"	Wrong view	...	Yes	(6)
7	"	"	...	Wrong view	No	(7)
8	"	"	...	Wrong view	Yes	(8)
9	Hatred	Displeasure	Aversion	...	No	(9)
10	"	"	"	...	Yes	(10)
11	Delusion	Equanimity	Doubt	...	...	(11)
12	"	"	Restlessness	...	...	(12)

The multisignificant word *sankhāra* is used here in a sense specific to the Abhidhamma to mean prompting, instigation, inducement (*payoga*), or the application of an expedient (*upāya*). This prompting may be imposed by others, or it may originate from within oneself; the means employed may be bodily, verbal, or purely mental. The instigation is bodily when someone induces us by bodily means to give rise to particular types of consciousness which may issue in corresponding actions. It is verbal when the means employed is another's command or power of persuasion. And it is mental when, either by reflection or the determination of the will, we make a deliberate endeavour, despite inner resistance, to generate certain types of consciousness. Prompting can be associated with either unwholesome or wholesome states of consciousness, as will be shown below. That consciousness which arises spontaneously, without prompting or inducement by expedient means, is called *unprompted*. That consciousness which arises with prompting or inducement by expedient means is called *prompted (sasankhārika)*. In the greed-rooted class of consciousness, four types are unprompted or spontaneous, and four types are prompted or induced.

§5 Consciousness Rooted in Hatred (*dosamūlacittāni*)—2

9. Domanassasahagataṁ paṭighasampayuttaṁ asankhārikam ekaṁ.

10. Domanassasahagataṁ paṭighasampayuttaṁ sasankhārikam ekan ti.

Imāni dve pi paṭighasampayuttacittāni nāma.

9. One consciousness, accompanied by displeasure, associated with aversion, unprompted.

10. One consciousness, accompanied by displeasure, associated with aversion, prompted.

These two types of consciousness are associated with aversion.

Guide to §5

Consciousness rooted in hatred (***dosamūlacittāni***): The second class of unwholesome consciousness analyzed by the Abhidhamma is that rooted in hatred, the second of the three unwholesome roots. This consciousness is of two kinds, distinguished simply as unprompted and prompted. In contrast to consciousness rooted in greed, which can arise with alternative types of feeling—either joy or equanimity—consciousness rooted in hatred arises with only one kind of feeling, that of displeasure. Again, unlike consciousness rooted in greed, consciousness rooted in hatred does not arise in association with wrong view. Although wrong view can motivate acts of hatred, according to the Abhidhamma the wrong view does not arise simultaneously with hate, in the same citta, but at an earlier time in a different type of citta.

Accompanied by displeasure (***domanassasahagata***): The feeling that accompanies states of consciousness rooted in hatred is displeasure. The Pali word *domanassa*, derived from *du* = bad + *manas* = mind, signifies unpleasant mental feeling. This feeling accompanies only consciousness rooted in hatred, and such consciousness is necessarily accompanied by this feeling. Thus displeasure, or unpleasant mental feeling, is always unwholesome; in this respect it differs from unpleasant bodily feeling, which is kammically indeterminate, and from joy and equanimity, which may be wholesome, unwholesome, or indeterminate.

Associated with aversion (***paṭighasampayutta***): Whereas consciousness rooted in greed is explicitly said to be accompanied by greed, consciousness rooted in hatred (*dosa*) is expounded under the synonymous term aversion (*paṭigha*). *Paṭigha* includes all degrees of aversion, from violent rage to subtle irritation. The word means literally "striking against," which indicates a mental attitude of resistance, rejection, or destruction.

Though displeasure and aversion always accompany each other, their qualities should be distinguished. Displeasure (*domanassa*) is the experience of unpleasant feeling, aversion (*paṭigha*) is the mental attitude of ill will or irritation. In terms of the five aggregates, displeasure is included in the aggregate of feeling (*vedanākkhandha*), while aversion is included in the aggregate of mental formations (*saṅkhārakkhandha*).

§6 Consciousness Rooted in Delusion (*mohamūlacittāni*)—2

11. Upekkhāsahagataṁ vicikicchāsampayuttam ekaṁ.
12. Upekkhāsahagataṁ uddhaccasampayuttam ekan ti.
Imāni dve momūhacittāni nāma.
Icc'evaṁ sabbathā pi dvādasākusalacittāni samattāni.

11. One consciousness, accompanied by equanimity, associated with doubt.

12. One consciousness, accompanied by equanimity, associated with restlessness.

These two types of consciousness involve sheer delusion.

Thus end, in all, the twelve types of unwholesome consciousness.

Guide to §6

Consciousness rooted in delusion (*mohamūlacittāni*): This last class of unwholesome consciousness comprises those cittas in which the other two unwholesome roots—greed and hatred—are absent. Usually delusion leads to the arising of greed or hatred as well. But though delusion is always present as a root in cittas accompanied by greed and hate, its function there is subordinate. In these last two types of unwholesome consciousness, however, delusion alone is present as an unwholesome root, and thus they are classified as consciousness rooted in delusion. Because the function of delusion is especially evident in these two types of consciousness, they are also described as consciousness *involving sheer delusion (momūhacitta)*, the Pali word *momūha* being an intensification of *moha*, delusion. There are two types of consciousness in which delusion is especially prominent: one is associated with doubt, the other with restlessness.

Accompanied by equanimity (*upekkhāsahagata*): Even if a desirable object is present when a delusion-rooted consciousness arises, it is not experienced as desirable and thus pleasant mental feeling (*somanassa*) does not arise. Similarly, an undesirable object is not experienced as such and thus unpleasant mental feeling (*domanassa*) does not arise. Moreover, when the mind is obsessed by doubt or restlessness, it is not capable of forming a determinate positive or negative evaluation of the object, and thus cannot be associated with either pleasant or painful feeling. For these reasons the feeling that accompanies these two cittas is neutral, the feeling of equanimity (*upekkhā*).

Associated with doubt (*vicikicchāsampayutta*): The commentators give two etymological explanations of the word *vicikicchā*: (i) vexation due to perplexed thinking; and (ii) being devoid of the remedy consisting in knowledge.[3] Both these explanations indicate that *vicikicchā*, doubt, means perplexity, skepticism or indecisiveness, due to the prevalence of delusion. The citta associated with this doubt is the first type of consciousness rooted in delusion.

Associated with restlessness (*uddhaccasampayutta*): Restlessness is disquietude, mental distraction, or agitation, and the citta infected by this restlessness is the second type of consciousness rooted in delusion. According to the Abhidhamma, the mental factor of restlessness is found in all twelve unwholesome cittas (see II, §13), but in the other eleven cittas its force (*satti*) is relatively weak and its function is secondary. However, in this last type of citta, restlessness becomes the chief factor; thus this last type alone is described as *consciousness associated with restlessness.*

It should be noted that no qualification in terms of prompted or unprompted is attached to the description of these two cittas rooted in delusion. The commentators offer different explanations for this omission. The *Vibhāvinī-Ṭīkā* and the *Mahā-Ṭīkā* to the *Visuddhimagga* maintain that the distinction in terms of prompting is omitted because neither alternative is applicable. They state that since these two cittas lack natural acuteness, they cannot be described as unprompted; and since there is no occasion when one deliberately tries to arouse them, they cannot be described as prompted. Ledi Sayadaw, however, rejects this position, holding these cittas to be exclusively unprompted. He contends: "Since these two cittas occur in beings naturally, by their own intrinsic nature, they need not be aroused by any inducement or expedient means. They always occur without trouble or difficulty. Therefore they are exclusively unprompted, and this should be seen as the reason the distinction by way of prompting is not mentioned here."

§7 Summary of Unwholesome Consciousness

Aṭṭhadhā lobhamūlāni
Dosamūlāni ca dvidhā
Mohamūlāni ca dve' ti
Dvādas' ākusalā siyuṁ.

Eight are rooted in greed, two in hatred, and two in delusion. Thus there are twelve types of unwholesome consciousness.

Guide to §7

The eight types of consciousness rooted in greed may be illustrated by the following cases:

1 With joy, holding the view that there is no evil in stealing, a boy spontaneously steals an apple from a fruit stall.

2 With joy, holding the same view, he steals an apple through the prompting of a friend.

3-4 The same as 1 and 2 except that the boy does not hold any wrong view.

5-8 These four are parallel to 1-4 except that the stealing is done with neutral feeling.

The two types rooted in hatred may be illustrated thus:

9 With hatred one man murders another in a spontaneous fit of rage.

10 With hatred one man murders another after premeditation.

The two types rooted in delusion may be illustrated thus:

11 A person, due to delusion, doubts the enlightenment of the Buddha or the efficacy of the Dhamma as a way to deliverance.

12 A person is so distracted in mind that he cannot focus his mind on any object.

Rootless Consciousness—18 (*ahetukacittāni*)

§8 Unwholesome-Resultant Consciousness (*akusalavipākacittāni*)—7

(1) Upekkhāsahagataṁ cakkhuviññāṇaṁ; tathā (2) sotaviññāṇaṁ, (3) ghānaviññāṇaṁ, (4) jivhāviññāṇaṁ; (5) dukkhasahagataṁ kāyaviññāṇaṁ; (6) upekkhāsahagataṁ sampaṭicchanacittaṁ; (7) upekkhāsahagataṁ santīraṇacittañ cā ti. Imāni satta pi akusala-vipākacittāni nāma.

(1) Eye-consciousness accompanied by equanimity; as are (2) ear-consciousness, (3) nose-consciousness, (4) tongue-consciousness; (5) body-consciousness accompanied by pain; (6) receiving consciousness accompanied by equanimity; (7) investigating consciousness accompanied by equanimity. These seven are the unwholesome-resultant types of consciousness.

Guide to §8

Rootless consciousness (***ahetukacittāni***): The word *ahetuka* means without roots, and qualifies those types of consciousness that are devoid of the mental factors called *hetu*, roots. These types, eighteen in number, do not contain any of the three unwholesome roots—greed, hatred, and delusion—nor do they contain the three bright roots—non-greed, non-hatred, and non-delusion—which may be either wholesome or indeterminate. Since a root is a factor which helps to establish stability in a citta, those cittas which lack roots are weaker than those which possess them. The eighteen cittas in this class fall into three groups: unwholesome-resultants, wholesome-resultants, and functional consciousness. (See Table 1.3.)

Unwholesome-resultant consciousness (***akusalavipākacittāni***): The first category of rootless consciousness comprises the seven types of consciousness that result from unwholesome kamma. These types of consciousness are not themselves unwholesome but kammically indeterminate (*abyākata*). The word "unwholesome" (*akusala*) here means that they are resultants produced by unwholesome kamma; the word qualifies, not these states of consciousness themselves, but the kamma from which they are born.

Eye-consciousness (*cakkhuviññāṇa*): The first five types of resultant consciousness in both classes, the unwholesome-resultants and the wholesome-resultants, are those that are based on the sensitive matter (*pasāda*) of the eye, ear, nose, tongue, and body. These ten cittas are collectively designated the "two sets of fivefold sense consciousness" (*dvi-pañcaviññāṇa*).

Eye-consciousness arises based upon eye-sensitivity (*cakkhu-pasāda*). Its function is simply to see, to cognize directly and immediately, the visible object. The other types of sense consciousness also arise based upon their respective sensitivity, and their function is simply to cognize their respective objects—to hear sounds, to smell smells, to taste tastes, and to feel tangibles. In the case of unwholesome-resultants, the object is unpleasant or undesirable (*aniṭṭha*). However, the impact of the object on the first four sense faculties is weak and thus the associated feeling is neutral, i.e. equanimity. But in the case of unwholesome-resultant body-consciousness, the object's impact on the body faculty is strong, and thus the accompanying feeling is bodily pain (*dukkha*).

Receiving consciousness (*sampaṭicchanacitta*): When a sense object impinges on a sense faculty at one of the five sense doors, e.g. a visible form on the eye, first there arises a citta adverting to the object. Immediately after this, eye-consciousness arises seeing that form. This act of seeing lasts only for a single mind-moment. Immediately thereafter arises a citta which apprehends or "receives" the object that had been seen by eye-consciousness. This is the receiving consciousness, which results from the same type of kamma that produced the eye-consciousness.

Investigating consciousness (*santīraṇacitta*): This is another rootless resultant consciousness, which arises immediately after the receiving consciousness. Its function is to investigate or examine the object that had just been cognized by the sense consciousness and apprehended by the receiving consciousness. The receiving consciousness and the investigating consciousness arise only in the five sense doors, and both are results of past kamma.

§9 Wholesome-Resultant Rootless Consciousness (*kusalavipāka-ahetukacittāni*)—8

(8) Upekkhāsahagataṁ cakkhuviññāṇaṁ; tathā (9) sotaviññāṇaṁ, (10) ghānaviññāṇaṁ, (11) jivhāviññāṇaṁ; (12) sukhasahagataṁ

kāyaviññāṇaṁ; (13) upekkhāsahagataṁ sampaṭicchanacittaṁ; (14) somanassasahagataṁ santīraṇacittaṁ; (15) upekkhāsahagataṁ santīraṇacittañ cā ti. Imāni aṭṭha pi kusalavipākāhetukacittāni nāma.

(8) Eye-consciousness accompanied by equanimity; as are (9) ear-consciousness, (10) nose-consciousness, (11) tongue-consciousness; (12) body-consciousness accompanied by pleasure; (13) receiving consciousness accompanied by equanimity; (14) investigating consciousness accompanied by joy; (15) investigating consciousness accompanied by equanimity. These eight are the wholesome-resultant types of rootless consciousness.

Guide to § 9

Wholesome-resultant rootless consciousness (***kusalavipāka-ahetukacittāni***): The eight types of consciousness in this category are results of wholesome kamma. In the designation of the previous class, the word *ahetuka* was not included because all unwholesome-resultants are rootless; there are no unwholesome-resultants that are accompanied by roots. However, as will be seen later, wholesome-resultants can be accompanied by roots, namely, by beautiful roots that are kammically indeterminate (*abyākata*). To distinguish the wholesome-resultants that are rootless from those with roots, the word *ahetuka* is included in their class designation.

Seven of these types of consciousness correspond to the unwholesome-resultants. But whereas the unwholesome-resultants arise in regard to an undesirable object, the wholesome-resultants arise in regard to an object that is desirable (*iṭṭha*) or extremely desirable (*ati-iṭṭha*). The first four sense consciousnesses here, like their counterparts, are associated with equanimity, that is, neutral feeling; but the impact of the object on the body being strong, the feeling associated with wholesome-resultant body-consciousness is that of bodily pleasure (*sukha*).

The rootless wholesome-resultants include one type of consciousness without a counterpart among the unwholesome-resultants. This is the investigating consciousness accompanied by joy (*somanassa*). Whereas the investigating consciousness resulting from unwholesome kamma is always accompanied by neutral feeling, that resulting from wholesome kamma is twofold: one accompanied by neutral feeling, arisen in regard to a moderately desirable object, and one accompanied by joy, which arises when the object is especially desirable. Thus there are eight types of consciousness in this class, in contrast to the seven types found in the former class.

TABLE 1.3: THE ROOTLESS CITTAS

	Kind	Feeling	Citta	No.
1	Unwholesome - resultant	Equanimity	Eye-consciousness	(13)
2	"	"	Ear - "	(14)
3	"	"	Nose - "	(15)
4	"	"	Tongue - "	(16)
5	"	Pain	Body - "	(17)
6	"	Equanimity	Receiving	(18)
7	"	"	Investigating	(19)
8	Wholesome-resultant	Equanimity	Eye-consciousness	(20)
9	"	"	Ear - "	(21)
10	"	"	Nose - "	(22)
11	"	"	Tongue - "	(23)
12	"	Pleasure	Body - "	(24)
13	"	Equanimity	Receiving	(25)
14	"	Joy	Investigating	(26)
15	"	Equanimity	Investigating	(27)
16	Functional	Equanimity	Five-door adverting	(28)
17	"	"	Mind-door adverting	(29)
18	"	Joy	Smile-producing	(30)

§10 Rootless Functional Consciousness (*ahetukakiriya-cittāni*)—3

(16) Upekkhāsahagataṁ pañcadvārāvajjanacittaṁ; tathā (17) manodvārāvajjanacittaṁ; (18) somanassasahagataṁ hasituppāda-cittañ cā ti. Imāni tīṇi pi ahetukakiriyacittāni nāma.

Icc'evaṁ sabbathā pi aṭṭhāras' āhetukacittāni samattāni.

(16) Five-sense-door adverting consciousness accompanied by equanimity; as is (17) mind-door adverting consciousness; (18) smile-producing consciousness accompanied by joy. These three are the rootless functional types of consciousness.

Thus end, in all, the eighteen types of rootless consciousness.

Guide to §10

Rootless functional consciousness (***ahetukakiriyacittāni***): The remaining three types of consciousness among the *ahetukas* are not kammic results. They belong to the category called *kiriya*, rendered here as "functional" to indicate that they perform tasks which do not have any kammic potency. Such types of consciousness are neither causal kamma nor the result of kamma. Within this category, three types of consciousness are rootless, the rest (described later) are with roots.

Five-sense-door adverting consciousness (***pañcadvārāvajjanacitta***): When an external sense object impinges on one of the five physical sense organs, before the appropriate sense consciousness can arise—e.g. eye-consciousness seeing a form—another consciousness must have arisen first. This consciousness is the five-sense-door adverting consciousness, which has the function of adverting (*āvajjana*) to whatever object is presenting itself at one of the five sense doors (*dvāra*). This consciousness does not see, hear, smell, taste, or touch the object. It simply turns to the object, thereby enabling the sense consciousness to arise in immediate succession.

Mind-door adverting consciousness (***manodvārāvajjanacitta***): This type of consciousness can arise either in a cognitive process occurring at the five sense doors or in a process occurring at the mind door. In each case it performs a different function. When it occurs in a five-door process it is called the *votthapanacitta*, determining consciousness. Its function then is to determine, or define, the object that has been cognized by sense consciousness. In the five-door process, determining consciousness succeeds the investigating consciousness. After the investigating consciousness has examined the object, the determining consciousness discriminates it.

In a mind-door process—a cognitive process that occurs through the internal ideation faculty—this same type of consciousness performs another function. Its function then is to advert to the object appearing at the mind door. In such a role this citta is known as the mind-door adverting consciousness.

Smile-producing consciousness (***hasituppādacitta***): This is a citta peculiar to Arahants, including Buddhas and Paccekabuddhas who are also types of Arahants. Its function is to cause Arahants to smile about sense-sphere phenomena. According to the Abhidhamma, Arahants may smile with one of five cittas—the four beautiful sense-sphere functional cittas (I, §15) and the rootless smile-producing consciousness mentioned here.

§11 Summary of Rootless Consciousness

Satt' ākusalapākāni puññapākāni aṭṭhadhā
Kriyācittāni tīṇī ti aṭṭhārasa ahetukā.

Seven are unwholesome-resultants. Wholesome-resultants are eightfold. Three are functionals. Thus the rootless are eighteen.

§12 Beautiful Consciousness (*sobhanacittāni*)

Pāpāhetukamuttāni sobhanānī ti vuccare
Ekūnasaṭṭhi cittāni ath' ekanavutī pi vā.

Excluding those that are evil and the rootless, the rest are called "beautiful." They number either fifty-nine or ninety-one.

Guide to §12

Beautiful consciousness (***sobhanacittāni***): Beautiful consciousness includes all cittas "excluding those that are evil," that is, the twelve types of unwholesome consciousness, and "the rootless," the eighteen types that are utterly devoid of roots. This type of consciousness is called beautiful because it is accompanied by beautiful mental factors (*cetasikas* —see II, §§ 5-8).

It should be understood that the beautiful (*sobhana*) has a wider range than the wholesome (*kusala*). The beautiful includes all wholesome cittas, but it also includes resultant and functional cittas that possess beautiful mental factors. These latter cittas are not wholesome but kammically indeterminate (*abyākata*). The beautiful comprises the twenty-four sense-sphere cittas (to be defined just below) as well as all fine-material-sphere cittas, immaterial-sphere cittas, and supramundane cittas. Those cittas other than the beautiful are called *asobhana*, non-beautiful.

Either fifty-nine or ninety-one: The fifty-nine beautiful cittas are obtained thus: 24 sense-sphere + 15 fine-material-sphere + 12 immaterial-sphere + 8 supramundane. A total of ninety-one is obtained by dividing the supramundane cittas into forty types rather than eight, as will be explained below (I, §§ 30-31).

Sense-Sphere Beautiful Consciousness—24
(*kāmāvacara-sobhanacittāni*)

§13 Sense-Sphere Wholesome Consciousness (*kāmāvacara-kusalacittāni*)—8

1. Somanassasahagataṁ ñāṇasampayuttaṁ asankhārikam ekaṁ.
2. Somanassasahagataṁ ñāṇasampayuttaṁ sasankhārikam ekaṁ.
3. Somanassasahagataṁ ñāṇavippayuttaṁ asankhārikam ekaṁ.
4. Somanassasahagataṁ ñāṇavippayuttaṁ sasankhārikam ekaṁ.
5. Upekkhāsahagataṁ ñāṇasampayuttaṁ asankhārikam ekaṁ.
6. Upekkhāsahagataṁ ñāṇasampayuttaṁ sasankhārikam ekaṁ.
7. Upekkhāsahagataṁ ñāṇavippayuttaṁ asankhārikam ekaṁ.
8. Upekkhāsahagataṁ ñāṇavippayuttaṁ sasankhārikam ekan ti.
Imāni aṭṭha pi sahetuka-kāmāvacara-kusalacittāni nāma.

1. One consciousness, accompanied by joy, associated with knowledge, unprompted.

2. One consciousness, accompanied by joy, associated with knowledge, prompted.

3. One consciousness, accompanied by joy, dissociated from knowledge, unprompted.

4. One consciousness, accompanied by joy, dissociated from knowledge, prompted.

5. One consciousness, accompanied by equanimity, associated with knowledge, unprompted.

6. One consciousness, accompanied by equanimity, associated with knowledge, prompted.

7. One consciousness, accompanied by equanimity, dissociated from knowledge, unprompted.

8. One consciousness, accompanied by equanimity, dissociated from knowledge, prompted.

These are the eight types of sense-sphere wholesome consciousness with roots.

Guide to §13

Sense-sphere wholesome consciousness (***kāmāvacara-kusala-cittāni***): This class of consciousness is divided into eight types on the basis of three principles of dichotomization. One is the concomitant feeling, which in four cases is joy (*somanassa*), i.e. pleasant mental feeling, and in four cases equanimity (*upekkhā*), i.e. neutral mental feeling; a second is the presence or absence of knowledge; and a third is the dyad of unprompted and prompted. (See Table 1.4.)

Associated with knowledge (***ñāṇasampayutta***): Knowledge comprehends things as they are (*yathāsabhāvaṁ*). In the consciousness associated with knowledge, the word *ñāṇa* refers to the mental factor of wisdom (*paññā-cetasika*), which also represents the root non-delusion (*amoha*). Consciousness *dissociated from knowledge* (*ñāṇavippayutta*) lacks this factor of wisdom, but it does not involve ignorance (*avijjā*) or delusion (*moha*), which pertains only to unwholesome consciousness.

Unprompted: According to the commentary, one does a good deed without prompting due to physical and mental fitness, good food and climate, etc., and as a result of having performed similar deeds in the

TABLE 1.4: THE SENSE-SPHERE BEAUTIFUL CITTAS

	Feeling	Knowledge	Prompted	Wh.	Rst.	Fnc.
1	Joy	Assoc. with	No	(31)	(39)	(47)
2	"	"	Yes	(32)	(40)	(48)
3	"	Dissoc. from	No	(33)	(41)	(49)
4	"	"	Yes	(34)	(42)	(50)
5	Equanimity	Assoc. with	No	(35)	(43)	(51)
6	"	"	Yes	(36)	(44)	(52)
7	"	Dissoc. from	No	(37)	(45)	(53)
8	"	"	Yes	(38)	(46)	(54)

past. Prompting occurs through inducement by another or by personal deliberation, as explained above (p.36).

With roots (***sahetuka***): The four wholesome cittas associated with knowledge possess all three wholesome roots; the four dissociated from knowledge possess non-greed or generosity and non-hate or loving-kindness, but lack non-delusion.

The eight types of wholesome sense-sphere consciousness may be illustrated by the following examples:

1 Someone joyfully performs a generous deed, understanding that this is a wholesome deed, spontaneously without prompting.

2 Someone performs the same good deed, with understanding, after deliberation or prompting by another.

3 Someone joyfully performs a generous deed, without prompting, but without understanding that this is a wholesome deed.

4 Someone joyfully performs a generous deed, without understanding, after deliberation or prompting by another.

5-8 These types of consciousness should be understood in the same way as the preceding four, but with neutral feeling instead of joyful feeling.

These eight types of consciousness are called wholesome (*kusala*) or meritorious (*puñña*) because they inhibit the defilements and produce good results. They arise in worldlings (*puthujjana*) and trainees (*sekkha*)—noble disciples at the three lower stages of stream-enterer, once-returner, and non-returner—whenever they perform wholesome bodily deeds and verbal deeds and whenever they generate wholesome states of mind pertaining to the sense sphere. These cittas do not arise in Arahants, whose actions are without kammic potency.

§14 Sense-Sphere Resultant Consciousness (*kāmāvacara-vipākacittāni*)—8

9. Somanassasahagataṁ ñāṇasampayuttaṁ asankhārikam ekaṁ.
10. Somanassasahagataṁ ñāṇasampayuttaṁ sasankhārikam ekaṁ.
11. Somanassasahagataṁ ñāṇavippayuttaṁ asankhārikam ekaṁ.
12. Somanassasahagataṁ ñāṇavippayuttaṁ sasankhārikam ekaṁ.
13. Upekkhāsahagataṁ ñāṇasampayuttaṁ asankhārikam ekaṁ.
14. Upekkhāsahagataṁ ñāṇasampayuttaṁ sasankhārikam ekaṁ.
15. Upekkhāsahagataṁ ñāṇavippayuttaṁ asankhārikam ekaṁ.
16. Upekkhāsahagataṁ ñāṇavippayuttaṁ sasankhārikam ekan ti.
Imāni aṭṭha pi sahetuka-kāmāvacara-vipākacittāni nāma.

9. One consciousness, accompanied by joy, associated with knowledge, unprompted.

10. One consciousness, accompanied by joy, associated with knowledge, prompted.

11. One consciousness, accompanied by joy, dissociated from knowledge, unprompted.

12. One consciousness, accompanied by joy, dissociated from knowledge, prompted.

13. One consciousness, accompanied by equanimity, associated with knowledge, unprompted.

14. One consciousness, accompanied by equanimity, associated with knowledge, prompted.

15. One consciousness, accompanied by equanimity, dissociated from knowledge, unprompted.

16. One consciousness, accompanied by equanimity, dissociated from knowledge, prompted.

These are the eight types of sense-sphere resultant consciousness with roots.

Guide to §14

Sense-sphere resultant consciousness with roots (***sahetuka-kāmāvacara-vipākacittāni***): As there are eight wholesome types of consciousness, there are also eight corresponding types of resultant consciousness. These eight cittas are kammic effects of the sense-sphere wholesome cittas. In order to differentiate them from the rootless resultants due to wholesome kamma, these are described as *sahetuka*, "with roots." Both the rootless wholesome-resultants and the rooted resultants are produced by the same eight wholesome cittas, but the two sets differ in their qualities and functions. These differences will become clearer when we discuss the functions of consciousness (III, §§8-11).

§15 Sense-Sphere Functional Consciousness (*kāmāvacara-kriyācittāni*)—8

17. *Somanassasahagataṁ ñāṇasampayuttaṁ asankhārikam ekaṁ*
18. *Somanassasahagataṁ ñāṇasampayuttaṁ sasankhārikam ekaṁ*
19. *Somanassasahagataṁ ñāṇavippayuttaṁ asankhārikam ekaṁ*
20. *Somanassasahagataṁ ñāṇavippayuttaṁ sasankhārikam ekaṁ*
21. *Upekkhāsahagataṁ ñāṇasampayuttaṁ asankhārikam ekaṁ.*
22. *Upekkhāsahagataṁ ñāṇasampayuttaṁ sasankhārikam ekaṁ.*

23. Upekkhāsahagataṁ ñāṇasampayuttaṁ asankhārikam ekaṁ.

24. Upekkhāsahagataṁ ñāṇasampayuttaṁ sasankhārikam ekan ti.

Imāni aṭṭha pi sahetuka-kāmāvacara-kriyācittāni nāma.

Icc' evaṁ sabbathā pi catuvīsati sahetuka-kāmāvacara-kusala-vipāka-kriyācittāni samattāni.

17. One consciousness, accompanied by joy, associated with knowledge, unprompted.

18. One consciousness, accompanied by joy, associated with knowledge, prompted.

19. One consciousness, accompanied by joy, dissociated from knowledge, unprompted.

20. One consciousness, accompanied by joy, dissociated from knowledge, prompted.

21. One consciousness, accompanied by equanimity, associated with knowledge, unprompted.

22. One consciousness, accompanied by equanimity, associated with knowledge, prompted.

23. One consciousness, accompanied by equanimity, dissociated from knowledge, unprompted.

24. One consciousness, accompanied by equanimity, dissociated from knowledge, prompted.

These are the eight types of sense-sphere functional consciousness with roots.

Thus end, in all, the twenty-four types of sense-sphere consciousness with roots—wholesome, resultant, and functional.

Guide to §15

Sense-sphere functional consciousness with roots (*sahetuka-kāmāvacara-kriyācittāni*): Whereas the eight wholesome sense-sphere cittas arise in worldlings and trainees, they do not arise in Buddhas and Arahants, who have transcended the cycle of kamma and future becoming in the realms of rebirth. However, in Buddhas and Arahants there arise eight types of consciousness which are their exact counterparts. These are called *kriyā* (*kiriya*) or functional cittas because they merely perform their functions without leaving any kammic deposit. Because a Buddha or an Arahant has eradicated all traces of ignorance and craving, the causes of rebirth, there is no way his good actions could generate future results. They merely arise, accomplish some function, and then fall away without residue.

§16 Summary of Sense-Sphere Beautiful Consciousness

Vedanā-ñāṇa-sankhārabhedena catuvīsati
Sahetu-kāmāvacarapuññapākakriyā matā.

The sense-sphere consciousness with roots—understood as wholesome, resultant, and functional—becomes twenty-four by classification according to feeling, knowledge, and prompting.

Guide to §16

Sense-sphere consciousness with roots becomes threefold as wholesome, resultant, and functional, and each of these divides into eight through permutation by way of feeling—either joyful or neutral; by way of presence or absence of knowledge; and by way of spontaneity or prompting. Thus there are twenty-four types of consciousness altogether—the twelve connected with knowledge having three roots, the other twelve having two roots. These three groups are often referred to as the *mahākusalas*, *mahāvipākas*, and *mahākiriyas*—the great wholesome cittas, the great resultants, and the great functionals—though the teachers give different explanations of the prefix *mahā*, meaning "great."

§17 Summary of Sense-Sphere Consciousness

Kāme tevīsapākāni puññāpuññāni vīsati
Ekādasa kriyā cā ti catupaññāsa sabbathā.

In the sense-sphere twenty-three are resultant, twenty are wholesome and unwholesome, and eleven are functional. Thus there are altogether fifty-four.

Guide to §17

All types of consciousness experienced in the sense-sphere total fifty-four. These are classified as follows:

By way of kind:

- 8 great wholesome
- 12 unwholesome
- 23 resultants:
  - 7 unwholesome-resultants
  - 8 rootless wholesome-resultants
  - 8 great wholesome-resultants

11 functionals:
3 rootless functionals
8 great functionals

By way of feeling:

18 with joy
32 with equanimity
2 with displeasure
1 with pleasure
1 with pain

By way of association with knowledge and views:

16 associated
16 dissociated
22 neither

By way of prompting:

17 unprompted
17 prompted
20 neither (= rootless and deluded).

The traditional monastic way of teaching Abhidhamma urges students not only to reflect on these lists but to know them well by heart. They are very important when one studies the mental factors comprised in these types of cittas, as expounded in the next chapter and in the Abhidhamma Piṭaka.

Fine-material-Sphere Consciousness—15 (*rūpāvacaracittāni*)

§18 Fine-material-Sphere Wholesome Consciousness (*rūpāvacara-kusalacittāni*)—5

1. Vitakka-vicāra-pīti-sukh'-ekaggatā-sahitaṁ paṭhamajjhāna-kusalacittaṁ.

2. Vicāra-pīti-sukh'-ekaggatā-sahitaṁ dutiyajjhāna-kusalacittaṁ.

3. Pīti-sukh'-ekaggatā-sahitaṁ tatiyajjhāna-kusalacittaṁ.

4. Sukh'-ekaggatā-sahitaṁ catutthajjhāna-kusalacittaṁ.

5. Upekkh'-ekaggatā-sahitaṁ pañcamajjhāna-kusalacittañ cā ti.

Imāni pañca pi rūpāvacara-kusalacittāni nāma.

1. First jhāna wholesome consciousness together with initial application, sustained application, zest, happiness, and one-pointedness.

2. Second jhāna wholesome consciousness together with sustained application, zest, happiness, and one-pointedness.

3. Third jhāna wholesome consciousness together with zest, happiness, and one-pointedness.

4. Fourth jhāna wholesome consciousness together with happiness and one-pointedness.

5. Fifth jhāna wholesome consciousness together with equanimity and one-pointedness.

These are the five types of fine-material-sphere wholesome consciousness.

§19 Fine-material-Sphere Resultant Consciousness (*rūpāvacara-vipākacittāni*)—5

1. Vitakka-vicāra-pīti-sukh'-ekaggatā-sahitaṁ paṭhamajjhāna-vipākacittaṁ.

2. Vicāra-pīti-sukh'-ekaggatā-sahitaṁ dutiyajjhāna-vipākacittaṁ.

3. Pīti-sukh'-ekaggatā-sahitaṁ tatiyajjhāna-vipākacittaṁ.

4. Sukh'-ekaggatā-sahitaṁ catutthajjhāna-vipākacittaṁ.

5. Upekkh'-ekaggatā-sahitaṁ pañcamajjhāna-vipākacittañ cā ti.

Imāni pañca pi rūpāvacara-vipākacittāni nāma.

1. First jhāna resultant consciousness together with initial application, sustained application, zest, happiness, and one-pointedness.

2. Second jhāna resultant consciousness together with sustained application, zest, happiness, and one-pointedness.

3. Third jhāna resultant consciousness together with zest, happiness, and one-pointedness.

4. Fourth jhāna resultant consciousness together with happiness and one-pointedness.

5. Fifth jhāna resultant consciousness together with equanimity and one-pointedness.

These are the five types of fine-material-sphere resultant consciousness.

§20 Fine-material-Sphere Functional Consciousness (*rūpāvacara-kriyācittāni*)—5

1. Vitakka-vicāra-pīti-sukh'-ekaggatā-sahitaṁ paṭhamajjhāna-kriyācittaṁ.

2. *Vicāra-pīti-sukh'-ekaggatā-sahitaṁ dutiyajjhāna-kriyācittaṁ.*
3. *Pīti-sukh'-ekaggatā-sahitaṁ tatiyajjhāna-kriyācittaṁ.*
4. *Sukh'-ekaggatā-sahitaṁ catutthajjhāna-kriyācittaṁ.*
5. *Upekkh'-ekaggatā-sahitaṁ pañcamajjhāna-kriyācittañ cā ti.*

Imāni pañca pi rūpāvacara-kriyācittāni nāma.

Icc'evaṁ sabbathā pi paṇṇarasa rūpāvacara-kusala-vipāka-kriyācittāni samattāni.

1. First jhāna functional consciousness together with initial application, sustained application, zest, happiness, and one-pointedness.
2. Second jhāna functional consciousness together with sustained application, zest, happiness, and one-pointedness.
3. Third jhāna functional consciousness together with zest, happiness, and one-pointedness.
4. Fourth jhāna functional consciousness together with happiness and one-pointedness.
5. Fifth jhāna functional consciousness together with equanimity and one-pointedness.

These are the five types of fine-material-sphere functional consciousness.

Thus end, in all, the fifteen types of fine-material-sphere wholesome, resultant, and functional consciousness.

Guide to §§18-20

Fine-material-sphere consciousness (***rūpāvacaracittāni***): This sphere of consciousness includes all the cittas which "move about in" or pertain to the fine-material plane of existence (*rūpabhūmi*), the realms in which gross matter is absent and only a subtle residue of matter remains. Rebirth into these realms is achieved by the attainment of the meditative states called *jhānas*,[4] high attainments in the development of concentration (*samādhi*). The states of consciousness which "frequent" this plane, in that they are qualitatively connected to it, are called "fine-material-sphere consciousness."

Fifteen cittas fall into this category—five wholesome, five resultant, and five functional (Table 1.5). The wholesome fine-material-sphere cittas are experienced by worldlings and trainees (*sekkha*) who develop the jhānas within this life itself. Their corresponding results (*vipāka*) arise only in the fine-material world, in the beings who have been reborn there as a consequence of developing the jhānas. The five functional (*kriyā*) jhāna cittas are experienced only by Arahants who attain the jhānas.

TABLE 1.5: THE FINE-MATERIAL-SPHERE CITTAS

	Citta	Together with					Wh.	Rst.	Fnc.
1	1st jhāna	In. applic.	Sus. applic.	Zest	Happiness	One-ptns.	(55)	(60)	(65)
2	2nd jhāna	....	Sus. applic.	Zest	Happiness	One-ptns.	(56)	(61)	(66)
3	3nd jhāna	....	....	Zest	Happiness	One-ptns.	(57)	(62)	(67)
4	4th jhāna	....	....	....	Happiness	One-ptns.	(58)	(63)	(68)
5	5th jhāna	....	....	....	Equanimity	One-ptns.	(59)	(64)	(69)

The commentators derive the Pali word *jhāna* from a root meaning "to contemplate," and again from another root meaning "to burn up." Thus the jhānas are so called because they closely contemplate the object and because they burn up the adverse states opposed to concentration.[5] The adverse states are the five hindrances (*nīvaraṇa*) of sensual desire, ill will, sloth and torpor, restlessness and worry, and doubt.

The jhānas are attained by the method of meditation called the development of calm or serenity (*samathabhāvanā*). This type of meditation involves the strengthening of the faculty of concentration (*samādhi*). By fixing the mind upon a single selected object, all mental distraction is eliminated. The hindrances are suppressed and the mind becomes fully absorbed in its object. The development of calm will be dealt with in detail later (see IX, §§2-21).

The object of the jhāna-consciousness is a mental image called the counterpart sign (*paṭibhāganimitta*). This sign is considered a conceptual object (*paññatti*), but it generally arises on the basis of a visible form, and hence these jhānas pertain to the fine-material sphere. The meditator aspiring to jhāna may select as the original object of concentration a contemplative device called a *kasiṇa*, such as a coloured disk, on which attention is fixed. When concentration matures, this physical device will give rise to a visualized replica of itself called the "learning sign" (*uggahanimitta*), and this in turn gives rise to the counterpart sign apprehended as the object of jhāna.

Fine-material-sphere wholesome consciousness: This category comprises five cittas distinguished by way of the five jhānas, each jhāna constituting a distinct type of citta. The jhānas are enumerated in the order given for two reasons: (i) because, when one meditates for the attainment of the jhānas, one achieves them in this order; and (ii) because the Buddha taught them in this order.

First jhāna wholesome consciousness: Each jhāna is defined by way of a selection of mental concomitants called its jhāna factors (*jhānanga*). From among the many mental factors contained in each jhāna consciousness, it is these that distinguish the specific jhāna from the other jhānas and bring about the process of absorption. The first jhāna contains five factors, as enumerated in the text. To attain the first jhāna, these five factors must all be present in a balanced way, closely contemplating the object and "burning up" the five hindrances that obstruct absorption.

Initial application (*vitakka*): In the Suttas the word *vitakka* is often used in the loose sense of thought, but in the Abhidhamma it is used in a precise technical sense to mean the mental factor that mounts or directs the mind onto the object.[6] Just as a king's favourite might conduct a villager to the palace, even so *vitakka* directs the mind onto the object. In the practice for attaining jhāna, *vitakka* has the special task of inhibiting the hindrance of sloth and torpor (*thīnamiddha*).

Sustained application (*vicāra*): The word *vicāra* usually means examination, but here it signifies the sustained application of the mind on the object. Whereas *vitakka* is the directing of the mind and its concomitants towards the object, *vicāra* is the continued exercise of the mind on the object. The Commentaries offer various similes to highlight the difference between these two jhāna factors. *Vitakka* is like a bird's spreading out its wings to fly, *vicāra* is like the bird's gliding through the air with outstretched wings. *Vitakka* is like a bee's diving towards a flower, *vicāra* is like the bee's buzzing above the flower. *Vitakka* is like the hand that holds a tarnished metal dish, *vicāra* is like the hand that wipes the dish.[7] *Vicāra* in the jhānas serves to temporarily inhibit the hindrance of doubt (*vicikicchā*).

Zest (*pīti*): *Pīti*, derived from the verb *pīnayati* meaning "to refresh," may be explained as delight or pleasurable interest in the object. The term is often translated as rapture, a rendering which fits its role as a jhāna factor but may not be wide enough to cover all its nuances.[8] The commentators distinguish five grades of *pīti* that arise when developing concentration: minor zest, momentary zest, showering zest, uplifting zest, and pervading zest. Minor zest is able to raise the hairs on the body. Momentary zest is like flashes of lightning. Showering zest breaks over the body again and again like waves on the sea shore. Uplifting zest can cause the body to levitate. And pervading zest pervades the whole body as an inundation fills a cavern. The latter is identified as the *pīti* present in jhāna.[9] As a factor of jhāna *pīti* inhibits the hindrance of ill will (*vyāpāda*).

Happiness (*sukha*): This jhāna factor is pleasant mental feeling. It is identical with *somanassa*, joy, and not with the *sukha* of pleasant bodily feeling that accompanies wholesome-resultant body-consciousness. This *sukha*, also rendered as bliss, is born of detachment from sensual pleasures; it is therefore explained as *nirāmisasukha*, unworldly or spiritual happiness. It counters the hindrance of restlessness and worry (*uddhaccakukkucca*).

Though *pīti* and *sukha* are closely connected, they are distinguished in that *pīti* is a conative factor belonging to the aggregate of mental formations (*sankhārakkhandha*), while *sukha* is a feeling belonging to the aggregate of feeling (*vedanākkhandha*). *Pīti* is compared to the delight a weary traveller would experience when coming across an oasis, *sukha* to his pleasure after bathing and drinking.[10]

One-pointedness (*ekaggatā*): The Pali term means literally a one (*eka*) pointed (*agga*) state (*tā*). This mental factor is the primary component in all five jhānas and the essence of concentration (*samādhi*). One-pointedness temporarily inhibits sensual desire, a necessary condition for any meditative attainment. *Ekaggatā* exercises the function of closely contemplating the object, the salient characteristic of jhāna, but it cannot perform this function alone. It requires the joint action of the other four jhāna factors each performing its own special function: *vitakka* applying the associated states on the object, *vicāra* sustaining them there, *pīti* bringing delight in the object, and *sukha* experiencing happiness in the jhāna.

Second jhāna wholesome consciousness, etc.: The higher jhānas are attained by successively eliminating the grosser jhāna factors and by refining the subtler factors through strengthened concentration. In the Suttas the Buddha expounds the jhānas as fourfold by teaching the simultaneous elimination of *vitakka* and *vicāra* in progressing from the first jhāna to the second. In the Abhidhamma the jhānas become fivefold by the inclusion of an intermediate jhāna in which *vitakka* has been eliminated while *vicāra* remains. This is the second jhāna in the Abhidhamma scheme.

In the third jhāna *vicāra* as well is eliminated, in the fourth *pīti* is made to fade away, and in the fifth jhāna *upekkhā*, equanimity or neutral feeling, replaces *sukha*, happiness, as the concomitant feeling. Thus, whereas the cittas of the first four jhānas are associated with joy (*somanassasahita*), the citta of the fifth jhāna is associated with equanimity (*upekkhāsahita*).

According to the Suttanta method, which enumerates four jhānas of the fine-material sphere, the first jhāna is identical in all respects with the first jhāna of the Abhidhamma method. However, the second jhāna of the Suttanta method is attained by the simultaneous subsiding of initial application and sustained application, and thus has only the three jhāna factors of zest, happiness, and one-pointedness, like the third jhāna of the Abhidhamma method. The third jhāna of the Suttanta method has the two factors of happiness and one-pointedness, the fourth jhāna the two factors of equanimity (i.e. neutral feeling) and one-pointedness. These two jhānas are equivalent to the fourth and fifth jhānas respectively of the Abhidhamma method.

Although the Suttas do not mention the fivefold analysis of jhāna in explicit terms, they provide an implicit basis for this analysis in the Buddha's distinction between three kinds of concentration: concentration accompanied by both initial application and sustained application; concentration without initial application but with sustained application; and concentration with neither initial application nor sustained application (*savitakka savicāra samādhi, avitakka vicāramatta samādhi, avitakka avicāra samādhi*: M.128/iii,162). The first is obviously the first jhāna in both systems, and the third is the second and higher jhānas of the Suttanta method and the third and higher jhānas of the Abhidhamma method. The second, however, is nowhere clarified within the Suttas themselves and only becomes intelligible as the second jhāna of the Abhidhamma method.

§21 Summary of Fine-material-Sphere Consciousness

Pañcadhā jhānabhedena rūpāvacaramānasaṁ
Puññapākakriyābhedā taṁ pañcadasadhā bhave.

Fine-material-sphere consciousness is fivefold when divided by way of the jhānas. It becomes of fifteen types when (further) divided by way of the wholesome, resultant, and functional.

Guide to §21

The five jhānas become of fifteen types by occurring as wholesome cittas, as resultants, and as functionals. Each jhāna citta of the same level is defined by the same set of factors, whether wholesome, resultant or functional. All cittas of the fine-material sphere are associated with knowledge (*ñāṇasampayutta*), though knowledge, not being a specific jhāna factor, is not mentioned in the formulas. Thus all the fine-material-sphere cittas have three roots, non-greed, non hatred, and non-delusion.

It should be noted that, in contrast with sense-sphere wholesome and unwholesome cittas, the fine-material-sphere cittas are not distinguished by way of prompted and unprompted (*sasankhārika-asankhārika*). The same distinction is also omitted from the exposition of the immaterial-sphere and supramundane cittas. This omission is made because, when one is practising meditation to attain a jhāna, a path, or a fruit, as long as one is dependent upon instigation from others or upon one's own self-prompting, the mind is not yet in a suitable condition to reach the attainment. The distinction of prompted and unprompted is appropriate in relation to the preliminary phase of practice leading up to the attainment, but the cittas with which the actual attainment takes place cannot involve prompting or inducement. Thus, in the absence of a real possibility of prompted jhāna and supramundane attainment, the very distinction between prompted and unprompted becomes untenable in relation to these types of cittas.

The view we have expressed here differs from the commonly accepted opinion of the *Vibhāvinī-Ṭīkā* that, since all jhāna attainment requires some preliminary exertion (*pubbābhisankhāra*), the jhāna cittas can never be called unprompted but only prompted. This view seems untenable because the preliminary exertion leading up to the jhāna should not be identified as a "prompting" concomitant with the jhāna cittas themselves. Thus, despite the prestigious authority of the *Vibhāvinī*, it still seems preferable to regard the prompted-unprompted distinction as irrelevant to the higher classes of consciousness.

Nevertheless, Ledi Sayadaw holds that this distinction may be understood to apply to the jhānas and supramundane states by reason of the distinction made in the texts in the mode of progress (*paṭipadā*) by which they are gained. The *Dhammasaṅgaṇī* distinguishes between attainments gained by difficult progress (*dukkhapaṭipadā*), when the defilements can only be suppressed by intense striving and much exertion, and easy progress (*sukhapaṭipadā*), when the defilements can be suppressed easily, in a pleasant mode. Ledi Sayadaw takes the jhāna or supramundane cittas of one who reaches attainment by difficult progress to be the counterpart of prompted cittas at the sense-sphere level, and the jhāna or supramundane cittas of one who proceeds by easy progress to be the counterpart of unprompted cittas.

However, while Ledi Sayadaw's view is noteworthy, the fact remains that: (1) the *Dhammasaṅgaṇī* initially classifies the jhāna and supramundane cittas without any reference to mode of progress; and (2) in the section where it does introduce classification by mode of progress, it does not use this distinction as a basis for enumerating distinct *types* of jhāna or supramundane cittas. It therefore seems preferable to exclude the prompted-unprompted distinction altogether from the jhāna cittas, as well as from the path and fruition cittas.

IMMATERIAL-SPHERE CONSCIOUSNESS—12
(*arūpāvacaracittāni*)

§22 Immaterial-Sphere Wholesome Consciousness (*arūpāvacara-kusalacittāni*)—4

1. Ākāsānañcāyatana-kusalacittaṁ.
2. Viññāṇañcāyatana-kusalacittaṁ.
3. Ākiñcaññāyatana-kusalacittaṁ.
4. N'evasaññān' āsaññāyatana-kusalacittañ cā ti.
Imāni cattāri pi arūpāvacara-kusalacittāni nāma.

1. Wholesome consciousness pertaining to the base of infinite space.

2. Wholesome consciousness pertaining to the base of infinite consciousness.

3. Wholesome consciousness pertaining to the base of nothingness.

4. Wholesome consciousness pertaining to the base of neither-perception-nor-non-perception.

These are the four types of immaterial-sphere wholesome consciousness.

§23 Immaterial-Sphere Resultant Consciousness (*arūpāvacara-vipākacittāni*)—4

1. Ākāsānañcāyatana-vipākacittaṁ.
2. Viññāṇañcāyatana-vipākacittaṁ.
3. Ākiñcaññāyatana-vipākacittaṁ.
4. N'evasaññān'āsaññāyatana-vipākacittañ cā ti.
Imāni cattāri pi arūpāvacara-vipākacittāni nāma.

1. Resultant consciousness pertaining to the base of infinite space.

2. Resultant consciousness pertaining to the base of infinite consciousness.

3. Resultant consciousness pertaining to the base of nothingness.

4. Resultant consciousness pertaining to the base of neither-perception-nor-non-perception.

These are the four types of immaterial-sphere resultant consciousness.

§24 Immaterial-Sphere Functional Consciousness (*arūpāvacara-kriyācittāni*)—4

1. Ākāsānañcāyatana-kriyācittaṁ.
2. Viññāṇañcāyatana-kriyācittaṁ.
3. Ākiñcaññāyatana-kriyācittaṁ.
4. N'evasaññān'āsaññāyatana-kriyācittañ cā ti.
Imāni cattāri pi arūpāvacara-kriyācittāni nāma.
Icc'evaṁ sabbathā pi dvādasa arūpāvacara-kusala-vipāka-kriyācittāni samattāni.

1. Functional consciousness pertaining to the base of infinite space.

2. Functional consciousness pertaining to the base of infinite consciousness.

3. Functional consciousness pertaining to the base of nothingness.
4. Functional consciousness pertaining to the base of neither- perception-nor-non-perception.

These are the four types of immaterial-sphere functional consciousness.

Thus end, in all, the twelve types of immaterial-sphere wholesome, resultant, and functional consciousness.

Guide to §§22-24

Immaterial-sphere consciousness (***arūpāvacaracittāni***): This sphere of consciousness comprises the cittas pertaining to the immaterial plane of existence (*arūpabhūmi*), four realms in which matter has been totally transcended and only consciousness and mental factors remain. Rebirth into these four realms comes about through the attainment of the *arūpajjhānas*, the four immaterial or formless absorptions, which are reached by developing concentration beyond the five jhānas of the fine-material sphere. The immaterial sphere consists of twelve cittas—the four wholesome cittas with which the immaterial attainments are experienced by worldlings and trainees, the four resultants which arise through rebirth in the immaterial realms, and the four functionals which occur to Arahants who enter upon the immaterial attainments.

The base of infinite space (***ākāsānañcāyatana***): The first of the four immaterial jhānas is the attainment of the base of infinite space. To reach this, a meditator who has mastered the fifth fine-material jhāna based on a kasina object spreads out the counterpart sign of the kasina until it becomes immeasurable in extent. Then he removes the kasina by attending only to the space it pervaded, contemplating it as "infinite space." Through repeated attention given in this way, there eventually arises in absorption a citta having as object the concept of infinite space (*ākāsapaññatti*). The expression "base of infinite space," strictly speaking, refers to the concept of infinite space which serves as the object of the first immaterial-sphere consciousness. Here, the word *āyatana*, "base," has the sense of a habitat or dwelling for the citta of the jhāna. However, in a derivative sense, the expression "base of infinite space" is also extended to the jhāna itself.

The base of infinite consciousness (***viññāṇañcāyatana***): The consciousness that is here said to be infinite is the consciousness of the first immaterial absorption. Since that first immaterial absorption has as its object the base or concept of infinite space, this implies that the consciousness which pervades that space as its object also partakes in its infinity. To reach this attainment, therefore, the meditator takes as object the consciousness of the base of infinite space, and contemplates it as "infinite consciousness" until the second immaterial absorption arises.

The base of nothingness (*ākiñcaññāyatana*): The third immaterial attainment has as its object the present non-existence, voidness, or secluded aspect of the consciousness pertaining to the base of infinite space. By giving attention to the absence of that consciousness, the third immaterial absorption arises taking as its object the concept of non-existence or nothingness (*natthibhāva-paññatti*) in respect of the first immaterial consciousness.

The base of neither-perception-nor-non-perception (*n'evasaññān' āsaññāyatana*): This fourth and final immaterial attainment is so called because it cannot be said either to include perception or to exclude perception. In this type of consciousness, the factor of perception (*saññā*) has become so subtle that it can no longer perform the decisive function of perception, and thus this state cannot be said to have perception. Yet perception is not altogether absent but remains in a residual form; thus it cannot be said not to have perception. Although perception alone is mentioned, all the other mental constituents in this citta also exist in a state of such extreme subtlety that they cannot be described as either existent or non-existent. This fourth immaterial absorption takes as its object the consciousness of the base of nothingness, the third immaterial absorption.

§25 Summary of Immaterial-Sphere Consciousness

Ālambanappabhedena catudh' āruppamānasaṁ
Puññapākakriyābhedā puna dvādasadhā ṭhitaṁ.

Immaterial-sphere consciousness is fourfold when classified by way of object. When again divided by way of the wholesome, resultant, and the functional, it stands at twelve types.

Guide to §25

When classified by way of object: In relation to each type of immaterial-sphere consciousness, there are two kinds of object (*ālambana*) to be understood: one is the object to be directly apprehended by the citta (*ālambitabba*); the other is the object to be transcended (*atikkamitabba*). Their correlations are shown in Table 1.6.

The *arūpajjhānas* differ from the *rūpajjhānas* in several important respects. While their *rūpajjhānas* can take various objects such as the different kasinas, etc., each *arūpajjhāna* apprehends just one object specific to itself. Also, the *rūpajjhānas* differ from each other with respect

TABLE 1.6: THE IMMATERIAL-SPHERE CITTAS

	Citta	Direct Object	Transcended Object	Wh.	Rst.	Fnc.
1	Base of inf. space	Concept of space	Concept of kasina	(70)	(74)	(78)
2	Base of inf. consness.	Consness. of inf. space	Concept of space	(71)	(75)	(79)
3	Base of nothingness	Concept of non-existence	Consness. of inf. space	(72)	(76)	(80)
4	Base of n.p. nor n-p.	Consness. of nothingness	Concept of non-existence	(73)	(77)	(81)

to their jhāna factors—the first having five factors, the second four, etc. The meditator who wishes to attain the higher jhānas keeps the same object and eliminates each successively subtler factor until he reaches the fifth jhāna. But to progress from the fifth *rūpajjhāna* to the first *arūpajjhāna*, and from one *arūpajjhāna* to the next, there are no more jhāna factors to be transcended. Instead the meditator progresses by transcending each successively subtler object.

The cittas of the *arūpajjhānas* all have the same two jhāna factors as the fifth *rūpajjhāna*, namely, equanimity and one-pointedness. For this reason the four *arūpajjhānas* are sometimes spoken of as being included in the fifth *rūpajjhāna*. As cittas they are different because they pertain to a different sphere and have different types of objects than the fifth jhāna. But because, as jhānas, they are constituted by the same two jhāna factors, they are sometimes considered by the teachers of Abhidhamma as modes of the fifth jhāna.

Collectively, the fifteen fine-material-sphere cittas and the twelve immaterial-sphere cittas are designated *mahaggatacitta*—sublime, lofty, or exalted consciousness—because they are free from the hindrances and are pure, elevated, great states of mind.

All the eighty-one types of consciousness discussed so far are termed *lokiyacitta*, mundane consciousness, because they pertain to the three worlds—the sensuous world (*kāmaloka*), the fine-material world (*rūpaloka*), and the immaterial world (*arūpaloka*).

Supramundane Consciousness—8
(*lokuttaracittāni*)

§26 Supramundane Wholesome Consciousness (*lokuttara-kusalacittāni*)—4

1. Sotāpatti-maggacittaṁ.
2. Sakadāgāmi-maggacittaṁ.
3. Anāgāmi-maggacittaṁ.
4. Arahatta-maggacittañ cā ti.
Imāni cattāri pi lokuttara-kusalacittāni nāma.

1. Path consciousness of stream-entry.
2. Path consciousness of once-returning.
3. Path consciousness of non-returning.
4. Path consciousness of Arahantship.

§27 Supramundane Resultant Consciousness (*lokuttara-vipākacittāni*)—4

1. Sotāpatti-phalacittaṁ.
2. Sakadāgāmi-phalacittaṁ.
3. Anāgāmi-phalacittaṁ.
4. Arahatta-phalacittañ cā ti.
Imāni cattāri pi lokuttara-vipākacittāni nāma.
Icc'evaṁ sabbathā pi aṭṭha lokuttara-kusala-vipāka-cittāni samattāni.

1. Fruition consciousness of stream-entry.
2. Fruition consciousness of once-returning.
3. Fruition consciousness of non-returning.
4. Fruition-consciousness of Arahantship.

These are the four types of supramundane resultant consciousness.

Thus end, in all, the eight types of supramundane wholesome and resultant consciousness.

§28 Summary of Supramundane Consciousness

Catumaggappabhedena catudhā kusalaṁ tathā
Pākaṁ tassa phalattā ti aṭṭhadh' ānuttaraṁ mataṁ.

The wholesome consciousness is fourfold, divided by way of the four paths. So too are the resultants, being their fruits. Thus the supramundane should be understood as eightfold.

Guide to §§26-28

Supramundane consciousness (*lokuttaracittāni*): Supramundane consciousness is consciousness that pertains to the process of transcending (*uttara*) the world (*loka*) consisting of the five aggregates of clinging. This type of consciousness leads to liberation from *saṁsāra*, the cycle of birth and death, and to the attainment of Nibbāna, the cessation of suffering. There are eight supramundane cittas. These pertain to the four stages of enlightenment—stream-entry, once-returning, non-returning, and Arahantship. Each stage involves two types of citta, path consciousness (*maggacitta*) and fruition consciousness (*phalacitta*), as seen in Table 1.7. All supramundane cittas take as object the unconditioned reality, Nibbāna, but they differ as paths and fruits according to their functions. The path consciousness has the function of eradicating (or of permanently attenuating)[11] defilements; the fruition consciousness has the function of experiencing the degree of liberation made possible by the corresponding path. The path consciousness is a *kusalacitta*, a wholesome state; the fruition consciousness is a *vipākacitta*, a resultant.

TABLE 1.7: THE EIGHT SUPRAMUNDANE CITTAS

	Path	Fruit
Stream-entry	(82)	(86)
Once-returning	(83)	(87)
Non-returning	(84)	(88)
Arahantship	(85)	(89)

Each path consciousness arises only once, and endures only for one mind-moment; it is never repeated in the mental continuum of the person who attains it. The corresponding fruition consciousness initially arises immediately after the path moment, and endures for two or three mind-moments. Subsequently it can be repeated, and with practice can be made to endure for many mind-moments, in the supramundane absorption called fruition attainment (*phalasamāpatti*—see below, IV, §22; IX, §42).

The paths and fruits are attained by the method of meditation called the development of insight (*vipassanābhāvanā*). This type of meditation involves the strengthening of the faculty of wisdom (*paññā*). By sustained attention to the changing phenomena of mind and matter, the meditator learns to discern their true characteristics of impermanence, suffering, and non-self. When these insights gain full maturity, they issue in the supramundane paths and fruits. (See IX, §§22-44.)

Path consciousness of stream-entry (***sotāpatti-maggacitta***): The entry upon the irreversible path to liberation is called stream-entry, and the citta that experiences this attainment is the path consciousness of stream-entry. The stream (*sota*) is the Noble Eightfold Path, with its eight factors of right view, right intention, right speech, right action, right livelihood, right effort, right mindfulness, and right concentration. As the current of the Ganges flows uninterrupted from the Himalayas to the ocean, so the supramundane Noble Eightfold Path flows uninterrupted from the arising of right view to the attainment of Nibbāna.

Though the factors of the eightfold path may arise in the mundane wholesome cittas of virtuous worldlings, these factors are not fixed in their destination, since a worldling may change character and turn away from the Dhamma. But in a noble disciple who has reached the experience of stream-entry, the path factors become fixed in destiny, and flow like a stream leading to Nibbāna.

The path consciousness of stream-entry has the function of cutting off the first three fetters—"personality view" or wrong views of self, doubt about the Triple Gem, and clinging to rites and ceremonies in the belief that they can lead to liberation. It further cuts off all greed, hatred and delusion strong enough to lead to a sub-human rebirth. This citta also permanently eliminates five other cittas, namely, the four cittas rooted in greed associated with wrong view, and the citta rooted in delusion associated with doubt. One who has undergone the experience of stream-entry is assured of reaching final deliverance in a maximum of seven lives, and of never being reborn in any of the woeful planes of existence.

Path consciousness of once-returning (***sakadāgāmi-maggacitta***): This citta is the consciousness associated with the Noble Eightfold Path that gives access to the plane of a once-returner. While it does not eradicate any fetters, this citta attenuates the grosser forms of sensual desire and ill will. The person who has reached this stage will be reborn in this world at most one more time before attaining liberation.

Path consciousness of non-returning (***anāgāmi-maggacitta***): One who attains the third path will never again be reborn in the sensuous plane. If such a person does not reach Arahantship in the same lifetime, he will be reborn in the fine-material world and there attain the goal. The path consciousness of non-returning cuts off the fetters of sensual desire and ill will; it also permanently eliminates the two cittas rooted in hate.

Path consciousness of Arahantship (***arahatta-maggacitta***): An Arahant is a fully liberated one, a person who has destroyed (*hata*) the enemy (*ari*) consisting of the defilements. The path consciousness of Arahantship is the citta that issues directly in the full liberation of Arahantship. This citta destroys the five subtle fetters—desire for fine-material and immaterial existence, conceit, restlessness, and ignorance. It also eliminates the remaining types of unwholesome cittas—the four rooted in greed dissociated from views and the one rooted in delusion associated with restlessness.

Fruition consciousness (***phalacitta***): Each path consciousness issues automatically in its respective fruition in the same cognitive series, in immediate succession to the path. Thereafter the fruition citta can arise many times when the noble disciple enters the meditative attainment of fruition. The fruition consciousness, as mentioned earlier, is classified by way of kind as a resultant (*vipāka*). It should be noted that there are no supramundane functional (*kiriya*) cittas. That is because when an Arahant enters fruition attainment, the cittas that occur in that attainment belong to the class of resultants, being fruits of the supramundane path.

§29 Comprehensive Summary of Consciousness

Dvādas' ākusalān' evaṁ kusalān' ekavīsati
Chattiṁs' eva vipākāni kriyācittāni vīsati.

Catupaññāsadhā kāme rūpe paṇṇaras' īraye
Cittāni dvādas' āruppe aṭṭhadh' ānuttare tathā.

Thus there are twelve unwholesome types of consciousness, and twenty-one wholesome types. Resultants are thirty-six in number, and functional types of consciousness are twenty.

There are fifty-four sense-sphere types of consciousness, and fifteen assigned to the fine-material sphere. There are twelve types of consciousness in the immaterial sphere, and eight that are supramundane.

Guide to §29

In these verses, Ācariya Anuruddha summarizes all the eighty-nine states of consciousness that he has so far expounded in this Compendium of Consciousness. In the first verse he divides these according to their nature or kind (*jāti*) into four classes (see Table 1.8):

12 unwholesome cittas (*akusala*);
21 wholesome cittas (*kusala*);
36 resultant cittas (*vipāka*);
20 functional cittas (*kiriya*).

The last two classes are grouped together as kammically indeterminate (*abyākata*), since they are neither wholesome nor unwholesome.

TABLE 1.8: THE 89 CITTAS BY KIND

	Unwholesome	Wholesome	Indeterminate	
			Resultant	Functional
SS	12	8	23	11
FMS	....	5	5	5
IS	....	4	4	4
SPM	....	4	4	....
	12	21	36	20

In the second verse he divides the same eighty-nine cittas by way of the plane of consciousness (*bhūmi*) into another four classes (see Table 1.9):

54 sense-sphere cittas (*kāmāvacara*);
15 fine-material-sphere cittas (*rūpāvacara*);
12 immaterial-sphere cittas (*arūpāvacara*);
8 supramundane cittas (*lokuttara*).

Thus, although citta is one in its characteristic of cognizing an object, it becomes manifold when it is divided according to different criteria into various types.

TABLE 1.9: THE 89 CITTAS BY PLANE

Mundane - 81															SUPRA - MUNDANE 8	
SENSE SPHERE 54									Sublime - 27							
Unwholesome 12			Rootless 18			Beautiful 24			FINE - MATERIAL SPHERE 15			IMMATERIAL SPHERE 12				
greed-rooted	hate-rooted	delusion-rooted	unwholesome-rst.	wholesome-rst.	functional	wholesome	resultant	functional	wholesome	resultant	functional	wholesome	resultant	functional	path	fruition
8	2	2	7	8	3	8	8	8	5	5	5	4	4	4	4	4

NOTE: Unbeautiful cittas = 12 unwholesome + 18 rootless (30). Beautiful cittas = the remainder (59 or 91).

121 Types of Consciousness
(*ekavīsasatāni cittāni*)

§30 In Brief

Ittham ekūnanavutippabhedaṁ pana mānasaṁ
Ekavīsasataṁ v' ātha vibhajanti vicakkhaṇā.

These different classes of consciousness, which thus number eighty-nine, the wise divide into one hundred and twenty-one.

§31 In Detail

Kathaṁ ekūnanavutividhaṁ cittaṁ ekavīsasataṁ hoti?

1. Vitakka-vicāra-pīti-sukh'-ekaggatā-sahitaṁ paṭhamajjhāna-sotāpatti-maggacittaṁ.

2. Vicāra-pīti-sukh'-ekaggatā-sahitaṁ dutiyajjhāna-sotāpatti-maggacittaṁ.

3. Pīti-sukh'-ekaggatā-sahitaṁ tatiyajjhāna-sotāpatti-magga-cittaṁ.

4. Sukh'-ekaggatā-sahitaṁ catutthajjhāna-sotāpatti-maggacittaṁ.

5. Upekkh'-ekaggatā-sahitaṁ pañcamajjhāna-sotāpatti-magga-cittañ cā ti.

Imāni pañca pi sotāpatti-maggacittāni nāma. Tathā sakadāgāmi-magga, anāgāmi-magga, arahatta-maggacittañ cā ti samavīsati maggacittāni. Tathā phalacittāni cā ti samacattāḷīsa lokuttaracittāni bhavantī ti.

How does consciousness which is analyzed into eighty-nine types become of one hundred and twenty-one types?

1. The first jhāna path consciousness of stream-entry together with initial application, sustained application, zest, happiness, and one-pointedness.

2. The second jhāna path consciousness of stream-entry together with sustained application, zest, happiness, and one-pointedness.

3. The third jhāna path consciousness of stream-entry together with zest, happiness, and one-pointedness.

4. The fourth jhāna path consciousness of stream-entry together with happiness and one-pointedness.

5. The fifth jhāna path consciousness of stream-entry together with equanimity and one-pointedness.

These are the five types of path consciousness of stream-entry.

So too for the path consciousness of once-returning, of non-returning, and of Arahantship, making twenty types of path consciousness. Similarly, there are twenty types of fruition consciousness. Thus there are forty types of supramundane consciousness.

Guide to §§30-31

All meditators reach the supramundane paths and fruits through the development of wisdom (*paññā*)—insight into the three characteristics of impermanence, suffering, and non-self. However, they differ among themselves in the degree of their development of concentration (*samādhi*). Those who develop insight without a basis of jhāna are called practitioners of bare insight (*sukkhavipassaka*). When they reach the path and fruit, their path and fruition cittas occur at a level corresponding to the first jhāna.

Those who develop insight on the basis of jhāna attain a path and fruit which corresponds to the level of jhāna they had attained before reaching the path. The ancient teachers advance different views on the question of what factor determines the jhāna level of the path and fruit. One school of thought holds that it is the basic jhāna (*pādakajjhāna*), i.e. the jhāna used as a basis for concentrating the mind before developing the insight that culminates in attainment of the supramundane path. A second theory holds that the jhāna level of the path is determined by the jhāna used as an object for investigation by insight, called the comprehended or investigated jhāna (*sammasitajjhāna*). Still a third school

TABLE 1.10: THE FORTY SUPRAMUNDANE CITTAS

	PATH				FRUIT			
Jhāna	S.E.	O.R.	N.R.	Arh.	S.E.	O.R.	N.R.	Arh.
1st	(82)	(87)	(92)	(97)	(102)	(107)	(112)	(117)
2nd	(83)	(88)	(93)	(98)	(103)	(108)	(113)	(118)
3rd	(84)	(89)	(94)	(99)	(104)	(109)	(114)	(119)
4th	(85)	(90)	(95)	(100)	(105)	(110)	(115)	(120)
5th	(86)	(91)	(96)	(101)	(106)	(111)	(116)	(121)

of thought holds that when a meditator has mastered a range of jhānas, he can control the jhāna level of the path by his personal wish or inclination (*ajjhāsaya*).[12]

Nevertheless, no matter what explanation is adopted, for bare insight meditator and jhāna meditator alike, all path and fruition cittas are considered types of jhāna consciousness. They are so considered because they occur in the mode of closely contemplating their object with full absorption, like the mundane jhānas, and because they possess the jhāna factors with an intensity corresponding to their counterparts in the mundane jhānas. The supramundane jhānas of the paths and fruits differ from the mundane jhānas in several important respects. First, whereas the mundane jhānas take as their object some concept, such as the sign of the kasina, the supramundane jhānas take as their object Nibbāna, the unconditioned reality. Second, whereas the mundane jhānas merely suppress the defilements while leaving their underlying seeds intact, the supramundane jhānas of the path eradicate defilements so that they can never again arise. Third, while the mundane jhānas lead to rebirth in the fine-material world and thus sustain existence in the round of rebirths, the jhānas of the path cut off the fetters binding one to the cycle and thus issue in liberation from the round of birth and death. Finally, whereas the role of wisdom in the mundane jhānas is subordinate to that of concentration, in the supramundane jhānas wisdom and concentration are well balanced, with concentration fixing the mind on the unconditioned element and wisdom fathoming the deep significance of the Four Noble Truths.

According to the constellation of their jhāna factors, the path and fruition cittas are graded along the scale of the five jhānas. Thus instead of enumerating the supramundane consciousness as eightfold by way of the bare paths and fruits, each path and fruition consciousness can be enumerated as fivefold according to the level of jhāna at which it may occur. When this is done, the eight supramundane cittas, each taken at all of the five jhānic levels, become forty in number, as shown in Table 1.10.

§32 Concluding Summary

Jhānangayogabhedena katv' ekekan tu pañcadhā
Vuccat' ānuttaraṁ cittaṁ cattāḷīsavidhan ti ca.

Yathā ca rūpāvacaraṁ gayhat' ānuttaraṁ tathā
Paṭhamādijhānabhede āruppañ cā pi pañcame.

Ekādasavidhaṁ tasmā paṭhamādikam īritaṁ
Jhānam ekekam ante tu tevīsatividhaṁ bhave.

Sattatiṁsavidhaṁ puññaṁ dvipaññāsavidhaṁ tathā
Pākam icc' āhu cittāni ekavīsasataṁ budhā ti.

Dividing each (supramundane) consciousness into five kinds according to different jhāna factors, the supramundane consciousness, it is said, becomes forty.

As the fine-material-sphere consciousness is treated by division into first jhāna consciousness and so on, even so is the supramundane consciousness. The immaterial-sphere consciousness is included in the fifth jhāna.

Thus the jhānas beginning from the first amount to eleven, they say. The last jhāna (i.e. the fifth) totals twenty-three.

Thirty-seven are wholesome, fifty-two are resultants; thus the wise say that there are one hundred and twenty-one types of consciousness.

Guide to §32

The immaterial-sphere consciousness is included in the fifth jhāna: As explained earlier, the *arūpajjhānas* have the same two jhāna factors as the fifth *rūpajjhāna*, and are therefore considered modes of the fifth jhāna. Thus when a meditator uses an *arūpajjhāna* as a basis for de-

TABLE 1.11: JHĀNA CITTAS — MUNDANE AND SUPRAMUNDANE

	Fine-material 15			Immaterial 12			Supramundane 40		
Jhāna	Wh.	Rst.	Fnc.	Wh.	Rst.	Fnc.	Wh.	Rst.	Total
1st	1	1	1	...	...	...	4	4	11
2nd	1	1	1	...	...	...	4	4	11
3rd	1	1	1	...	...	...	4	4	11
4th	1	1	1	...	...	...	4	4	11
5th	1	1	1	4	4	4	4	4	23
	5	5	5	4	4	4	20	20	

veloping insight, his path and fruition consciousness become fifth jhāna supramundane cittas.

The jhānas beginning from the first amount to eleven: Each jhāna from the first to the fourth occurs one each as fine-material-sphere wholesome, resultant, and functional (= 3), and four each by way of the paths and fruits (= 8); thus eleven.

The last ... totals twenty-three: The fifth jhāna considered as embracing both the last *rūpajjhāna* and the four *arūpajjhānas* thus comprises five each as wholesome, resultant, and functional (= 15), and eight as supramundane, for a total of twenty-three. (See Table 1.11.)

The thirty-seven wholesome and fifty-two resultants are obtained by replacing the four supramundane wholesome and resultant cittas with twenty each. Thus the total number of cittas in the Compendium of Consciousness increases from 89 to 121.

Iti Abhidhammatthasangahe
Cittasangahavibhāgo nāma
paṭhamo paricchedo.

Thus ends the first chapter
in the Manual of Abhidhamma entitled
the Compendium of Consciousness.

CHAPTER II
COMPENDIUM OF MENTAL FACTORS
(*Cetasikasangahavibhāga*)

§1 Introductory

Ekuppāda-nirodhā ca ekālambana-vatthukā
Cetoyuttā dvipaññāsa dhammā cetasikā matā.

The fifty-two states associated with consciousness that arise and cease together (with consciousness), that have the same object and base (as consciousness), are known as mental factors.

Guide to § 1

States associated with consciousness (***cetoyuttā dhammā***): The second chapter of the *Abhidhammattha Sangaha* is devoted to the classification of the second type of ultimate reality, the *cetasikas* or mental factors. The cetasikas are mental phenomena that occur in immediate conjunction with citta or consciousness, and assist citta by performing more specific tasks in the total act of cognition. The mental factors cannot arise without citta, nor can citta arise completely segregated from the mental factors. But though the two are functionally interdependent, citta is regarded as primary because the mental factors assist in the cognition of the object depending upon citta, which is the principal cognitive element. The relationship between citta and the cetasikas is compared to that between a king and his retinue. Although one says "the king is coming," the king does not come alone, but he always comes accompanied by his attendants. Similarly, whenever a citta arises, it never arises alone but always accompanied by its retinue of cetasikas.[1]

In the Compendium of Mental Factors, Ācariya Anuruddha will first enumerate all the mental factors in their appropriate classes (§§2-9). Thereafter he will investigate the mental factors from two complementary points of view. The first of these is called the method of association (*sampayoganaya*). This method takes the mental factors as the basis of inquiry and seeks to determine which types of citta each mental factor is associated with (§§10-17). The second point of view is called the method of combination or inclusion (*sangahanaya*). This method takes the citta as primary and seeks to determine, for each type of citta, which mental factors are combined within it (§§18-29).

That arise and cease together (with consciousness): The first verse defines the mental factors by way of four characteristics that are common to them all:

(1) arising together with consciousness (*ekuppāda*);
(2) ceasing together with consciousness (*ekanirodha*);
(3) having the same object as consciousness (*ekālambana*);
(4) having the same base as consciousness (*ekavatthuka*).

These four characteristics delineate the relationship between the citta and its concomitant cetasikas. If only "arising together" were mentioned, the definition would include (wrongly) as cetasikas those material phenomena that arise simultaneously with the citta, that is, material phenomena produced by mind and by kamma. However, these material phenomena do not all perish at the same time as the co-arisen citta, but mostly endure for seventeen mind-moments. Thus to exclude them the characteristic "ceasing together" is introduced.

Again, there are two material phenomena—bodily intimation and vocal intimation[2]—which arise and cease together with consciousness. However, these material phenomena do not take an object, and this distinguishes mental phenomena—both citta and cetasikas—from material phenomena: all mental phenomena experience an object, co-arisen citta and cetasikas experience the same object, while material phenomena do not experience any object at all. Thus the third characteristic is stated, that of having the same object.

Finally, in those realms in which the aggregate of material form is found, i.e. in the sensuous world and the fine-material world, the citta and its cetasikas have the same physical base, that is, they arise with the common support of either one of the material sense organs or the heart-base.[3] This is the fourth characteristic of cetasikas.

The Fifty-Two Mental Factors

The Ethically Variable Factors—13 (*aññasamānacetasika*)

§2 The Universals (*sabbacittasādhāraṇa*)—7

Katham? I. (1) Phasso, (2) vedanā, (3) saññā, (4) cetanā, (5) ekaggatā, (6) jīvitindriyaṁ, (7) manasikāro cā ti satt' ime cetasikā sabbacittasādhāraṇā nāma.

How? I. (1) Contact, (2) feeling, (3) perception, (4) volition, (5) one-pointedness, (6) mental life faculty, and (7) attention: these seven mental factors are termed universals, i.e. common to every consciousness.

Guide to § 2

The fifty-two mental factors: The Abhidhamma philosophy recognizes fifty-two cetasikas, which are classified into four broad categories, as may be seen in Table 2.1:

(1) seven universals;
(2) six occasionals;
(3) fourteen unwholesome factors; and
(4) twenty-five beautiful factors.

The ethically variable factors (*aññasamānacetasika*): The first two categories of mental factors—the seven universals and the six occasionals—are united under the designation *aññasamāna*, freely rendered here as "ethically variable." The expression literally means "common to the other." The non-beautiful cittas are called "other" (*añña*) in relation to the beautiful cittas, and the beautiful cittas are called "other" in relation to the non-beautiful cittas. The thirteen cetasikas of the first two categories are common (*samāna*) to both beautiful and non-beautiful cittas, and assume the ethical quality imparted to the citta by the other cetasikas, particularly the associated roots (*hetu*). In wholesome cittas they become wholesome, in unwholesome cittas they become unwholesome, and in kammically indeterminate cittas they become kammically indeterminate. For this reason they are called "common to the other," that is, ethically variable.

The universals (*sabbacittasādhāraṇa*): The seven universals are the cetasikas common (*sādhāraṇa*) to all consciousness (*sabbacitta*). These factors perform the most rudimentary and essential cognitive functions, without which consciousness of an object would be utterly impossible.

(1) **Contact (*phassa*)**: The word *phassa* is derived from the verb *phusati*, meaning "to touch," but contact should not be understood as the mere physical impact of the object on the bodily faculty. It is, rather, the mental factor by which consciousness mentally "touches" the object that has appeared, thereby initiating the entire cognitive event. In terms of the fourfold defining device used in the Pali Commentaries,[4] contact has the characteristic of touching. Its function is impingement, as it causes consciousness and the object to impinge. Its manifestation is the concurrence of consciousness, sense faculty, and object. Its proximate cause is an objective field that has come into focus.[5]

TABLE 2.1: THE 52 MENTAL FACTORS AT A GLANCE

Ethically Variables—13

Universals—7

(1) Contact
(2) Feeling
(3) Perception
(4) Volition
(5) One-pointedness
(6) Life faculty
(7) Attention

Occasionals—6

(8) Initial application
(9) Sustained application
(10) Decision
(11) Energy
(12) Zest
(13) Desire

Unwholesome Factors—14

Unwholesome Universals—4

(14) Delusion
(15) Shamelessness
(16) Fearlessness of wrong
(17) Restlessness

Unwholesome Occasionals—10

(18) Greed
(19) Wrong view
(20) Conceit
(21) Hatred
(22) Envy
(23) Avarice
(24) Worry
(25) Sloth
(26) Torpor
(27) Doubt

Beautiful Factors—25

Beautiful Universals—19

(28) Faith
(29) Mindfulness
(30) Shame
(31) Fear of wrong
(32) Non-greed
(33) Non-hatred
(34) Neutrality of mind
(35) Tranquillity of mental body
(36) Tranquillity of consciousness
(37) Lightness of mental body
(38) Lightness of consciousness
(39) Malleability of mental body
(40) Malleability of consciousness
(41) Wieldiness of mental body
(42) Wieldiness of consciousness
(43) Proficiency of mental body
(44) Proficiency of consciousness
(45) Rectitude of mental body
(46) Rectitude of consciousness

Abstinences—3

(47) Right speech
(48) Right action
(49) Right livelihood

Illimitables—2

(50) Compassion
(51) Appreciative joy

Non-Delusion—1

(52) Wisdom faculty

(2) **Feeling** (***vedanā***): Feeling is the mental factor that feels the object: it is the affective mode in which the object is experienced. The Pali word *vedanā* does not signify emotion (which appears to be a complex phenomenon involving a variety of concomitant mental factors), but the bare affective quality of an experience, which may be either pleasant, painful or neutral. Feeling is said to have the characteristic of being felt (*vedayita*). Its function is experiencing, or its function is to enjoy the desirable aspect of the object. Its manifestation is the relishing of the associated mental factors. Its proximate cause is tranquillity.[6] Whereas the other mental factors experience the object only derivatively, feeling experiences it directly and fully. In this respect, the other factors are compared to a cook who prepares a dish for a king and only samples the food while preparing it, while feeling is compared to the king who enjoys the meal as much as he likes.

(3) **Perception** (***saññā***): The characteristic of perception is the perceiving of the qualities of the object. Its function is to make a sign as a condition for perceiving again that "this is the same," or its function is recognizing what has been previously perceived. It becomes manifest as the interpreting of the object (*abhinivesa*) by way of the features that had been apprehended. Its proximate cause is the object as it appears. Its procedure is compared to a carpenter's recognition of certain kinds of wood by the mark he has made on each.

(4) **Volition** (***cetanā***): *Cetanā*, from the same root as *citta*, is the mental factor that is concerned with the actualization of a goal, that is, the conative or volitional aspect of cognition. Thus it is rendered volition. The Commentaries explain that *cetanā* organizes its associated mental factors in acting upon the object. Its characteristic is the state of willing, its function is to accumulate (kamma), and its manifestation is coordination. Its proximate cause is the associated states. Just as a chief pupil recites his own lesson and also makes the other pupils recite their lessons, so when volition starts to work on its object, it sets the associated states to do their own tasks as well. Volition is the most significant mental factor in generating kamma, since it is volition that determines the ethical quality of the action.

(5) **One-pointedness** (***ekaggatā***): This is the unification of the mind on its object. Although this factor comes to prominence in the jhānas, where it functions as a jhāna factor, the Abhidhamma teaches that the germ of that capacity for mental unification is present in all types of consciousness, even the most rudimentary. It there functions as the factor which fixes the mind on its object. One-pointedness has non-wandering or non-distraction as its characteristic. Its function is to conglomerate or unite the associated states. It is manifested as peace, and its proximate cause is happiness.[7]

(6) **Mental life faculty** (*jīvitindriya*): There are two kinds of life faculty, the mental, which vitalizes the associated mental states, and the physical, which vitalizes material phenomena. The mental life faculty alone is intended as a cetasika. It has the characteristic of maintaining the associated mental states, the function of making them occur, manifestation as the establishing of their presence, and its proximate cause is the mental states to be maintained.

(7) **Attention** (*manasikāra*): The Pali word literally means "making in the mind." Attention is the mental factor responsible for the mind's advertence to the object, by virtue of which the object is made present to consciousness. Its characteristic is the conducting (*sāraṇa*) of the associated mental states towards the object. Its function is to yoke the associated states to the object. It is manifested as confrontation with an object, and its proximate cause is the object. Attention is like the rudder of a ship, which directs it to its destination, or like a charioteer who sends the well-trained horses (i.e. the associated states) towards their destination (the object). *Manasikāra* should be distinguished from *vitakka*: while the former turns its concomitants towards the object, the latter applies them onto the object. *Manasikāra* is an indispensable cognitive factor present in all states of consciousness; *vitakka* is a specialized factor which is not indispensable to cognition.

§3 The Occasionals (*pakiṇṇaka*)—6

II. (1) Vitakko, (2) vicāro, (3) adhimokkho, (4) viriyaṁ, (5) pīti, (6) chando cā ti cha ime cetasikā pakiṇṇakā nāma. Evam ete terasa cetasikā aññasamānā ti veditabbā.

II. (1) Initial application, (2) sustained application, (3) decision, (4) energy, (5) zest, and (6) desire: these six mental factors are termed occasionals.

Thus these thirteen mental factors should be understood as the ethically variables.

Guide to § 3

The occasionals (*pakiṇṇaka*): The six cetasikas in this group are similar to the universals in being ethically variable factors, which take on the moral quality of the citta as determined by other concomitants. They differ from the universals in that they are found only in particular types of conciousness, not in all.

(1) **Initial application** (*vitakka*): *Vitakka* was already introduced in the discussion of the jhānas, where it appears as the first of the five jhāna

factors.[8] *Vitakka* is the application of the mind to the object. Its characteristic is the directing of the mind onto the object.[9] Its function is to strike at and thresh the object. It is manifested as the leading of the mind onto an object. Though no proximate cause is mentioned in the Commentaries, the object may be understood as its proximate cause.

Ordinary *vitakka* simply applies the mind to the object. But when *vitakka* is cultivated through concentration it becomes a factor of jhāna. It is then termed *appanā*, the absorption of the mind in the object. *Vitakka* is also called *sankappa*, intention, and as such is distinguished as *micchāsankappa* or wrong intention and *sammāsankappa* or right intention. The latter is the second factor of the Noble Eightfold Path.

(2) **Sustained application (*vicāra*)**: *Vicāra*, also a jhāna factor, has the characteristic of continued pressure on the object,[10] in the sense of examining it. Its function is sustained application of the associated mental phenomena to the object. It is manifested as the anchoring of those phenomena in the object. The object may be understood to be its proximate cause. The difference between *vitakka* and *vicāra* has been discussed above (p. 56).

(3) **Decision (*adhimokkha*)**: The word *adhimokkha* means literally the releasing of the mind onto the object. Hence it has been rendered decision or resolution. It has the characteristic of conviction, the function of not groping, and manifestation as decisiveness. Its proximate cause is a thing to be convinced about. It is compared to a stone pillar owing to its unshakable resolve regarding the object.

(4) **Energy (*viriya*)**: *Viriya* is the state or action of one who is vigorous. Its characteristic is supporting, exertion, and marshalling. Its function is to support its associated states. Its manifestation is non-collapse. Its proximate cause is a sense of urgency (*saṁvega*) or a ground for arousing energy, that is, anything that stirs one to vigorous action. Just as new timbers added to an old house prevent it from collapsing, or just as a strong reinforcement enables the king's army to defeat the enemy, so energy upholds and supports all the associated states and does not allow them to recede.

(5) **Zest (*pīti*)**: Already introduced among the jhāna factors, *pīti* has the characteristic of endearing (*sampiyāyana*). Its function is to refresh mind and body, or its function is to pervade (to thrill with rapture). It is manifested as elation. Mind-and-body (*nāmarūpa*) is its proximate cause.

(6) **Desire (*chanda*)**: *Chanda* here means desire to act (*kattu-kāmatā*), that is, to perform an action or achieve some result. This kind of desire must be distinguished from desire in the reprehensible sense, that is, from *lobha*, greed, and *rāga*, lust.[11] Whereas the latter terms are invariably unwholesome, *chanda* is an ethically variable factor which, when con-

joined with wholesome concomitants, can function as the virtuous desire to achieve a worthy goal. The characteristic of *chanda* is desire to act, its function is searching for an object, its manifestation is need for an object, and that same object is its proximate cause. It should be regarded as the stretching forth of the mind's hand towards the object.

§4 The Unwholesome Factors—14 (*akusalacetasika*)

III. (1) Moho, (2) ahirikaṁ, (3) anottappaṁ, (4) uddhaccaṁ, (5) lobho, (6) diṭṭhi, (7) māno, (8) doso, (9) issā, (10) macchariyaṁ, (11) kukkuccaṁ, (12) thīnaṁ, (13) middhaṁ, (14) vicikicchā cā ti cuddas' ime cetasikā akusalā nāma.

III. (1) Delusion, (2) shamelessness, (3) fearlessness of wrongdoing, (4) restlessness, (5) greed, (6) wrong view, (7) conceit, (8) hatred, (9) envy, (10) avarice, (11) worry, (12) sloth, (13) torpor, and (14) doubt: these fourteen mental factors are termed the unwholesome.

Guide to §4

(1) **Delusion (*moha*)**: Moha is a synonym for *avijjā*, ignorance. Its characteristic is mental blindness or unknowing (*aññāṇa*). Its function is non-penetration, or concealment of the real nature of the object. It is manifested as the absence of right understanding or as mental darkness. Its proximate cause is unwise attention (*ayoniso manasikāra*). It should be seen as the root of all that is unwholesome.

(2, 3) **Shamelessness (*ahirika*) and fearlessness of wrongdoing (*anottappa*)**: The characteristic of shamelessness is the absence of disgust at bodily and verbal misconduct; the characteristic of fearlessness of wrongdoing (or moral recklessness) is absence of dread on account of such misconduct. Both have the function of doing evil things. They are manifest as not shrinking away from evil. Their proximate cause is the lack of respect for self and lack of respect for others, respectively.[12]

(4) **Restlessness (*uddhacca*)**: Restlessness (or agitation) has the characteristic of disquietude, like water whipped up by the wind. Its function is to make the mind unsteady, as wind makes a banner ripple. It is manifested as turmoil. Its proximate cause is unwise attention to mental disquiet.

(5) **Greed (*lobha*)**: Greed, the first unwholesome root, covers all degrees of selfish desire, longing, attachment, and clinging. Its character-

istic is grasping an object. Its function is sticking, as meat sticks to a hot pan. It is manifested as not giving up. Its proximate cause is seeing enjoyment in things that lead to bondage.

(6) **Wrong view** (***diṭṭhi***): *Diṭṭhi* here means seeing wrongly. Its characteristic is unwise (unjustified) interpretation of things. Its function is to preassume. It is manifested as a wrong interpretation or belief. Its proximate cause is unwillingness to see the noble ones (*ariya*), and so on.[13]

(7) **Conceit** (***mana***): Conceit has the characteristic of haughtiness. Its function is self-exaltation. It is manifested as vainglory.[14] Its proximate cause is greed dissociated from views.[15] It should be regarded as madness.

(8) **Hatred** (***dosa***): *Dosa*, the second unwholesome root, comprises all kinds and degrees of aversion, ill will, anger, irritation, annoyance, and animosity. Its characteristic is ferocity. Its function is to spread, or to burn up its own support, i.e. the mind and body in which it arises. It is manifestated as persecuting, and its proximate cause is a ground for annoyance.[16]

(9) **Envy** (***issā***): Envy has the characteristic of being jealous of other's success. Its function is to be dissatisfied with others' success. It is manifested as aversion towards that. Its proximate cause is others' success.

(10) **Avarice** (***macchariya***): The characteristic of avarice (or stinginess) is concealing one's own success when it has been or can be obtained. Its function is not to bear sharing these with others. It is manifest as shrinking away (from sharing) and as meanness or sour feeling. Its proximate cause is one's own success.

(11) **Worry** (***kukkucca***): *Kukkucca* is worry or remorse after having done wrong. Its characteristic is subsequent regret. Its function is to sorrow over what has and what has not been done. It is manifested as remorse. Its proximate cause is what has and what has not been done (i.e. wrongs of commission and omission).

(12) **Sloth** (***thīna***): Sloth is sluggishness or dullness of mind. Its characteristic is lack of driving power. Its function is to dispel energy. It is manifested as the sinking of the mind. Its proximate cause is unwise attention to boredom, drowsiness, etc.

(13) **Torpor** (***middha***): Torpor is the morbid state of the mental factors. Its characteristic is unwieldiness. Its function is to smother. It is manifested as drooping, or as nodding and sleepiness. Its proximate cause is the same as that of sloth.

Sloth and torpor always occur in conjunction, and are opposed to energy (*viriya*). Sloth is identified as sickness of consciousness (*cittagelañña*), torpor as sickness of the mental factors (*kāyagelañña*). As a pair they constitute one of the five hindrances, which is overcome by initial application (*vitakka*).

(14) **Doubt** (***vicikicchā***): Doubt here signifies spiritual doubt, from a Buddhist perspective the inability to place confidence in the Buddha, the Dhamma, the Sangha, and the training. Its characteristic is doubting. Its function is to waver. It is manifested as indecisiveness and as taking various sides. Its proximate cause is unwise attention.

The Beautiful Factors—25
(*sobhanacetasika*)

§5 The Universal Beautiful Factors (*sobhanasādhāraṇa*)—19

IV. (1) Saddhā, (2) sati, (3) hiri, (4) ottappaṁ, (5) alobho, (6) adoso, (7) tatramajjhattatā, (8) kāyapassaddhi, (9) cittapassaddhi, (10) kāyalahutā, (11) cittalahutā, (12) kāyamudutā, (13) cittamudutā, (14) kāyakammaññatā, (15) cittakammaññatā, (16) kāyapāguññatā, (17) cittapāguññatā, (18) kāyujjukatā, (19) cittujjukatā cā ti ekūnavīsat' ime cetasikā sobhanasādhāraṇā nāma.

IV. (1) Faith, (2) mindfulness, (3) shame, (4) fear of wrongdoing, (5) non-greed, (6) non-hatred, (7) neutrality of mind, (8) tranquillity of the (mental) body, (9) tranquillity of consciousness, (10) lightness of the (mental) body, (11) lightness of consciousness, (12) malleability of the (mental) body, (13) malleability of consciousness, (14) wieldiness of the (mental) body, (15) wieldiness of consciousness, (16) proficiency of the (mental) body, (17) proficiency of consciousness, (18) rectitude of the (mental) body, and (19) rectitude of consciousness: these nineteen mental factors are termed the universal beautiful factors.

Guide to §5

The universal beautiful factors (***sobhanasādhāraṇa***): The beautiful mental factors are subdivided into four groups. First come the universal beautiful factors, nineteen cetasikas that are invariably present in all beautiful consciousness. Following this come three groups of beautiful cetasikas which are variable adjuncts not necessarily contained in beautiful consciousness.

(1) **Faith** (***saddhā***): The first of the beautiful cetasikas is faith, which has the characteristic of placing faith or of trusting. Its function is to clarify, as a water-clearing gem causes muddy water to become clear;

or its function is to set forth, as one might set forth to cross a flood.[17] It is manifested as non-fogginess, i.e. the removal of the mind's impurities, or as resolution. Its proximate cause is something to place faith in, or the hearing of the Good Dhamma, etc., that constitute the factors of stream-entry.

(2) **Mindfulness** (***sati***): The word *sati* derives from a root meaning "to remember," but as a mental factor it signifies presence of mind, attentiveness to the present, rather than the faculty of memory regarding the past. It has the characteristic of not wobbling, i.e. not floating away from the object.[18] Its function is absence of confusion or non-forgetfulness. It is manifested as guardianship, or as the state of confronting an objective field. Its proximate cause is strong perception (*thirasaññā*) or the four foundations of mindfulness (see VII, §24).

(3, 4) **Shame** (***hiri***) and **fear of wrongdoing** (***ottappa***): Shame has the characteristic of disgust at bodily and verbal misconduct, fear of wrongdoing has the characteristic of dread in regard to such misconduct. They both have the function of not doing evil, and are manifested as the shrinking away from evil. Their proximate cause is respect for self and respect for others, respectively. These two states are called by the Buddha the guardians of the world because they protect the world from falling into widespread immorality.

(5) **Non-greed** (***alobha***): Non-greed has the characteristic of the mind's lack of desire for its object, or non-adherence to the object like a drop of water on a lotus leaf. Its function is not to lay hold, and its manifestation is detachment. It should be understood that non-greed is not the mere absence of greed, but the presence of positive virtues such as generosity and renunciation as well.

(6) **Non-hatred** (***adosa***): Non-hatred has the characteristic of lack of ferocity, or of non-opposing. Its function is to remove annoyance, or to remove fever, and its manifestation is agreeableness. Non-hatred comprises such positive virtues as loving-kindness, gentleness, amity, friendliness, etc.

When non-hatred appears as the sublime quality of loving-kindness (*mettā*) it has the characteristic of promoting the welfare of living beings. Its function is to prefer their welfare. Its manifestation is the removal of ill will. Its proximate cause is seeing beings as lovable. Such loving-kindness must be distinguished from selfish affection, its "near enemy."

(7) **Neutrality of mind** (***tatramajjhattatā***): The Pali term for this cetasika literally means "there in the middleness." It is a synonym for equanimity (*upekkhā*), not as neutral feeling, but as a mental attitude of balance, detachment, and impartiality. It has the characteristic of conveying consciousness and the mental factors evenly. Its function is to

prevent deficiency and excess, or to prevent partiality. It is manifested as neutrality. It should be seen as the state of looking on with equanimity in the citta and cetasikas, like a charioteer who looks on with equanimity at the thoroughbreds progressing evenly along the roadway.

Neutrality of mind becomes the sublime quality of equanimity towards living beings. As such it treats beings free from discrimination, without preferences and prejudices, looking upon all as equal. This equanimity should not be confused with its "near enemy," the worldly-minded indifference due to ignorance.

The next twelve universal beautiful cetasikas fall into six pairs, each containing one term that extends to the "mental body" (*kaya*) and another that extends to consciousness (*citta*). In this context the mental body is the collection of associated cetasikas, called "body" in the sense of an aggregation.

(8, 9) **Tranquillity** (***passaddhi***) : The twofold tranquillity has the characteristic of the quieting down of disturbances (*daratha*) in the mental body and consciousness, respectively. Its function is to crush such disturbances. It is manifested as peacefulness and coolness. Its proximate cause is the mental body and consciousness. It should be regarded as opposed to such defilements as restlessness and worry, which create distress.

(10, 11) **Lightness** (***lahutā***): The twofold lightness has the characteristic of the subsiding of heaviness (*garubhāva*) in the mental body and consciousness, respectively. Its function is to crush heaviness. It is manifested as non-sluggishness. Its proximate cause is the mental body and consciousness. It should be regarded as opposed to such defilements as sloth and torpor, which create heaviness.

(12, 13) **Malleability** (***mudutā***): The twofold malleability has the characteristic of the subsiding of rigidity (*thambha*) in the mental body and consciousness, respectively. Its function is to crush rigidity. It is manifested as non-resistance, and its proximate cause is the mental body and consciousness. It should be regarded as opposed to such defilements as wrong views and conceit, which create rigidity.

(14, 15) **Wieldiness** (***kammaññatā***): The twofold wieldiness has the characteristic of the subsiding of unwieldiness (*akammaññabhāva*) in the mental body and consciousness, respectively. Its function is to crush unwieldiness. It is manifested as success of the mental body and consciousness in making something an object. Its proximate cause is the mental body and consciousness. It should be regarded as opposed to the remaining hindrances, which create unwieldiness of the mental body and consciousness.

(16, 17) **Proficiency** (***pāguññatā***): The twofold proficiency has the characteristic of healthiness of the mental body and consciousness, respectively. Its function is to crush unhealthiness of the mental body and consciousness. It is manifested as absence of disability. Its proximate cause is the mental body and consciousness. It should be regarded as opposed to lack of faith, etc., which cause unhealthiness of the mental body and consciousness.

(18, 19) **Rectitude** (***ujjukatā***): Rectitude is straightness. The twofold rectitude has the characteristic of uprightness of the mental body and consciousness, respectively. Its function is to crush tortuousness of the mental body and consciousness, and its manifestation is non-crookedness. Its proximate cause is the mental body and consciousness. It should be regarded as opposed to hypocrisy and fraudulence, etc., which create crookedness in the mental body and consciousness.

§6 The Abstinences (*virati*)—3

V. (1) Sammāvācā, (2) sammākammanto, (3) sammā-ājīvo cā ti tisso viratiyo nāma.

V. (1) Right speech, (2) right action, and (3) right livelihood: these three are termed abstinences.

Guide to § 6

The abstinences: The *viratis* are three beautiful mental factors which are responsible for the deliberate abstinence from wrong conduct by way of speech, action, and livelihood. In mundane consciousness, the *viratis* are operative only on an occasion when one intentionally refrains from a wrong mode of conduct for which an opportunity has arisen. When a person refrains from evil deeds without an opportunity for their performance arising, this is not a case of *virati* but of pure moral conduct (*sīla*).

The commentators distinguish three types of *virati*: (1) natural abstinence; (2) abstinence by undertaking precepts; and (3) abstinence by eradication.[19]

(1) Natural abstinence (*sampattavirati*) is the abstinence from evil deeds when the opportunity arises to engage in them, due to the consideration of one's social position, age, level of education, etc. An example is refraining fom theft out of concern that one's reputation would be hurt if one is caught.

(2) Abstinence by undertaking precepts (*samādānavirati*) is the abstinence from evil deeds because one has undertaken to observe precepts, for example, the Five Precepts of abstaining from killing, stealing, sexual misconduct, false speech, and intoxicants.

(3) Abstinence by eradication (*samucchedavirati*) is the abstinence associated with the supramundane path consciousness, which arises eradicating the dispositions towards evil deeds. Whereas the previous two *viratis* are mundane, this one is supramundane.

The *viratis* comprise three distinct mental factors mentioned in the text: right speech, right action, and right livelihood.

(1) **Right speech** (***sammāvācā***): Right speech is the deliberate abstinence from wrong speech: from false speech, slander, harsh speech, and frivolous talk.

(2) **Right action** (***sammākammanta***): Right action is the deliberate abstinence from wrong bodily action: from killing, stealing, and sexual misconduct.

(3) **Right livelihood** (***sammā-ājīva***): Right livelihood is the deliberate abstinence from wrong livelihood, such as dealing in poisons, intoxicants, weapons, slaves, or animals for slaughter.

The three *viratis* have the respective characteristics of non-transgression by bodily misconduct, by wrong speech, and by wrong livelihood. Their function is to shrink back from evil deeds. They are manifested as the abstinence from such deeds. Their proximate causes are the special qualities of faith, shame, fear of wrongdoing, fewness of wishes, etc. They should be regarded as the mind's aversion to wrongdoing.

§7 The Illimitables (*appamaññā*)—2

VI. (1) Karuṇā, (2) muditā pana appamaññāyo nāmā ti.

VI. (1) Compassion, (2) appreciative joy: these are termed illimitables.

Guide to § 7

The illimitables: There are four attitudes towards living beings called the illimitables (or immeasurables) because they are to be developed towards all living beings and thus have a potentially limitless range. The four illimitable states are loving-kindness (*mettā*), compassion (*karuṇā*), appreciative joy (*muditā*), and equanimity (*upekkhā*). These four are also called *brahmavihāras*, "divine abodes" or sublime states.

Although four illimitables are recognized as ideal attitudes towards beings, only two—compassion and appreciative joy—are included as cetasikas under the heading of the illimitables. This is because loving-kindness, as we have seen, is a mode of the cetasika *adosa*, non-hatred, and equanimity is a mode of the cetasika *tatramajjhattatā*, neutrality of mind. Non-hatred does not necessarily manifest as loving-kindness; it can appear in other modes as well. But when loving-kindness does arise in the mind, it does so as a manifestation of the cetasika non-hatred. A similar relationship holds between the cetasika neutrality of mind and the sublime state of equanimity as impartiality towards living beings.

The two illimitables that appear as mental factors in their own right, not as manifestations of other mental factors, are compassion and appreciative joy. Whereas non-hatred and mental neutrality—the factors underlying loving-kindness and equanimity—are present in all beautiful cittas, these two are present only on occasions when their functions are individually exercised.

(1) **Compassion:** *Karuṇā*, or compassion, has the characteristic of promoting the removal of suffering in others. Its function is not being able to bear others' suffering. It is manifested as non-cruelty. Its proximate cause is seeing helplessness in those overwhelmed by suffering. It succeeds when it causes cruelty to subside, and it fails when it produces sorrow.

(2) **Appreciative joy:** *Muditā*, or appreciative joy, has the characteristic of gladness at the success of others. Its function is being unenvious at others' success. It is manifested as the elimination of aversion. Its proximate cause is seeing the success of others. It succeeds when it causes aversion to subside, and it fails when it produces merriment.

§8 Non-Delusion (*amoha*)—1

VII. Sabbathā pi paññindriyena saddhiṁ pañcavīsat' ime cetasikā sobhanā ti veditabbā.

VII. Together with the faculty of wisdom these twenty-five, in all, are to be understood as beautiful mental factors.

Guide to §8

The wisdom faculty: ***Paññā*** is wisdom, or knowing things as they really are. It is here called a faculty because it exercises predominance in comprehending things as they really are. In the Abhidhamma, the three terms—wisdom (*paññā*), knowledge (*ñāṇa*), and non-delusion (*amoha*)—are used synonymously. Wisdom has the characteristic of penetrating things according to their intrinsic nature (*yathāsabhāvapaṭivedha*). Its function is to illuminate the objective field like a lamp. It is manifested as non-bewilderment. Its proximate cause is wise attention (*yoniso manasikāra*).

§9 Summary

Ettāvatā ca:

Teras' aññasamānā ca cuddas' ākusalā tathā
Sobhanā pañcavīsā ti dvipaññāsa pavuccare.

Thus:

Thirteen are ethically variable, and fourteen are unwholesome. Twenty-five are beautiful. Thus fifty-two have been enumerated.

Association of Mental Factors —16
(*cetasikasampayoganaya*)

§10 Introductory Verse

Tesaṁ cittāviyuttānaṁ yathāyogam ito paraṁ
Cittuppādesu paccekaṁ sampayogo pavuccati.
Satta sabbattha yujjanti yathāyogaṁ pakiṇṇakā
Cuddas' ākusalesv' eva sobhanesv' eva sobhanā.

In the following we will explain, in the appropriate ways, the association of each of these mental adjuncts with the different states of consciousness.

Seven are linked with every type of consciousness. The occasionals are linked in the appropriate ways. Fourteen are linked only with the unwholesome types, and the beautiful factors only with the beautiful types (of consciousness).

The Ethically Variable Factors—7
(*aññasamānacetasika*)

§11 Analysis

Kathaṁ?

(i) Sabbacittasādhāraṇā tāva satt' ime cetasikā sabbesu pi ekūnanavuti cittuppādesu labbhanti.

Pakiṇṇakesu pana:

(ii) Vitakko tāva dvipañcaviññāṇa-vajjita-kāmāvacaracittesu c' eva ekādasasu paṭhamajjhānacittesu cā ti pañcapaññāsa cittesu uppajjati.

(iii) Vicāro pana tesu c' eva ekādasasu dutiyajjhānacittesu cā ti chasaṭṭhi cittesu jāyati.

TABLE 2.2: ASSOCIATION OF MENTAL FACTORS

CETASIKA	CITTAS	TOTAL
Variables		
Universals	All cittas	89, 121
Initial application	1-12, 18, 19, 25-54, 55, 60, 65, 82, 87, 92, 97, 102, 107, 112, 117	55
Sustained application	Same + 56, 61, 66, 83, 88, 93, 98, 103, 108, 113, 118	66
Decision	1-10, 12, 18, 19, 25-89 (or: 25-121)	78, 110
Energy	1-12, 29-89 (or: 29-121)	73, 105
Zest	1-4, 26, 30, 31-34, 39-42, 47-50, 55-57, 60-62, 65-67, 82-84, 87-89, 92-94, 97-99, 102-104, 107-109, 112-114, 117-119	51
Desire	1-10, 31-89 (or: 31-121)	69, 101
Unwholesome		
Unwh. universals	1-12	12
Greed	1-8	8
Wrong view	1, 2, 5, 6	4
Conceit	3, 4, 7, 8	4
Hatred, envy, avarice, worry	9, 10	2
Sloth, torpor	2, 4, 6, 8, 10	5
Doubt	11	1
Beautiful		
Btf. universals	31-89 (or: 31-121)	59, 91
Abstinences	31-38, 82-89 (or: 82-121)	16, 48
Illimitables	31-38, 47-54, 55-58, 60-63, 65-68	28
Wisdom	31, 32, 35, 36, 39, 40, 43, 44, 47, 48, 51, 52, 55-89 (or: 55-121)	47, 79

Unfixed adjuncts = 11

Envy, avarice, worry	3	separately and occasionally	
Abstinences	3	" " "	(mundane)
Abstinences	3	conjoined always	(supramundane)
Illimitables	2	separately and occasionally	
Conceit	1	occasionally	
Sloth, torpor	2	conjoined and occasionally	

Fixed adjuncts = remaining 41

(iv) Adhimokkho dvipañcaviññāṇa-vicikicchāsahagata-vajjita-cittesu.

(v) Viriyaṁ pañcadvārāvajjana-dvipañcaviññāṇa-sampaṭicchana-santīraṇa-vajjita-cittesu.

(vi) Pīti domanass'-upekkhāsahagata-kāyaviññāṇa-catutthajjhāna-vajjita-cittesu.

(vii) Chando ahetuka-momūha-vajjita-cittesu labbhati.

In what way?

(i) In the first place, the seven universal mental factors are found in all the eighty-nine types of consciousness.

Among the particular mental factors:

(ii) Initial application arises in fifty-five types of consciousness: in all types of sense-sphere consciousness except the two sets of fivefold sense consciousness (54 – 10 = 44); and also in the eleven types of first jhāna consciousness (44 + 11 = 55).

(iii) Sustained application arises in sixty-six types of consciousness: in those fifty-five and in the eleven types of second jhāna consciousness (55 + 11 = 66).

(iv) Decision arises in all types of consciousness excluding the two sets of fivefold sense consciousness and consciousness accompanied by doubt (89 – 11 = 78).

(v) Energy arises in all types of consciousness excluding the five-sense-door adverting consciousness, the two sets of fivefold sense consciousness, receiving consciousness, and investigating consciousness (89 – 16 = 73).

(vi) Zest arises in all types of consciousness excluding those accompanied by displeasure and equanimity, body-consciousness, and the fourth jhāna consciousness (121 – (2 + 55 + 2 + 11) = 51).

(vii) Desire arises in all types of consciousness excluding the rootless and the two types of consciousness accompanied by delusion (89 – 20 = 69).

Guide to § 11

Initial application: The two sets of fivefold sense consciousness, being the most rudimentary types of citta, do not contain any cetasikas with more complex functions to perform than the seven universal mental factors. *Vitakka* is excluded from these cittas because of their elementary nature, and from all sublime and supramundane cittas above the level of the first jhāna because it has been overcome by meditative development. On the eleven types of first jhāna consciousness, see I, §32 and Guide.

Sustained application is present in the second jhāna consciousness, but is excluded from all higher jhānas.

Decision is excluded from the doubting consciousness because a decision cannot be made while the mind is obstructed by doubt.

Energy is excluded from the five-door adverting consciousness, the two kinds of receiving consciousness, and the three kinds of investigating consciousness (see I, §§8-10) because these cittas are still of a relatively weak and passive nature.

Zest is always accompanied by joyful feeling (*somanassa*), but the cittas of the fourth jhāna contain joyful feeling without zest.

Desire here is desire to act, to achieve a purpose, and the two cittas rooted in delusion are so dense that they exclude purposeful action.

§12 Summary

Te pana cittuppādā yathākkamaṁ:

> *Chasaṭṭhi pañcapaññāsa ekādasa ca soḷasa*
> *Sattati vīsati c'eva pakiṇṇakavivajjitā.*
> *Pañcapaññāsa chasaṭṭhi 'ṭṭhasattati tisattati*
> *Ekapaññāsa c' ekūnasattati sapakiṇṇakā.*

Those types of consciousness in order are:

Sixty-six, fifty-five, eleven, sixteen, seventy, and twenty without the occasionals.

Fifty-five, sixty-six, seventy-eight, seventy-three, fifty-one, and sixty-nine with the occasionals.

Guide to §12

The first line of the summary cites the number of cittas without each of the six occasionals, the second line cites the number with the same occasionals. It should be noted, by adding the two figures, that the 121-fold scheme has been used when the jhānic levels of the path and fruition cittas are relevant to the computation, the 89-fold scheme when such distinctions are irrelevant.

The Unwholesome Factors—5
(*akusalacetasika*)

§13 Analysis

(i) Akusalesu pana moho ahirikaṁ, anottappaṁ, uddhaccañ cā ti cattāro' me cetasikā sabbākusalasādhāraṇā nāma. Sabbesu pi dvādas' ākusalesu labbhanti.

(ii) Lobho aṭṭhasu lobhasahagatesv' eva labbhati.

(iii) Diṭṭhi catūsu diṭṭhigatasampayuttesu.

(iv) Māno catūsu diṭṭhigatavippayuttesu.

(v) Doso, issā, macchariyaṁ, kukkuccañ ca dvīsu paṭigha-sampayuttacittesu.

(vi) Thīnaṁ, middhaṁ pañcasu sasankhārikacittesu.

(vii) Vicikicchā vicikicchāsahagatacitte yeva labbhatī ti.

(i) Of the unwholesome mental factors, these four factors—delusion, shamelessness, fearlessness of wrongdoing, and restlessness—are called universal unwholesome factors. They are found in all twelve unwholesome types of consciousness.

(ii) Greed is found only in the eight types of consciousness accompanied by greed.

(iii) Wrong view arises in the four types of (greed-rooted) consciousness associated with wrong view.

(iv) Conceit is found in the four types of (greed-rooted) consciousness dissociated from wrong view.

(v) Hatred, envy, avarice, and worry are found in the two types of consciousness associated with aversion.

(vi) Sloth and torpor are found in the five types of prompted consciousness.

(vii) Doubt is found only in the type of consciousness associated with doubt.

Guide to §13

Universal unwholesome factors: These four factors occur in all twelve unwholesome cittas, for every unwholesome citta involves a mental blindness to the danger in evil (i.e. delusion), a lack of shame and moral dread, and an underlying current of agitation (i.e. restlessness).

Wrong view, conceit: Both of these factors are found only in the cittas rooted in greed, for they involve some degree of holding to the five aggregates. However, the two exhibit contrary qualities, and thus they cannot coexist in the same citta. Wrong view occurs in the mode of misapprehending, i.e. interpreting things in a manner contrary to actuality; conceit occurs in the mode of self-evaluation, i.e. of taking oneself to be superior, equal, or inferior to others. Whereas wrong view is necessarily present in the four cittas rooted in greed accompanied by wrong view, conceit is not a necessary concomitant of the four greed-rooted cittas dissociated from wrong view. It does not arise apart from these cittas, but these cittas can occur without conceit.

Hatred, envy, avarice, worry: These four factors occur only in the cittas associated with aversion. Hatred, being a synonym for aversion, is necessarily found in these two cittas; the other three factors occur variably, depending on conditions. All three partake in the characteristic of aversion: envy involves resentment against the success of others; avarice involves resistance to sharing one's belongings with others; worry here means remorse—self-recrimination for one's commissions and omissions.

Sloth and torpor: These two factors make the cittas dull and sluggish. Hence they cannot arise in the unprompted cittas, which are naturally keen and active, but only in the prompted unwholesome cittas.

§14 Summary

Sabbāpuññesu cattāro lobhamūle tayo gatā
Dosamūlesu cattāro sasankhāre dvayaṁ tathā
Vicikicchā vicikicchācitte cā ti catuddasa
Dvādas' ākusalesv' eva sampayujjanti pañcadhā.

Four are found in all unwholesome states, three in those rooted in greed, four in those rooted in hatred, and so are two in the prompted.

Doubt is found in the consciousness accompanied by doubt. Thus the fourteen (factors) are conjoined only with the twelve unwholesome (types of consciousness) in five ways.

The Beautiful Factors—4
(*sobhanacetasika*)

§15 Analysis

(i) Sobhanesu pana sobhanasādhāraṇā tāva ekūnavīsat' ime cetasikā sabbesu pi ekūnasaṭṭhi sobhanacittesu saṁvijjanti.

(ii) Viratiyo pana tisso pi lokuttaracittesu sabbathā pi niyatā ekato'va labbhanti. Lokiyesu pana kāmāvacarakusalesv' eva kadāci sandissanti visuṁ visuṁ.

(iii) Appamaññāyo pana dvādasasu pañcamajjhānavajjita-mahaggatacittesu c'eva kāmāvacarakusalesu ca sahetuka-kāmāvacarakiriyacittesu cā ti—aṭṭhavīsaticittesv' eva—kadāci nānā hutvā jāyanti. Upekkhāsahagatesu pan' ettha karuṇā muditā na santī ti keci vadanti.

(iv) Paññā pana dvādasasu ñāṇasampayutta-kāmāvacaracittesu c'eva sabbesu pañcatiṁsa mahaggata-lokuttaracittesu cā ti sattacattāḷīsa cittesu sampayogaṁ gacchatī ti.

(i) Of the beautiful, firstly, the nineteen universal beautiful factors are found in all the fifty-nine types of beautiful consciousness.

(ii) The three abstinences are necessarily found together in their entirety in every supramundane type of consciousness. But in the mundane sense-sphere wholesome types of consciousness they are only sometimes present (and then) separately (8 + 8 = 16).

(iii) The illimitables arise at times variably in twenty-eight types of consciousness—namely, the twelve sublime types of consciousness excluding the fifth jhāna, the (eight types of) sense-sphere wholesome consciousness, and the (eight types of) sense-sphere functional consciousness with roots (12 + 8 + 8 = 28). Some, however, say that compassion and appreciative joy are not present in the types of consciousness accompanied by equanimity.

(iv) Wisdom goes into combination with forty-seven types of consciousness—namely, the twelve types of sense-sphere consciousness associated with knowledge, and all the thirty-five sublime and supramundane types of consciousness (12 + 35 = 47).

Guide to §15

The three abstinences: In the supramundane path and fruition cittas, the abstinences are always present together as the right speech, right action, and right livelihood of the Noble Eightfold Path. But in mundane cittas they are only present, as explained earlier, on occasions when one deliberately refrains from wrongdoing. Since one deliberately refrains from an evil deed with a consciousness that is aware of the opportunity for transgression, the mundane abstinences can occur only in the sense-sphere wholesome cittas; they cannot occur in sublime cittas, which take the counterpart sign of the jhāna as their object, nor do they occur in resultant sense-sphere cittas, which do not exercise the function of restraint. They also do not occur in the great functional cittas of an Arahant, since an Arahant has altogether overcome the disposition towards transgression and thus has no need for abstinence.

In the supramundane cittas the three abstinences are necessarily present (*niyata*). In the path cittas they are present as the three moral factors of the eightfold path, performing the functions of eradicating the inclinations to wrong speech, wrong action, and wrong livelihood respectively. In the fruition cittas they reappear representing the moral purity of speech, action, and livelihood accomplished by the work of the path.

Since transgressions in speech, action, and livelihood each have a different sphere, in mundane consciousness the three abstinences are mutually exclusive: if one is present, the other two must be absent. Moreover, any abstinence that arises can arise only in part, as determined by the type of transgression one refrains from: if one meets the opportunity to take life, then right action arises as abstinence only from taking life; if one meets the opportunity to steal, then it arises as abstinence only from stealing. However, when the abstinences arise in the supramundane cittas they always occur together (*ekato*), all three being present simultaneously. And as present, each one functions in its entirety (*sabbathā*); that is, right speech eliminates the dispositions to all forms of wrong speech, right action to all forms of wrong action, and right livelihood to all forms of wrong livelihood.

The illimitables: While non-hatred and mental neutrality—which can also become the illimitables of loving-kindness and equanimity—are present in all wholesome cittas, the other two illimitables—compassion and appreciative joy—are only present when the citta occurs in the appropriate mode: either as commiserating with those in suffering, when compassion arises, or as rejoicing in the fortune of others, when appreciative joy arises.

The twelve sublime types of consciousness here are the first four jhānas in the three aspects of wholesome, resultant, and functional. These two illimitables (as well as loving-kindness) do not arise in the fifth jhāna cittas because, at the level of jhāna, they are necessarily connected to joyful mental feeling (*somanassa*), which in the fifth jhāna is replaced by equanimous feeling (*upekkhā*). Some teachers deny that the illimitables are found in the sense-sphere cittas accompanied by equanimity, but from the author's use of the expression "some, however, say," he apparently does not share their view.[20]

Wisdom: The character of wisdom varies in accordance with the types of cittas in which it arises, but all beautiful cittas except the sense-sphere cittas dissociated from knowledge include some measure of right understanding.

§16 Summary

Ekūnavīsati dhammā jāyant' ekūnasaṭṭhisu
Tayo soḷasacittesu aṭṭhavīsatiyaṁ dvayaṁ
Paññā pakāsitā sattacattāḷīsavidhesu pi
Sampayuttā catudh' evaṁ sobhanesv' eva sobhanā.

Nineteen states arise in fifty-nine, three in sixteen, two in twenty-eight types of consciousness.

Wisdom is declared to be found in forty-seven types. Thus beautiful (factors) are found only in the beautiful (types of consciousness), combined in four ways.

§17 Fixed and Unfixed Adjuncts (*niyatāniyatabheda*)

Issā-macchera-kukkucca-viratī-karuṇādayo
Nānā kadāci māno ca thīna-middhaṁ tathā saha.
Yathāvuttānusārena sesā niyatayogino
Sangahañ ca pavakkhāmi tesaṁ dāni yathārahaṁ.

Envy, avarice, worry, abstinences, compassion, etc. (i.e. appreciative joy), and conceit arise separately and occasionally. So do sloth and torpor, but in combination.

The remaining factors, apart from those mentioned above (52 – 11 = 41), are fixed adjuncts. Now I shall speak of their combination accordingly.

Guide to § 17

Of the fifty-two cetasikas, eleven are called unfixed adjuncts (*aniyatayogī*) because they do not necessarily arise in the types of consciousness to which they are allied. The remaining forty-one factors are called fixed adjuncts (*niyatayogī*) because they invariably arise in their assigned types of consciousness.

In the sections to follow, Ācariya Anuruddha will analyze each of the 121 cittas in terms of its constellation of associated cetasikas. This method of analysis is called the *sangahanaya*, the method of combinations.

COMBINATIONS OF MENTAL FACTORS—33
(*cetasikasangahanaya*)

§18 Introductory Verse

Chattiṁs' ānuttare dhammā pañcatiṁsa mahaggate
Aṭṭhatiṁsā pi labbhanti kāmāvacarasobhane.
Sattavīsaty' apuññamhi dvādas'āhetuke ti ca
Yathāsambhavayogena pañcadhā tattha sangaho.

Thirty-six factors arise in the supramundane (consciousness), thirty-five in the sublime, thirty-eight in the sense-sphere beautiful. Twenty-seven in the unwholesome, twelve in the rootless. According to the way they arise their combination therein is fivefold.

Supramundane Consciousness—5
(*lokuttaracittāni*)

§19 Analysis

Kathaṁ?

(i) Lokuttaresu tāva aṭṭhasu paṭhamajjhānikacittesu aññasamānā terasa cetasikā appamaññāvajjitā tevīsati sobhanacetasikā cā ti chattiṁsa dhammā sangahaṁ gacchanti.

(ii) Tathā dutiyajjhānikacittesu vitakkavajjā.

(iii) Tatiyajjhānikacittesu vitakka-vicāravajjā.

(iv) Catutthajjhānikacittesu vitakka-vicāra-pītivajjā.

(v) Pañcamajjhānikacittesu pi upekkhāsahagatā te eva sangayhantī ti. Sabbathā pi aṭṭhasu lokuttaracittesu pañcakajjhānavasena pañcadhā va sangaho hotī ti.

How?

(i) First, in the eight types of supramundane first jhāna consciousness, thirty-six factors enter into combination, namely, thirteen ethically variables and twenty-three beautiful mental factors, excluding the two illimitables (13 + 23 = 36).

(ii) Similarly, in the supramundane second jhāna types of consciousness, all the above are included except initial application (35).

(iii) In the third jhāna types of consciousness (all those) excluding initial application and sustained application (34).

(iv) In the fourth jhāna types of consciousness (all those) excluding initial application, sustained application, and zest (33).

TABLE 2.3: COMBINATIONS OF MENTAL FACTORS

CITTA	NO.	CETASIKAS	TOTAL
Supramundane			
1st jhāna	8	1-13, 28-49, 52	36
2nd jhāna	8	1-7, 9-13, 28-49, 52	35
3rd jhāna	8	1-7, 10-13, 28-49, 52	34
4th jhāna	8	1-7, 11-13, 28-49, 52	33
5th jhāna	8	1-7, 11-13, 28-49, 52	33
Sublime			
1st jhāna	3	1-13, 28-46, 50-52	35
2nd jhāna	3	1-7, 9-13, 28-46, 50-52	34
3rd jhāna	3	1-7, 10-13, 28-46, 50-52	33
4th jhāna	3	1-7, 11-13, 28-46, 50-52	32
5th jhāna	15	1-7, 11-13, 28-46, 52	30
SS Beautiful			
Wholesome	31, 32	1-13, 28-52	38
"	33, 34	1-13, 28-51	37
"	35, 36	1-11, 13, 28-52	37
	37, 38	1-11, 13, 28-51	36
Resultant	39, 40	1-13, 28-46, 52	33
"	41, 42	1-13, 28-46	32
"	43, 44	1-11, 13, 28-46, 52	32
"	45, 46	1-11, 13, 28-46	31
Functional	47, 48	1-13, 28-46, 50-52	35
"	49, 50	1-13, 28-46, 50, 51	34
"	51, 52	1-11, 13, 28-46, 50-52	34
"	53, 54	1-11, 13, 28-46, 50-51	33
Unwholesome			
Greed-rooted	1	1-19	19
"	2	1-19, 25, 26	21
"	3	1-18, 20	19
"	4	1-18, 20, 25, 26	21
"	5	1-11, 13, 14-19	18
"	6	1-11, 13, 14-19, 25, 26	20
"	7	1-11, 13, 14-18, 20	18
"	8	1-11, 13, 14-18, 20, 25, 26	20
Hate-rooted	9	1-11, 13, 14-17, 21-24	20
"	10	1-11, 13, 14-17, 21-24, 25, 26	22
Delus.-rooted	11	1-9, 11, 14-17, 27	15
"	12	1-11, 14-17	15
Rootless			
Sense consness.	13-17	1-7	7
" "	20-24	1-7	7
Receiving	18, 25	1-10	10
Investigating	19, 27	1-10	10
Investigating	26	1-10, 12	11
Five door-advt.	28	1-10	10
Mind-door-advt.	29	1-11	11
Smile-producing	30	1-12	12

(v) In the fifth jhāna types of consciousness, those (same factors of the fourth jhāna) are included accompanied by equanimity (instead of happiness) (33).

Thus altogether, for the eight types of supramundane consciousness, the combination is fivefold by way of the five kinds of jhāna.

Guide to §19

Supramundane first jhāna consciousness: On the supramundane jhānas, see I, §§31-32.

Excluding the two illimitables: The illimitables of compassion and appreciative joy are not found in the supramundane cittas because they always take the concept of living beings as their object, while the path and fruition cittas take Nibbāna as their object.[21] The exceptions in (ii)-(v) should be understood by way of the elimination of the grosser jhāna factors at the different levels of supramundane jhāna.

§20 Summary

Chattiṁsa pañcatiṁsā ca catuttiṁsa yathākkamaṁ
Tettiṁsa dvayam icc' evaṁ pañcadh' ānuttare ṭhitā.

Respectively there are thirty-six, thirty-five, thirty-four, and thirty-three in the last two. Thus in five ways they exist in the supramundane.

Sublime Consciousness—5 (*mahaggatacittāni*)

§21 Analysis

Mahaggatesu pana:

(i) Tīsu paṭhamajjhānikacittesu tāva aññasamānā terasa cetasikā viratittayavajjitā dvāvīsati sobhanacetasikā cā ti pañcatiṁsa dhammā sangahaṁ gacchanti. Karuṇā-muditā pan' ettha paccekam eva yojetabbā.

(ii) Tathā dutiyajjhānikacittesu vitakkavajjā.

(iii) Tatiyajjhānikācittesu vitakka-vicāravajjā.

(iv) Catutthajjhānikacittesu vitakka-vicāra-pītivajjā.

(v) Pañcamajjhānikacittesu pana paṇṇarasasu appamaññāyo na labbhantī ti.

Sabbathā pi sattavīsati mahaggatacittesu pañcakajjhānavasena pañcadhā va sangaho hotī ti.

(i) In the sublime types of consciousness, first in the three types of first jhāna consciousness, thirty-five states enter into combination, namely, the thirteen ethically variable mental factors and twenty-two beautiful mental factors, excluding the three abstinences (13 + 22 = 35). But here compassion and appreciative joy should be combined separately.

(ii) Similarly, in the second jhāna consciousness (all those are included) except initial application (34).

(iii) In the third jhāna consciousness, all except initial application and sustained application (33).

(iv) In the fourth jhāna consciousness, all except initial application, sustained application, and zest (32).

(v) In the fifteen (types of) fifth jhāna consciousness the illimitables are not obtained (30).

Thus altogether, for the twenty-seven types of sublime consciousness, the combination is fivefold by way of the five kinds of jhāna.

Guide to § 21

Three types of first jhāna consciousness: that is, wholesome, resultant, and functional.

Excluding the three abstinences: The abstinences are not included in the sublime consciousness because one who is absorbed in jhāna is not, at that time, deliberately refraining from some type of wrongdoing.

Compassion and appreciative joy should be combined separately: Compassion takes as object beings who are afflicted by suffering, appreciative joy takes as object beings who have achieved success and happiness. Compassion occurs in the mode of commiseration, appreciative joy in the mode of rejoicing. Hence because of their contrary objects and modes of occurrence, the two cannot coexist in the same citta. While one or the other may be associated with this consciousness, they both may be absent.

§22 Summary

Pañcatiṁsa catuttiṁsa tettiṁsa ca yathākkamaṁ
Battiṁsa c'eva tiṁseti pañcadhā va mahaggate.

There are respectively thirty-five, thirty-four, thirty-three, thirty-two, and thirty. Fivefold is the combination in the sublime.

Sense-Sphere Beautiful Consciousness—12
(*kāmāvacara-sobhanacittāni*)

§23 Analysis

(i) Kāmāvacara-sobhanesu pana kusalesu tāva paṭhamadvaye aññasamānā terasa cetasikā pañcavīsati sobhanacetasikā cā ti aṭṭhatiṁsa dhammā sangahaṁ gacchanti. Appamaññā viratiyo pan' ettha pañca pi paccekam eva yojetabbā.

(ii) Tathā dutiyadvaye ñāṇavajjitā.

(iii) Tatiyadvaye ñāṇasampayuttā pītivajjitā.

(iv) Catutthadvaye ñāṇapītivajjitā te eva sangayhanti.

Kiriyacittesu pi virativajjitā tath' eva catūsu pi dukesu catudhā va sangayhanti.

Tathā vipākesu ca appamañña-virati-vajjitā te eva sangayhantī ti.

Sabbathā pi catuvīsati kāmāvacara-sobhanacittesu dukavasena dvādasadhā va sangaho hotī ti.

(i) In the sense-sphere beautiful types of consciousness, first in the wholesome types of consciousness, in the first couplet thirty-eight states enter into combination, namely, the thirteen ethically variable mental factors and the twenty-five beautiful mental factors (13 + 25 = 38). But here the (two) illimitables and the (three) abstinences should be combined separately.

(ii) Similarly in the second couplet, (all those are included) excluding knowledge (37).

(iii) In the third couplet, associated with knowledge, (all those are included) excluding zest (37).

(iv) In the fourth couplet (all) those are included excluding knowledge and zest (36).

In the functional types of consciousness, in the four couplets those (mental factors) are included in the same four ways, except that the abstinences are excluded (35, 34, 34, 33).

So too, in the resultant types of consciousness, those (mental factors) are included except that the illimitables and the abstinences are excluded (33, 32, 32, 31).

Thus altogether, for the twenty-four sense-sphere beautiful types of consciousness, the combination is twelvefold by way of the couplets.

Guide to §23

The first couplet: The couplets spoken of in this passage are the pairs of prompted and unprompted cittas. These do not differ in their constituency of cetasikas, and thus may be analyzed together.

The (three) abstinences should be combined separately: Because the abstinences have different spheres of application—speech, action, and livelihood—only one can occur in any given citta, as determined by the kind of wrong deed one is intending to refrain from. Since the abstinences only arise on occasions of deliberate restraint, they need not be present in this type of consciousness.

Excluding zest: The third and fourth couplets are the cittas accompanied by equanimous feeling (*upekkhā*); these exclude zest (*pīti*), which can occur only in connection with joyful feeling (*somanassa*).

Functional types of consciousness: Functional cittas of the beautiful class arise only in Arahants. These cittas exclude the abstinences because Arahants, having cut off all defilements, do not need to deliberately refrain from evil deeds.

Resultant types: Sense-sphere resultants exclude the illimitables because they take solely sense-sphere phenomena as their object, while the illimitables take the concept of beings as their object; they exclude the abstinences because there is no refraining from wrong deeds on the occasion of sense-sphere resultants.

§24 Summary

Aṭṭhatiṁsa sattatiṁsa dvayaṁ chattiṁsakaṁ subhe
Pañcatiṁsa catuttiṁsa dvayaṁ tettiṁsakaṁ kriye.
Tettiṁsa pāke battiṁsa dvay' ekatiṁsakaṁ bhave
Sahetukāmāvacara puñña-pāka-kriyā mane.

With respect to sense-sphere consciousness with roots—wholesome, resultant, and functional—there arise in the wholesome (first pair) thirty-eight, twice thirty-seven (in the second and third pairs), and thirty-six (in the fourth pair). In the functional there are thirty-five (in the first pair), twice thirty-four (in the second and third pairs), and thirty-three (in the fourth pair). In the resultant there are thirty-three (in the first pair), twice thirty-two (in the second and third pairs), and thirty-one (in the fourth pair).

§25 Distinctions among the Beautiful Types

Na vijjant' ettha viratī kriyāsu ca mahaggate
Anuttare appamaññā kāmapāke dvayaṁ tathā.

Anuttare jhānadhammā appamaññā ca majjhime
Viratī ñāṇapīti ca parittesu visesakā.

Herein, the abstinences are not found in the functional consciousness or the sublime consciousness, nor are the illimitables found in the supramundane, nor is the pair (the illimitables and abstinences) present in the sense-sphere resultants.

In the supreme (i.e. the supramundane) the jhāna factors are the basis of distinctions, in the middle (i.e. the sublime) the illimitables (and jhāna factors), and in the limited (i.e. the sense-sphere beautiful) the abstinences, knowledge, and zest are the basis of distinctions.

Guide to § 25

The *Vibhāvinī-Ṭīkā* adds that in the "limited" or sense-sphere cittas the illimitables (compassion and appreciative joy) are also a basis of distinctions, since they distinguish the wholesome and functionals, in which they may be found, from the resultants, from which they are necessarily absent.

Unwholesome Consciousness—7
(*akusalacittāni*)

§26 Analysis

(i) Akusalesu pana lobhamūlesu tāva paṭhame asankhārike aññasamānā terasa cetasikā akusalasādhāraṇā cattāro cā ti sattarasa lobhadiṭṭhīhi saddhiṁ ekūnavīsati dhammā sangahaṁ gacchanti.

(ii) Tath'eva dutiye asankhārike lobhamānena.

(iii) Tatiye tath'eva pītivajjitā lobhadiṭṭhīhi saha aṭṭhārasa.

(iv) Catutthe tath'eva lobhamānena.

(i) In the unwholesome types of consciousness, first in those rooted in greed, in the first unprompted consciousness nineteen states enter into combination, namely, the thirteen ethically variable mental factors and the four universal unwholesome mental factors, making seventeen, together with greed and wrong view (13 + 4 + 2 = 19).

(ii) Similarly, in the second unprompted consciousness, (the same seventeen are found together) with greed and conceit (13+4+2 = 19).

(iii) Similarly, in the third unprompted consciousness, there are eighteen states, together with greed and wrong view but excluding zest (12 + 4 + 2 = 18).

(iv) Similarly, in the fourth (there are eighteen) with greed and conceit (12 + 4 + 2 = 18).

(v) Pañcame pana paṭighasampayutte asankhārike doso issā macchariyaṁ kukkuccañ cā ti catūhi saddhiṁ pītivajjitā te eva vīsati dhammā sangayhanti. Issā-macchariya-kukkuccāni pan' ettha paccekam eva yojetabbāni.

(vi) Sasankhārikapañcake pi tath'eva thīna-middhena visesetvā yojetabbā.

(v) In the fifth unprompted consciousness, that associated with aversion, these twenty states enter into combination—the above excluding zest but including the four: hatred, envy, avarice, and worry. But here envy, avarice and worry should be combined separately (12 + 4 + 4 = 20).

(vi) In the five types of prompted consciousness the above states should similarly be combined with this difference, that sloth and torpor are included. (Thus: 21; 21; 20; 20; 22.)

(vii) Chanda-pīti-vajjitā pana aññasamānā ekādasa akusalasādhāraṇā cattāro cā ti paṇṇarasa dhammā uddhaccasahagate sampayujjanti.

(viii) Vicikicchāsahagatacitte ca adhimokkhavirahitā vicikicchāsahagatā tath'eva paṇṇarasa dhammā samupalabbhantī ti.

Sabbathā pi dvādas' ākusalacittuppādesu paccekaṁ yojiyamānā pi gaṇanavasena sattadhā va sangahitā bhavantī ti.

(vii) In the type of consciousness connected with restlessness fifteen mental states occur, namely, eleven ethically variable factors excluding desire and zest, and the four universal unwholesome factors (11 + 4 = 15).

(viii) In the type of consciousness connected with doubt fifteen states are similarly obtained by excluding decision and incorporating doubt (10 + 4 + 1 = 15).

Thus altogether, for the twelve types of unwholesome consciousness, the combination becomes sevenfold when reckoned according to their different adjuncts.

Guide to § 26

Those rooted in greed: The first and third unprompted cittas rooted in greed invariably include wrong view; the third, being accompanied by equanimity, excludes zest. The second and fourth may include conceit, but not as a matter of necessity. Thus when conceit is absent they will contain eighteen and seventeen cetasikas, respectively.

That associated with aversion: This type of citta includes twelve ethically variable factors, four unwholesome universals, and the four additional states of the aversion class—hatred, envy, avarice, and worry. The last three are mutually exclusive and may all be absent from this citta.

Connected with restlessness: The two cittas rooted in delusion exclude desire, as they are incapable of sustaining purposive activity. In the doubting consciousness, decision is replaced by doubt, the two being mutually incompatible.

§27 Summary

Ekūnavīs' aṭṭhārasa vīs' ekavīsa vīsati
Dvāvīsa paṇṇarase ti sattadh' ākusale ṭhitā.
Sādhāraṇā ca cattāro samānā ca dasā' pare
Cuddas' ete pavuccanti sabbākusalayogino.

Nineteen, eighteen, twenty, twenty-one, twenty, twenty-two, fifteen—thus they stand in seven ways in the unwholesome consciousness.

These fourteen mental states—namely, the four unwholesome universals and ten variables—are said to be associated with all the unwholesome types of consciousness.

Rootless Consciousness—4
(*ahetukacittāni*)

§28 Analysis

(i) Ahetukesu pana hasanacitte tāva chandavajjitā aññasamānā dvādasa dhammā sangahaṁ gacchanti.

(ii) Tathā votthapane chanda-pīti-vajjitā.

(iii) Sukhasantīraṇe chanda-viriya-vajjitā.

(iv) Manodhātuttika-ahetukapaṭisandhiyugale chanda-pīti-viriya-vajjitā.

(v) Dvipañcaviññāṇe pakiṇṇakavajjitā te yeva sangayhantī ti.

Sabbathā pi aṭṭhārasasu ahetukesu gaṇanavasena catudhā va sangaho hotī ti.

(i) In the rootless types of consciousness, first in the smile-producing consciousness, twelve ethically variable states, excluding desire, enter into combination (7 + 5 = 12).

(ii) Likewise they occur in the determining consciousness, excluding desire and zest (7 + 4 = 11).

(iii) In the investigating consciousness accompanied by joy, all those except desire and energy occur (7 + 4 = 11).

(iv) In the triple mind element and in the pair of rootless rebirth-linking types of consciousness, all those except desire, zest, and energy occur (7 + 3 = 10).

(v) In the two types of fivefold sense consciousness, all those enter into combination except the occasionals (7).

Thus altogether, for the eighteen types of rootless consciousness, the combinations, numerically considered, constitute four groups.

Guide to § 28

The determining consciousness (*votthapana*): This consciousness is the same as the mind-door adverting consciousness, which in the five sense doors performs the function of determining the object.

The investigating consciousness accompanied by joy: This citta, a wholesome kamma resultant arisen in regard to an exceptionally desirable object, includes zest because the associated feeling is joy. In this citta and those to follow, energy is excluded, because these rootless types of consciousness are weak and passive.

The triple mind element (*manodhātuttika*): This is a collective term for the five-door adverting consciousness (*pañcadvārāvajjana*) and the two types of receiving consciousness (*sampaṭicchana*).

Pair of rootless rebirth-linking types of consciousness (*paṭisandhi*): These are the two kinds of investigating consciousness accompanied by equanimity. Their role in rebirth-linking is explained at III, §9.

§29 Summary

Dvādas' ekādasa dasa satta cā ti catubbidho
Aṭṭhāras' āhetukesu cittuppādesu sangaho.
Ahetukesu sabbattha satta sesā yathārahaṁ
Iti vitthārato vutto tettiṁsavidhasangaho.

Twelve, eleven, ten, seven—thus the combination in the eighteen rootless types of consciousness is fourfold.

In all the rootless the seven (universals) occur. The rest (the occasionals) arise according to the type. Thus in detail the combinations are told in thirty-three ways.

§30 Conclusion

Itthaṁ cittāviyuttānaṁ sampayogañ ca sangahaṁ
Ñatvā bhedaṁ yathāyogaṁ cittena samam uddise.

Understanding thus the associations and combinations of the mental adjuncts, let one explain their classification through their union with consciousness as is fit.

Guide to § 30

The associations ... of the mental adjuncts: This refers to the association of each cetasika with the different cittas in which it is found, explained in §§10-17.

The combinations of the mental adjuncts: This refers to the analysis of each citta into its component cetasikas, explained in §§18-29. For a comprehensive view of both the method of association and the method of combination together, see Table 2.4 at the end of this chapter.

Let one explain their classification, etc.: The author advises the student to categorize the cetasikas by way of the cittas to which they pertain. For example, the seven universals are eighty-ninefold because they arise in all cittas. Initial application is fifty-fivefold because it arises in fifty-five cittas. The cetasikas can further be divided by way of plane, kind, associations, etc., in accordance with their host consciousness.

Iti Abhidhammatthasangahe
Cetasikasangahavibhāgo nāma
dutiyo paricchedo.

Thus ends the second chapter
in the Manual of Abhidhamma entitled
the Compendium of Mental Factors.

TABLE 2.4:
COMPREHENSIVE CHART ON MENTAL FACTORS

← METHOD OF COMBINATION →

↑ METHOD OF ASSOCIATION

CITTAS		CETASIKAS Universals 7	In. Application	Sus. Application	Decision	Energy	Zest	Desire	Unwh. Univs. 4	Greed	Wrong View	Conceit	Hate, Envy, Avarice, Worry	Sloth, Torpor	Doubt	Btf. Univs. 19	Abstinences 3	Illimitables 2	Wisdom	Totals
Greed - rtd.	1	■	■	■	■	■	■	■	■	■	■									19
"	2	■	■	■	■	■	■	■	■	■	■			■						21
"	3	■	■	■	■	■	■	■	■	■		■								19
"	4	■	■	■	■	■	■	■	■	■		■		■						21
"	5	■	■	■	■	■		■	■	■	■									18
"	6	■	■	■	■	■		■	■	■	■			■						20
"	7	■	■	■	■	■		■	■	■		■								18
"	8	■	■	■	■	■		■	■	■		■		■						20
Hate - rtd.	1	■	■	■	■	■		■	■				■							20
"	2	■	■	■	■	■		■	■				■	■						22
Delusion-rtd.	1	■	■	■		■			■						■					15
"	2	■	■	■	■	■			■											15
Sense consness.	10	■																		7
Receiving	2	■	■	■	■															10
Investigating - eqn.	2	■	■	■	■															10
Investigating - joy	1	■	■	■	■		■													11
Five-door advert.	1	■	■	■	■															10
Mind-door advert.	1	■	■	■	■	■														11
Smile-producing	1	■	■	■	■	■	■													12

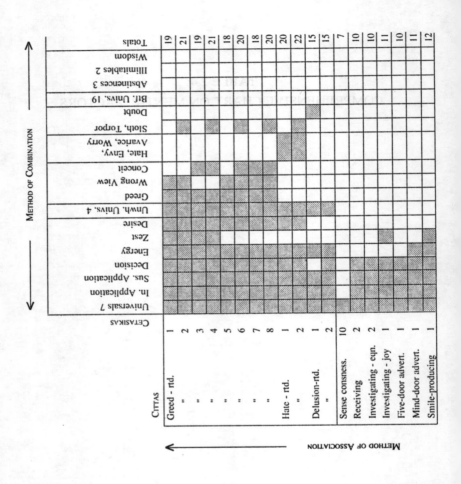

METHOD OF ASSOCIATION →

SS Wholesome	1, 2																			38
"	3, 4																			37
"	5, 6																			37
"	7, 8																			36
SS Resultant	1, 2																			33
"	3, 4																			32
"	5, 6																			32
"	7, 8																			31
SS Functional	1, 2																			35
"	3, 4																			34
"	5, 6																			34
"	7, 8																			33
FMS 1st Jhana	3																			35
" 2nd "	3																			34
" 3rd "	3																			33
" 4th "	3																			32
" 5th "	3																			30
IS 5th Jhana	12																			30
4 Path Cittas 1st Jhana	4																			36
2nd "	4																			35
3rd "	4																			34
4th "	4																			33
5th "	4																			33
4 Fruit Cittas 1st Jhana	4																			36
2nd "	4																			35
3rd "	4																			34
4th "	4																			33
5th "	4																			33
Totals		89	55	66	78	73	51	69	12	8	4	4	2	5	1	59	16	28	47	
		121			110	105		101								91	48	79		

CHAPTER III
COMPENDIUM OF THE MISCELLANEOUS
(Pakiṇṇakasangahavibhāga)

§1 Introductory Verse

Sampayuttā yathāyogaṁ tepaṇṇāsa sabhāvato
Cittacetasikā dhammā tesaṁ dāni yathārahaṁ.
Vedanā-hetuto kicca-dvār'-ālambana-vatthuto
Cittuppādavasen' eva sangaho nāma nīyate.

Having explained accordingly the fifty-three associated states—consciousness and mental factors—with respect to their intrinsic nature, now, taking consciousness alone, we will deal concisely with its classification by way of feelings, roots, functions, doors, objects, and bases.

Guide to §1

The fifty-three associated states: Though 89 (or 121) types of consciousness are recognized in the Abhidhamma, these are treated collectively as a single *dhamma* or reality because they all have the same characteristic, namely, the cognizing of an object. However, the fifty-two cetasikas are considered to be each a separate reality because they all have different characteristics. Thus there are altogether fifty-three associated mental phenomena.

Taking consciousness alone *(cittuppādavasen' eva)*: The Pali term *cittuppāda* literally means an arising of consciousness. In other contexts it implies the citta together with its collection of cetasikas but here it denotes citta itself. Nevertheless, it should be understood that consciousness always occurs in indissoluble union with its cetasikas, which often form the basis for its analysis and classification.

Compendium of Feeling
(*vedanāsangaha*)

§2 Analysis of Feeling

Tattha vedanāsangahe tāva tividhā vedanā: sukhā, dukkhā, adukkhamasukhā cā ti. Sukhaṁ, dukkhaṁ, somanassaṁ, domanassaṁ, upekkhā ti ca bhedena pana pañcadhā hoti.

In the compendium of feeling there are first three kinds of feeling, namely, pleasant, painful, and that which is neither painful nor pleasant. Again, feeling is analyzed as fivefold: pleasure, pain, joy, displeasure, and equanimity.

Guide to §2

Analysis of feeling: As we have seen, feeling (*vedanā*) is a universal mental factor, the cetasika with the function of experiencing the "flavour" of the object. Since some sort of feeling accompanies every citta, feeling serves as an important variable in terms of which consciousness can be classified. In this section the author's main concern is to classify the totality of cittas by way of their concomitant feeling.

Three kinds of feeling: Feeling may be analyzed as either threefold or fivefold. When it is analyzed simply in terms of its affective quality, it is threefold: pleasant, painful, and neither-painful-nor-pleasant. In this threefold classification, pleasant feeling includes both bodily pleasure and mental pleasure or joy, and painful feeling includes both bodily pain and mental pain or displeasure.

Feeling is analyzed as fivefold: When feeling is analyzed by way of the governing faculty (*indriya*), it becomes fivefold. These five types of feelings are called faculties because they exercise lordship or control (*indra*) over their associated states with respect to the affective mode of experiencing the object.

When the fivefold analysis of feeling is considered, the pleasant feeling of the threefold scheme becomes divided into pleasure and joy, the former bodily and the latter mental; the painful feeling of the threefold scheme becomes divided into pain and displeasure, again the former bodily and the latter mental; and neither-painful-nor-pleasant feeling becomes identified with equanimity or neutral feeling.

In the Suttas the Buddha sometimes also speaks of feeling as twofold, pleasure (*sukha*) and pain (*dukkha*). This is a loose or metaphorical method of analysis, arrived at by merging the blameless neutral feeling in pleasure and the blameworthy neutral feeling in pain. The

Buddha further declares that whatever is felt is included in suffering (*yaṁ kiñci vedayitaṁ taṁ dukkhasmiṁ*, S.36:11/iv, 216). In this statement the word *dukkha* does not bear the narrow meaning of painful feeling, but the broader meaning of the suffering inherent in all conditioned things by reason of their impermanence.

Pleasure (***sukha***) has the characteristic of experiencing a desirable tangible object, the function of intensifying associated states, manifestation as bodily enjoyment, and its proximate cause is the body faculty.

Pain (***dukkha***) has the characteristic of experiencing an undesirable tangible object, the function of withering associated states, manifestation as bodily affliction, and its proximate cause is also the body faculty.

Joy (***somanassa***) has the characteristic of experiencing a desirable object, the function of partaking of the desirable aspect of the object, manifestation as mental enjoyment, and its proximate cause is tranquillity.[1]

Displeasure (***domanassa***) has the characteristic of experiencing an undesirable object, the function of partaking of the undesirable aspect of the object, manifestation as mental affliction, and its proximate cause is the heart-base.[2]

Equanimity (***upekkhā***) has the characteristic of being felt as neutral, the function of neither intensifying nor withering associated states, manifestation as peacefulness, and its proximate cause is consciousness without zest.[3]

§3 Classification by way of Consciousness

Tattha sukhasahagataṁ kusalavipākaṁ kāyaviññāṇaṁ ekam eva.

Tathā dukkhasahagataṁ akusalavipākaṁ kāyaviññāṇaṁ.

Somanassasahagatacittāni pana lobhamūlāni cattāri, dvādasa kāmāvacarasobhanāni, sukhasantīraṇa-hasanāni ca dve ti aṭṭhārasa kāmāvacaracittāni c'eva paṭhama-dutiya-tatiya-catutthajjhāna-saṅkhātāni catucattāḷīsa mahaggata-lokuttaracittāni cā ti dvāsaṭṭhividhāni bhavanti.

Domanassasahagatacittāni pana dve paṭighasampayuttacittān'eva.

Sesāni sabbāni pi pañcapaññāsa upekkhāsahagatacittān' evā ti.

Of them, wholesome-resultant body-consciousness is the only one accompanied by pleasure.

Similarly, unwholesome-resultant body-consciousness is the only one accompanied by pain.

There are sixty-two kinds of consciousness accompanied by joy, namely:

(a) eighteen types of sense-sphere consciousness—four rooted in greed, twelve types of sense-sphere beautiful consciousness, the two (rootless) types, i.e. joyful investigating and smiling consciousness (4 + 12 + 2);

(b) forty-four types of sublime and supramundane consciousness pertaining to the first, second, third, and fourth jhānas (12 + 32).

Only the two types of consciousness connected with aversion are accompanied by displeasure.

All the remaining fifty-five types of consciousness are accompanied by equanimity.

Guide to §3

The remaining fifty-five: Those cittas accompanied by equanimity are:

(1) six unwholesome cittas, four rooted in greed, two in delusion;
(2) fourteen rootless cittas;
(3) twelve sense-sphere beautiful cittas (four each wholesome, resultant, and functional);
(4) three cittas of the fifth jhāna;
(5) twelve cittas of the immaterial jhānas; and
(6) eight supramundane cittas, i.e. the paths and fruits pertaining to the fifth supramundane jhāna.

§4 Summary

Sukhaṁ dukkhaṁ upekkhā ti tividhā tattha vedanā
Somanassaṁ domanassam iti bhedena pañcadhā.
Sukham ekattha dukkhañ ca domanassaṁ dvaye ṭhitaṁ
Dvāsaṭṭhīsu somanassaṁ pañcapaññāsake'tarā.

Feeling, therein, is threefold, namely, pleasure, pain, and equanimity. Together with joy and displeasure it is fivefold.

Pleasure and pain are each found in one, displeasure in two, joy in sixty-two, and the remaining (i.e. equanimity) in fifty-five.

Guide to §4

Pleasure and pain are each found in one: It should be noted that while the four pairs of sense consciousness other than body-consciousness are accompanied by equanimous feeling, body-consciousness arises in connection with either pleasure or pain. The *Aṭṭhasālinī* explains that in the case of the four doors—eye, ear, nose, and tongue—the sense object, which is derived matter, impinges on the sense faculty, which is also derived matter. When this happens, the impact is not strong, as when four balls of cotton placed on anvils are struck by four other balls of cotton. Thus the resulting feeling is neutral. But in the case of the body, the object consists of three of the primary elements—earth, fire, and air. Thus when the object impinges on body-sensitivity, its impact is strong and is conveyed to the primary elements of the body. This is comparable to four balls of cotton being struck by hammers: the hammer breaks through the cotton and hits the anvil. In the case of a desirable object the body-consciousness is a wholesome-resultant and the concomitant bodily feeling is physical pleasure, in the case of an undesirable object the body-consciousness is an unwholesome-resultant and the concomitant bodily feeling is physical pain.[4]

TABLE 3.1: COMPENDIUM OF FEELING

	RTLS.			SS BTF.			FMS			IS			PATH				FRUIT			
Unwholesome	Unwh.-result	Wh.-result	Rtls. result	Wholesome	Resultant	Functional	Wholesome	Resultant	Functional	Wholesome	Resultant	Functional	Stream-entry	Once-return	Non-return	Arahant	Stream-entry	Once-return	Non-return	Arahant
●				●	●	●	●	●	●				●	●	●	●	●	●	●	●
●				●	●	●	●	●	●				●	●	●	●	●	●	●	●
●				●	●	●	●	●	●				●	●	●	●	●	●	●	●
●				●	●	●	●	●	●				●	●	●	●	●	●	●	●
○	○	○	○	○	○	○	○	○	○	○	○	○	○	○	○	○	○	○	○	○
○	○	○	○	○	○	○				○	○	○								
○	○	○	●	○	○	○				○	○	○								
○	○	○		○	○	○				○	○	○								
∗	□	■																		
∗	○	○																		
○		●																		
○	○	○																		

KEY:

●	joy	62	■	pleasure	1
○	equanimity	55	□	pain	1
∗	displeasure	2			

Though it may seem that pleasure and pain also accompany the other four kinds of sense consciousness, the Abhidhamma maintains that the immediate moment of sense consciousness in these cases is necessarily accompanied by neutral feeling. In the javana phase belonging to the same cognitive process as the moment of sense consciousness, and in subsequent mind-door processes taking the same object, mental pleasure (that is, *somanassa* or joy) may arise towards an agreeable sight, sound, smell, or taste; mental pain (that is, *domanassa* or displeasure) may arise towards a disagreeable sight, etc.; and equanimity or neutral feeling (*upekkhā*) may arise towards an object regarded with indifference or detachment. These, however, are mental feelings rather than physical feelings, and they arise subsequent to the moment of bare sense consciousness rather than in immediate association with the bare sense consciousness. As they occur in the javana phase, these feelings are associated with wholesome or unwholesome consciousness, or—in the case of the joy and equanimity experienced by Arahants—with functional consciousness.[5]

Compendium of Roots
(*hetusangaha*)

§5 Analysis of Roots

Hetusangahe hetū nāma lobho doso moho alobho adoso amoho cā ti chabbidhā bhavanti.

In the compendium of roots there are six roots, namely, greed, hatred, delusion, non-greed, non-hatred, and non-delusion.

Guide to §5

Analysis of roots: In this section all types of consciousness are classified by way of their concomitant *hetus* or "roots." In the Suttas the word *hetu* is used in the general sense of cause or reason (*kāraṇa*). There it is synonymous with the word *paccaya*, condition, with which it is often conjoined, and it applies to any phenomenon that functions as a cause or reason for other things. In the Abhidhamma, however, *hetu* is used exclusively in the specialized sense of root (*mūla*), and it is restricted in application to six mental factors representing ethically significant qualities.

Formally defined, a root is a mental factor which establishes firmness and stability in the cittas and cetasikas with which it is associated.[6] For it is said that those cittas that possess roots are firm and stable, like trees, while those that are rootless are weak and unstable, like moss.[7]

Of the six roots enumerated in the text, three—greed, hatred, and delusion—are exclusively unwholesome, while three—non-greed, non-hatred, and non-delusion—may be either wholesome or indeterminate. They are wholesome when they arise in wholesome cittas and indeterminate when they arise in resultant and functional cittas. In either case, whether wholesome or indeterminate, these three roots are beautiful (*sobhana*) cetasikas.

§6 Classification by way of Consciousness

Tattha pañcadvārāvajjana-dvipañcaviññāṇa-sampaṭicchana-santīraṇa-votthapana-hasana-vasena aṭṭhārasa ahetukacittāni nāma. Sesāni sabbāni pi ekasattati cittāni sahetukān' eva.

Tatthā pi dve momūhacittāni ekahetukāni. Sesāni dasa akusala-cittāni c' eva ñāṇavippayuttāni dvādasa kāmāvacarasobhanāni cā ti dvāvīsati dvihetukacittāni.

Dvādasa ñāṇasampayutta-kāmāvacarasobhanāni c' eva pañcatiṁsa mahaggata-lokuttaracittāni cā ti sattacattāḷīsa tihetukacittāni.

Therein, eighteen types of consciousness are without roots, namely, five-door adverting, the two sets of fivefold sense consciousness, receiving, investigating, determining, and smiling (1 + 5 + 5 + 2 + 3 + 1 + 1). All the remaining seventy-one types of consciousness are with roots.

Of them the two types of consciousness associated with sheer delusion have only one root. The remaining ten unwholesome types of consciousness and the twelve sense-sphere beautiful types of consciousness dissociated from knowledge—thus totalling twenty-two—are with two roots.

The twelve sense-sphere beautiful types of consciousness associated with knowledge, and the thirty-five sublime and supramundane types of consciousness—thus totalling forty-seven—are with three roots.

Guide to §6

The remaining ten unwholesome types of consciousness: The eight cittas accompanied by greed have greed and delusion as roots; the two cittas accompanied by aversion have hatred and delusion as roots.

The twelve ... dissociated from knowledge: These sense-sphere beautiful cittas—four each wholesome, resultant, and functional—are conditioned by non-greed and non-hatred; non-delusion is excluded because they are dissociated from knowledge.

Forty-seven ... with three roots: These cittas are conditioned by the three beautiful roots.

§7 Summary

Lobho doso ca moho ca hetū akusalā tayo
Alobhādosāmoho ca kusalābyākatā tathā.
Ahetuk' aṭṭhāras' ekahetukā dve dvāvīsati
Dvihetukā matā sattacattāḷīsa tihetukā.

Greed, hatred, and delusion are the three unwholesome roots. Non-greed, non-hatred, and non-delusion are (the three roots that are) wholesome and indeterminate.

TABLE 3.2: COMPENDIUM OF ROOTS

Roots \ Cittas	Greed-rooted 8	Hate-rooted 2	Delusion-rooted 2	Rootless 18	SS Btf. w. Knwl. 12	SS Btf. wo. Knwl. 12	Sublime 27	Supramundane 8	Total
Greed	■								8
Hate		■							2
Delusion	■	■	■						12
Non-greed					■	■	■	■	59
Non-hate					■	■	■	■	59
Non-delusion					■		■	■	47
	2	2	1	0	3	2	3	3	

It should be understood that eighteen (types of consciousness) are without roots, two with one root, twenty-two with two roots, and forty-seven with three roots.

Compendium of Functions
(*kiccasangaha*)

§8 Analysis of Functions

Kiccasangahe kiccāni nāma paṭisandhi-bhavanga-āvajjana-dassana-savana-ghāyana-sāyana-phusana-sampaṭicchana-santīraṇa-votthapana-javana-tadārammaṇa-cutivasena cuddasavidhāni bhavanti.

Paṭisandhi-bhavanga-āvajjana-pañcaviññāṇa-ṭṭhānādivasena pana tesaṁ dasadhā ṭhānabhedo veditabbo.

In the compendium of functions there are fourteen functions, namely: (1) rebirth-linking, (2) life-continuum, (3) adverting, (4) seeing, (5) hearing, (6) smelling, (7) tasting, (8) touching, (9) receiving, (10) investigating, (11) determining, (12) javana, (13) registration, and (14) death.

Their further classification should be understood by way of stage as tenfold, namely: (1) rebirth-linking, (2) life-continuum, (3) adverting, (4) fivefold sense consciousness, and so forth.

Guide to §8

Analysis of functions: In this section the eighty-nine types of consciousness are classified by way of function. The Abhidhamma posits altogether fourteen functions performed by different kinds of consciousness. These are exercised either at distinct phases within the cognitive process (3-13) or on occasions when consciousness is occurring outside the cognitive process, that is, in process-freed (*vīthimutta*) consciousness (1, 2, 14).

(1) **Rebirth-linking (*paṭisandhi*)**: This function exercised at conception is called rebirth-linking because it links the new existence to the previous one. The consciousness that performs this function, the *paṭisandhicitta* or rebirth-linking consciousness, occurs only once in any individual existence, at the moment of rebirth.

(2) **Life-continuum (*bhavanga*)**: The word *bhavanga* means factor (*anga*) of existence (*bhava*), that is, the indispensable condition of existence. *Bhavanga* is the function of consciousness by which the conti-

nuity of the individual is preserved through the duration of any single existence, from conception to death. After the *paṭisandhicitta* has arisen and fallen away, it is then followed by the *bhavangacitta*, which is a resultant consciousness of the same type as the *paṭisandhicitta* but which performs a different function, namely, the function of preserving the continuity of the individual existence. *Bhavangacittas* arise and pass away every moment during life whenever there is no active cognitive process taking place. This type of consciousness is most evident during deep dreamless sleep, but it also occurs momentarily during waking life countless times between occasions of active cognition.

When an object impinges on a sense door, the bhavanga is arrested and an active cognitive process ensues for the purpose of cognizing the object. Immediately after the cognitive process is completed, again the bhavanga supervenes and continues until the next cognitive process arises. Arising and perishing at every moment during this passive phase of consciousness, the bhavanga flows on like a stream, without remaining static for two consecutive moments.

(3) **Adverting (*āvajjana*):** When an object impinges at one of the sense doors or at the mind door, there occurs a mind-moment called *bhavanga-calana,* vibration of the life-continuum, by which the bhavanga consciousness "vibrates" for a single moment. This is followed by another moment called *bhavanga-upaccheda,* arrest of the life-continuum, by which the flow of the bhavanga is cut off. Immediately after this, a citta arises turning to the object, either at one of the five physical sense doors or at the mind door. This function of turning to the object is termed adverting.

(4-8) **Seeing, etc.**: In a cognitive process at the sense doors, after the moment of adverting, there arises a citta which directly cognizes the impingent object. This citta, and the specific function it performs, is determined by the nature of the object. If the object is a visible form, eye-consciousness arises seeing it; if it is a sound, ear-consciousness arises hearing it, and so forth. In this context, the functions of seeing and hearing, etc., do not refer to the cognitive acts which explicitly identify the objects of sight and hearing, etc., as such. They signify, rather, the rudimentary momentary occasions of consciousness by which the sense datum is experienced in its bare immediacy and simplicity prior to all identificatory cognitive operations.

(9-11) **Receiving, etc.**: In the case of a cognitive process through any of the five sense doors, following the citta that performs the function of seeing, etc., there arise in succession cittas that perform the functions of receiving (*sampaṭicchana*), investigating (*santīraṇa*), and determining (*votthapana*) the object. In the case of a cognitive process occurring in the mind door independently of the physical senses, these three functions do not occur; rather, mind-door adverting follows immediately upon the cutting off of the bhavanga without any intermediate functions.

(12) **Javana**: *Javana* is a technical term of Abhidhamma usage that is best left untranslated. The literal meaning of the word is running swiftly. As a function of consciousness it applies to the stage of the cognitive process that immediately follows the determining stage,[8] and consists of a series of cittas (normally seven, all identical in kind) which "run swiftly" over the object in the act of apprehending it. The javana stage is the most important from an ethical standpoint, for it is at this point that wholesome or unwholesome cittas originate.[9]

(13) **Registration (*tadārammaṇa*):** The word *tadārammaṇa* means literally "having that object," and denotes the function of taking as object the object that had been apprehended by the javanas. This function is exercised for two mind-moments immediately after the javana phase in a sense-sphere cognitive process when the object is either very prominent to the senses or clear to the mind. When the object lacks special prominence or clarity, as well as in other types of cognitive process apart from the sense-sphere process, this function is not exercised at all. Following registration (or the javana phase when registration does not occur) the stream of consciousness again lapses back into the bhavanga.

(14) **Death (*cuti*):** The death consciousness is the last citta to occur in an individual existence; it is the citta which marks the exit from a particular life. This citta is of the same type as the rebirth-linking consciousness and the bhavanga, and like them it pertains to the process-freed side of existence, the passive flow of consciousness outside an active cognitive process. It differs from them in that it performs a different function, namely, the function of passing away.

By way of stage as tenfold: The word "stage" (*ṭhāna*) means a moment or occasion between two other cittas at which a given citta is able to arise. Although there are fourteen functions of consciousness, the five sensory functions of seeing, etc., all occupy the same stage of the cognitive process, between the two stages of adverting and receiving. Thus the fourteen functions can be condensed into ten stages of consciousness.

§9 Classification by way of Consciousness

Tattha dve upekkhāsahagatasantīraṇāni c'eva aṭṭha mahāvipākāni ca nava rūpārūpavipākāni cā ti ekūnavīsati cittāni paṭisandhi-bhavanga-cutikiccāni nāma.

Āvajjanakiccāni pana dve. Tathā dassana-savana-ghāyana-sāyana-phusana-sampaṭicchanakiccāni ca.

Tīṇi santīraṇakiccāni.

Manodvārāvajjanam eva pañcadvāre votthapanakiccaṁ sādheti.

Āvajjanadvayavajjitāni kusalākusala-phala-kriyā cittāni pañcapaññāsa javanakiccāni.

Aṭṭha mahāvipākāni c'eva santīraṇattayañ cā ti ekādasa tadārammaṇakiccāni.

Of them, nineteen types of consciousness perform the functions of rebirth-linking, life-continuum, and death. They are: two types of investigating consciousness accompanied by equanimity; eight great resultants; and nine fine-material-sphere and immaterial-sphere resultants (2 + 8 + 9 = 19).

Two perform the function of adverting.

Similarly, two perform each of the functions of seeing, hearing, smelling, tasting, touching, and receiving.

Three perform the function of investigating.

The mind-door adverting consciousness performs the function of determining in the five sense doors.

With the exception of the two types of adverting consciousness, the fifty-five types of unwholesome, wholesome, fruition and functional consciousness perform the function of javana.

The eight great resultants and the three types of investigating consciousness, totalling eleven, perform the function of registration.

Guide to §9

Classification by way of consciousness: The present section will be less likely to cause perplexity if it is recognized that there is a distinction between a type of consciousness and the function after which it is commonly named. Although certain types of consciousness are named after a single function that they perform, this name is chosen as a convenient designation and does not mean that the type of consciousness so named is confined to that particular function. To the contrary, a given type of consciousness may perform several functions completely different from the one with reference to which it is named.

The functions of rebirth-linking, life-continuum, and death: As pointed out above, in any single life it is the same type of consciousness that performs the three functions of rebirth-linking, life-continuum, and death. At the moment of conception this type of consciousness arises linking the new existence to the old one; throughout the course of life this same type of consciousness arises countless times as the passive flow of the bhavanga, maintaining the continuity of existence; and at death this same type of consciousness again occurs as the passing away from the old existence.

There are nineteen cittas which perform these three functions. The unwholesome-resultant investigating consciousness (*santīraṇa*) does so in the case of those beings who take rebirth into the woeful planes—the hells, the animal realm, the sphere of petas, and the host of asuras. The wholesome-resultant investigating consciousness accompanied by equanimity performs these functions in the case of a human rebirth as one who is congenitally blind, deaf, dumb, etc., as well as among certain lower classes of gods and spirits. While the deformity itself is due to unwholesome kamma, the human rebirth is the result of wholesome kamma, though of a relatively weak degree. It should not be thought that investigation occurs at the moment of rebirth or during the life-continuum, for a consciousness can perform only one function at a time.

The eight great resultants—the beautiful sense-sphere resultants with two and three roots—perform these three functions for those reborn in the fortunate sensuous realms as gods and humans free from congenital defects.

The above ten cittas pertain to rebirth in the sensuous plane.

The five fine-material-sphere resultants serve as rebirth consciousness, life-continuum, and death consciousness for those reborn into the fine-material plane of existence, and the four immaterial-sphere resultants for those reborn into the respective immaterial planes of existence.

The function of adverting: The five-sense-door adverting consciousness (*pañcadvārāvajjana*) performs this function when a sense object impinges on one of the five physical sense doors. The mind-door adverting consciousness (*manodvārāvajjana*) does so when an object arises at the mind door. Both these cittas are rootless functionals (*ahetukakiriya*).

The function of seeing, etc.: The two cittas that perform each of these five functions are the wholesome-resultant and unwholesome-resultant eye-consciousness, etc.

Receiving: The function of receiving is performed by the two types of receiving consciousness (*sampaṭicchanacitta).*

The function of investigating: The three cittas that perform this function are the two rootless resultants accompanied by equanimity—one wholesome-resultant, the other unwholesome-resultant—and the rootless wholesome-resultant accompanied by joy.

The function of determining: There is no distinct citta known as determining consciousness. It is the same type of citta—a rootless functional consciousness accompanied by equanimity (see I, §10)—that

TABLE 3.3: COMPENDIUM OF FUNCTIONS

FUNCTIONS / CITTAS	Unwholesome	Eye-consness.	Ear-consness.	Nose-consness.	Tongue-consness.	Body-consness.	Receiving	Invs. - eqn.	Invs. - joy	Five-door-advt.	Mind-door-advt.	Smiling	SS Wholesome	SS Resultant	SS Functional	Sbl. Wholesome	Sbl. Resultant	Sbl. Functional	Supramundane	Total
1-3 Rebirth, bhavanga, death								■						■			■			19
4 Adverting										■	■									2
5 Seeing		■																		2
6 Hearing			■																	2
7 Smelling				■																2
8 Tasting					■															2
9 Touching						■														2
10 Receiving							■													2
11 Investigating								■	■											3
12 Determining											■									1
13 Javana	■											■	■		■	■		■	■	55
14 Registration								■	■					■						11
No. of functions	1	1	1	1	1	1	1	5	2	1	2	1	1	4	1	1	3	1	1	
Total of cittas	12	2	2	2	2	2	2	2	1	1	1	1	8	8	8	9	9	9	8	

performs the function of mind-door adverting in the mind-door process and the function of determining in a process in the five physical sense doors.

The function of javana: The fifty-five cittas that function as javanas are the twelve unwholesome cittas, twenty-one wholesome cittas, four resultants (i.e. the supramundane fruits), and eighteen functionals (the two adverting cittas being excepted).

The function of registration: These eleven are resultant cittas. When the three investigating consciousnesses perform the function of registration, they do not simultaneously perform the function of investigating.

§10 Classification by Numbers of Functions

Tesu pana dve upekkhāsahagatasantīraṇacittāni paṭisandhi-bhavanga-cuti-tadārammaṇa-santīraṇavasena pañcakiccāni nāma.

Mahāvipākāni aṭṭha paṭisandhi-bhavanga-cuti-tadārammaṇa-vasena catukiccāni.

Mahaggatavipākāni nava paṭisandhi-bhavanga-cutivasena tikiccāni.

Somanassasahagataṁ santīraṇaṁ santīraṇa-tadārammaṇavasena dukiccaṁ.

Tathā votthapanañ ca votthapanāvajjanavasena.

Sesāni pana sabbāni pi javana-manodhātuttika-dvipañcaviññāṇāni yathāsambhavam ekakiccānī ti.

Of them, the two types of investigating consciousness accompanied by equanimity perform five functions—rebirth-linking, life-continuum, death, registration, and investigating.

The eight great resultants perform four functions—rebirth-linking, life-continuum, death, and registration.

The nine sublime resultants perform three functions—rebirth-relinking, life-continuum, and death.

The investigating consciousness accompanied by joy performs two functions—investigating and registration.

Similarly, the determining consciousness performs two functions—determining and adverting.

All the remaining types of consciousness—javana, the triple mind element, and the fivefold sense consciousness—perform only one function as they arise.

Guide to §10

Javana: The fifty-five cittas that perform the function of javana occur solely in the role of javana and do not perform any other functions.

The triple mind element: the five-door adverting consciousness and the two types of receiving consciousness.

§11 Summary

Paṭisandhādayo nāma kiccabhedena cuddasa
Dasadhā ṭhānabhedena cittuppādā pakāsitā.
Aṭṭhasaṭṭhi tathā dve ca nav' aṭṭha dve yathākkamaṁ
Eka-dvi-ti-catu-pañca kiccaṭṭhānāni niddise.

The types of consciousness are declared to be fourteen according to functions such as rebirth-linking and so forth, and ten according to analysis by stages.

It is stated that those which perform one function are sixty-eight; two functions, two; three functions, nine; four functions, eight; and five functions, two respectively.

Compendium of Doors
(*dvārasangaha*)

§12 Analysis of Doors

Dvārasangahe dvārāni nāma cakkhudvāraṁ sotadvāraṁ ghānadvāraṁ jivhādvāraṁ kāyadvāraṁ manodvārañ cā ti chabbidhāni bhavanti.

Tattha cakkhum eva cakkhudvāraṁ tathā sotādayo sotadvārādīni. Manodvāraṁ pana bhavangan ti pavuccati.

In the compendium of doors, there are six doors, namely: eye door, ear door, nose door, tongue door, body door, and mind door.

Therein, the eye itself is the eye door; and so for the ear door and the others. But the life-continuum is called the mind door.

Guide to §12

Analysis of doors: The term "door" (*dvāra*) is used metaphorically in the Abhidhamma to denote the media through which the mind interacts with the objective world. Three doors of action are specified—body, speech, and mind—the channels through which the mind acts upon the world (see V, §§22-24). Again, six doors of cognition are recognized: the six sense doors by which the citta and cetasikas go out to meet the object and by which objects enter into range of the citta and cetasikas. In the present section the author will first enumerate the six sense doors. Then he will identify the cittas that arise through each door and classify the cittas according to the number of doors through which they arise.

The eye itself is the eye door: Five of the doors are material phenomena (*rūpa*), namely, the sensitive matter (*pasādarūpa*) in each of the five sense organs. Each of these serves as a door by which the citta and cetasikas occurring in a cognitive process gain access to their object, and by which the object becomes accessible to the cittas and cetasikas. Eye-sensitivity is the door for the cittas belonging to an eye-door process, enabling them to cognize visible forms through the eye. The same holds for the other sensitivities of the sense organs in relation to their respective processes and objects.

The life-continuum is called the mind door: Unlike the first five doors, the mind door (*manodvāra*) is not material but mental (*nāma*), namely, the bhavanga consciousness. When an object is to be cognized by a mind-door process, the cittas belonging to that process gain access to the object solely through the mind door, without immediate dependence on any material sense faculty.

Different commentaries express contrary opinions about the precise denotation of the mind door. The *Vibhāvinī-Ṭīkā* states that the bhavanga citta immediately preceding the mind-door adverting consciousness, i.e. the arrest bhavanga (*bhavanga-upaccheda*), is the mind door. Other Abhidhamma commentaries identify the mind door as the bhavanga citta together with the mind-door adverting. However, Ledi Sayadaw and the commentary to the *Vibhanga* both state that the entire bhavanga without distinction is the mind door. Ācariya Anuruddha did not make any specifications but simply stated that the bhavanga is called the mind door.

§13 Classification by way of Consciousness

Tattha pañcadvārāvajjana-cakkhuviññāṇa-sampaṭicchana-santīraṇa-votthapana-kāmāvacarajavana-tadārammaṇavasena chacattāḷīsa cittāni cakkhudvāre yathārahaṁ uppajjanti. Tathā pañcadvārāvajjana-sotaviññāṇādivasena sotadvārādīsu pi chacattāḷīs' eva bhavantī ti. Sabbathā pi pañcadvāre catupaññāsa cittāni kāmāvacarān' evā ti veditabbāni.

Manodvāre pana manodvārāvajjana-pañcapaññāsajavana-tadārammaṇavasena sattasaṭṭhi cittāni bhavanti.

Ekūnavīsati paṭisandhi-bhavanga-cutivasena dvāravimuttāni.

Therein, forty-six types of consciousness arise in the eye door according to circumstances: five-door adverting, eye-consciousness, receiving, investigating, determining, sense-sphere javanas, and registration.

Likewise in the ear door, etc., forty-six types of consciousness arise, five-door adverting, ear-consciousness, and so forth.

It should be understood that altogether the fifty-four types of sense-sphere consciousness occur in the five doors.

In the mind door sixty-seven types of consciousness arise: mind-door adverting, fifty-five javanas, and registration.

Nineteen types of consciousness are door-freed, occurring by way of rebirth-linking, life-continuum, and death.

Guide to §13

Forty-six types of consciousness arise in the eye door: The forty-six cittas are as follows:

1	five-door adverting consciousness
2	eye-consciousnesses
3	investigating consciousnesses
1	determining consciousness
29	sense-sphere javanas (12 unwholesome, 8 wholesome, 8 beautiful functional, 1 smile-producing functional)
8	registration (= sense-sphere beautiful resultants; the other three being included under investigating consciousness—see §9).

The same types of cittas arise in the other four physical sense doors with their respective objects, except that in each case the pair of sense consciousnesses are to be replaced in correlation with the sense door.

According to circumstances (*yathārahaṁ*): Although a total of forty-six cittas arise in the eye door, they cannot all arise together in one process, but only as determined by conditions. Ledi Sayadaw specifies these conditions as: (i) the object, (ii) the plane of existence, (iii) the individual, and (iv) attention.

(i) For example, if the object is undesirable, then the eye-consciousness, receiving, investigating, and registration are unwholesome-resultants, while if the object is desirable, then they are wholesome-resultants. If the object is exceptionally desirable, the investigating and registration consciousnesses are accompanied by joy, while if the object is only moderately desirable, they are accompanied by equanimity.

(ii) If an eye-door process occurs in the sensuous plane (*kāmabhūmi*), all forty-six cittas can arise, but if the process occurs in the fine-material plane (*rūpabhūmi*), registration consciousness cannot arise, the function of registration being confined to the sensuous plane.

(iii) If the individual is a worldling or a trainee, the javana cittas will be wholesome or unwholesome (according to the level of attainment in the case of trainees),[10] while if the individual is an Arahant the javanas will be functional.

(iv) If a worldling or a trainee applies wise attention (*yoniso manasikāra*), wholesome javanas will arise, while if unwise attention is applied, unwholesome javanas will arise.

Similarly, whether prompted or unprompted cittas arise is also governed by circumstances.

The fifty-four types of sense-sphere consciousness occur in the five doors: In any single door, all types of sense-sphere consciousness occur except for the four pairs of sense consciousness pertaining to the other four sense faculties. Thus when these are totalled, all types of sense-sphere consciousness occur in the five doors.

In the mind door: All fifty-five types of javana occur in the mind door. Only twenty-two cittas do not occur in the mind door: the five-door adverting, the two sets of fivefold sense consciousness, the two types of receiving consciousness, the five fine-material resultants, and the four immaterial resultants.

Door-freed (*dvāravimutta*): These nineteen cittas, enumerated in §9, are known as "door-freed" because their particular functions of rebirth, bhavanga, and death do not occur in the sense doors and because they do not receive any new object but apprehend only the object determined by the last cognitive process of the preceding existence (see below, §17).

§14 Classification by Number of Doors

Tesu pana dvipañcaviññāṇāni c' eva mahaggata-lokuttarajavanāni cā ti chattiṁsa yathārahaṁ ekadvārikacittāni nāma.

Manodhātuttikaṁ pana pañcadvārikaṁ.

Sukhasantīraṇa-votthapana-kāmāvacarajavanāni chadvārikacittāni.

Upekkhāsahagatasantīraṇa-mahāvipākāni chadvārikāni c' eva dvāravimuttāni ca.

Mahaggatavipākāni dvāravimuttān' evā ti.

Of those (that arise through doors), thirty-six types of consciousness—the two sets of fivefold sense consciousness and the sublime and supramundane javanas—are with one door accordingly.

The three mind elements arise through five doors.

TABLE 3.4: COMPENDIUM OF DOORS

	Five-door advt.	Eye-consness.	Ear-consness.	Nose-consness.	Tongue-consness.	Body-consness.	Receiving	Invs. - eqn.	Invs. - joy	Determining (=mind-door-advt.)	SS Javana	Sbl. & Spm. Javana	SS Result	Sbl. Result	Total
Eye door	■	■					■	■	■	■	■		■		46
Ear door	■		■				■	■	■	■	■		■		46
Nose door	■			■			■	■	■	■	■		■		46
Tongue door	■				■		■	■	■	■	■		■		46
Body door	■					■	■	■	■	■	■		■		46
Mind door								■	■	■	■	■	■		67
Door-freed								■					■	■	19
No. of doors	5	1	1	1	1	1	5	6	6	6	6	1	6	0	
Total of cittas	1	2	2	2	2	2	2	2	1	1	29	26	8	9	

Joyful investigation, determining, and the sense-sphere javanas arise through six doors.

Investigating consciousness accompanied by equanimity and the great resultants arise either through the six doors or as door-freed.

The sublime resultants always arise as door-freed.

Guide to §14

Accordingly: The two sets of fivefold sense consciousness arise only in their respective sense doors, the sublime and supramundane javanas arise only in the mind door.

Joyful investigating: This citta arises with the functions of investigating and registration in the five sense doors and with the function of registration alone in the mind door.

Determining: This citta performs the function of determining in the five sense doors and the function of adverting in the mind door.

The great resultants: These eight cittas, like the two types of investigating consciousness accompanied by equanimity, arise through the six doors in the role of registration, and as door-freed in the roles of rebirth, bhavanga, and death consciousness.

The sublime resultants: These nine cittas—the five fine-material-sphere resultants and the four immaterial-sphere resultants—arise exclusively in their respective planes as rebirth, bhavanga, and death consciousness. Hence they are always free of doors.

§15 Summary

Ekadvārikacittāni pañcadvārikāni ca
Chadvārikavimuttāni vimuttāni ca sabbathā.
Chattiṁsati tathā tīṇi ekatiṁsa yathākkamaṁ
Dasadhā navadhā cā ti pañcadhā paridīpaye.

Thirty-six types of consciousness arise through one door, three through five doors, thirty-one through six doors, ten through six doors or as door-freed, nine wholly free from a door. Thus in five ways they are shown.

Compendium of Objects (*ālambanasangaha*)

§16 Analysis of Objects

Ālambanasangahe ālambanāni nāma rūpārammaṇaṁ saddārammaṇaṁ gandhārammaṇaṁ rasārammaṇaṁ phoṭṭhabbārammaṇaṁ dhammārammaṇañ cā ti chabbidhāni bhavanti.

Tattha rūpam eva rūpārammaṇaṁ. Tathā saddādayo saddārammaṇādīni. Dhammārammaṇaṁ pana pasāda-sukhumarūpa-citta-cetasika-nibbāna-paññattivasena chadhā sangayhanti.

In the compendium of objects, there are six kinds of objects, namely, visible form object, sound object, smell object, taste object, tangible object, and mental object.

Therein, visible form itself is visible form object. Likewise, sound, etc., are sound object, etc. But mental object is sixfold: sensitive matter, subtle matter, consciousness, mental factors, Nibbāna, and concepts.

Guide to §16

Analysis of objects: Every consciousness, along with its associated mental factors, necessarily takes an object, for consciousness itself essentially consists in the activity of cognizing an object. In Pali two principal words are used to denote an object. One is *ārammaṇa*, derived from a root meaning "to delight in." The other is *ālambana*, derived from an altogether different root meaning "to hang on to." Thus the object is that which consciousness and its concomitants delight in or that which they hang on to. In this section the author will first specify the kinds of objects. Then he will determine which kinds of objects occur through each of the six doors as well as to door-freed consciousness. Finally he will determine the range of objects taken by each type of consciousness.

Six kinds of objects: In the Abhidhamma six kinds of objects are recognized, corresponding to the six senses. The first five are all included in the category of materiality.[11] Four of these—visible form, sound, smell, and taste—are considered to be kinds of derived matter (*upādā rūpa*), that is, secondary material phenomena dependent on the primary elements of matter. The tangible object is identified with three of the four primary elements themselves: the earth element, or solidity, which is experienced by touch as hardness or softness; the fire element, which is experienced as heat or cold; and the air element, which is experienced as distension or pressure. The fourth primary element, the water element, has the characteristic of cohesion, and this, according to the Abhidhamma, cannot be experienced as a datum of touch but can only be cognized through the mind door.[12]

Mental object is sixfold: Each of the first five objects can be cognized in any of these ways: (1) through its own respective sense-door process; (2) through a mind-door process; and (3) by the process-freed cittas occurring in the roles of rebirth-linking, bhavanga, and death. Mental objects—the objects of the sixth class—cannot be cognized at all through a sense-door process. They can be cognized only by the cittas of a mind-door process or by the process-freed cittas that occur independent of the sense doors.

Six kinds of objects fall into the category of mental object (*dhammārammaṇa*). *Sensitive matter* (*pasādarūpa*) is the sensory receptive substance in the five sense organs; it is fivefold, eye-sensitivity, ear-sensitivity, etc. *Subtle matter* (*sukhumarūpa*) includes sixteen species of material phenomena enumerated below (VI, §6), among them the water element. *Citta* is also a type of mental object. Though citta experiences objects, citta in turn can become an object. It should be noted that a citta in its immediacy cannot become its own object, for the cognizer cannot cognize itself; but a citta in an individual mental continuum can experience earlier cittas in that same continuum as well as the cittas of other beings. The fifty-two *cetasikas* can also become objects of a mind-door process, as for example, when one becomes aware of one's feelings, volitions, and emotions. *Nibbāna* becomes the object of cittas occurring in the mental processes of noble individuals, both trainees and Arahants. *Concepts*—the class of conventional realities, things which do not exist in the ultimate sense—also fall into the category of mental object.

§17 Classification by way of Doors

Tattha cakkhudvārikacittānaṁ sabbesam pi rūpam eva ārammaṇaṁ. Tañ ca paccuppannam eva. Tathā sotadvārikacittādīnam pi saddādīni. Tāni ca paccuppannāni yeva.

Manodvārikacittānaṁ pana chabbidham pi paccuppannam atītaṁ anāgataṁ kālavimuttañ ca yathāraham ālambanaṁ hoti.

Dvāravimuttānañ ca pana paṭisandhi-bhavanga-cuti-sankhātānaṁ chabbidham pi yathāsambhavaṁ yebhuyyena bhavantare chadvāragahitaṁ paccuppannam atītaṁ paññattibhūtaṁ vā kammakammanimitta-gatinimittasammataṁ ālambanaṁ hoti.

For all types of eye-door consciousnesses, visible form alone is the object, and that pertains only to the present. Likewise, sounds, etc., are the object of ear-door consciousnesses, etc., and those too pertain only to the present.

But the object of mind-door consciousnesses is of six kinds, and that object may be present, past, future, or independent of time, according to circumstances.

Further, in the case of the door-freed-consciousnesses—that is, rebirth-linking, life-continuum, and death (consciousness)—the object is sixfold, and according to the situation (that object) has usually been apprehended in (one of) the six doors in the immediately preceding existence, as either a present or past object or as a concept. It is known as kamma, or as sign of kamma, or as sign of destiny.

Guide to §17

For all types of eye-door consciousnesses: In an eye-door cognitive process, all the cittas pertaining to that process take the visible form as their object. The visible form is not the object solely of eye-consciousness. The five-door adverting consciousness, the receiving, investigating and determining consciousnesses, the javanas, and the registration cittas also occur with the same visible form as their object. Further, these cittas occurring in an eye-door process take "visible form alone" (*rūpam eva*) as object. Within that process they cannot cognize any other kind of object.

And that pertains only to the present: The word "present" is used here in the sense of "momentary present" (*khaṇikapaccuppanna*), that is, in reference to what has actual being at the present moment of experience. Since material phenomena have a slower rate of change than mental phenomena, a single visible form can remain present to all the cittas in a process occurring in the eye door. So too for the objects of the other physical senses. (See below, pp. 156-57)

The object of mind-door consciousness: The cittas that arise in a mind-door process can cognize any of the five physical sense objects as well as all types of mental objects inaccessible to the cittas in a sense-door process. Mind-door cittas can also cognize an object belonging to any of the three periods of time—past, present, or future—or one that is independent of time (*kālavimutta*). This last expression applies to Nibbāna and concepts. Nibbāna is timeless because its intrinsic nature (*sabhāva*) is without arising, change and passing away; concepts are timeless because they are devoid of intrinsic nature.

According to circumstances: The *Vibhāvinī-Ṭīkā* explains: according to whether the cittas are sense-sphere javanas, direct-knowledge javanas, the remaining sublime javanas, etc. For the sense-sphere javanas, except the smile-producing consciousness, take objects of the three times and timeless objects. The smile-producing consciousness takes only objects of the three times. The direct-knowledge cittas (or *abhiññās*—see Guide to §18) take objects of the three times as well as the timeless. The sublime javanas take timeless objects (i.e. concepts), except for the second and fourth immaterial jhānas, which take past cittas as objects. The supramundane javanas take a timeless object, Nibbāna.

In the case of the door-freed consciousness, etc.: The door-freed consciousness is the citta that performs, in any single life, the three functions of rebirth-linking, bhavanga, and death. It is of nineteen types, as explained earlier (§9). The object of this citta can be of six kinds: it can be any of the five sense objects, either past or present, or it can be a mental object. In all three of its functions, this citta retains the same object from the rebirth moment to the moment of decease. That same object is grasped at the moment of rebirth by the relinking consciousness; during the course of life it is held to by every bhavanga citta; and at the moment of death it is held to by the death consciousness.

The object of the door-freed consciousness in any given existence is generally identical with the object of the last cognitive process in the immediately preceding existence. When a person is on the verge of death, in the last phase of active consciousness some object will present itself to the cognitive process, determined by previous kamma and present circumstances. This object can be one of three kinds:

(1) It can be a *kamma*, a good or evil deed performed earlier during the same lifetime.

(2) It can be a sign of kamma (*kammanimitta*), that is, an object or image associated with the good or evil deed that is about to determine rebirth or an instrument used to perform it. For example, a devout person may see the image of a monk or temple, a physician may see the image of patients, a butcher may hear the groans of slaughtered cattle or see an image of a butcher knife.

(3) It can be a sign of destiny (*gatinimitta*), that is, a symbol of the realm into which the dying person is about to be reborn. For example, a person heading for a heavenly rebirth may see celestial mansions, a person heading for an animal rebirth may see forests or fields, a person heading for a rebirth in hell may see infernal fires.

According to the situation (*yathāsambhavaṁ*): The *Vibhāvinī-Ṭīkā* explains this phrase to mean that the object cognized by the door-freed citta varies according to the door at which it was originally apprehended by the last mental process of the preceding life; according to whether it is a present or past object or a concept; and according to whether it is a kamma, a sign of kamma, or a sign of destiny. The explanation is as follows:

In the case of a sense-sphere rebirth, any one of the five sense objects apprehended in any of the six doors in the last javana process of the preceding existence may become an object as sign of kamma. Such an object, on the occasions of rebirth-linking and the first series of bhavangas, can be either past or present. It can be present because the sense object apprehended by the last javana process of the previous existence may still persist as far as the first few mind-moments of the new existence. Thereafter for the bhavanga, and for the death consciousness of the new existence, that object is necessarily past.

A mental object apprehended in the mind door in the last javana process of the previous existence may become an object of the rebirth-linking, bhavanga, and death consciousnesses of the new existence as a kamma or as a sign of kamma that is past. If the object should be a sign of destiny, it is usually a visible form apprehended in the mind door and is present.

In the case of a fine-material-sphere rebirth, the object of the three process-freed cittas is a mental object apprehended in the mind-door process of the preceding existence; it is a concept (hence timeless) and is considered a sign of kamma. So too in the case of rebirth into the first and third immaterial planes. In the case of rebirth into the second and fourth immaterial planes, the object, being a citta, is a mental object; it is past and is also considered a sign of kamma.

Usually (*yebhuyyena*): This qualification is added with reference to those reborn after passing away from the realm of non-percipient beings (*asaññasattā*), a realm in the fine-material plane where consciousness is altogether absent (see V, §31). For such beings the object of the door-freed cittas cannot be something apprehended in the immediately preceding existence, since in that existence there was no consciousness. For these beings the object presents itself to the rebirth, bhavanga, and death consciousness as a sign of kamma, etc., entirely through the power of a past kamma from an existence prior to that in the non-percipient realm.

§18 Classification by Type of Consciousness

Tesu cakkhuviññāṇādīni yathākkamaṁ rūpādi-ekekālambanān' eva. Manodhātuttikaṁ pana rūpādipañcālambanaṁ. Sesāni kāmāvacaravipākāni hasanacittañ cā ti sabbathā pi kāmāvacarālambanān' eva.

Akusalāni c'eva ñāṇavippayuttakāmāvacarajavanāni cā ti lokuttaravajjita-sabbālambanāni.

Ñāṇasampayuttakāmāvacarakusalāni c'eva pañcamajjhāna-sankhātaṁ abhiññākusalañ cā ti arahattamaggaphalavajjita-sabbālambanāni.

Ñāṇasampayuttakāmāvacarakriyā c'eva kriyābhiññā-votthapanañ cā ti sabbathā pi sabbālambanāni.

Āruppesu dutiyacatutthāni mahaggatālambanāni. Sesāni mahaggatacittāni pana sabbāni pi paññattālambanāni. Lokuttaracittāni nibbānālambanānī ti.

Of these, eye-consciousness, etc., each take a single object, respectively, visible form, etc. But the triple mind element takes (all) five kinds of (sense) object, visible form, etc. The remaining sense-sphere resultants and the smiling consciousness always have only sense-sphere objects.

The unwholesome (consciousnesses) and the sense-sphere javanas that are dissociated from knowledge take all objects except supramundane states.

The sense-sphere wholesome (consciousnesses) associated with knowledge, and the wholesome direct-knowledge consciousness consisting in the fifth jhāna, take all objects except the path and fruit of Arahantship.

The sense-sphere functionals associated with knowledge, the functional direct-knowledge consciousness, and the determining consciousness can all take all kinds of objects.

Among the immaterial (consciousnesses), the second and fourth take sublime objects. All the remaining sublime consciousnesses take concepts as objects. The supramundane consciousnesses take Nibbāna as object.

Guide to §18

The triple mind element: The five-door adverting consciousness and the two kinds of receiving consciousness—collectively known as the triple mind element—take all five kinds of sense objects, visible form, etc., since they arise in all five doors.

The remaining sense-sphere resultants: These resultants—the three investigating cittas and the eight great resultants—take all kinds of sense-sphere objects presented at the six doors when they occur by way of registration. Again, these same resultants—excluding the investigating consciousness accompanied by joy—take the six objects freed from doors when they occur as rebirth, bhavanga, and death consciousness. The smile-producing consciousness of Arahants also takes all six kinds of sense-sphere objects.

The unwholesome, etc.: The nine supramundane states—the four paths, their fruits, and Nibbāna—because of their extreme purity and profundity, cannot be apprehended by any unwholesome cittas nor by wholesome and functional cittas devoid of knowledge.

The sense-sphere wholesome, etc.: Worldlings and trainees cannot know the path and fruition consciousness of an Arahant. Since they have not attained these states themselves, these two cittas remain inaccessible to the wholesome sense-sphere cittas associated with knowledge that arise in their mental process.

The path and fruition cittas of trainees are inaccessible to the cittas of worldlings. The path and fruition cittas of trainees at a higher stage are inaccessible to the cittas of trainees at a lower stage. The wholesome sense-sphere cittas associated with knowledge can know the path and

TABLE 3.5: COMPENDIUM OF OBJECTS

Citta		Object
Eye-consciousness Ear- " Nose- " Tongue- " Body- "	2 2 2 2 2	Present visible form Present sound Present smell Present taste Present tangible
Mind element	3	Present five objects
Invs. 3, smiling 1, SS btf. rst. 8	12	SS citta 54, cetas. 52, mat. 28
Unwh. 12, SS btf. dissoc. knwl. wh. 4, fnc. 4	20	Mundane citta 81, cetas. 52, mat. 28, concepts
SS. btf. assoc. knwl. wh. 4, wh. abhiññā 1	5	87 citta (all exc. arh. path & frt.), cetas. 52, mat. 28, Nibbāna, concepts
SS btf. assoc. knwl. fnc. 4, fnc. abhiññā 1, m-d-advt.	6	All objects (= citta 89, cetas. 52, mat. 28, Nibbāna, concepts)
IS 2nd & 4th	6	Sublime : 1st & 3rd IS cittas resp.
FMS 15, IS 1st & 3rd	21	Concepts
Supramundane	8	Nibbāna

fruition cittas as well as Nibbāna when trainees review their own supramundane attainments. These same cittas take Nibbāna as object on the occasion called change-of-lineage (*gotrabhū*) immediately preceding the arising of the supramundane path (see IX, §34).

The wholesome direct-knowledge consciousness: The direct knowledges (*abhiññā*) are types of higher knowledge accessible to those who have mastery over the five jhānas. Five kinds of mundane direct knowledge are mentioned in the texts: supernormal powers, the divine ear, knowledge of others' minds, the recollection of past lives, and the divine eye (see below, IX, §21). These knowledges are acquired through a special application of the fifth-jhāna citta, wholesome in the case of worldlings and trainees, functional in the case of Arahants. By the third direct knowledge trainees with mastery of the fifth jhāna can cognize the path and fruition cittas of trainees on a level equal to or lower than their own, but they cannot know the path and fruition cittas of those on a higher level. The path and fruition consciousness of Arahantship is utterly beyond range of the wholesome direct-knowledge citta.

The sense-sphere functional, etc: By means of the sense-sphere functional cittas associated with knowledge, an Arahant can know his own path and fruition cittas when reviewing his attainment, and by the functional direct-knowledge citta he can know the path and fruition cittas of other noble disciples, both trainees and Arahants. The determining con-

TABLE 3.6: CONCEPTUAL OBJECTS OF SUBLIME CITTAS

CITTAS		OBJECTS → Kasinas 10	Foulness 10	Body 1	Breath 1	Beings (love) 1	Beings (comp.) 1	Beings (joy) 1	Beings (eqn.) 1	Infinite space 1	Nothingness 1	Total
FMS 1st Jhāna	3	■	■	■	■	■	■	■				25
" 2nd Jhāna	3	■			■	■	■	■				14
" 3rd Jhāna	3	■			■	■	■	■				14
" 4th Jhāna	3	■			■	■	■	■				14
" 5th Jhāna	3	■			■				■			12
IS 1st Jhāna	3									■		1
" 3rd Jhāna	3										■	1

sciousness apprehends the five sense objects in a sense-door process and all six objects in its role as the mind-door adverting consciousness.

Among the immaterial, etc.: The second immaterial citta takes the first immaterial citta as object, while the fourth immaterial citta takes the third as object. Thus these two cittas take sublime entities as object.

All the remaining sublime consciousnesses: The fine-material jhāna cittas take as object a conceptual entity such as the counterpart sign in the case of the kasinas (see I, Guide to §§18-20), or living beings in the case of the illimitables. The first immaterial citta takes as object the concept of infinite space, the third takes as object the concept of nothingness or non-existence. (See Table 3.6.)

§19 Summary

Pañcavīsa parittamhi cha cittāni mahaggate
Ekavīsati vohāre aṭṭha nibbānagocare.
Vīsānuttaramuttamhi aggamaggaphalujjhite
Pañca sabbattha chacceti sattadhā tattha sangaho.

Twenty-five types of consciousness are connected with lower objects; six with the sublime; twenty-one with concepts; eight with Nibbāna.

Twenty are connected with all objects except the supramundane; five with all except the highest path and fruit; and six with all. Thus sevenfold is their grouping.

Guide to §19

Twenty-five types: The twenty-three sense-sphere resultants, the five-door adverting, and the smile-producing consciousness take lower, i.e. sense-sphere, objects only.

Six with the sublime: These are the second and fourth immaterial jhānas, as wholesome, resultant, and functional.

Twenty-one with concepts: These are the five fine-material jhānas and the first and third immaterial jhānas, all considered as wholesome, resultant, and functional.

Eight with Nibbāna: These are the paths and fruits.

Twenty ... except the supramundane: The twelve unwholesome, and the four wholesome and four functionals dissociated from knowledge.

Five: the four sense-sphere wholesomes with knowledge and the wholesome direct-knowledge citta.

Six with all: the four great functionals with knowledge, the functional fifth jhāna direct-knowledge citta, and the determining citta.

Compendium of Bases
(*vatthusangaha*)

§20 Analysis of Bases

Vatthusangahe vatthūni nāma cakkhu-sota-ghāna-jivhā-kāya-hadayavatthu cā ti chabbidhāni bhavanti.

Tāni kāmaloke sabbāni pi labbhanti. Rūpaloke pana ghānādittayaṁ natthi. Arūpaloke pana sabbāni pi na saṁvijjanti.

In the summary of bases, there are six bases, namely, eye-, ear-, nose-, tongue-, body-, and heart-base.

All these, too, are found in the sense world. But in the fine-material world three bases—nose, tongue, and body—are not found. In the immaterial world no base exists.

Guide to §20

Analyses of bases: In those planes of existence where materiality obtains, cittas and cetasikas arise in dependence on a condition called a base (*vatthu*). A base is a physical support for the occurrence of consciousness. Although the first five bases coincide with the first five doors—namely, the sensitive matter of the five sense faculties—a base is not identical with a door, since it plays a different role in the origination of consciousness. A door is a channel through which the cittas and cetasikas of a cognitive process gain access to the object; a base is a physical support for the occurrence of cittas and cetasikas.

This difference in functions implies important consequences. In an eye-door process many types of cittas apart from eye-consciousness occur with eye-sensitivity as their door; but eye-sensitivity is the base solely of eye-consciousness, not of the other cittas that utilize the eye door. In relation to the doors, the various cittas that function as rebirth-linking, bhavanga, and death consciousness are considered "door-freed," that is, as occurring without any door. But in planes of existence which include both mind and matter, no cittas occur without a base.

In the present section, the author will enumerate the bases and classify cittas by way of the bases on which they depend.

Heart-base (*hadayavatthu*): According to the Pali commentators, the heart serves as the physical support for all cittas other than the two sets of fivefold sense consciousness, which take their respective sensitivities as their bases. In the canonical Abhidhamma the heart-base is not expressly mentioned. The *Paṭṭhāna*, the last book of the Abhidhamma Piṭaka, simply speaks of "that matter in dependence on which the mind element and mind-consciousness element occur" (i,4). The Commentaries, however, subsequently specify "that matter" to be the heart-base, a cavity situated within the physical heart.[13]

In the sense world, etc.: In the sensuous plane of existence all six bases are found, except in the case of those who are born blind or deaf. In the fine-material world the three bases of nose, tongue, and body—the supports for the corresponding types of sensuous experience—are absent, since these types of sense experience are coarser in quality than the other two (sight and hearing) and thus are excluded from this elevated plane. The commentators say that the beings there possess the physical forms of these organs, but these organs lack sensitivity and hence cannot serve as bases for smelling, tasting and touching, sensory experiences that therefore do not occur in the fine-material realm. In the immaterial world no bases exist because all the bases are made of matter.

§21 Classification by way of Consciousness

Tattha pañcaviññāṇadhātuyo yathākkamaṁ ekantena pañcappasādavatthūni nissāy'eva pavattanti. Pañcadvārāvajjana-sampaṭicchanasankhātā pana manodhātu ca hadayaṁ nissitā yeva pavattanti. Avasesā pana manoviññāṇadhātusankhātā ca santīraṇa-mahāvipāka-paṭighadvaya-paṭhamamagga-hasana-rūpāvacaravasena hadayaṁ nissāy'eva pavattanti.

Avasesā kusal'-ākusala-kriyā' -nuttaravasena pana nissāya vā anissāya vā. Āruppavipākavasena hadayaṁ anissāy'evā ti.

Therein, the five elements of sense consciousness occur entirely dependent on the five sensitive parts (of the sense organs) as their respective bases (2 x 5 = 10). But the mind element—namely, the five-door-adverting consciousness and the (two types of) receiving consciousness—occurs in dependence on the heart. Likewise those that remain—namely, the mind-consciousness element comprising the investigating consciousness, the great resultants, the two accompanied by aversion, the first path consciousness, smiling consciousness, and fine-material-sphere consciousness—occur in dependence on the heart (3 + 3 + 8 + 2 + 1+ 1+ 15 = 33).

The remaining classes of consciousness, whether wholesome, unwholesome, functional, or supramundane, may be either dependent on, or independent of, the heart-base (12 + 10 + 13 + 7 = 42). The immaterial-sphere resultants are independent of the heart-base (4).

Guide to §21

The five elements of sense consciousness, etc.: In the Abhidhamma all eighty-nine types of citta are distributed among seven consciousness elements (*viññāṇadhātu*) as follows:

TABLE 3.7: THE SEVEN CONSCIOUSNESS ELEMENTS

Element	Cittas	
Eye-cons. element	Eye-consciousness	2
Ear-cons. element	Ear-consciousness	2
Nose-cons. element	Nose-consciousness	2
Tongue-cons. element	Tongue-consciousness	2
Body-cons. element	Body-consciousness	2
Mind-element	5-d-advt., recv. cons.	3
Mind-cons. element	All remaining cittas	76

The three cittas called mind element (*manodhātu*) involve a very weak grasp of the object: the five-door adverting consciousness because it encounters an utterly novel object and is followed by a citta with a different base, the twofold receiving consciousness because it follows a citta with a different base. The five elements of sense consciousness are slightly stronger because they directly see, hear, smell, taste, or touch the object, but they are still relatively weak because they come between two cittas with bases different than their own. The cittas collected under mind-consciousness element (*manoviññāṇadhātu*), being preceded and followed by cittas which share their own base, are capable of a fuller and clearer cognitive grasp of their object.

But the mind-element ... occurs in dependence on the heart: The thirty-three cittas enumerated here do not arise in the immaterial world, but only in worlds where matter exists. Hence they are always supported by the heart-base. The cittas accompanied by aversion do not occur in the fine-material and immaterial planes because aversion has been well suppressed as a prerequisite for attaining jhāna. The first path consciousness, the path consciousness of stream-entry, cannot occur in the immaterial realms because it is contingent on hearing the Dhamma, which presupposes the ear faculty. The smile-producing consciousness, of course, requires a body to exhibit the smile.

The remaining classes of consciousness: They are: ten unwholesome cittas (excluding the two accompanied by aversion), the eight great wholesome cittas, the eight great functionals, four immaterial wholesome, four immaterial functionals, seven supramundane (excluding the first path), and the mind-door adverting—a total of forty-two. These cittas are dependent on the heart-base when they occur in the planes where

TABLE 3.8: COMPENDIUM OF BASES

BASE \ CITTAS	Greed-rtd. 8	Hate-rtd. 2	Delusion-rtd. 2	Eye-cons. 2	Ear-cons. 2	Nose-cons. 2	Tongue-cons. 2	Body-cons. 2	Mind elem. 3	Invs. 3	M-d-advt. 1	Smiling 1	SS Wh. 8	SS Rst. 8	SS Fnc. 8	FMS 15	IS Wh. 4	IS Rst. 4	IS Fnc. 4	S.E. Path 1	Other Spm. 7	Total
Eye-base				■																		2
Ear-base					■																	2
Nose-base						■																2
Tongue-base							■															2
Body-base								■														2
Heart-base (A)		■							■	■		■		■		■				■		33
Heart-base (S)	■		■								■		■		■		■		■		■	42
No base																		■				4

NOTE : (A) = always; (S) = sometimes, i.e. only in sensuous and fine-material planes, not in immaterial plane.

matter exists, i.e. in the sensuous plane and the fine-material plane, and independent of the heart-base when they occur in the immaterial plane. The immaterial-sphere resultants occur only in the immaterial plane and thus do not depend on any base. On the three planes, see V, §§3-7.

§22 Summary

Chavatthuṁ nissitā kāme satta rūpe catubbidhā
Tivatthuṁ nissit' āruppe dhātv' ekānissitā matā.
Tecattāḷīsa nissāya dvecattāḷīsa jāyare
Nissāya ca anissāya pāk' āruppā anissitā ti.

It should be known that in the sensuous plane seven elements are dependent on the six bases, in the fine-material plane four are dependent on three bases, in the immaterial plane the one single element is not dependent on any.

Forty-three (types of consciousness) arise dependent on a base. Forty-two arise with or without a base. The immaterial resultants arise without any base.

Guide to §22

In the sense world, etc.: In the sensuous plane five consciousness elements arise each dependent on their own base, the mind element and mind-consciousness element in dependence on the heart-base. In the fine-material plane the nose-, tongue-, and body-bases, along with their corresponding consciousness elements, are absent. In the immaterial plane only mind-consciousness element occurs, and that without a base.

Iti Abhidhammatthasangahe
Pakiṇṇakasangahavibhāgo nāma
tatiyo paricchedo.

Thus ends the third chapter
in the Manual of Abhidhamma entitled
the Compendium of the Miscellaneous.

CHAPTER IV
COMPENDIUM OF THE COGNITIVE PROCESS
(*Vīthisangahavibhāga*)

§1 Introductory Verse

Cittuppādānam icc' evaṁ katvā sangaham uttaraṁ
Bhūmi-puggalabhedena pubbāparaniyāmitaṁ
Pavattisangahaṁ nāma paṭisandhippavattiyaṁ
Pavakkhāmi samāsena yathāsambhavato kathaṁ.

Having thus completed the excellent compendium of states of consciousness, I shall briefly explain in due order the occurrence of consciousness both at rebirth-linking and during the course of existence, according to the planes and individuals, and as determined by what (states of consciousness) precede and follow.

Guide to §1

I shall briefly explain, etc.: In the preceding chapter the author has classified the states of consciousness with their mental concomitants in terms of such categories as feelings, roots, functions, and so forth. In the next two chapters he will deal with the dynamics of consciousness as it occurs in the process of life. The present chapter examines the occurrence of consciousness in the cognitive process (*cittavithi*), the next chapter the occurrence of consciousness outside the cognitive process (*vīthimutta*), on the occasions of rebirth, bhavanga, and death.

As determined by what (states of consciousness) precede and follow (*pubbāparaniyāmitaṁ*): This phrase means that the cittas in any one cognitive process, as well as in the preceding and following processes, occur in due order in accordance with natural law.

Enumeration of Categories

§2 The Six Sixes

Cha vatthūni, cha dvārāni, cha ālambanāni, cha viññāṇāni, cha vīthiyo, chadhā visayappavatti cā ti vīthisangahe cha chakkāni veditabbāni.

Vīthimuttānaṁ pana kamma-kammanimitta-gatinimitta-vasena tividhā hoti visayappavatti.

Tattha vatthu-dvār'-ālambanāni pubbe vuttanayen' eva.

In the compendium of the cognitive process, six classes each with six members should be understood:

(i) six bases;
(ii) six doors;
(iii) six objects;
(iv) six types of consciousness;
(v) six processes; and
(vi) sixfold presentation of objects.

The presentation of objects to the process-freed consciousness is threefold, namely, kamma, sign of kamma, and sign of destiny. The bases, doors, and objects therein are as described before.

§3 Six Types of Consciousness

Cakkhuviññāṇaṁ, sotaviññāṇaṁ, ghānaviññāṇaṁ, jivhāviññāṇaṁ, kāyaviññāṇaṁ manoviññāṇañ cā ti cha viññāṇāni.

The six types of consciousness are: eye-consciousness, ear-consciousness, nose-consciousness, tongue-consciousness, body-consciousness, and mind-consciousness.

§4 Six Processes

Cha vīthiyo pana cakkhudvāravīthi, sotadvāravīthi, ghānadvāravīthi, jivhādvāravīthi, kāyadvāravīthi, manodvāravīthi cā ti dvāravasena vā cakkhuviññāṇavīthi, sotaviññāṇavīthi, ghānaviññāṇavīthi, jivhāviññāṇavīthi, kāyaviññāṇavīthi manoviññāṇavīthi cā ti viññāṇavasena vā dvārappavattā cittappavattiyo yojetabbā.

According to the doors the six cognitive processes are:

(i) the process connected with the eye door;
(ii) the process connected with the ear door;
(iii) the process connected with the nose door;
(iv) the process connected with the tongue door;
(v) the process connected with the body door; and
(vi) the process connected with the mind door.

Or, according to consciousness, the cognitive processes are:

(i) the process connected with eye-consciousness;
(ii) the process connected with ear-consciousness;
(iii) the process connected with nose-consciousness;
(iv) the process connected with tongue-consciousness;
(v) the process connected with body-consciousness; and
(vi) the process connected with mind-consciousness.

The cognitive processes connected with the doors should be co-ordinated (with the corresponding consciousness).

Guide to §4

The six cognitive processes: The word *vīthi* literally means street, but here it is used in the sense of process. When cittas arise cognizing an object at the sense doors or the mind door, they do not occur at random or in isolation, but as phases in a series of discrete cognitive events leading one to the other in a regular and uniform order. This order is called *cittaniyāma*, the fixed order of consciousness.

For a cognitive process to occur, all the essential conditions must be present. According to the Commentaries, the essential conditions for each type of process are as follows:

(i) For an eye-door process:
- (a) eye-sensitivity (*cakkhuppasāda*);
- (b) visible object (*rūpārammaṇa*);
- (c) light (*āloka*);
- (d) attention (*manasikāra*).

(ii) For an ear-door process:
- (a) ear-sensitivity (*sotappasāda*);
- (b) sound (*saddārammaṇa*);
- (c) space (*ākāsa*);
- (d) attention.

(iii) For a nose-door process:
- (a) nose-sensitivity (*ghānappasāda*);
- (b) smell (*gandhārammaṇa*);
- (c) air element (*vayodhātu*);
- (d) attention.

(iv) For a tongue-door process:
- (a) tongue-sensitivity (*jivhāppasāda*);
- (b) taste (*rasārammaṇa*);
- (c) water element (*āpodhātu*);
- (d) attention.

(v) For a body-door process:
- (a) body-sensitivity (*kāyappasāda*);
- (b) tangible object (*phoṭṭhabbārammaṇa*)
- (c) earth element (*paṭhavīdhātu*);
- (d) attention.

(vi) For a mind-door process:
- (a) the heart-base (*hadayavatthu*);
- (b) mental object (*dhammārammaṇa*);
- (c) the bhavanga.[1]

The six types of cognitive processes are conveniently divided into two groups—the five-door process (*pañcadvāravīthi*), which includes the five processes occurring at each of the physical sense doors; and the mind-door process (*manodvāravīthi*), which comprises all processes that occur solely at the mind door. Since the bhavanga is also the channel from which the five-door processes emerge, the latter are sometimes called mixed door processes (*missaka-dvāravīthi*) as they involve both the mind door and a physical sense door. The processes that occur solely at the mind door are then called bare mind-door processes (*suddha-manodvāravīthi*) since they emerge from the bhavanga alone without the instrumentality of a physical sense door. As will be seen, the first five processes all follow a uniform pattern despite the difference in the sense faculty through which they occur, while the sixth comprises a variety of processes which are alike only in that they occur independently of the external sense doors.

§5 Sixfold Presentation of Objects

Atimahantaṁ mahantaṁ parittaṁ atiparittañ cā ti pañcadvāre, manodvāre pana vibhūtam avibhūtañ cā ti chadhā visayappavatti veditabbā.

The sixfold presentation of objects should be understood as follows:

a. At the five sense doors, it is: (i) very great, (ii) great, (iii) slight, (iv) very slight.

b. At the mind door, it is: (v) clear and (vi) obscure.

Guide to §5

Presentation of objects: The Pali expression *visayappavatti* means the presentation of an object to consciousness at one of the six doors, or the occurrence of states of consciousness upon the presentation of an object. The sixfold presentation of objects is analyzed into four alternatives at the five sense doors—very great, great, slight, and very slight; and two alternatives at the mind door—clear and obscure.

In this context the words "great" (*mahā*) and "slight" (*paritta*) are not used with reference to the size or grossness of the object, but to the force of its impact on consciousness. Even though a large or gross visible object is present at the eye door, if the sensitive matter of the eye is weak, or the object impinges on the eye after it has passed its prime, or the light is dim, the object will not make a distinct impression and thus will fall into the categories of slight or very slight. On the other hand, if a small or subtle form impinges on the eye while it is at its prime, and the sensitive matter of the eye is strong, and the light is bright, then the object will make a distinct impression and will fall into the categories of great or very great.

Therefore the terms "great object" and "slight object," etc., indicate, not the size of the object, but the number of process cittas (*vīthicitta*) that arise from the moment the object enters the avenue of a sense door until the moment the presentation of the object to consciousness ceases. A similar principle distinguishes the presentation of objects in the mind door into the clear and the obscure.

The Five-Door Process
(*pañcadvāravīthi*)

§6 The Very Great Object

Kathaṁ? Uppāda-ṭṭhiti-bhanga-vasena khaṇattayaṁ ekacittakkhaṇaṁ nāma. Tāni pana sattarasa cittakkhaṇāni rūpadhammānam āyu. Ekacittakkhaṇātītāni vā bahucittakkhaṇātītāni vā ṭhitippattān' eva pañcālambanāni pañcadvāre āpātham āgacchanti.

How (is the intensity in the presentation of objects determined)? One mind-moment consists of the three (sub-) moments—arising, presence, and dissolution. The duration of material phenomena consists of seventeen such mind-moments. The five sense objects enter the avenue of the five sense doors at the stage of presence, when one or several mind-moments have passed.

Tasmā yadi ekacittakkhaṇātītakaṁ rūpārammaṇaṁ cakkhussa āpātham āgacchati, tato dvikkhattuṁ bhavange calite bhavangasotaṁ vocchinditvā tam eva rūpārammaṇaṁ āvajjantaṁ pañcadvār-āvajjanacittaṁ uppajjitvā nirujjhati. Tato tass' ānantaraṁ tam eva rūpaṁ passantaṁ cakkhuviññāṇaṁ, sampaṭicchantaṁ sampaṭicchanacittaṁ, santīrayamānaṁ santīraṇacittaṁ, vavatthapentaṁ votthapanacittañ cā ti yathākkamaṁ uppajjitvā nirujjhanti.

Therefore, if a visible form as object, having passed one mind-moment (i), enters the avenue of the eye, the life-continuum vibrates for two mind-moments and is arrested (ii, iii). Then a five-door adverting consciousness arises and ceases adverting to that same visible form as object (iv). Immediately after there arise and cease in due order:

(v) eye-consciousness seeing that form;
(vi) receiving consciousness receiving it;
(vii) investigating consciousness investigating it;
(viii) determining consciousness determining it.

Tato paraṁ ekūnatiṁsakāmāvacarajavanesu yaṁ kiñci laddhappaccayaṁ yebhuyyena sattakkhattuṁ javati. Javanānubandhāni ca dve tadārammaṇapākāni yathārahaṁ pavattanti. Tato paraṁ bhavangapāto.

Following this, any one of the twenty-nine sense-sphere javanas which has gained the right conditions runs its course, generally for seven mind-moments (ix-xv). After the javanas, two registration resultants arise accordingly (xvi-xvii). Then comes the subsidence into the life-continuum.

Ettāvatā cuddasa vīthicittuppādā dve bhavangacalanāni pubb' ev' atītakam ekacittakkhaṇan ti katvā sattarasa cittakkhaṇāni paripūrenti. Tato paraṁ nirujjhati. Ālambanam etaṁ atimahantaṁ nāma gocaraṁ.

TABLE 4.1: A COMPLETE EYE-DOOR PROCESS

14 acts of process consciousness

Moment	Sub-moments	Function
	***	Stream of bhavanga
1	***	Past bhavanga
2	***	Vibrational bhavanga
3	***	Arrest bhavanga
4	***	Five-door adverting
5	***	Eye-consciousness
6	***	Receiving
7	***	Investigating
8	***	Determining
9	***	Javana
10	***	Javana
11	***	Javana
12	***	Javana
13	***	Javana
14	***	Javana
15	***	Javana
16	***	Registration
17	***	Registration
	***	Stream of bhavanga

NOTE: The triple asterisks beneath the numbers represent the three sub-moments of each mind-moment: arising, presence, and dissolution.

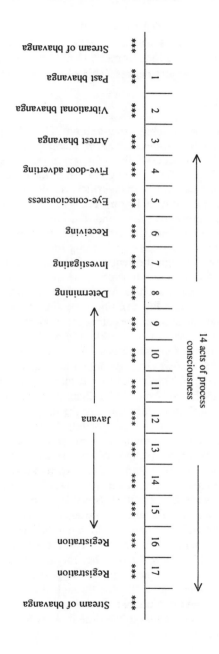

To this extent seventeen mind-moments are completed, namely, fourteen acts of process consciousness, two vibrations of the life-continuum, and one mind-moment that had passed prior to (the process). Then the object ceases. This object is called "very great."

Guide to §6

The duration of material phenomena: The life-span of a citta is termed, in the Abhidhamma, a mind-moment (*cittakkhaṇa*). This is a temporal unit of such brief duration that, according to the commentators, in the time that it takes for lightning to flash or the eyes to blink, billions of mind-moments can elapse. Nevertheless, though seemingly infinitesimal, each mind-moment in turn consists of three sub-moments—arising (*uppāda*), presence (*ṭhiti*), and dissolution (*bhanga*). Within the breadth of a mind-moment, a citta arises, performs its momentary function, and then dissolves, conditioning the next citta in immediate succession. Thus, through the sequence of mind-moments, the flow of consciousness continues uninterrupted like the waters in a stream.

Some commentators, such as Ācariya Ānanda (author of the *Mūla-Ṭīkā* to the Abhidhamma Piṭaka), reject the sub-moment of presence in relation to mental phenomena, appealing for support to the Citta-Yamaka chapter of the *Yamaka*, which speaks only of the arising moment and dissolution moment of consciousness, but not of a presence moment. Ācariya Anuruddha, however, does not endorse this position, nor do his commentators. The *Vibhāvinī* points out that the sub-moment of presence is a stage in the occurrence of a dhamma separate from the stages of arising and dissolution, during which the dhamma "stands facing its own dissolution" (*bhangābhimukhāvatthā*). Ledi Sayadaw regards the moment of presence as the midpoint between the two phases of arising and falling (*udaya-vaya*), just as, when a stone is thrown upwards, a moment is needed before it starts falling downwards. He also says that the presence moment can be taken to cover the entire life-span of a dhamma between the first point of its arising and the end of its falling away. Many commentators take the presence moment to be implied by the Buddha's statement: "There are three conditioned characteristics of the conditioned: arising, passing away, and the alteration of that which stands" (A.3:47/i,152). Here the presence moment is identified with "the alteration of that which stands" (*ṭhitassa aññathatta*).

Material phenomena as well pass through the same three stages of arising, presence, and dissolution, but for them the time required for these three stages to elapse is equal to the time it takes for seventeen cittas to arise and perish. The stages of arising and dissolution are equal in duration for both material and mental phenomena, but in the case of material phenomena the stage of presence is equal to forty-nine sub-moments of mental phenomena.[2]

The five sense objects enter ... at the stage of presence: The five sense objects—visible forms, etc.—are material phenomena and thus endure for seventeen mind-moments. Since the sense object is still weak at the sub-moment of arising, it can enter the avenue of sense only when it reaches the stage of presence.

Therefore, if a visible form as object, etc.: When no active cognitive process is taking place, the bhavanga flows on as a series of cittas all of the same type, hanging on to a single object—either a kamma, a sign of kamma, or a sign of destiny—the same as the object of the last javana process in the immediately preceding existence. At the very moment a sense object enters a sense door, one bhavanga citta passes, known as *atīta-bhavanga*, the past life-continuum. Then another two bhavanga cittas vibrate owing to the impact of the object, the second interrupting the stream of the bhavanga. In the sub-commentaries these are distinguished as *bhavanga-calana*, vibrational life-continuum, and *bhavang'-upaccheda*, arrest life-continuum. Thereafter, with the arising of the five-door adverting citta, the stream of consciousness emerges from the "process-freed" state and launches into a cognitive process (*vīthipāta*).

The twenty-nine sense-sphere javanas: that is, twelve unwholesome types, eight each of the great wholesome and great functional types, and the functional smile-producing citta. Only one type of citta runs for all seven occasions of the javana process.

This object is called "very great": In the process with a very great object, the object arises simultaneously with the arising sub-moment of the *atīta-bhavanga*. Since the sense object and the sensitive matter of the sense organ both have a duration of seventeen mind-moments, they both perish simultaneously with the second registration citta. Thus this kind of cognitive process runs for a full seventeen mind-moments, of which fourteen cittas, beginning with the five-door adverting citta, are considered process cittas proper. This cognitive process is also known as *tadārammaṇavāra*, a course ending with registration. (See Table 4.1.)

The connection of the cognitive process described in the text with the "six sixes" may be understood as follows. When a visible form impinges on the eye-sensitivity, then, supported by the eye-base, there arises an eye-consciousness taking as object the visible form that has impinged on the eye. For the eye-consciousness, the eye-sensitivity is the base and the door, the visible form is the object. The other cittas in the process—the five-door adverting, the receiving, investigating, and determining consciousnesses, the javanas, and registration—are states of mind-consciousness. They take the same visible form as object and the eye-sensitivity as door, but they arise with the support of the heart-base. For all the cittas in the process, the bhavanga is also considered a door, since the entire process emerges from the bhavanga. Thus all sense-door processes are considered to have two doors, the material sensitivity as a differentiating door and the mind door or bhavanga as a common door. Because it has arisen specifically in the eye door this process is called an "eye-door process," and because it is distinguished by eye-consciousness it is also called an "eye-consciousness process." Since it has arisen with a very powerful object capable of impinging on the sense faculty after only one mind-moment has passed, it is called a process with a very great object. The cognitive processes in the other senses may be understood accordingly, with the necessary substitutions.

The ancient teachers of the Abhidhamma illustrate the cognitive process occurring in the sense doors with the simile of the mango.[3] A certain man with his head covered went to sleep at the foot of a fruiting mango tree. Then a ripe mango loosened from the stalk fell to the ground, grazing his ear. Awakened by the sound, he opened his eyes and looked; then he stretched out his hand, took the fruit, squeezed it, and smelt it. Having done so, he ate the mango, swallowed it appreciating its taste, and then went back to sleep.

Here, the time of the man's sleeping at the foot of the mango tree is like the time when the bhavanga is occurring. The instant of the ripe mango falling from its stalk and grazing his ear is like the instant of the object striking one of the sense organs, for instance, the eye. The time of awaking through the sound is like that of the five-door adverting consciousness turning towards the object. The time of the man's opening his eyes and looking is like eye-consciousness accomplishing its function of seeing. The time of stretching out his hand and taking the mango is like that of the receiving consciousness receiving the object. The time of squeezing the fruit is like that of the investigating consciousness investigating the object. The time of smelling the mango is like that of the determining consciousness determining the object. The time of eating the mango is like that of javana experiencing the flavour of the object. The swallowing of the fruit while appreciating its taste is like the registration consciousness taking the same object as the javana phase. And the man's going back to sleep is like the subsidence back into the bhavanga.

It should be noted that the entire cognitive process occurs without any self or subject behind it as an enduring experiencer or inner controller, a "knower" outside the scope of the process itself. The momentary cittas themselves exercise all the functions necessary to cognition, and the unity of the cognitive act derives from their coordination through laws of conditional connectedness. Within the cognitive process each citta comes into being in accordance with the lawful order of consciousness (*cittaniyāma*). It arises in dependence on a variety of conditions, including the preceding citta, the object, a door, and a physical base. Having arisen, it performs its own unique function within the process, and then it dissolves, becoming a condition for the next citta.

§7 The Great Object

Yāva tadārammaṇ' uppādā pana appahontātītakam āpātham āgataṁ ālambanaṁ mahantaṁ nāma. Tattha javanāvasāne bhavangapāto va hoti. Natthi tadārammaṇ' uppādo.

The object is called "great" when it enters the avenue of sense after having passed (a few moments) and is unable to survive till the arising of the registration mind-moments. In that case, at the end of the javanas, there is subsidence into the life-continuum and no arising of registration consciousness.

Guide to §7

The object is called "great," etc.: In this kind of cognitive process, after the object has arisen two or three *atīta-bhavanga* cittas pass before its impact causes the bhavanga to vibrate. Since the object and sense door can only endure for seventeen mind-moments, this process does not give any scope for the registration cittas to arise; registration cannot occur even when there are two *atīta-bhavangas,* since registration occurs either for two mind-moments or not at all.

When there are two *atīta-bhavanga* cittas, fifteen more cittas can arise during the life-span of the object. In such a case both the object and the sense door perish simultaneously with the dissolution moment of the first bhavanga citta following the javana phase. When there are three *atīta-bhavanga* cittas, scope remains for fourteen more cittas to arise, and in this case the sense object and sense door perish simultaneously with the last javana citta. This kind of cognitive process is also called a *javana-vāra,* a course ending with javana.

§8 The Slight Object

Yāva javan' uppādā pi appahontātītakam āpātham āgataṁ ālambanaṁ parittaṁ nāma. Tattha javanam pi anuppajjitvā dvattikkhattuṁ votthapanam eva pavattati. Tato paraṁ bhavangapāto va hoti.

The object is called "slight" when it enters the avenue of sense after having passed (a few moments) and is unable to survive till the arising of the javanas. In that case even the javanas do not arise, but the determining consciousness occurs for two or three moments, and then there is subsidence into the life-continuum.

Guide to §8

The object is called "slight," etc.: In the process with a slight object, from four to nine *atīta-bhavangas* will pass initially, and no javanas will arise. The determining citta will occur two or three times, after which the cognitive process will subside into the bhavanga. Depending on the number of *atīta-bhavangas* there are six types of process with a slight object. This kind of process is also called *votthapanavāra*, a course ending with determining.

§9 The Very Slight Object

Yāva votthapan' uppādā ca pana appahontātītakam āpātham āgataṁ nirodhāsannam ālambanaṁ atiparittaṁ nāma. Tattha bhavangacalanam eva hoti. Natthi vīthicittuppādo.

The object is called "very slight" when it enters the avenue of sense as it is on the verge of ceasing and, after having passed (a few moments), is unable to survive until the arising of the determining consciousness. In that case there is merely vibration of the life-continuum, but no arising of a cognitive process.

Guide to §9

The object is called "very slight," etc.: In this course of cognition there are no process cittas but only vibrations of the bhavanga. During the seventeen moments of the object's life-span, ten to fifteen moments will be occupied by *atīta-bhavanga* cittas, two moments by vibrational bhavangas, and the rest by the bhavangas subsequent to the vibration. This type of process, of which there are six sub-types, is also termed *moghavāra*, the futile course.

§10 Fourfold Presentation of Objects

Icc' evaṁ cakkhudvāre tathā sotadvārādīsu cā ti sabbathā pi pañcadvāre tadārammaṇa-javana-votthapana-moghavāra-

TABLE 4.2: GRADES OF SENSE-DOOR PROCESSES

The Very Great Object																			
1	B	{P	V	A	F	E	Rc	I	D	J	J	J	J	J	J	J	Rg	Rg }	B
The Great Object																			
2	B	{P	P	V	A	F	E	Rc	I	D	J	J	J	J	J	J	J	B }	B
3	B	{P	P	P	V	A	F	E	Rc	I	D	J	J	J	J	J	J	J }	B
The Slight Object																			
4	B	{P	P	P	P	V	A	F	E	Rc	I	D	D	D	B	B	B	B }	B
5	B	{P	P	P	P	P	V	A	F	E	Rc	I	D	D	D	B	B	B }	B
6	B	{P	P	P	P	P	P	V	A	F	E	Rc	I	D	D	D	B	B }	B
7	B	{P	P	P	P	P	P	P	V	A	F	E	Rc	I	D	D	D	B }	B
8	B	{P	P	P	P	P	P	P	P	V	A	F	E	Rc	I	D	D	D }	B
9	B	{P	P	P	P	P	P	P	P	P	V	A	F	E	Rc	I	D	D }	B
The Very Slight Object																			
10	B	{P	P	P	P	P	P	P	P	P	P	V	V	B	B	B	B	B }	B
11	B	{P	P	P	P	P	P	P	P	P	P	P	V	V	B	B	B	B }	B
12	B	{P	P	P	P	P	P	P	P	P	P	P	P	V	V	B	B	B }	B
13	B	{P	P	P	P	P	P	P	P	P	P	P	P	P	V	V	B	B }	B
14	B	{P	P	P	P	P	P	P	P	P	P	P	P	P	P	V	V	B }	B
15	B	{P	P	P	P	P	P	P	P	P	P	P	P	P	P	P	V	V }	B

KEY: B = stream of bhavanga; P = past bhavanga; V = vibrational bhavanga; A = arrest bhavanga; F = five-door adverting; E = eye-consciousness; Rc = receiving; I = investigation; D = determining; J = javana; Rg = registration; { } = the life of the object.

NOTE: For eye-consciousness, substitute ear-, nose-, tongue-, or body-consciousness. All fifteen types of cognitive process can occur through each of the five doors, making a total of seventy-five processes occuring at the five sense doors.

sankhātānaṁ catunnaṁ vārānaṁ yathākkamaṁ ālambanabhūtā visayappavatti catudhā veditabbā.

As in the eye door, so in the ear door, etc. Thus in all the five doors, the fourfold presentation of objects should be understood, in due order, in the four ways known as:

(i) the course (ending with) registration;
(ii) the course (ending with) javana;
(iii) the course (ending with) determining; and
(iv) the futile course.

Guide to §10

Thus in all the five doors, etc.: When these four courses are divided by way of their sub-types, there are altogether fifteen kinds of sense-door cognitive process. Since each of these can occur in all the five sense doors, this makes a total of seventy-five sense-door processes. (See Table 4.2.)

§11 Summary

Vīthicittāni satt' eva cittuppādā catuddasa
Catupaññāsa vitthārā pañcadvāre yathārahaṁ.

Ayam ettha pañcadvāre
vīthicittappavattinayo.

There are seven modes and fourteen different states of consciousness in the cognitive process. In detail there are accordingly fifty-four in the five doors.

Herein, this is the method
of the cognitive process in the five sense doors.

Guide to §11

There are seven modes, etc.: The seven modes in which the process cittas occur are: five-door adverting, sense consciousness (one of five), receiving, investigating, determining, javana and registration. The fourteen states of consciousness are obtained by taking the javana seven times and registration twice. The fifty-four cittas that occur in the five-door process comprise all the sense-sphere cittas.

The Mind-Door Process (*manodvāravīthi*)

§12 The Limited Javana Process

Manodvāre pana yadi vibhūtam ālambanaṁ āpātham āgacchati, tato paraṁ bhavangacalana-manodvārāvajjana-javanāvasāne tadārammaṇapākāni pavattanti. Tato paraṁ bhavangapāto.

When a clear object enters the avenue of the mind door, then the vibration of the life-continuum, mind-door adverting, javanas, and at the end of the javanas, registration resultants, all take place. Following this there is subsidence into the life-continuum.

Avibhūte pan' ālambane javanāvasāne bhavangapāto va hoti. Natthi tadārammaṇ' uppādo ti.

In the case of an obscure object there is subsidence into the life-continuum at the end of the javanas, without giving rise to the registration resultants.

Guide to §12

The mind-door process: When a cognitive process occurs in one of the sense doors, two doors are actually involved: the physical sense door and the mind door, which is the bhavanga from which the cognitive process emerges. What is called a mind-door process is a cognitive process that occurs exclusively through the mind door, without any admixture of the sense doors. This kind of process is also called, for the sake of clarity, a bare mind-door process (*suddha-manodvāravīthi*).

The mind-door process includes both the "limited" or sense-sphere process (*paritta-vīthi*), dealt with in §§12-13, and the cognitive process in absorption pertaining to the sublime (*mahaggata*) and supramundane (*lokuttara*) attainments, dealt with in §§14-16.

The limited or sense-sphere mind-door process is itself twofold: (1) that consequent to a five-door process (*pañcadvārānubandhakā*), and (2) the independent process (*visuṁsiddhā*).

(1) Just as when a gong is struck once by a baton, the gong sends forth a continuous stream of reverberations, so when one of the five sense doors has been impinged upon once by a sense object, after the five-door process has ceased the past sense object comes into range at the mind door and sets off many sequences of mind-door processes. Because these cognitive processes come as the sequel to a five-door process, they

are known as *consequent processes*. They are counted as fivefold by way of the five sense-door processes which they follow.

Ledi Sayadaw explains that it is in these consequent processes that distinct recognition of the object occurs; such recognition does not occur in a bare five-door process itself. An eye-door process, for example, is followed first by a conformational mind-door process (*tadanuvattikā manodvāravīthi*), which reproduces in the mind door the object just perceived in the sense-door process. Then comes a process grasping the object as whole (*samudāyagāhikā*); then a process recognizing the colour (*vaṇṇasallakkhaṇā*); then a process grasping the entity (*vatthugāhikā*); then a process recognizing the entity (*vatthu sallakkhaṇā*); then a process grasping the name (*nāmagāhikā*); then a process recognizing the name (*nāmasallakkhaṇā*).

"The process grasping the object as a whole" is the mind-door process perceiving as a whole the forms repeatedly perceived in individual frames by the two preceding processes, the original sense-door process and the conformational mind-door process. This process exercises a synthesizing function, fusing the perception of distinct "shots" of the object into the perception of a unity, as in the case of a whirling firebrand perceived as a circle of fire. It is only when this has occurred that recognition of the colour is possible. When the recognition of the colour occurs, one recognizes the colour, "I see blue." When the recognition of the entity occurs, one recognizes the entity or shape. When the recognition of the name occurs, one recognizes the name. Thus, Ledi Saydaw asserts, it is only when a recognitional process referring to one or another specific feature occurs that one knows, "I see this or that specific feature."

(2) An *independent mind-door process* occurs when any of the six objects enters the range of cognition entirely on its own, not as a consequence of an immediately preceding sense-door process. The question may be raised how an object can enter the range of the mind door independently of a proximate sensory impingement. Ledi Sayadaw cites various sources: through what was directly perceived earlier, or by inference from what was directly perceived; through what was learnt by oral report, or by inference from what was learnt by oral report; on account of belief, opinion, reasoning, or reflective acceptance of a view; by the power of kamma, psychic power, disturbance of the bodily humours, the influence of a deity, comprehension, realization, etc. He explains that if one has clearly experienced an object even once, at a later time—even after a hundred years or in a future life—dependent on that object a condition may be set for the vibration of the bhavanga. The mind that has been nurtured on such an input of prior experiences

is extremely susceptible to their influence. When it encounters any sense object, that object may trigger off in a single moment mental waves extending to many thousands of objects previously perceived.

The mental continuum, constantly being excited by these causal influences, is always seeking an opportunity to emerge from the bhavanga and acquire a clear cognition of an object. Therefore the mental factor of attention present in the bhavanga repeatedly causes the bhavanga to vibrate, and it directs consciousness again and again to advert to objects which have gained conditions to appear. Even though the bhavanga citta has its own object, Ledi Sayadaw explains, it occurs in the mode of inclining towards some other object. As a result of this perpetual "buzz" of activity in the bhavanga, when an object acquires sufficient prominence through other operative conditions, it draws the continuum of consciousness out of the bhavanga, and then that object comes into the range of cognition at the mind door.

The independent process is analyzed as sixfold: the process based on what was directly perceived; the process based on inference from what was directly perceived; the process based on oral report; the process based on inference from oral report; the process based on the cognized; the process based on inference from the cognized. "The cognized" here includes belief, opinion, comprehension, and realization; "inference from the cognized" includes judgements arrived at by inductive and deductive reasoning.

When a clear object enters, etc.: There are two types of mind-door process pertaining to the sense sphere, distinguished by the intensity of the object. In a process with a clear object (*vibhūtālambana*), when the object enters the avenue of the mind door, the bhavanga vibrates and is arrested. Then a mind-door adverting consciousness turns to the object, followed by seven moments of javana and two of registration, after which the cognitive process subsides into the bhavanga. This is in the case of beings in the sense-sphere plane; but for beings in the fine-material and immaterial planes, moments of registration do not occur even when the object is exceptionally clear (see below §§19-20).

In the case of an obscure object: In the process with an obscure object (*avibhūtālambana*) the two moments of registration do not occur under any conditions.

Ledi Sayadaw holds that the subsidence into the bhavanga at the end of the javanas should be understood as the maximum type of process with an obscure object. However, he maintains that when the object is obscure, a course ending with two or three occurrences of the mind-door adverting is also found, and a course ending with the mere vibration of the bhavanga may also be admitted. For in the case of the bare mind-

TABLE 4.3: THE LIMITED JAVANA PROCESS

The Clear Object

B { V A M J J J J J J J Rg Rg } B

The Obscure Object

B { V A M J J J J J J J } B B B

KEY: M = mind-door adverting; { } = extent of the process; rest as in Table 4.2.

door process, on countless occasions an object enters the range of cognition and causes the bhavanga to vibrate two or three times, after which the disturbance subsides with no occurrence of cittas belonging to a cognitive process proper. Thus, according to Ledi Sayadaw, in the mind door too there is a fourfold presentation of objects. The course ending with registration can be called a very clear (*ati-vibhūta*) presentation; the course ending with javanas, a clear (*vibhūta*) presentation; the course ending with mind-door adverting, an obscure (*avibhūta*) presentation; and the course ending with mere vibration of the bhavanga, a very obscure (*ati-avibhūta*) presentation. The clarity of the presentation depends on either the prominence of the object or the strength of consciousness. For a prominent object can appear clearly even when consciousness is weak, while a strong consciousness can clearly cognize even a subtle abstruse object.

§13 Summary

Vīthicittāni tīṇ' eva cittuppādā das' eritā
Vitthārena pan' etth' ekacattāḷīsa vibhāvaye.

Ayam ettha parittajavanavāro.

Three modes and ten different states (of consciousness) in the cognitive process are told. It should be explained that, in detail, there are forty-one kinds here.

Herein, this is the limited javana section.

Guide to §13

Three modes, etc.: The three modes of the process cittas are mind-door adverting, javana, and registration. The ten states of consciousness are obtained by taking the javana seven times and registration twice. The forty-one cittas here include all the sense-sphere cittas except the two sets of fivefold sense consciousness, the five-door adverting, and the two kinds of receiving consciousness. The three investigating cittas occur here with the function of registration, the determining citta with the function of mind-door adverting.

The Process of Absorption Javanas in the Mind Door (*appanājavana-manodvāravīthi*)

§14 The Process of Absorption

Appanājavanavāre pana vibhūtāvibhūtabhedo natthi. Tathā tadāramman' uppādo ca. Tattha hi ñāṇasampayuttakāmāvacaraja-vanānam aṭṭhannaṁ aññatarasmiṁ parikamm'-opacār'-ānuloma-gotrabhū nāmena catukkhattuṁ tikkhattum eva vā yathākkamaṁ uppajjitvā niruddhe tadanantaram eva yathārahaṁ catutthaṁ pañcamaṁ vā chabbīsati mahaggata-lokuttarajavanesu yathābhi-nīhāravasena yaṁ kiñci javanaṁ appanāvīthim otarati. Tato paraṁ appanāvasāne bhavangapāto va hoti.

In the occurrence of javanas in absorption, there is no distinction between clear and obscure (objects). Likewise there is no arising of registration consciousness. In this case (i.e. in the process of absorption), any one of the eight sense-sphere javanas accompanied by knowledge arises and ceases four times or three times, in due order as preparation, access, conformity, and change-of-lineage. Immediately after they cease, in the fourth or fifth moment as the case may be, any one of the javanas among the twenty-six types of sublime or supramundane javanas enters upon the process of absorption in accordance with the way the mind is conveyed. After that, at the end of absorption, there is subsidence into the life-continuum.

Guide to §14

Absorption (*appanā*): *Appanā* primarily signifies a highly developed form of *vitakka*, initial application of mind, which thrusts the associated mental states so deeply into the object that they become absorbed in it. Although *vitakka* is absent in the jhānas beyond the first, because the mind that has entered jhāna becomes fixed one-pointedly on its object, the word *appanā* comes to be extended to all meditative attainments pertaining to the fine-material, immaterial, and supramundane planes.

There is no distinction between clear and obscure (objects): This distinction is not found in relation to absorption because the meditative attainments are only possible when the object is clearly apprehended.

In this case ... any one of the eight sense-sphere javanas ... arises: When the meditator is about to achieve a jhāna, a path, or fruition, first there arises mind-door adverting. Then, in the same cognitive process as the attainment, immediately preceding it, a series of sense-sphere javanas runs its course in quick succession, leading the mind from the sense-sphere plane to the absorption. In the case of a worldling or a trainee, these javanas will be one of the four wholesome sense-sphere cittas accompanied by knowledge; in the case of an Arahant, one of the four functional sense-sphere cittas accompanied by knowledge.

In due order as preparation, etc.: In an individual with average faculties, these preliminary javanas occur four times, each one exercising a different preliminary function. The first is called preparation (*parikamma*) because it prepares the mental continuum for the attainment to follow. The next is called access (*upacāra*) because it arises in proximity to the attainment. The third moment is called conformity (*anuloma*) because it arises in conformity with both the preceding moments and the subsequent absorption. The fourth moment is called change-of-lineage (*gotrabhū*). In the case of jhāna attainment it receives this name because it overcomes the sense-sphere lineage and evolves the lineage of sublime consciousness. In the case of the first path attainment, this moment is called change-of-lineage because it marks the transition from the lineage of worldlings to the lineage of the noble ones (*ariya*). The expression continues to be used figuratively for the moment of transition to the higher paths and fruits, though sometimes it is designated by a different name, *vodāna*, meaning "cleansing."[4]

In an individual with especially keen faculties, the moment of preparation (*parikamma*) is omitted, and thus only three preliminary sense-sphere javanas occur prior to absorption.

Immediately after they cease, etc.: Immediately after the change-of-lineage citta, as the fourth javana in an individual with keen faculties, or as the fifth javana in one with average faculties, there arises the first javana citta at the level of absorption. This citta may be one of the five fine-material-sphere cittas either wholesome or functional (10), one of the four immaterial-sphere cittas either wholesome or functional (8), or one of the four paths or fruits (8). Thus it can be of twenty-six types.

It should be noted that in an absorption cognitive process, the javana cittas can be of different types, even of different planes, while in a sense-sphere process they are all uniform.

In accordance with the way the mind is conveyed (*yathābhinīhāravasena*): This means that the absorption citta that arises is conditioned by the direction the meditator gives to his mind. If he wishes to attain the first jhāna, then he conveys his mind towards that jhāna through the development of calm concentration (*samatha*), and so too for the attainment of the higher jhānas. If the meditator aims at reaching the path and fruit, then he conveys his mind towards the path and fruit through the development of insight (*vipassanā*).

At the end of absorption: After absorption there is immediate subsidence into the bhavanga, with no occurrence of registration cittas.

TABLE 4.4: THE ABSORPTION JAVANA PROCESS

The Initial Attainment of Jhāna
Avrg: B { V A M Pr Ac Cn Ch Jh } B B B
Keen: B { V A M Ac Cn Ch Jh } B B B B

Attainment of Path and Fruit
Avrg: B { V A M Pr Ac Cn Ch Pa Fr Fr } B
Keen: B { V A M Ac Cn Ch Pa Fr Fr Fr } B

KEY: Avrg = one of average faculties; keen = one of keen faculties; Pr = preparation; Ac = access; Cn = conformity; Ch = change-of-lineage; Jh = jhāna; Pa = path; Fr = fruition; rest as in Tables 4.2 and 4.3.

§15 Correlations in Absorption

Tattha somanassasahagatajavanānantaraṁ appanā pi somanassasahagatā va pāṭikankhitabbā. Upekkhāsahagatajavanānantaraṁ upekkhāsahagatā va. Tatthā pi kusalajavanānantaraṁ kusalajavanañ c'eva heṭṭhimañ ca phalattayam appeti. Kriyājavanānantaraṁ kriyājavanaṁ arahattaphalañ cā ti.

Therein, immediately after a javana accompanied by joy, absorption accompanied by joy may be expected. Immediately after a javana accompanied by equanimity, absorption (occurs) accompanied by equanimity.

Therein, too, immediately after a wholesome javana, absorption occurs through a wholesome javana and the three lower fruits. Immediately after a functional javana, absorption occurs through a functional javana and the fruit of Arahantship.

Guide to §15

The purpose of this passage is to establish the correlations between the preliminary cittas of the cognitive process issuing in absorption and the absorption cittas themselves. The verses to follow will provide the detailed application of the general principles stated in the present passage.

§16 Summary

Dvattiṁsa sukhapuññamhā dvādas' opekkhakā paraṁ
Sukhitakriyato aṭṭha cha sambhonti upekkhakā.
Puthujjanāna sekkhānaṁ kāmapuññā tihetuto
Tihetukāmakriyato vītarāgānam appanā.

Ayam ettha manodvāre
vīthicittappavattinayo.

Following wholesome consciousness accompanied by joy, thirty-two (classes of absorption javanas) arise. After (wholesome consciousness) accompanied by equanimity, twelve (classes of absorption javanas arise). After functionals accompanied by joy, eight classes arise, and after (functionals) accompanied by equanimity, six classes arise.

For worldlings and trainees, absorption occurs following a three-rooted wholesome sense-sphere consciousness. For those free from lust (i.e. Arahants), absorption follows a three-rooted sense-sphere functional consciousness.

Herein, this is the method
of the cognitive process in the mind door.

Guide to §16

Following wholesome consciousness accompanied by joy, etc.: When the preliminary functions in the absorption process are performed by either of the two wholesome sense-sphere cittas accompanied by joy and knowledge—that is, in the case of worldlings or trainees—then there can arise thirty-two cittas as javanas in absorption: the sublime wholesome cittas of the first four jhānas (those accompanied by happiness); the four path cittas at the level of any of the first four jhānas; and the lower three fruition cittas at the same four levels (4 + 16 + 12 = 32).

After (wholesome consciousness) accompanied by equanimity, etc.: When the preliminary functions are performed by either of the two wholesome sense-sphere cittas accompanied by equanimity and knowledge—also in the case of worldlings or trainees—then there can arise twelve absorption javanas: the sublime wholesome cittas of the fifth jhāna and the four immaterial jhānas; the four path cittas at the level of the fifth jhāna; and the lower three fruition cittas at the level of the fifth jhāna (5 + 4 + 3 = 12).

After functionals accompanied by joy, etc.: Following the two functional sense-sphere cittas accompanied by joy and knowledge—that is, in the case of Arahants only—there arise eight javanas in absorption: the sublime functional javanas of the first four jhānas and the fruition of Arahantship at the level of the first four jhānas (4 + 4 = 8).

After (functionals) accompanied by equanimity, etc.: Following the two functional sense-sphere cittas accompanied by equanimity and knowledge there arise six javanas in absorption: five sublime functional javanas and the fruition of Arahantship at the level of the fifth jhāna (5 + 1 = 6).

For worldlings and trainees, etc.: In the case of worldlings and trainees who have attained the three lower paths and fruits, after any of the four wholesome sense-sphere javanas accompanied by knowledge there arises one of the forty-four absorption javanas described above (32 + 12 = 44). After the four functional sense-sphere javanas accompanied by knowledge, there arises to the Arahant one of the above fourteen absorption javanas (8 + 6 = 14).

The Procedure of Registration (*tadārammaṇaniyama*)

§17 Analysis of Registration

Sabbatthā pi pan' ettha aniṭṭhe ārammaṇe akusalavipākān' eva pañcaviññāṇa-sampaṭicchana-santīraṇa-tadārammaṇāni; iṭṭhe kusalavipākāni; ati-iṭṭhe pana somanassasahagatān' eva santīraṇa-tadārammaṇāni.

Here, under all circumstances, when an object is undesirable, the fivefold sense consciousness, reception, investigation, and registration (that arise) are unwholesome-resultants. When (the object is) desirable, they are wholesome-resultants. If the object is extremely desirable, investigation and registration are accompanied by joy.

Tatthā pi somanassasahagatakriyājavanāvasāne somanassa-sahagatān' eva tadārammaṇāni bhavanti. Upekkhāsahagata-kriyājavanāvasāne ca upekkhāsahagatān' eva honti.

In this connection, too, at the end of functional javanas accompanied by joy, there arise registration mind-moments also accompanied by joy. At the end of functional javanas accompanied by equanimity, the registration mind-moments are also accompanied by equanimity.

Guide to §17

When an object is undesirable, etc.: Sense objects are distinguished into three classes: the undesirable (*aniṭṭha*), the moderately desirable (*iṭṭha*, also called *iṭṭhamajjhatta*, desirable-neutral), and the extremely desirable (*ati-iṭṭha*). While the desirable object is thus subdivided into two, all undesirable objects are comprised within a single class called simply "the undersirable."

According to the Abhidhamma philosophy, this distinction in the quality of objects pertains to the intrinsic nature of the object itself; it is not a variable determined by the individual temperament and preferences of the experiencer. The *Sammohavinodanī*, the commentary to the *Vibhanga*, contends that when a person considers a desirable object to be undesirable, or an undesirable object to be desirable, he does so due to a perversion of perception (*saññāvipallāsa*). The object itself, however, remains inherently desirable or undesirable independently of the perceiver's personal preferences. The *Sammohavinodanī* states that the distinction between the intrinsically desirable and undesirable obtains by way of the average being (*majjhima-satta*): "It is distinguishable according to what is found desirable at one time and undesirable at another time by average (men such as) accountants, government officials, burgesses, land owners and merchants."[5]

Whether on a given occasion one experiences an undesirable, a moderately desirable, or an extremely desirable object is governed by one's past kamma. Thus the object experienced provides the opportunity for kamma to ripen in the form of resultant states of consciousness (*vipākacitta*). The resultant cittas accord with the nature of the object spontaneously, without deliberation, just as a facial reflection in a mirror accords with the features of the face.

Through the force of unwholesome kamma one encounters an undesirable object, and thus the resultant cittas in the cognitive process by which that object is cognized will be generated by the maturation of that unwholesome kamma. In this case the sense consciousness, reception, investigation, and registration cittas are necessarily unwholesome-resultants (*akusalavipāka*). The accompanying feeling is always equanimity (*upekkhā*), except in the case of body-consciousness, which is accompanied by pain.

Conversely, a desirable-neutral or a very desirable object is encountered through the force of wholesome kamma, and the resultant cittas in the cognitive process will be generated by the maturation of that wholesome kamma. In this case the same four resultant positions will be occupied by wholesome-resultants (*kusalavipāka*). These cittas will generally be accompanied by equanimity, except that body-consciousness is accompanied by pleasure and, in the experience of an extremely desirable object, investigation and registration are accompanied by joy.

When the object is undesirable, the function of registration is exercised exclusively by the unwholesome-resultant investigating consciousness. Registration in regard to a moderately desirable object is exercised by the wholesome-resultant investigating consciousness accompanied by equanimity or by one of the four great resultants accompanied by equanimity. When the object is very desirable, registration is generally performed by the investigating consciousness accompanied by joy or by one of the four great resultants accompanied by joy.

It should be noted that while the resultant cittas are governed by the nature of the object, the javanas are not, but vary in accordance with the temperament and proclivities of the experiencer. Even when the object is extremely desirable, the javanas may occur in the mode of indifference as wholesome or unwholesome cittas accompanied by equanimity; for example, at the sight of the Buddha a skeptic may experience cittas accompanied by doubt, while at the sight of a beautiful woman a meditative monk may experience wholesome cittas accompanied by knowledge and equanimity. It is even possible for javanas accompanied by aversion and displeasure to arise towards a very desirable object. Again, towards an undesirable object, the javanas may occur in the mode normally appropriate for a desirable object. Thus a masochist may respond to physical pain with cittas rooted in greed and accompanied by joy, while a meditative monk may contemplate a decaying corpse with wholesome cittas accompanied by knowledge and joy.

In this connection, too, etc.: This passage is included to show that it is not only the resultant cittas that accord with the object but also the Arahant's functional sense-sphere javanas. When an Arahant experiences an extremely desirable object, his javanas occur as one of the four functional cittas accompanied by joy and the registration cittas as one of the five resultants accompanied by joy. When he experiences an undesirable or desirable-neutral object, the javanas occur accompanied by equanimity and the registration cittas as one of the six resultants accompanied by equanimity.

Ledi Sayadaw points out that this correlation between the object and the functional javanas of Arahants is stated only with reference to the natural mode in which their javanas occur. However, with the appropriate mental determination, an Arahant can arouse cittas accompanied by equanimity towards an extremely desirable object and cittas accompanied by joy towards an undesirable object. Ledi Sayadaw quotes in this connection the Indriyabhāvanā Sutta (M.152/iii, 301-302):

Here, Ānanda, when a bhikkhu sees a form with the eye, there arises what is agreeable, there arises what is disagreeable, there arises what is both agreeable and disagreeable. If he wishes, he dwells perceiving what is repulsive as unrepulsive; if he wishes, he dwells perceiving what is unrepulsive as repulsive; ... if he wishes, he avoids both the repulsive and unrepulsive and dwells in equanimity, mindful and clearly comprehending.

§18 The Adventitious Bhavanga

Domanassasahagatajavanāvasāne ca pana tadārammaṇāni c' eva bhavangāni ca upekkhāsahagatān' eva bhavanti. Tasmā yadi somanassapaṭisandhikassa domanassasahagatajavanāvasāne tadārammaṇasambhavo natthi, tadā yaṁ kiñci paricitapubbaṁ parittārammaṇam ārabbha upekkhāsahagatasantīraṇaṁ uppajjati. Tam anantaritvā bhavangapāto va hotī ti pi vadanti ācariyā.

But at the end of javanas accompanied by displeasure, the registration mind-moments and the life-continuum are both accompanied by equanimity. Therefore, in the case of one whose rebirth-consciousness is accompanied by joy, if at the end of javanas accompanied by displeasure there is no occurrence of registration mind-moments, then, the teachers explain, there arises an investigating consciousness accompanied by equanimity apprehending any familiar trivial object. Immediately after that there is subsidence into the life-continuum.

Guide to §18

But at the end of javanas accompanied by displeasure, etc.: Because pleasant feeling and painful feeling are diametrical opposites, cittas accompanied by the one cannot arise in immediate succession to cittas accompanied by the other. However, cittas accompanied by either of these opposed feelings can be immediately preceded or followed by cittas accompanied by neutral feeling. Thus, when the javanas are accompanied by displeasure (*domanassa*), i.e. as cittas rooted in hatred, if there is occasion for registration cittas they must be accompanied by equanimity.[6] If there is no scope for registration cittas, javanas accompanied by displeasure will be followed immediately by the bhavanga only if the latter is accompanied by equanimous feeling.

Therefore, in the case of one, etc.: For someone whose bhavanga is one of the four great resultants accompanied by joy, if there are no registration cittas following a javana process accompanied by displeasure, the last javana citta cannot be followed by an immediate descent into the bhavanga, owing to the law that cittas with opposite feelings cannot arise in immediate succession. In such a case, the ancient teachers of the Abhidhamma hold that an investigating consciousness accompanied by equanimity occurs for a single mind-moment, serving as a buffer between the displeasure (= painful mental feeling) of the javana and the joy (= pleasant mental feeling) of the bhavanga. On such an occasion this citta does not perform the function of investigating. It takes an object different from that of the cognitive process—some unrelated sense-sphere object with which one is already familiar—and functions simply to pave the way back to the normal flow of the root bhavanga. This special citta is termed *āgantuka-bhavanga*, "the adventitious life-continuum."

§19 The Law of Registration

Tathā kāmāvacarajavanāvasāne kāmāvacarasattānaṁ kāmāvacaradhammesv' eva ārammaṇabhūtesu tadārammaṇaṁ icchantī ti.

Likewise, they hold that registration occurs (only) at the end of sense-sphere javanas, (only) to sense-sphere beings, only when sense-sphere phenomena become objects.

§20 Summary

Kāme javanasattārammaṇānaṁ niyame sati
Vibhūte 'timahante ca tadārammaṇam īritaṁ.

Ayam ettha tadārammaṇaniyamo.

Registration occurs, they say, in connection with clear and very great objects when there is certainty as regards sense-sphere javanas, beings, and objects.

Herein, this is the procedure of registration.

The Procedure of Javana (*javananiyama*)

§21 Sense-Sphere Javana

Javanesu ca parittajavanavīthiyaṁ kāmāvacarajavanāni sattakkhattuṁ chakkhattum eva vā javanti. Mandappavattiyaṁ pana maraṇakālādīsu pañcavāram eva. Bhagavato pana yamaka-pāṭihāriyakālādīsu lahukappavattiyaṁ cattāri pañca vā paccavekkhaṇacittāni bhavantī ti pi vadanti.

Among the javanas, in a limited javana process, the sense-sphere javanas run only for seven or six times. But in the case of a feeble process such as at the time of dying, etc., they run only five times. To the Exalted One, at the time of the Twin Miracle and the like, when the procedure is rapid, only four or five occasions of reviewing consciousness occur, they also say.

Guide to §21

In a limited javana process: That is, in a sense-sphere cognitive process, the general rule is for the javanas to run seven times, though if the object is extremely weak they may run only six times. In the last javana process preceding death (and, the commentators add, at times such as fainting) the javanas run only five times, because of the weakness of the heart-base.

To the Exalted One, etc.: The Twin Miracle (*yamakapāṭihāriya*) was a feat of psychic power the Buddha performed on several occasions during his lifetime, when it helped to inspire others with confidence in his Enlightenment. By this miracle the Buddha displays his body as emitting streams of fire and water simultaneously (Pṭs.i,125) He performs this feat by entering into the fifth jhāna separately, in quick succession, in the fire kasina and the water kasina, and then determining to display fire and water issuing forth from his body. After emerging from each jhāna, the Buddha reviews its factors, and he does this by an extremely rapid javana process which runs for only four or five cittas. While the Twin Miracle itself is exercised by the fifth-jhāna direct-knowledge citta, the reviewing of the jhāna factors is performed by a sense-sphere process, the quickest possible in the sense sphere.

§22 Javana in Attainments

Ādikammikassa pana paṭhamakappanāyaṁ mahaggatajavanāni abhiññājavanāni ca sabbadā pi ekavāram eva javanti. Tato paraṁ bhavangapāto.

The sublime javanas for a beginner during the first (cognitive process of) absorption, and the direct-knowledge javanas always, run only once. Then comes subsidence into the life-continuum.

Cattāro pana magg' uppādā ekacittakkhaṇikā. Tato paraṁ dve tīṇi phalacittāni yathārahaṁ uppajjanti. Tato paraṁ bhavangapāto.

The arising of the four paths endures for only one mind-moment. Thereafter, two or three occasions of fruition consciousness arise according to the case. Then comes subsidence into the life-continuum.

Nirodhasamāpattikāle dvikkhattuṁ catutthāruppajavanaṁ javati. Tato paraṁ nirodhaṁ phusati. Vuṭṭhānakāle ca anāgāmiphalaṁ vā arahattaphalaṁ vā yathāraham ekavāraṁ uppajjitvā niruddhe bhavangapāto va hoti.

At the time of the attainment of cessation, the fourth immaterial javana runs twice and then contacts cessation. When emerging (from cessation), either the fruition consciousness of non-returning or the fruition consciousness of Arahantship arises accordingly for a single occasion. When it ceases, there is subsidence into the life-continuum.

Sabbatthā pi samāpattivīthiyaṁ pana bhavangasoto viya vīthiniyamo natthī ti katvā bahūni pi labbhantī ti.

In the cognitive process of attainments, as in the stream of the life-continuum, there is no fixed procedure regarding the processes. It should be understood that even many (sublime and supramundane) javanas take place (in immediate succession).

Guide to §22

The sublime javanas for a beginner, etc.: During the first cognitive process in the attainment of any of the jhānas, a sublime javana occurs for only a single occasion owing to its weakness due to the lack of repetition. The javana of the fifth jhāna that performs the role of direct knowledge (*abhiññā*) always occurs for only one occasion, even in those who have mastered it, because a single occasion is sufficient for it to accomplish its task.

The arising of the four paths, etc.: Each path consciousness also lasts for only one mind-moment, during which it accomplishes the abandoning of the defilements to be eradicated or attenuated by that particular path. In an individual with average faculties, the preliminary portion of the cognitive process of the path includes the moment called preparation (*parikamma*); for such a person two fruition cittas arise following the path. In an individual with keen faculties the moment of preparation is bypassed and thus three fruition cittas follow the path.

At the time of the attainment of cessation: Non-returners and Arahants who have mastery over the fine-material and immaterial jhānas can, by mental development, enter a meditative attainment in which the stream of consciousness and its concomitants is temporarily arrested. In such a state—known as *nirodhasamāpatti*, the attainment of cessation—all mental activity has ceased, though the body remains alive retaining its vital heat.

To attain cessation the meditator must enter each jhāna, emerge from it, and contemplate its factors with insight as impermanent, suffering, and non-self. After reaching the base of nothingness and emerging from it, the meditator performs certain preparatory tasks, and then resolves to enter the attainment. Thereupon two cittas of the fourth *arūpajjhāna* arise and cease, after which the stream of consciousness is cut off.

The duration of the attainment is governed by the meditator's prior determination, and with training can be extended up to seven days. On emerging there arises first one moment of fruition consciousness, either of non-returning or Arahantship, the former in the case of a non-returner, the latter in the case of an Arahant. Thereafter the mind lapses into the bhavanga. For details, see IX, §§43-44.

In the cognitive process of attainments, etc.: This is said to show that in the attainments of jhāna and fruition, through practice it is possible to extend the duration of the absorption. For beginners the attainment occurs for only one javana moment. With practice the attainment can gradually be increased to two, three, four javanas, etc., while for those who have achieved mastery over the attainment absorption cittas occur in unbroken succession for long periods of time, even for days on end.

§23 Summary

Sattakkhattuṁ parittāni maggābhiññā sakiṁ matā
Avasesāni labbhanti javanāni bahūni pi.

Ayam ettha javananiyamo.

It should be known that limited javanas arise seven times, the path and direct knowledge only once, the rest (sublime and supramundane) many times.

Herein, this is the procedure of javanas.

Analysis by way of Individuals (*puggalabheda*)

§24 Rootless and Double Rooted

Duhetukānam ahetukānañ ca pan' ettha kriyājavanāni c'eva appanājavanāni ca na labbhanti. Tathā ñāṇasampayuttavipākāni ca sugatiyaṁ. Duggatiyaṁ pana ñāṇavippayuttāni ca mahāvipākāni na labbhanti.

Herein, to those with double-rooted and rootless (rebirth consciousness), functional javanas and absorption javanas do not arise. Likewise, in a blissful plane, resultants accompanied by knowledge also do not arise. But in a woeful plane great resultants dissociated from knowledge are not found.

Guide to §24

Those beings for whom the functions of rebirth, bhavanga, and death are performed by either of the two types of investigating consciousness accompanied by equanimity have a rootless (*ahetuka*) rebirth consciousness. Those for whom these functions are performed by one of the great resultants dissociated from knowledge have a double-rooted (*duhetuka*) rebirth consciousness, the root of non-delusion or wisdom being absent. In such beings the functional javanas, which are exclusive to Arahants, cannot arise, nor can such beings attain absorption either by way of jhānas or the path. Moreover, the only cittas that can perform the role of registration for these beings are the three types of rootless investigating consciousness.

In a blissful plane, such as the human world or the sense-sphere heavens, for those reborn by a relinking citta devoid of wisdom, owing to the inferiority of the rebirth consciousness three-rooted great resultants do not arise in the role of registration; for these beings, the registration cittas are only rootless or double-rooted. In a woeful plane, where the rebirth consciousness is invariably rootless, even two-rooted great resultants do not perform the role of registration; only the rootless resultants can arise in this role.

§25 Triple Rooted

Tihetukesu ca khīṇāsavānaṁ kusalākusalajavanāni na labbhanti. Tathā sekkhaputhujjanānaṁ kriyājavanāni. Diṭṭhigatasampayutta-vicikicchājavanāni ca sekkhānaṁ. Anāgāmipuggalānaṁ pana paṭighajavanāni ca na labbhanti. Lokuttarajavanāni ca yathārahaṁ ariyānam eva samuppajjantī ti.

Amongst those with triple-rooted (rebirth consciousness), to Arahants, no wholesome or unwholesome javanas arise. Similarly, to trainees and worldlings, functional javanas do not arise. Nor do javanas associated with wrong view and doubt arise to the trainees. To non-returner individuals there are no javanas associated with aversion. But the supramundane javanas are experienced only by noble ones according to their respective capacities.

Guide to §25

Those reborn by a relinking consciousness associated with knowledge are said to have a triple-rooted rebirth (*tihetuka*). These individuals may be worldlings, trainees, or Arahants (who have, of course, become such after taking rebirth, not by virtue of their rebirth consciousness).

At the path of stream-entry, the defilements of wrong views and doubt are eradicated; thus javanas associated with wrong views or doubt cannot arise in trainees. Non-returners have eliminated the defilement of aversion, and therefore no longer experience cittas rooted in aversion.

§26 Summary

Asekkhānaṁ catucattāḷīsa sekkhānam uddise
Chapaññās' āvasesānaṁ catupaññāsa sambhavā.

Ayam ettha puggalabhedo.

According to circumstances, it is said, those beyond training experience forty-four classes of consciousness, trainees fifty-six, and the rest fifty-four.

Herein, this is the analysis by way of individuals.

Guide to §26

Worldlings with a triple-rooted rebirth consciousness can experience a maximum of fifty-four cittas: 12 unwholesome + 17 wholesome (minus the 4 paths) + 23 sense-sphere resultants + 2 adverting.

However, beings arisen in the woeful planes, having a rootless rebirth consciousness, experience only thirty-seven cittas: 12 unwholesome + 8 great wholesome + 15 rootless resultants + 2 adverting. Those taking rebirth in a happy plane with either a rootless or a double-rooted rebirth consciousness also experience the four great resultants dissociated from knowledge, making a total of forty-one. The total of fifty-four for those with triple roots includes all nine jhānas; this total should, of course, be reduced for those who lack particular jhānas.

At the path of stream-entry, the defilements of wrong view and doubt are eradicated; thus the four cittas associated with wrong view and the one citta accompanied by doubt are eliminated. Stream-enterers and once-returners can experience the following fifty cittas, inclusive of the jhānas: 7 unwholesome + 17 wholesome + 23 sense-sphere resultants + 2 adverting + 1 fruition; the latter will be either the fruition of stream-entry or the fruition of once-returning, according to their respective level. Non-returners, having further eliminated aversion, no longer experience the two cittas rooted in hatred and experience the fruition of non-returning, a maximum of forty-eight. The fifty-six cittas mentioned in the text for trainees is arrived at by grouping the three fruitions together and adding the four path cittas.

Arahants, referred to here as "those beyond training" (*asekkha*), have eliminated all defilements and thus no longer experience any unwholesome cittas. The forty-four cittas they can experience are: 18 rootless + 8 great functionals + 8 great resultants + 5 fine-material functionals + 4 immaterial functionals + 1 fruition of Arahantship.

These figures are for those in the sense-sphere plane. As the next section will show, they should be reduced for those in the fine-material and immaterial planes by subtracting the cittas that cannot arise in those planes.

For a tabular presentation of §26 and §27 combined, see Table 4.5.

Analysis by way of Planes (*bhūmibheda*)

§27 Analysis

Kāmāvacarabhūmiyaṁ pan' etāni sabbāni pi vīthicittāni yathārahaṁ upalabbhanti.

Rūpāvacarabhūmiyaṁ paṭighajavana-tadārammaṇa-vajjitāni.

Arūpāvacarabhūmiyaṁ paṭhamamagga-rūpāvacara-hasana-heṭṭhimāruppa-vajjitāni ca labbhanti.

In the sense-sphere plane all these foregoing cognitive processes occur according to circumstances.

In the fine-material-sphere plane (all occur) with the exception of javanas connected with aversion and registration moments.

TABLE 4.5: INDIVIDUALS, PLANES, AND CITTAS

INDIV. TYPE	SENSE-SPHERE PLANE	FINE-MATER. PLANE	IMMATERIAL PLANE
Woeful Rootless Reb. Consness.	12 unwh., 17 rtls., 8wh. (37)	....	....
Blissful Rootless Reb. Consness.	Above + 4 btf. rst. dissoc. knwl. (41)	....	....
2-rooted Reb. Consness.	Same as above (41)	....	....
3-rooted Worldling	Above + 4 btf. rst. assoc. knwl. + 9 sbl. (54)	10 unwh., 11 rtls., 8 SS wh., 9 sbl. wh., 5 sbl. rst. (43)	10 unwh., m-d-ad., 8 SS wh., 4 sbl. wh., 4 sbl. rst. (27)
Stream-enterer	Above, less 5 unwh., + S.E. frt. (50)	Above, less 5 unwh., + S.E. frt. (39)	Above, less 5 unwh., + S.E. frt. (23)
Once-returner	Above, but with O.R. frt. (50)	Above, but with O.R. frt. (39)	Above, but with O.R. frt. (23)
Non-returner	Above, less 2 unwh., with N.R. frt. (48)	Above, but with N.R. frt. (39)	Above, but with N.R. frt. (23)
Arahant	18 rtls., 8 SS btf. fnc., 8 SS btf. rst., 9 sbl. fnc., Arh. frt. (44)	12 rtls., 8 SS btf. fnc., 9 sbl. fnc., 5 sbl. rst., Arh. frt. (35)	M-d-ad., 8 SS btf. fnc., 4 sbl. fnc., 4 sbl. rst., Arh. frt. (18)

NOTE: The above classification does not take into account the momentary path cittas, which mark the attainment of the path.

In the immaterial-sphere plane (all occur) with the (further) exception of the first path, fine-material-sphere consciousness, smiling consciousness, and the lower immaterial classes of consciousness.

Guide to §27

In the present passage, "plane" (*bhūmi*) refers to planes of existence, not to planes of consciousness. Cittas connected with aversion do not occur in the fine-material plane because aversion was well suppressed in the preliminary training for attaining the jhāna. Aversion and registration are also absent in the immaterial plane. Smiling cannot occur without a physical body. Those reborn into any immaterial realm do not attain the fine-material-sphere jhānas or lower immaterial-sphere jhānas.

§28 Special Cases

Sabbatthā pi ca taṁtaṁ pasādarahitānaṁ taṁtaṁ dvārikavīthicittāni na labbhant' eva.

Asaññasattānaṁ pana sabbathā pi cittappavatti natth' evā ti.

In all planes, to those who are devoid of particular sense organs, cognitive processes connected with the corresponding doors do not arise.

To the non-percipient beings there is absolutely no cognitive process whatsoever.

Guide to §28

To those who are devoid of particular sense organs: Those who are blind, deaf, etc., in the sense-sphere plane and the beings in the fine-material plane, who lack the senses of smell, taste and touch.

To the non-percipient beings: These beings are completely devoid of consciousness and thus have no cignitive process. See V, §31.

§29 Summary

Asīti vīthicittāni kāme rūpe yathārahaṁ
Catusaṭṭhi tathāruppe dvecattāḷīsa labbhare.

Ayam ettha bhūmivibhāgo.

In the sense-sphere plane, according to circumstances, eighty kinds of process consciousness are found, in the fine-material plane there are sixty-four, and in the immaterial plane, forty-two.

Herein, this is the analysis by way of planes.

Guide to §29

The eighty process cittas found in the sense-sphere plane include all cittas except the nine sublime resultants, which never occur in a cognitive process.

The sixty-four process cittas in the fine-material plane are as follows: 10 unwholesome (excluding the two with aversion) + 9 rootless resultants (excluding the pairs of nose -, tongue -, and body-consciousness) + 3 rootless functionals + 16 great wholesome and functionals + 10 fine-material wholesome and functionals + 8 immaterial wholesome and functionals + 8 supramundane.

The forty-two in the immaterial plane are as follows: 10 unwholesome + 1 mind-door adverting + 16 great wholesome and functionals + 8 immaterial wholesome and functionals + 7 supramundane (excluding the path of stream-entry).

§30 Conclusion

Icc' evaṁ chadvārikacittappavatti yathāsambhavaṁ bhavangantaritā yāvatāyukam abbocchinnā pavattati.

Thus the cognitive process connected with the six doors according to circumstances continues on uninterrupted as long as life lasts, intercepted by the life-continuum.

Iti Abhidhammatthasangahe
Vīthisangahavibhāgo nāma
catuttho paricchedo.

Thus ends the fourth chapter
in the Manual of Abhidhamma entitled
the Compendium of the Cognitive Process.

CHAPTER V
COMPENDIUM OF THE PROCESS-FREED
(*Vīthimuttasangahavibhāga*)

§1 Introductory Verse

Vīthicittavasen' evaṁ pavattiyam udīrito
Pavattisangaho nāma sandhiyaṁ dāni vuccati.

Thus the compendium of the occurrence (of consciousness) has been explained by way of the cognitive process during the course of existence. Now the compendium of the occurrence (of consciousness) at rebirth will be told.

Guide to §1

In the preceding chapter the author explained the active aspect of the flow of consciousness, its occurrence in cognitive processes during the course of a lifetime. In the present chapter he will explain the occurrence of passive or "process-freed" consciousness. Although, in the opening verse, the author specifies "at rebirth" (*sandhiyaṁ*), this chapter will deal with process-freed consciousness in the roles of bhavanga and death as well.

§2 Enumeration of Categories

Catasso bhūmiyo, catubbidhā paṭisandhi, cattāri kammāni, catudhā maraṇ'uppatti cā ti vīthimuttasangahe cattāri catukkāni veditabbāni.

In the compendium of process-freed consciousness, four sets of four should be understood as follows:

(i) four planes of existence;
(ii) four modes of rebirth-linking;
(iii) four kinds of kamma; and
(iv) fourfold advent of death.

TABLE 5.1: THE 31 REALMS OF EXISTENCE

Plane			Realm	Life-Span	
Immaterial-Sphere Plane 4			31. Neither perception nor non-perception	84,000	G.A.
			30. Nothingness	60,000	"
			29. Infinite consciousness	40,000	"
			28. Infinite space	20,000	"
Fine-material-Sphere Plane 16	4th Jhāna Plane	Pure Abodes 23-27	27. Highest Pure Abode	16,000	G.A.
			26. Clear-sighted " "	8,000	"
			25. Beautiful " "	4,000	"
			24. Serene " "	2,000	"
			23. Durable " "	1,000	"
			22. Non-percipient Realm	500	"
			21. Great Reward	500	"
	3rd Jhāna Plane		20. Steady Aura	64	G.A.
			19. Infinite Aura	32	"
			18. Minor Aura	16	"
	2nd Jhāna Plane		17. Radiant Lustre	8	G.A.
			16. Infinite Lustre	4	"
			15. Minor Lustre	2	"
	1st Jhāna Plane		14. Mahā Brahmā	1	I.A.
			13. Brahmā's Ministers	1 / 2	"
			12. Brahma's Retinue	1 / 3	"

TABLE 5.1 — Continued

PLANE	REALM		LIFE-SPAN
Sense - Sphere Plane 11	Sensuous Blissful Plane	11. Paranimmitavasavatti	16,00 C.Y.
		10. Nimmānarati	8,000 "
		9. Tusita	4,000 "
		8. Yāma	2,000 "
		7. Tāvatiṁsa	1,000 "
		6. Cātummahārājika	500 "
		5. Human	Indefinite
	Woeful Plane	4. Asura	Indefinite
		3. Peta	"
		2. Animal	"
		1. Hell	"

G.A. = great aeon
I.A. = incalculable aeon
C.Y. = celestial years

Guide to §2

The compendium of process-freed consciousness opens with a survey of the topography of the phenomenal world, charting the planes of existence and the various realms within each plane (see Table 5.1). The author undertakes this survey before examining the types of process-freed consciousness because the external universe, according to the Abhidhamma, is an outer reflection of the internal cosmos of mind, registering in concrete manifest form the subtle gradations in states of consciousness. This does not mean that the Abhidhamma reduces the outer world to a dimension of mind in the manner of philosophical idealism. The outer world is quite real and possesses objective existence. However, the outer world is always a world apprehended by consciousness, and the type of consciousness determines the nature of the world that appears. Consciousness and the world are mutually dependent and inextricably connected to such an extent that the hierarchical structure of the realms of existence exactly reproduces and corresponds to the hierarchical structure of consciousness.

Because of this correspondence, each of the two—the objective hierarchy of existence and the inner gradation of consciousness—provides the key to understanding the other. The reason why a living being is reborn into a particular realm is because he has generated, in a previous life, the kamma or volitional force of consciousness that leads to rebirth into that realm, and thus in the final analysis all the realms of existence are formed, fashioned, and sustained by the mental activity of living beings. At the same time these realms provide the stage for consciousness to continue its evolution in a new personality and under a fresh set of circumstances.

Each realm is keyed to a particular type of rebirth consciousness, which becomes the bhavanga or life-continuum flowing on through the course of existence until the termination of the life-process at death. Thus in dependence on kamma ripening in the sense-sphere plane, a sense-sphere rebirth consciousness is generated and sense-sphere existence becomes manifest. In dependence on kamma ripening in the fine-material plane, a fine-material rebirth consciousness is generated and fine-material existence becomes manifest. And in dependence on kamma ripening in the immaterial plane, an immaterial rebirth consciousness is generated and immaterial existence becomes manifest. As the Buddha says: "Kamma is the field, consciousness is the seed, and craving is the moisture, for the consciousness of beings obstructed by ignorance and fettered by craving to be established in a new realm of existence—either low, middling, or superior" (A.3:76/i,223). As determined by past kamma, the seed of consciousness falls into an appropriate realm, sends down roots, and nurtured by its store of kammic accumulations, unfolds according to its hidden potentials.

The Four Planes of Existence (*bhūmicatukka*)

§3 Overview

Tattha apāyabhūmi, kāmasugatibhūmi, rūpāvacarabhūmi, arūpāvacarabhūmi cā ti catasso bhūmiyo nāma.

Of these, the four planes are:

(i) the woeful plane;
(ii) the sensuous blissful plane;
(iii) the fine-material-sphere plane;
(iv) the immaterial-sphere plane.

Guide to §3

The four planes: Though a distinction is made here between the woeful plane and the sensuous blissful plane, both planes are actually subdivisions of the sense-sphere plane, as is pointed out at the end of §5.

§4 The Woeful Plane (*apāyabhūmi*)

Tāsu nirayo, tiracchānayoni, pettivisayo, asurakāyo cā ti apāyabhūmi catubbidhā hoti.

Among these, the woeful plane is fourfold, namely:

(i) hell;
(ii) the animal kingdom;
(iii) the sphere of petas; and
(iv) the host of asuras.

Guide to §4

The woeful plane: The word *apāya* means literally that which is devoid (*apa*) of happiness (*aya*). This is the collective name for those realms of existence in which pain and misery greatly exceed happiness. They are the realms where evildoers are reborn as a consequence of their evil deeds.

Hell (*niraya*) is the lowest plane of existence in the Buddhist cosmos, the place of the most intense suffering. It is said that the beings in hell have to suffer the results of their evil deeds from the beginning of their lives until the end, without a moment's respite. The commentators state that there are eight great hells, of increasing intensity of torment. They are named Sañjīva, Kāḷasutta, Sanghāta, Roruva, Mahā Roruva, Tāpana, Mahā Tāpana, and Avīci. Of these, Avīci is the lowest and most terrible. Each great hell is surrounded on each of its four sides by five minor hells, bringing the total to 168 hells.

The animal kingdom: Buddhism maintains that the animal realm is a woeful plane into which beings may be reborn as a result of evil kamma. According to the Buddha, human beings who have committed evil may be reborn as animals, and animals may, as a result of some accumulated good kamma, be reborn as human beings or even as gods in a heavenly world. Although the animal realm does not involve as much misery as the hells, it is included in the woeful planes because the suffering there greatly exceeds the amount of happiness and because it does not provide suitable conditions for the performance of meritorious deeds.

The sphere of petas: The word *peta*, often translated as "hungry ghosts," refers to a class of beings who are tormented by intense hunger and thirst as well as other afflictions from which they cannot find relief. The petas have no world of their own. They live in the same world as human beings—in forests, bogs, cemeteries, etc.—though they remain invisible to humans except when they display themselves or are perceived by those with the divine eye.

The host of asuras: The word *asura,* often translated "titans," is used to refer to various classes of beings. As a realm within the woeful plane the commentators identify the asuras with a group of tormented spirits similar to the petas. These asuras are to be distinguished from the asuras that combat the gods of the Tāvatiṁsa heaven, who are included among the Tāvatiṁsa gods.

§5 The Sensuous Blissful Plane *(kāmasugatibhūmi)*

Manussā, cātummahārājikā, tāvatiṁsā, yāmā, tusitā, nimmānarati, paranimmitavasavattī cā ti kāmasugatibhūmi sattavidhā hoti.

Sā pan' āyaṁ ekādasavidhā pi kāmāvacarabhūmicc' eva sankhaṁ gacchati.

The sensuous blissful plane is sevenfold, namely:

(i) the human realm;
(ii) the Realm of the Four Great Kings;
(iii) the Realm of the Thirty-three Gods;
(iv) the Realm of the Yāma Gods;
(v) the Delightful Realm;

(vi) the Realm of the Gods who rejoice in (their own) Creations;
(vii) the Realm of the Gods who lord over the Creations of Others.

These eleven realms constitute the sense-sphere plane.

Guide to §5

The human realm: The word *manussa*, human, literally means those who have sharp or developed minds. As the human mind is very sharp, this makes man much more capable of weighty moral and immoral action than any other class of living beings. The human being is capable of development up to Buddhahood, and also of such serious crimes as matricide and parricide. The human realm is a mixture of both pain and pleasure, suffering and happiness, but because if offers the opportunity for attaining the highest happiness, it is considered a blissful realm.

The Realm of the Four Great Kings: The next six realms are the sense-sphere heavens, the abodes of the *devas* or gods.These planes involve a longer life-span than the human world and a richer variety of sensual pleasures which, however, are inevitably impermanent.

The Cātummahārājikā heaven, the Realm of the Four Great Kings, has four divisions corresponding to the four directions. Each is ruled over by its own guardian deity and inhabited by a different class of demigods. To the east, the divine king Dhataraṭṭha rules over the *gandhabbas,* the celestial musicians; to the south, Virūḷhaka presides over the *kumbhaṇḍas*, the gnomic caretakers of forests, mountains, and hidden treasures; in the western region the divinity Virūpakkha rules over the *nāgas*, demigods in the form of dragons; and in the north reigns Vessavaṇa, ruler of the *yakkhas* or spirits.

The Realm of the Thirty-three Gods: This heaven, Tāvatiṁsa, is so named because according to legend, a group of thirty-three noble-minded men who dedicated their lives to the welfare of others were reborn here as the presiding deity and his thirty-two assistants. The chief of this realm is Sakka, also known as Indra, who resides in the Vejayanta Palace in the realm's capital city, Sudassana.

The Realm of the Yāma Gods, etc.: Each of these heavens is depicted in the celestial hierarchy as situated above its predecessor. The heaven of the *Yāma* gods is a realm of great happiness presided over by their ruler, the divine king Suyāma or Yāma. *Tusita*, the Delightful Realm, is the abode of a Bodhisatta in his last existence before attaining Buddhahood. The gods in the *Nimmānarati* heaven have the power to create objects of sensual enjoyment by thought, in accordance with their desires. The gods of the *Paranimmitavasavatti* realm cannot create such objects themselves, but they control the objects of enjoyment created for their use by their attendants.

§6 The Fine-material-Sphere Plane (*rupāvacarabhūmi*)

Brahmapārisajjā, brahmapurohitā, mahābrahmā cā ti paṭhamajjhānabhūmi.

Parittābhā, appamāṇābhā, ābhassarā cā ti dutiyajjhānabhūmi.

Parittasubhā, appamāṇasubhā, subhakiṇhā cā ti tatiyajjhānabhūmi.

Vehapphalā, asaññasattā, suddhāvāsā cā ti catutthajjhānabhūmī ti rūpāvacarabhūmi soḷasavidhā hoti.

Avihā, atappā, sudassā, sudassī, akaniṭṭhā cā ti suddhāvāsabhūmi pañcavidhā hoti.

The fine-material-sphere plane is sixteenfold, namely:

I. The first jhāna plane: (i) the Realm of Brahmā's Retinue; (ii) the Realm of Brahmā's Ministers; and (iii) the Mahā Brahmā Realm.

II. The second jhāna plane: (iv) the Realm of Minor Lustre; (v) the Realm of Infinite Lustre; and (vi) the Realm of Radiant Lustre.

III. The third jhāna plane: (vii) the Realm of Minor Aura; (viii) the Realm of Infinite Aura; and (ix) the Realm of Steady Aura.

IV. The fourth jhāna plane: (x) the Realm of Great Reward; (xi) the realm of non-percipient beings; and the Pure Abodes.

The Pure Abodes are fivefold: (xii) the Durable Realm; (xiii) the Serene Realm; (xiv) the Beautiful Realm; (xv) the Clear-sighted Realm; and (xvi) the Highest Realm.

Guide to §6

The fine-material-sphere plane is sixteenfold: The fine-material-sphere plane is the realm of rebirth for those who have developed, during their life, one or another of the fine-material jhānas, and at the time of death still possess that jhāna in the sense that they still have potential access to it, not having lost it owing to negligence and obsession by obstructive states. This plane is divided into four tiers in accordance with the four jhānas of the Suttanta system. In the Suttas only four jhānas are mentioned, as the transition from the first to the second jhāna takes place by the simultaneous abandoning of initial application (*vitakka*) and sustained application (*vicāra*). Thus the second-jhāna plane of existence corresponds to the second and third jhānas of the Abhidhamma system, the third-jhāna plane to the fourth jhāna, and the fourth-jhāna plane to the fifth jhāna.

Each of the four jhāna planes is divided into three realms, except that in the fourth-jhāna plane the last realm is subdivided into five abodes. The principle according to which rebirth takes place into the jhāna realms is explained at §31 below.

The Pure Abodes (*suddhāvāsa*) are five realms of rebirth open only to non-returners, noble disciples who have attained the third stage of sanctity. Those who take rebirth in these abodes never return to the lower realms but attain final deliverance there.

§7 The Immaterial-Sphere Plane (*arūpāvacarabhūmi*)

Ākāsānañcāyatanabhūmi, viññāṇañcāyatanabhūmi, ākiñcaññāyatanabhūmi, n'evasaññān'āsaññāyatanabhūmi cā ti arūpabhūmi catubbidhā hoti.

The immaterial-sphere plane is fourfold, namely:

(i) the realm of infinite space;
(ii) the realm of infinite consciousness;
(iii) the realm of nothingness; and
(iv) the realm of neither-perception-nor-non-perception.

Guide to §7

These are the four planes of rebirth for those who, at the time of death, possess an immaterial meditative attainment. Each immaterial attainment leads to rebirth into the corresponding realm.

§8 By way of Individuals

Puthujjanā na labbhanti suddhāvāsesu sabbathā
Sotāpannā ca sakadāgāmino cā pi puggalā.
Ariyā n'opalabbhanti asaññāpāyabhūmisu
Sesaṭṭhānesu labbhanti ariyā' nariyā pi ca.

Idam ettha bhūmicatukkaṁ.

In the Pure Abodes no worldlings, stream-enterers, or once-returners are found in any way.

Noble ones are not found in the non-percipient realm and in the woeful planes. In other planes are found both noble ones and non-noble ones.

Herein, these are the four planes.

The Four Types of Rebirth-Linking (*paṭisandhicatukka*)

§9 Overview

Apāyapaṭisandhi, kāmasugatipaṭisandhi, rūpāvacarapaṭisandhi, arūpāvacarapaṭisandhi cā ti catubbidhā hoti paṭisandhi nāma.

Rebirth-linking is fourfold, namely:

(i) rebirth-linking in the woeful plane;
(ii) rebirth-linking in the sensuous blissful plane;
(iii) rebirth-linking in the fine-material sphere; and
(iv) rebirth-linking in the immaterial sphere.

§10 Rebirth-Linking in the Woeful Plane

Tattha akusalavipāk' opekkhāsahagata-santīraṇaṁ apāya-bhūmiyaṁ okkantikkhaṇe paṭisandhi hutvā tato paraṁ bhavangaṁ pariyosāne cavanaṁ hutvā vocchijjati. Ayam ekā v' āpāyapaṭisandhi nāma.

Therein, the unwholesome-resultant investigating consciousness accompanied by equanimity becomes the rebirth-linking (consciousness) at the moment of descent into the woeful plane. Then it lapses into the life-continuum and finally it becomes the death (consciousness) and is cut off. This is the one single woeful rebirth-linking.

§11 Rebirth-Linking in the Sensuous Blissful Plane

Kusalavipāk' opekkhāsahagata-santīraṇaṁ pana kāmasugatiyaṁ manussānañ c' eva jaccandhādihīnasattānaṁ bhummassitānañ ca vinipātikāsurānaṁ paṭisandhi-bhavanga-cutivasena pavattati.

Mahāvipākāni pan' aṭṭha sabbatthā pi kāmasugatiyaṁ paṭisandhi-bhavanga-cutivasena pavattanti.

Imā nava kāmasugatipaṭisandhiyo nāma.

Sā pan' āyaṁ dasavidhā pi kāmāvacarapaṭisandhicc' eva sankhaṁ gacchati.

The wholesome-resultant investigating consciousness accompanied by equanimity occurs as the rebirth-linking, life-continuum and death (consciousness) of deformed human beings of the sensuous blissful plane, such as those born blind, etc., as well as of (some) earth-bound (deities) and of (some) fallen asuras.

The eight great resultants act as the rebirth-linking, life-continuum, and death (consciousness) everywhere in the sensuous blissful plane.

These nine comprise rebirth-linking in the sensuous blissful plane.

The (foregoing) ten modes are reckoned as sense-sphere rebirth-linking.

Guide to §§10-11

For a detailed explanation of the types of consciousness that perform the functions of rebirth-linking, life-continuum, and death, see III, §9.

Such as those born blind, etc.: The "etc." (*ādi*) here is intended to include those born deaf, mute, mentally retarded, mentally deranged, and also those born as eunuchs, hermaphrodites, and sexually indeterminate. The commentators explain that the expression "born blind" refers to one whose rebirth-consciousness is produced by a kamma that, owing to deficiency of merit, is incapable of generating eyes with the capacity for vision. The expression does not apply to those who emerge from the womb blind because of some accident or illness incurred during the stay in the womb, for blindness under such circumstances may occur also to those with a double- or triple-rooted rebirth consciousness. The same principle applies to those born deaf, etc. In all such cases the rebirth consciousness is invariably rootless only when the defect is already inherent in the kamma that generates rebirth.

(Some) earth-bound (deities): Buddhist cosmology recognizes a class of deities who do not dwell in the heavenly realms but in proximity to the earth, in remote regions such as forests, mountains, and shrines. These beings are called earth-gods (*bhummadeva*). While the more powerful deities in this class may possess double- or triple-rooted types of rebirth consciousness, they are often accompanied by retinues which may include deities of defective merit who manage to maintain their lives with difficulty. It is these, according to Ledi Sayadaw, that are intended here as the earth-bound deities reborn with a rootless rebirth consciousness.

And (some) fallen asuras: These beings are said to dwell in villages or in the vicinity of villages living off the remains of food discarded by the residents. They also haunt or oppress human beings when they fail to obtain food.

The (foregoing) ten modes: The ten modes of sense-sphere rebirth-linking are obtained by way of the ten types of consciousness that perform the function of rebirth-linking in the sense sphere.

§12 Sensuous Plane Life-Spans

Tesu catunnaṁ apāyānaṁ manussānaṁ vinipātikāsurānañ ca āyuppamāṇagaṇanāya niyamo natthi.

Cātummahārājikānaṁ pana devānaṁ dibbāni pañcavassasatāni āyuppamāṇaṁ. Manussagaṇanāya navutivassasatasahassappamāṇaṁ hoti.

Tato catugguṇaṁ tāvatiṁsānaṁ, tato catugguṇaṁ yāmānaṁ, tato catugguṇaṁ tusitānaṁ, tato catugguṇaṁ nimmānaratīnaṁ, tato catugguṇaṁ paranimmitavasavattīnaṁ devānaṁ āyuppamāṇaṁ.

> *Navasatañ c'ekavīsa vassānaṁ koṭiyo tathā*
> *Vassasatasahassāni saṭṭhi ca vasavattisu.*

There is no definite limit to the duration of life of beings in the four woeful planes, or amongst humans and fallen asuras.

The life-span of Gods of the Realm of the Four Great Kings is five hundred celestial years, that is, according to human reckoning, 9,000,000 years.

The life-span of the Thirty-three Gods is four times this amount. The life-span of Yāma Gods is four times that of the Thirty-three. Four times that amount is the life-span of the Delightful Gods. Four times that amount is the life-span of the Gods who rejoice in their Creations. Four times that amount is the life-span of the Gods who lord over the Creations of Others.

In the plane of Gods who lord over Others' Creations, the life-span, according to human reckoning, is nine-hundred and twenty-one koṭis of years plus sixty-hundred-thousand years (9,216,000,000).

Guide to §12

There is no definite limit: In the four planes of woe the life-span is highly variable, depending on the potency of the evil kamma that produces rebirth there. Thus in the hells some undergo torment only for a few days and then pass on to rebirth elsewhere, while others must endure torment for millions of years. In the human realm, too, the life-span can vary from minutes to over a hundred years. Further, according to Buddhist cosmology, the average span of human life also varies over time, ranging between a minimum of ten years and a maximum of many thousands of years.

Celestial years: The *Vibhanga* (§1023) states that one celestial day (CD) in the Cātummāhārājika heaven equals fifty human years (HY);

thirty such days amount to one celestial month; twelve such months constitute one celestial year (CY). In the Tāvatiṁsa heaven one celestial day equals one hundred human years; in the Yāma heaven, two hundred human years; and so on, doubling in each higher heaven.

On this basis, the life-spans in the six heavenly worlds would be computed as in the following table:

TABLE 5.2: LIFE-SPANS IN THE SENSE-SPHERE HEAVENS

Realm	CD	CY	HY
1 Cātummahārājika	50 HY	500	9 million
2 Tāvatiṁsa	100 HY	1000	36 million
3 Yāma	200 HY	2000	144 million
4 Tusita	400 HY	4000	576 million
5 Nimmānarati	800 HY	8000	2,304 million
6 Paranimmitavasavatti	1,600 HY	16,000	9,216 million

§13 Rebirth-Linking in the Fine-material Sphere

Paṭhamajjhānavipākaṁ paṭhamajjhāna bhūmiyaṁ paṭisandhi-bhavanga-cutivasena pavattati.

Tathā dutiyajjhānavipākaṁ tatiyajjhānavipākañ ca dutiyajjhānabhūmiyaṁ, catutthajjhānavipākaṁ tatiyajjhānabhūmiyaṁ, pañcamajjhānavipākaṁ catutthajjhānabhūmiyaṁ. Asaññasattānaṁ pana rūpam eva paṭisandhi hoti. Tathā tato paraṁ pavattiyaṁ cavanakāle ca rūpam eva pavattitvā nirujjhati.

Imā cha rūpāvacarapaṭisandhiyo nāma.

The first jhāna resultant occurs in the first jhāna plane as the rebirth-linking, life-continuum, and death (consciousness); similarly, the second jhāna resultant and the third jhāna resultant (occur thus) in the second jhāna plane; the fourth jhāna resultant in the third jhāna plane; the fifth jhāna resultant in the fourth jhāna plane. But for non-percipient beings material form itself occurs as rebirth-linking. Similarly thereafter, during the course of existence and at the moment of death, only material form exists and perishes.

These are the six modes of rebirth-linking in the fine-material sphere.

§14 Life-Spans in the Fine-material Sphere

Tesu brahmapārisajjānaṁ devānaṁ kappassa tatiyo bhāgo āyuppamāṇaṁ. Brahmapurohitānaṁ upaḍḍhakappo, mahābrahmānaṁ eko kappo, parittābhānaṁ dve kappāni, appamāṇābhānaṁ cattāri kappāni, ābhassarānaṁ aṭṭha kappāni, parittasubhānaṁ soḷasa kappāni, appamāṇasubhānaṁ dvattiṁsa kappāni, subhakiṇhānaṁ catusaṭṭhi kappāni, vehapphalānaṁ asaññasattānañ ca pañcakappasatāni, avihānaṁ kappasahassāni, atappānaṁ dve kappasahassāni, sudassānaṁ cattāri kappasahassāni, sudassīnaṁ aṭṭha kappasahassāni, akaniṭṭhānaṁ soḷasa kappasahassāni āyuppamāṇaṁ.

Among these, the life-span of the Gods of Brahmā's Retinue is one-third of an aeon; of Brahmā's Ministers, half an aeon; of Mahā Brahmās, one aeon; of the Gods of Minor Lustre, two aeons; of Infinite Lustre, four aeons; of Radiant Lustre, eight aeons; of Minor Aura, sixteen aeons; of Infinite Aura, thirty-two aeons; of Steady Aura, sixty-four aeons; of Great Reward and non-percipient beings, 500 aeons; of Durable Gods, 1000 aeons; of Serene Gods, 2000 aeons; of Beautiful Gods, 4000 aeons; of Clear-sighted Gods, 8000 aeons; of the Highest Gods, 16,000 aeons.

Guide to §14

An aeon (*kappa*): The Buddhist texts speak of three kinds of aeon—an interim aeon, an incalculable aeon, and a great aeon. An interim aeon (*antarakappa*) is the period of time required for the life-span of human beings to rise from ten years to the maximum of many thousands of years, and then fall back to ten years. Twenty such interim aeons equal one incalculable aeon (*asankheyyakappa*), and four incalculable aeons constitute one great aeon (*mahākappa*). The length of a great aeon is said by the Buddha to be longer than the time it would take for a man to wear away a mountain of solid granite one *yojana* (about 7 miles) high and wide by stroking it once every hundred years with a silk cloth (S.15:5/ii,181-82).

According to the commentators, the aeon referred to in the figures on the life-spans in the first-jhana plane is the *asankheyyakappa*, while the aeon referred to from the Gods of Minor Lustre up through the higher planes is the *mahākappa*.[1]

§15 Rebirth-Linking in the Immaterial Sphere

Paṭham' āruppādivipākāni paṭhamāruppādibhūmisu yathākkamaṁ paṭisandhi-bhavanga-cutivasena pavattanti. Imā catasso āruppa-paṭisandhiyo nāma.

The first immaterial resultant occurs as the rebirth-linking, life-continuum, and death (consciousness) in the first immaterial plane, and the others occur in the same functions in their respective planes. These are the four modes of rebirth-linking in the immaterial sphere.

§16 Life-Spans in the Immaterial Sphere

Tesu pana ākāsānañcāyatanūpagānaṁ devānaṁ vīsati kappa-sahassāni āyuppamāṇaṁ. Viññāṇañcāyatanūpagānaṁ devānaṁ cattāḷīsa kappasahassāni, ākiñcaññāyatanūpagānaṁ devānaṁ saṭṭhi kappasahassāni, n'evasaññānāsaññāyatanūpagānaṁ devānaṁ caturāsīti kappasahassāni āyuppamāṇaṁ.

Among them, the life-span of gods who have attained to the realm of infinite space is 20,000 aeons; of those who have attained to the realm of infinite consciousness, 40,000 aeons; of those who have attained to the realm of nothingness, 60,000 aeons; of those who have attained to the realm of neither-perception-nor-non-perception, 84,000 aeons.

§17 Summary

Paṭisandhi bhavangañ ca tathā cavanamānasaṁ
Ekam eva tath' ev' ekavisayañ c'ekajātiyaṁ.

Idam ettha paṭisandhicatukkaṁ.

The rebirth-linking consciousness, life-continuum consciousness, and the death consciousness in one (particular) birth are similar and have an identical object.

Herein, these are the four types of rebirth-linking.

Four Types of Kamma
(*kammacatukkaṁ*)

§18 By way of Function

Janakaṁ, upatthambakaṁ, upapīḷakaṁ, upaghātakañ cā ti kicca-vasena.

I. With respect to function there are four kinds of kamma, namely:

(i) productive kamma;
(ii) supportive kamma;
(iii) obstructive kamma; and
(iv) destructive kamma.

Guide to §18

Four types of kamma: The Pali term *kammacatukka*, the name of this section, means a fourfold division of kamma. This section will actually introduce four fourfold divisions, in all sixteen types of kamma obtained by applying four different methods of analysis.

The word *kamma* means literally action or deed, but in the Buddha's teaching it refers exclusively to volitional action. From a technical standpoint, kamma denotes wholesome or unwholesome volition (*cetanā*), volition being the factor responsible for action. Thus the Buddha declares: "It is volition, monks, that I call kamma, for having willed, one performs an action through body, speech or mind" (A.6:63/iii,415). All volitional action, except that of a Buddha or an Arahant, constitutes kamma. The Buddhas and the Arahants do not accumulate kamma, since they have eradicated ignorance and craving, the roots of kamma. Nevertheless, even the Buddhas and Arahants are bound to experience the ripening of their past kamma as long as their psycho-physical personality persists, that is, until they pass away.

The law of kamma (*kammaniyāma*) is self-subsistent in its operation, ensuring that willed deeds produce their effects in accordance with their ethical quality just as surely as seeds bear fruit in accordance with their species. The direct products of kamma are the resultant (*vipāka*) states of consciousness and mental factors that arise when kamma finds the right conditions to fructify. Kamma also produces a distinct type of matter in the organic bodies of living beings, called materiality originating from kamma (*kammasamuṭṭhānarūpa*—see VI, §10).

With respect to function: Kammas perform different functions (*kicca*), of which four are mentioned here. Any kamma, under different circumstances, can perform any or several of these functions.

TABLE 5.3: FOURFOLD KAMMA AT A GLANCE

I. By way of function
1. Productive kamma
2. Supportive "
3. Obstructive "
4. Destructive "

II. By order of ripening
1. Weighty kamma
2. Death-proximate "
3. Habitual "
4. Reserve "

III. By time of ripening
1. Immediately effective kamma
2. Subsequently effective "
3. Indefinitely effective "
4. Defunct "

IV. By place of ripening
1. Unwholesome kamma
2. Sense-sphere wholesome "
3. Fine-material-sphere wholesome "
4. Immaterial-sphere wholesome "

Productive (*janaka*) kamma is wholesome or unwholesome volition which produces resultant mental states and kamma-born materiality, both at the moment of rebirth-linking and during the course of existence. At the moment of conception, productive kamma generates the rebirth-linking consciousness and the kamma-born types of materiality constituting the physical body of the new being. During the course of existence it produces other resultant cittas and the continuities of kamma-born materiality, such as the sense faculties, sexual determination, and the heart-base. Only a kamma that has attained the status of a full course of action (see §22 below) can perform the function of producing rebirth-linking, but all wholesome and unwholesome kammas without exception can produce results during the course of existence.

Supportive (*upatthambaka*) kamma is kamma which does not gain an opportunity to produce its own result, but which, when some other kamma is exercising a productive function, supports it either by enabling it to produce its pleasant or painful results over an extended time without obstruction or by reinforcing the continuum of aggregates produced by another kamma. For example, when through the productive function of wholesome kamma one is reborn as a human being, supportive kamma may contribute to the extension of one's life-span and ensure that one is healthy and well provided with the necessities of life. When an unwholesome kamma has exercised its productive function by causing a painful disease, other unwholesome kamma may support it by preventing medicines from working effectively, thereby prolonging the disease. When a being has been reborn as an animal through the productive force of unwholesome kamma, supportive kamma may facilitate the ripening of more unwholesome kamma productive of painful results, and may also lead to an extension of the life-span so that the continuity of unwholesome-resultants will endure long.

Obstructive (*upapīḷaka*) kamma is kamma which cannot produce its own result but nevertheless obstructs and frustrates some other kamma, countering its efficacy or shortening the duration of its pleasant or painful results. Even though a productive kamma may be strong at the time it is accumulated, an obstructive kamma directly opposed to it may counteract it so that it becomes impaired when producing its results. For example, a wholesome kamma tending to produce rebirth in a superior plane of existence may be impeded by an obstructive kamma so that it generates rebirth in a lower plane. A kamma tending to produce rebirth among high families may produce rebirth among low families; kamma tending to longevity may tend towards shortness of life; kamma tending to produce beauty may produce a plain appearance, etc. In the opposite way, an unwholesome kamma tending to produce rebirth in the great hells may be counteracted by an obstructive wholesome kamma and produce rebirth in the minor hells or among the petas.

During the course of existence many instances may be found of the operation of obstructive kamma. For example, in the human realm such kamma will obstruct the continuum of aggregates produced by kamma, facilitating the maturation of kamma that results in suffering and causing failures in regard to property and wealth or family and friends, etc. In the lower realms obstructive kamma may counteract the rebirth-producing kamma, contributing to occasions of ease and happiness.

Destructive (*upaghātaka*) kamma is wholesome or unwholesome kamma which supplants other weaker kamma, prevents it from ripening, and produces instead its own result. For example, somebody born as a human being may, through his productive kamma, have been originally destined for a long life-span, but a destructive kamma may arise and bring about a premature death. At the time of death, at first a sign of a bad destination may appear by the power of an evil kamma, heralding a bad rebirth, but then a good kamma may emerge, expel the bad kamma, and having caused the sign of a good destination to appear, produce rebirth in a heavenly world. On the other hand, a bad kamma may suddenly arise, cut off the productive potential of a good kamma, and generate rebirth in a woeful realm. According to Ledi Sayadaw, destructive kamma can also be responsible for cutting off the efficacy of any of the sense faculties—the eye, ear, etc.—causing blindness or deafness, etc., and can also cause sexual mutation.

The *Vibhāvinī-Ṭīkā* distinguishes between productive kamma and destructive kamma on the ground that productive kamma produces its result without cutting off the result of some other kamma while destructive kamma does so after first cutting off another kamma's result. But other teachers cited by the *Vibhāvinī* hold that destructive kamma does not produce its own result at all; it completely cuts off the result of the other kamma, giving still a third kamma the opportunity to ripen.

Ledi Sayadaw gives the example of intentional killing to illustrate how one kamma may exercise all four functions. When one person takes another's life, as long as the volition of killing does not get the opportunity to ripen it exercises any function among the other three functions: it may support the ripening of other unwholesome kamma, or obstruct the ripening of wholesome kamma, or cut off entirely the efficacy of wholesome kamma. When the act of killing gains the opportunity to ripen, then each volition involved in the act has the power to produce one rebirth in the woeful planes; thereafter such volition has no more power to produce rebirth-linking. However, such kamma can continue to exercise the other three functions, as well as the function of producing results during the course of existence, even for a hundred thousand aeons or more into the future.

§19 By Order of Ripening

Garukaṁ, āsannaṁ, āciṇṇaṁ, kaṭattā kammañ cā ti pākadāna-pariyāyena.

II. With respect to the order in which the effect of kamma takes place, there are four kinds of kamma, namely:

(i) weighty kamma;
(ii) death-proximate kamma;
(iii) habitual kamma; and
(iv) reserve kamma.

Guide to §19

The order in which the effect of kamma takes place: This section concerns the order of precedence among different kammas in taking on the role of generating rebirth-linking in the next existence.

Weighty (*garuka*) kamma is kamma of such powerful moral weight that it cannot be replaced by any other kamma as the determinant of rebirth. On the wholesome side, this kamma is the attainment of the jhānas. On the unwholesome side, it is the five heinous crimes together with a fixed wrong view that denies the basis for morality. The five heinous crimes (*ānantariyakamma*) are: parricide, matricide, the murder of an Arahant, the wounding of a Buddha, and maliciously creating a schism in the Sangha. If someone were to develop the jhānas and later were to commit one of the heinous crimes, his good kamma would be obliterated by the evil deed, and the latter would generate rebirth into a state of misery. For example, the Buddha's ambitious cousin Devadatta lost his psychic powers and was reborn in hell for wounding the Buddha and causing a schism in the Sangha. But if someone were first to commit one of the heinous crimes, he could not later reach a sublime or supramundane attainment, because the evil kamma would create an insurmountable obstruction. Thus King Ajātasattu, while listening to the Buddha speak the Sāmaññaphala Sutta, the Discourse on the Fruits of Recluseship, had all the other conditions for reaching stream-entry; but because he had killed his father, King Bimbisāra, he could not attain the path and fruit.

Death-proximate (*āsanna*) kamma is a potent kamma remembered or done shortly before death, that is, immediately prior to the last javana process. If a person of bad character remembers a good deed he has done, or performs a good deed just before dying, he may receive a fortunate rebirth; and conversely, if a good person dwells on an evil deed done earlier, or performs an evil deed just before dying, he may undergo an unhappy rebirth. For this reason in Buddhist countries it is customary to remind a dying person of his good deeds or to urge him to arouse good thoughts during the last moments of his life.

When there is no weighty kamma, and a potent death-proximate kamma is performed, this kamma will generally take on the role of generating rebirth. This does not mean that a person will escape the fruits of the other good and bad deeds he has committed during the course of life. When they meet with conditions, these kammas too will produce their due results.

Habitual (*āciṇṇa*) kamma is a deed that one habitually performs, either good or bad. In the absence of weighty kamma and a potent death-proximate kamma, this type of kamma generally assumes the rebirth-generative function.

Reserve (*kaṭattā*) kamma is any other deed, not included in the three aforementioned categories, which is potent enough to take on the role of generating rebirth. This type of kamma becomes operative when there is no kamma of the other three types to exercise this function.

§20 By Time of Ripening

Diṭṭhadhammavedanīyaṁ, upapajjavedanīyaṁ, aparāpariyavedanīyaṁ, ahosikammañ cā ti pākakālavasena cattāri kammāni nāma.

III. With respect to the time of taking effect, there are four kinds of kamma, namely:

(i) immediately effective kamma;
(ii) subsequently effective kamma;
(iii) indefinitely effective kamma; and
(iv) defunct kamma.

Guide to §20

Immediately effective (*diṭṭhadhammavedanīya*) kamma is kamma which, if it is to ripen, must yield its results in the same existence in which it is performed; otherwise, if it does not meet the opportunity to ripen in the same existence, it becomes defunct. According to the Abhidhamma, of the seven javanas in a javana process, the first javana moment, being the weakest of all, generates immediately effective kamma.

Subsequently effective (*upapajjavedanīya*) kamma is kamma which, if it is to ripen, must yield its results in the existence immediately following that in which it is performed; otherwise it becomes defunct. This type of kamma is generated by the last javana moment in a javana process, which is the second weakest in the series.

Indefinitely effective (*aparāpariyavedanīya*) kamma is kamma which can ripen at any time from the second future existence onwards, whenever it gains an opportunity to produce results. This kamma, generated by the five intermediate javana moments of a cognitive process, never becomes defunct so long as the round of rebirths continues. No one, not even a Buddha or an Arahant, is exempt from experiencing the results of indefinitely effective kamma.

Defunct (*ahosi*) kamma: This term does not designate a special class of kamma, but applies to kamma that was due to ripen in either the present existence or the next existence but did not meet conditions conducive to its maturation. In the case of Arahants, all their accumulated kamma from the past which was due to ripen in future lives becomes defunct with their final passing away.

§21 By Place of Ripening

Tathā akusalaṁ, kāmāvacarakusalaṁ, rūpāvacarakusalaṁ, arūpāvacarakusalañ cā ti pākaṭṭhānavasena.

IV. With respect to the place in which the effect takes place, there are four kinds of kamma, namely:

(i) unwholesome kamma;
(ii) wholesome kamma pertaining to the sense sphere;
(iii) wholesome kamma pertaining to the fine-material sphere; and
(iv) wholesome kamma pertaining to the immaterial sphere.

Unwholesome and Wholesome Kamma

§22 Unwholesome Kamma

Tattha akusalaṁ kāyakammaṁ, vacīkammaṁ, manokammañ cā ti kammadvāravasena tividhaṁ hoti.

Of them, unwholesome kamma is threefold according to the doors of action, namely: bodily action, verbal action, and mental action.

Kathaṁ? Pāṇātipāto, adinnādānaṁ, kāmesu micchācāro cā ti kāyaviññāttisankhāte kāyadvāre bāhullavuttito kāyakammaṁ nāma.

How? Killing, stealing, and sexual misconduct are bodily actions generally occurring through the door of the body, known as bodily intimation.

Musāvādo, pisuṇavācā, pharusavācā, samphappalāpo cā ti vacīviññattisankhāte vacīdvāre bāhullavuttito vacīkammaṁ nāma.

False speech, slandering, harsh speech, and frivolous talk are verbal actions generally occurring through the door of speech, known as vocal intimation.

Abhijjhā, vyāpādo, micchādiṭṭhi cā ti aññatrā pi viññattiyā manasmiṁ yeva bāhullavuttito manokammaṁ nāma.

Covetousness, ill will, and wrong view are mental actions generally occurring only in the mind without (bodily or vocal) intimation.

Guide to §22

The above passage enumerates the ten unwholesome courses of action (*akusalakammapatha*). As shown, three are bodily, four are verbal, and three are purely mental. The first seven courses are identified with the volition initiating an effort to accomplish the respective action. Such volition is an unwholesome kamma regardless of whether or not it completes the action, but if it does reach completion of the action and achieves its aim (e.g. the death of the intended victim, the appropriation of another's property, etc.) then it becomes a full course of action. The characteristic of a full course of action is being a kamma with the potency to take on the rebirth-generating role.[2]

Generally occurring through the door of the body (*kāyadvāra*): In relation to action, the doors (*dvāra*) are the media through which kamma is performed. The door of the body is bodily intimation (*kāyaviññatti*), a type of mind-produced material phenomenon by which a person expresses, through the medium of the body, a volition arisen in the mind (see VI, §4). The expression "generally occurring" (*bāhullavuttito*) is used because such actions as killing and stealing can also be done by speech, i.e. by command, yet even in such cases these actions are still considered bodily kamma.

The door of speech (*vacīdvāra*), similarly, denotes vocal intimation (*vacīviññatti*), the mind-originated material phenomenon by means of which volition is expressed verbally (see VI, §4). Though such actions as false speech, etc., may also be done bodily, i.e. by writing or by hand signals, because their main medium of execution is the door of speech, they are still considered verbal kamma.

Covetousness, etc.: The last three courses of action generally occur only in the mind without reaching intentional expression through body or speech. Such action is said to occur through the mind door (*manodvāra*), which here is a collective designation for consciousness in its entirety.

Covetousness (*abhijjhā*) is the mental factor of greed, arisen as the wish to acquire another person's property. Even though greed arises for another's property, it does not become a full course of action unless one gives rise to the wish to take possession of that property.

Ill will (*vyāpāda*) is the mental factor of hatred, which becomes a full course of action when it arises with the wish that another being meets with harm and affliction.

Wrong view (*micchādiṭṭhi*) becomes a full course of action when it assumes the form of one of the morally nihilistic views which deny the validity of ethics and the retributive consequences of action. Three such views are mentioned often in the Sutta Piṭaka:

(i) nihilism (*natthika-diṭṭhi*), which denies the survival of the personality in any form after death, thus negating the moral significance of deeds;

(ii) the inefficacy of action view (*akiriya-diṭṭhi*), which claims that deeds have no efficacy in producing results and thus invalidates moral distinctions; and

(iii) the acausality view (*ahetukadiṭṭhi*), which states that there is no cause or condition for the defilement and purification of beings, that beings are defiled and purified by chance, fate, or necessity.[3]

§23 By way of Roots and Consciousness

Tesu pāṇātipāto pharusavācā vyāpādo ca dosamūlena jāyanti. Kāmesu micchācāro abhijjhā micchādiṭṭhi ca lobhamūlena. Sesāni cattāri pi dvīhi mūlehi sambhavanti. Cittuppādavasena pan' etaṁ akusalaṁ sabbathā pi dvādasavidhaṁ hoti.

Of them, killing, harsh speech, and ill will spring from the root of hatred; sexual misconduct, covetousness, and wrong view from the root of greed; the remaining four arise from the two roots. According to the classes of consciousness this unwholesome kamma is altogether twelvefold.

Guide to §23

Strictly speaking, ill will is a mode of the root hatred and covetousness is a mode of the root greed; wrong view is a mode of the cetasika wrong view. These three courses of action are thus identifiable with the corresponding cetasikas. The other seven courses of action are identifiable with the cetasika of volition (*cetanā*) arisen along with the unwholesome roots. Although instances may be found where, for example, greed may be the underlying motivation for killing and hatred may be the underlying motivation for sexual misconduct, the Abhidhamma holds that the volition that drives the act of cutting off the life faculty of another being is always rooted in hatred, i.e. aversion towards the continued existence of the being, while the volition that drives the act of sexual transgression is always rooted in greed, i.e. desire to enjoy sexual pleasure with the illicit partner. The volition driving the other four acts—stealing, lying, slandering, and frivolous talk—may be accompanied by either greed or hatred. All unwholesome courses of action are invariably accompanied by the root delusion. Unwholesome kamma is also identifiable with the twelve unwholesome cittas. In this case the citta itself as a composite whole rather than the individual factor of volition is considered to be the kamma.

§24 Wholesome Kamma of the Sense Sphere

Kāmāvacarakusalaṁ pi kāyadvāre pavattaṁ kāyakammaṁ, vacīdvāre pavattaṁ vacīkammaṁ, manodvāre pavattaṁ manokammañ cā ti kammadvāravasena tividhaṁ hoti.

Wholesome kamma of the sense sphere is threefold according to the doors of action, namely, bodily action pertaining to the door of the body; verbal action pertaining to the door of speech; and mental action pertaining to the door of the mind.

Tathā dāna-sīla-bhāvanāvasena. Cittuppādavasena pan' etaṁ aṭṭhavidhaṁ hoti.

Similarly, it is threefold as giving, virtue, and meditation. But it is eightfold according to the classes of consciousness.

Dāna-sīla-bhāvanā-apacāyana-veyyāvacca-pattidāna-pattānumodana-dhammasavana-dhammadesanā-diṭṭhijjukammavasena dasavidhaṁ hoti.

It is also tenfold as: (i) giving; (ii) virtue; (iii) meditation; (iv) reverence; (v) service; (vi) transference of merit; (vii) rejoicing in (others') merit; (viii) hearing the Dhamma; (ix) teaching the Dhamma; and (x) straightening out one's views.

Tam pan' etaṁ vīsatividham pi kāmāvacarakammam icc' eva saṅkhaṁ gacchati.

All these twenty kinds (unwholesome and wholesome) are known as kamma pertaining to the sense sphere.

Guide to §24

According to the doors of action: By way of door of action, ten courses of wholesome kamma are enumerated. The three of body are abstinence from the three unwholesome bodily deeds; the four of speech are abstinence from the four unwholesome verbal deeds; the three of mind are non-covetousness, non-ill will, and right view. In terms of ultimate realities, the first seven are identified as two of the abstinences, i.e. the cetasikas of right action and right speech, and also as the volitions arisen along with those abstinences. The last three are modes of the three wholesome roots, non-greed, non-hatred, and non-delusion.

Similarly, it is threefold, etc.: The threefold and tenfold lists given here are commonly known as the three and ten bases of meritorious deeds (*puññakiriyavatthu*). The eight classes of consciousness by which such wholesome kamma is created are the eight great wholesome cittas.

All these twenty kinds: Kamma arising from the twelve unwholesome cittas and the eight great wholesome cittas.

§25 Wholesome Kamma of the Fine-material Sphere

Rūpāvacarakusalaṁ pana manokammam eva. Tañ ca bhāvanāmayaṁ appanāppattaṁ jhānangabhedena pañcavidhaṁ hoti.

Wholesome kamma of the fine-material sphere is purely mental action. It consists in meditation that has reached absorption and is fivefold by distinction of the jhāna factors.

§26 Wholesome Kamma of the Immaterial Sphere

Tathā arūpāvacarakusalañ ca manokammaṁ. Tam pi bhāvanāmayaṁ appanāppattaṁ ālambanabhedena catubbidhaṁ hoti.

So too, wholesome kamma of the immaterial sphere is purely mental action. It consists in meditation that has reached absorption and is fourfold by distinction of the object.

Guide to §§25–26

Fivefold by distinction of the jhāna factors: the five fine-material-sphere jhānas.

Fourfold by distinction of the object: the four immaterial sphere attainments.

Results of Kamma

§27 Results of Unwholesome Kamma

Ettha akusalakammam uddhaccarahitaṁ apāyabhūmiyaṁ paṭisandhiṁ janeti. Pavattiyaṁ pana sabbam pi dvādasavidhaṁ satt'ākusalapākāni sabbatthā pi kāmaloke rūpaloke ca yathārahaṁ vipaccati.

Herein, unwholesome kamma excluding restlessness produces rebirth-linking in the woeful plane. But during the course of existence all twelve (unwholesome classes of consciousness) give effect to the seven unwholesome resultants anywhere in the sensuous world or the fine-material world, according to circumstances.

Guide to §27

Unwholesome kamma excluding restlessness: The citta rooted in delusion and accompanied by restlessness is the weakest of all the unwholesome cittas, and for this reason it cannot take on the role of generating rebirth. Any of the other eleven unwholesome cittas can generate the unwholesome-resultant investigating consciousness which functions as rebirth-linking, bhavanga, and death consciousness for the beings reborn in the four woeful realms. All twelve unwholesome cittas can generate the seven unwholesome-resultant cittas anywhere in the sensuous world during the course of existence—the five kinds of sense consciousness, and the receiving and investigating consciousnesses. In the fine-material world they produce only four unwholesome-resultants, the threefold sense consciousness of nose, tongue, and body being excluded. See Table 5.4—p.212.

§28 Results of Sense-Sphere Wholesome Kamma

Kāmāvacarakusalam pi kāmasugatiyam eva paṭisandhiṁ janeti, tathā pavattiyañ ca mahāvipākāni. Ahetukavipākāni pana aṭṭha pi sabbatthā pi kāmaloke rūpaloke ca yathārahaṁ vipaccati.

Wholesome kamma of the sense sphere produces rebirth-linking in the sensuous blissful plane, and so too, (it produces) the great resultants in the course of existence. But it gives effect to the eight rootless resultants anywhere in the sensuous world or the fine-material world, according to circumstances.

Guide to §28

In §§29-30 the author will explain the correlations between each type of wholesome citta and the resultants it is capable of producing.

The great resultants occur in four modes: with the three process-freed functions of rebirth-linking, bhavanga, and death, and within the cognitive process, with the function of registration. These resultants ripen only in the sensuous world.

The eight rootless resultants are the fivefold sense consciousness, receiving consciousness, and the twofold investigating consciousness.

TABLE 5.4: KAMMA AND ITS RESULTS

Kamma		Results										
	Sense-Sphere Volitions	At Rebirth	During Life	Realms of Existence		Unwh.-rst. Invs. - Eqn.	Other Rtls. Unwh.-rsts.	Wh.-rst. Invs. - Eqn.	Other Rtls. Wh.-rsts.	Great Rsts. dissoc. Knwl.	Great Rsts. assoc. Knwl.	Total
1	11 unwholesome (exc. restlessness)	*		Woeful	4	1						1
2	12 unwholesome		*	SS All	11	7						7
			*	FMS	15	4						4
3	4 3-rtd. superior wholesome	*		SS Blissful	7						4	4
			*	SS All	11			8		8		16
			*	FMS	15			5		8		13
4	4 3-rtd. inferior 4 2-rtd. superior wholesome	*		SS Blissful	7					4		4
			*	SS All	11			8		4		12
			*	FMS	15			5		4		9
5	4 2-rtd. inferior wholesome	*		Human, gods	2			1				1
			*	SS All	11			8				8
			*	FMS	15			5				5

NOTE: The gods referred to in No. 5 are from the Cātummahārājika realm only.

TABLE 5.4 — Continued

	Sublime Volitions	Realms of Existence	Reb., Bhv., Dth.
6	1st jhāna - infr. " " - med. " " - supr.	Brahmā's Retinue Brahmā's Ministers Mahā Brahmās	1st jhāna resultant
7	2nd jhāna - infr. " " - med. " " - supr.	Minor Lustre Infinite Lustre Radiant Lustre	2nd jhāna resultant
8	3rd jhāna - infr. " " - med. " " - supr.	Minor Lustre Infinite Lustre Radiant Lustre	3rd jhāna resultant
9	4th jhāna - infr. " " - med. " " - supr.	Minor Aura Infinite Aura Steady Aura	4th jhāna resultant
10	5th jhāna - normal	Great Reward	5th jhāna resultant
11	5th jhāna with dispassion for perception	Non-percipient beings	None
12	5th jhāna of non-returner	Pure Abodes	5th jhāna resultant
13	Base of infinite space	Infinite space	1st IS resultant
14	Base of infinite consness.	Infinite consciousness	2nd IS resultant
15	Base of nothingness	Nothingness	3rd IS resultant
16	Base of neither perc. nor non-perc.	Neither perception nor non-perception	4th IS resultant

The latter can occur within the cognitive process in the role of registration as well, while the one accompanied by equanimity can also function as the rebirth, bhavanga, and death consciousness for those of defective birth. All eight rootless resultants ripen in the sensuous world, but three types of sense consciousness—of nose, tongue, and body—do not ripen in the fine-material world, as the beings there lack the requisite sense faculties.

§29 Wholesome Results and the Roots

Tatthā pi tihetukam ukkaṭṭhaṁ kusalaṁ tihetukaṁ paṭisandhiṁ datvā pavatte soḷasa vipākāni vipaccati.

Therein, superior wholesome kamma accompanied by three roots produces rebirth-linking similarly accompanied by three roots, and during the course of existence it gives effect to sixteen kinds of resultants.

Tihetukam omakaṁ dvihetukam ukkaṭṭhañ ca kusalaṁ dvihetukaṁ paṭisandhiṁ datvā pavatte tihetukarahitāni dvādasa pi vipākāni vipaccati.

Wholesome kamma of an inferior grade accompanied by three roots, and that of a superior grade accompanied by two roots, produces rebirth-linking with two roots, and gives effect to twelve kinds of resultants, excluding those with three roots, during the course of existence.

Dvihetukam omakaṁ pana kusalam ahetukam eva paṭisandhiṁ deti. Pavatte ca ahetukavipākān' eva vipaccati.

But wholesome kamma of an inferior grade accompanied by two roots produces rebirth-linking without roots, and gives effect to rootless resultants during the course of existence.

Guide to §29

Superior wholesome kamma: Wholesome kamma is distinguished by way of its capacity to produce results into two grades, the superior and the inferior. The superior grade (*ukkaṭṭha*) of wholesome kamma is that done with a mind that has been well cleansed of the defilements and is attended with good causes before and after the commission of the deed; for example, giving alms to the virtuous with wealth righteously obtained, while rejoicing before and after the act of giving. The inferior grade (*omaka*) is that done with a mind that before and after the performance of the wholesome deed is tainted by such defiled states as self-exaltation, the disparagement of others, and subsequent regret.

Rebirth linking ... accompanied by three roots, etc.: This occurs by way of the four great resultants accompanied by knowledge. The sixteen resultants that arise in the course of existence are the eight that are rootless and the eight great resultants.

Twelve kinds of resultants: excluding the four great resultants accompanied by knowledge.

Rebirth-linking without roots: the wholesome-resultant investigating consciousness accompanied by equanimity.

§30 An Alternative View

Asankhāraṁ sasankhāravipākāni na paccati
Sasankhāram asankhāravipākānī ti kecana.
Tesaṁ dvādasapākāni das' aṭṭha ca yathākkamaṁ
Yathāvuttānusārena yathāsambhavam uddise.

Some (teachers) say that unprompted (states of consciousness) do not produce prompted resultants and prompted (states of consciousness) do not produce unprompted resultants.

According to them, as stated above, the arising of the resultants should be set forth in due order as twelve, ten, and eight.

Guide to §30

Some teachers say: The view on resultants stated in §29 was advanced by the ancient master Tipiṭaka Cūḷanāga Thera and is the prevalent opinion among teachers of the Abhidhamma. In §30 the author states an alternative view held by the teachers of the school of Mahā Dhammarakkhita Thera, an Abhidhamma master at the ancient Moravāpi Monastery in Sri Lanka.[4]

Twelve, ten, and eight: On this view, both at rebirth and during the course of existence, unprompted wholesome cittas produce only unprompted resultants and prompted wholesome cittas produce only prompted resultants. This means that during life, the superior three-rooted wholesome cittas produce only twelve resultants each, the eight rootless resultants and either the four unprompted or the four prompted resultants, corresponding to their own nature as unprompted or prompted. The wholesome cittas of the second grade produce ten resultants each, the eight rootless resultants and either the two unprompted or the two prompted two-rooted resultants, again corresponding to their own nature

TABLE 5.5:
RESULTS OF SENSE-SPHERE WHOLESOME KAMMA

SS Wholesome Citta	Rebirth Resultant	Resultants during Life		
		Rootless Resultants	With Roots: Gen. View	With Roots: Alt. View
1st supr.	3 roots	All 8	1-8	1, 3, 5, 7
1st infr.	2 roots	"	3, 4, 7, 8	3, 7
2nd supr.	3 roots	"	1-8	2, 4, 6, 8
2nd infr.	2 roots	"	3, 4, 7, 8	4, 8
3rd supr.	2 roots	"	3, 4, 7, 8	3, 7
3rd infr.	Rootless	"	None	None
4th supr.	2 roots	"	3, 4, 7, 8	4, 8
4th infr.	Rootless	"	None	None
5th supr.	3 roots	"	1-8	1, 3, 5, 7
5th infr.	2 roots	"	3, 4, 7, 8,	3, 7
6th supr.	3 roots	"	1-8	2, 4, 6, 8
6th infr.	2 roots	"	3, 4, 7, 8	4, 8
7th supr.	2 roots	"	3, 4, 7, 8	3, 7
7th infr.	Rootless	"	None	None
8th supr.	2 roots	"	3, 4, 7, 8	4, 8
8th infr.	Rootless	"	None	None

NOTE: For the numbers of the sense-sphere wholesome and resultant cittas, see Table 1.4.

as unprompted or prompted. As in the prevalent view, so in this view too the weakest grade of wholesome cittas produce only rootless rebirth-linking and only the eight rootless resultants during the course of existence. For a tabular comparison of the two views, see Table 5.5.

§31 Results of Fine-material-Sphere Wholesome Kamma

Rūpāvacarakusalaṁ pana paṭhamajjhānaṁ parittaṁ bhāvetvā brahmapārisajjesu uppajjanti. Tad eva majjhimaṁ bhāvetvā brahmapurohitesu, paṇītaṁ bhāvetvā mahābrahmesu.

As regards wholesome kamma of the fine-material sphere, those who develop the first jhāna to a limited degree are reborn into Brahmā's Retinue. Developing the same to a medium degree, they are reborn among Brahmā's Ministers. Developing it to a superior degree, they are reborn among the Mahā Brahmās.

Tathā dutiyajjhānaṁ tatiyajjhānañ ca parittaṁ bhāvetvā parittābhesu; majjhimaṁ bhāvetvā appamāṇābhesu; paṇītaṁ bhāvetvā ābhassaresu.

Similarly, developing the second jhāna and the third jhāna to a limited degree, they are reborn among the Gods of Minor Lustre. Developing them to a medium degree, they are reborn among the Gods of Infinite Lustre. Developing them to a superior degree, they are reborn among the Gods of Radiant Lustre.

Catutthajjhānaṁ parittaṁ bhāvetvā parittasubhesu; majjhimaṁ bhāvetvā appamāṇasubhesu; paṇītaṁ bhāvetvā subhakiṇhesu.

Developing the fourth jhāna to a limited degree, they are reborn among the Gods of Minor Aura. Developing it to a medium degree, they are reborn among the Gods of Infinite Aura. Developing it to a superior degree, they are reborn among the Gods of Steady Aura.

Pañcamajjhānaṁ bhāvetvā vehapphalesu. Tad eva saññāvirāgaṁ bhāvetvā asaññasattesu. Anāgāmino pana suddhāvāsesu uppajjanti.

Developing the fifth jhāna, they are reborn among the Gods of Great Reward. Developing dispassion towards perception, they are reborn among the non-percipient beings. But non-returners are reborn in the Pure Abodes.

Guide to §31

Wholesome kamma of the fine-material sphere: Each of the five fine-material-sphere jhānas produces, as its kammic result, the resultant fine-material-sphere citta that is its own exact counterpart. This citta is the only resultant produced by the wholesome jhāna citta itself. The wholesome cittas generated in the preparatory stages of meditation culminating in jhāna are sense-sphere wholesome cittas, and their results accordingly are sense-sphere resultants, not fine-material resultants. The fine-material-sphere resultant citta performs only the three functions of rebirth-linking, bhavanga, and death. This means that it occurs only as a process-freed consciousness. It does not occur within the cognitive process, nor does the wholesome jhāna citta produce any resultants occurring in the cognitive process. All resultant cittas occurring in the cognitive process, with the exception of the supramundane fruits, are sense-sphere resultants.

Each wholesome jhāna citta generates rebirth in the fine-material realm that corresponds with its own level. However, the fine-material realms are structured in accordance with the four jhānas of the Suttanta system into four broad tiers rather than five, and thus the second and third jhāna cittas of the Abhidhamma fivefold analysis of jhāna both produce rebirth into the fine-material realms corresponding to the second jhāna of the Suttanta system.

The lower three tiers of the fine-material world each consist of three distinct realms. These realms are the spheres of rebirth for those who develop the corresponding jhāna to three degrees of mastery: limited, medium, and superior. The jhāna citta itself is not distinguished into different types according to the three degrees of development. The citta is defined as a jhāna citta of a particular type in terms of its constellation of cetasikas, and for any given jhāna these remain the same no matter whether the jhāna is developed to an inferior, middling, or superior degree of mastery. However, the degree of development affects the potency of the citta to generate rebirth, and thus in each tier three different realms are found as the objective counterparts of their different potencies. In the case of a meditator who has developed several jhānas, the highest one he still possesses at the end of his life is the one that will take on the role of generating rebirth. See Table 5.4—p.213.

Developing the fifth jhāna: The principle according to which this plane is divided differs from that which divides the previous three. In this plane, all worldlings, stream-enterers, and once-returners who develop the fifth jhāna in the normal way—whether to a limited, medium or superior degree—are reborn in the Realm of Great Reward. Some worldlings, however, adopt the attitude that consciousness and perception are the root of all misery, and they develop the fifth jhāna conjoined with a strong sense of dispassion towards perception. Because their fifth jhāna citta is permeated by the wish for perception to cease, they are reborn in the realm of non-percipient beings. There they exist as mere animate material bodies—the vital nonad (see VI, §28)—until they pass away and take rebirth elsewhere.

But non-returners are reborn in the Pure Abodes: It is said that their rebirth into these five realms is determined by their predominant spiritual faculty. Non-returners in whom faith is the dominant faculty are reborn into the Aviha realm; those in whom energy is dominant, into the Atappa realm; those in whom mindfulness is dominant, into the Sudassa realm; those in whom concentration is dominant, into the Sudassī realm; and those in whom wisdom is dominant, into the Akaniṭṭha realm. Although none but non-returners are reborn into the Pure Abodes, there is no fixed law holding that all non-returners are reborn there. It may be that the Pure Abodes are open only to non-returners who possess the fifth jhāna, while non-returners with a lower jhāna attainment will be reborn elsewhere in the fine-material plane. However, all non-returners must be reborn in the fine-material plane because they have eradicated sensual desire (*kāmarāga*), the fetter which leads to rebirth in the sensuous plane.

§32 Results of Immaterial-Sphere Wholesome Kamma

Arūpāvacarakusalañ ca yathākkamaṁ bhāvetvā āruppesu uppajjanti.

Developing wholesome kamma of the immaterial sphere, they are reborn in the immaterial planes corresponding (to their attainments).

Guide to §32

That is, one who has developed the base of infinite space, and at the time of death has not lost it due to negligence and other hindrances, will be reborn into the realm of infinite space. Similarly with respect to the other immaterial attainments: the highest attainment preserved at the time of death will generate rebirth into the corresponding realm.

As in the case of the fine-material-sphere cittas, each immaterial-sphere wholesome citta produces as its result only its corresponding resultant citta, which fulfils only the three functions of rebirth, bhavanga, and death in the immaterial realm to which it pertains.

§33 Conclusion

Itthaṁ mahaggataṁ puññaṁ yathābhūmi vavatthitaṁ
Janeti sadisaṁ pākaṁ paṭisandhippavattiyaṁ.

Idam ettha kammacatukkaṁ.

Thus sublime merit, determined according to planes, produces similar results (both) at rebirth-linking and in the course of existence.

Herein, this is the fourfold kamma.

The Process of Death and Rebirth (*cutipaṭisandhikkama*)

§34 Four Causes of Death

Āyukkhayena, kammakkhayena, ubhayakkhayena, upacchedakakammunā cā ti catudhā maraṇ' uppatti nāma.

The advent of death is fourfold, namely: (i) through the expiration of the life-span; (ii) through the expiration of the (productive) kammic force; (iii) through the (simultaneous) expiration of both; and (iv) through (the intervention of) a destructive kamma.

Guide to §34

The advent of death: Death is formally defined as the cutting off of the life faculty (*jīvitindriya*) included within the limits of a single existence.

Through the expiration of the life-span: This is the kind of death that comes about for the beings in those realms of existence where the life-span is bounded by a definite limit (see §§12, 14, 16). In the human realm too this should be understood as death in advanced old age due to natural causes. If the productive kamma is still not exhausted when death takes place through reaching the maximum age, the kammic force can generate another rebirth on the same plane or on some higher plane, as in the case of the devas.

Through the expiration of the (productive) kammic force: This is the kind of death that takes place when the kamma generating rebirth expends its force even though the normal life-span is not exhausted and there are otherwise favourable conditions for the prolongation of life. When both the life-span and kammic force simultaneously come to an end, this is death by the *expiration of both.*

Through (the intervention of) a destructive kamma: This is a term for the death that occurs when a powerful destructive kamma cuts off the force of the rebirth-generating kamma even before the expiration of the life-span (see §18).

The first three types of death are known as timely death (*kālamaraṇa*), the last as untimely death (*akālamaraṇa*). An oil lamp, for example, may be extinguished due to the exhaustion of the wick, the exhaustion of the oil, the simultaneous exhaustion of both, or some extraneous cause, like a gust of wind.

§35 The Signs at the Time of Death

Tathā ca marantānaṁ pana maraṇakāle yathārahaṁ abhimukhībhūtaṁ bhavantare paṭisandhijanakaṁ kammaṁ vā taṁkammakaraṇakāle rūpādikam upaladdhapubbam upakaraṇabhūtañ ca kammanimittaṁ vā anantaram uppajjamānabhave upalabhitabbaṁ upabhogabhūtañ ca gatinimittaṁ vā kammabalena channaṁ dvārānaṁ aññatarasmiṁ paccupaṭṭhāti.

Now in the case of those who are about to die, at the time of death one of the following presents itself through any of the six (sense) doors:

(i) a kamma that is to produce rebirth-linking in the next existence, which according to circumstances confronts (the dying person); or

(ii) a sign of kamma, that is, a form, etc., that had been apprehended previously at the time of performing the kamma or something that was instrumental in performing the kamma; or

(iii) a sign of destiny, that is, (a symbol of the state) to be obtained and experienced in the immediately following existence.

Guide to §35

For an explanation of the three types of object presented to the mind of the dying individual, see III, §17. It should be stressed that this object presents itself to the javana process of the dying person, not to the death consciousness itself. The death consciousness (*cuticitta*), the final citta in a life term, apprehends the same object grasped by the rebirth consciousness and bhavanga of the existence that is about to end. The object of the last javana process then serves as the object of the rebirth consciousness and bhavanga in the next existence, and becomes in turn the object of the death consciousness at the end of that existence.

§36 The Mind at the Time of Death

Tato paraṁ tam eva tath' opaṭṭhitaṁ ālambanaṁ ārabbha vipaccamānakakammānurūpaṁ parisuddham upakkiliṭṭhaṁ vā upalabhitabbabhavānurūpaṁ tatth' onataṁ va cittasantānaṁ abhiṇhaṁ pavattati bāhullena. Tam eva vā pana janakabhūtaṁ kammam abhinavakaraṇavasena dvārappattaṁ hoti.

Thereafter, attending to that object thus presented, the stream of consciousness—in accordance with the kamma that is to be matured, whether pure or corrupted, and in conformity with the state into which one is to be reborn—continually flows, inclining mostly towards that state. Or that rebirth-productive kamma presents itself to a sense door in the way of renewing.

Guide to §36

In the way of renewing (*abhinavakaraṇavasena*): that is, the kamma presenting itself does not appear as a memory image of something that was previously done, but it appears to the mind door as if it were being done at that very moment.

§37 Death and Rebirth-Linking

Paccāsannamaraṇassa tassa vīthicittāvasāne bhavangakkhaye vā cavanavasena paccuppannabhavapariyosānabhūtaṁ cuticittam uppajjitvā nirujjhati. Tasmiṁ niruddhāvasāne tass' ānantaram eva tathāgahitaṁ ālambanam ārabbha savatthukaṁ avatthukam eva vā yathārahaṁ avijjānusayaparikkhittena taṇhānusayamūlakena sankhārena janīyamānaṁ sampayuttehi pariggayhamānaṁ sahajātānam adhiṭṭhānabhāvena pubbangamabhūtaṁ bhavantara-paṭisandhānavasena paṭisandhisankhātaṁ mānasaṁ uppajjamānam eva patiṭṭhāti bhavantare.

To one who is on the verge of death, either at the end of a cognitive process or at the dissolution of the life-continuum, the death consciousness, the consummation of the present life, arises and ceases in the way of death.

Immediately after that (death consciousness) has ceased, a rebirth-linking consciousness arises and is established in the subsequent existence, apprehending the object thus obtained, either supported by the heart-base or baseless, as is appropriate; it is generated by a volitional formation that is enveloped by latent ignorance and rooted in latent craving. That rebirth-linking consciousness, so called because it links together the two consecutive existences, is conjoined with its mental adjuncts, and acts as the forerunner to the conascent states as their locus (or foundation).

Guide to §37

To one who is on the verge of death: The last cognitive process begins when the bhavanga is interrupted, vibrates for one moment, and is then arrested. Thereafter follows either a sense-door process taking as object some sense object presenting itself at one of the five sense doors or a bare mind-door process taking as object either some sense object or a mental object presenting itself at the mind door. Within this terminal process the javana phase, by reason of its weakness, runs for only five mind-moments rather than the usual seven. This process lacks original productive kammic potency, but acts rather as the channel for the past kamma that has assumed the rebirth-generative function. Following the javana stage two registration cittas (*tadārammaṇa*) may or may not follow. In some cases the bhavanga may follow the last process cittas. Then, as the very last citta, the death consciousness arises performing the function of passing away from the present life. With the ceasing of the death consciousness, the life faculty is cut off. Then the body remains a mass of inanimate material phenomena born of temperature, and continues as such until the corpse is reduced to dust.

Immediately after that has ceased: Following the dissolution moment of the death consciousness, there arises in a new existence the rebirth-linking consciousness *apprehending the object thus obtained* in the final javana process of the previous life. This citta is *supported by the heart-base* in realms which include matter, but is *baseless* in the immaterial realms. It is *generated by a volitional formation*, i.e. the kamma of the previous javana process, which in turn is grounded in the twin roots of the round of existence, *latent ignorance and latent craving*. The rebirth consciousness is *conjoined with its mental adjuncts*, i.e. the cetasikas, which it serves as a forerunner not in the sense that it precedes them, but in that it acts as *their locus* (or *foundation*).

§38 Objects of Sense-Sphere Rebirth Consciousness

Maraṇāsannavīthiyaṁ pan' ettha mandappavattāni pañc' eva javanāni pāṭikankhitabbāni. Tasmā yadā paccuppannālambanesu āpātham āgatesu dharantesv' eva maraṇaṁ hoti, tadā paṭisandhibhavangānam pi paccuppannālambanatā labbhatī ti katvā kāmāvacarapaṭisandhiyā chadvāragahitaṁ kammanimittaṁ gatinimittañ ca paccuppannam atītam ālambanaṁ upalabbhati. Kammaṁ pana atītam eva, tañ ca manodvāragahitaṁ. Tāni pana sabbāni pi parittadhammabhūtān' ev' ālambanāni.

Herein, in the death-proximate cognitive process, only five feebly occurring javanas should be expected. Therefore, when death takes place while present objects are occurring and have entered the avenue of sense, then the rebirth-linking and life-continuum (of the new existence) also take a present object. In the case of a sense-sphere rebirth-linking, when the object is a sign of kamma or a sign of destiny perceived at any of the six doors, that object may be present or it may be past. But kamma (as object) is only past, and it is perceived only at the mind door. All these objects (of sense-sphere rebirth) are limited phenomena only.

Guide to §38

The rebirth-linking and life-continuum ... also take a present object: A present object apprehended at the time of death may persist through the occasion of rebirth-linking and the first few bhavangas, and thus these too may take a present object.

In the case of a sense-sphere rebirth-linking, etc.: If the object of the rebirth consciousness is a kamma, then it is necessarily past and must be a mental object apprehended at the mind door. If the object is a sign of kamma, then it can be apprehended at any of the six doors and may be either past or present. In the case of the sign of destiny as object, different teachers advance conflicting interpretations. Some commentators, including the author of the *Vibhāvinī-Ṭīkā*, hold that the sign of destiny is necessarily a present visible form apprehended at the mind door. They interpret Ācariya Anuruddha's statement in the text as meaning: "When the object is a sign of kamma it may be perceived at any of the six doors and may be present or past; when it is a sign of destiny it is perceived at the sixth door, i.e. the mind door, and is present." Other commentators, including Ledi Sayadaw, reject this interpretation as forced and too narrow. They argue that Ācariya Anuruddha must be taken at his word as holding the wider view that the sign of destiny can be past or present and may appear at any of the six doors. Ledi Sayadaw asserts that when the Abhidhamma texts commonly speak of the sign of destiny as a present visible object appearing at the mind door, this is said by way of its usual manifestation but does not mean that it does not become manifest in other ways, for example, as the groans of those in hell or as celestial music or fragrance, etc.

§39 Objects of Sublime Rebirth Consciousness

Rūpāvacarapaṭisandhiyā pana paññattibhūtaṁ kammanimittam ev' ālambanaṁ hoti. Tathā āruppapaṭisandhiyā ca mahaggatabhūtaṁ paññattibhūtañ ca kammanimittam eva yathārahaṁ ālambanaṁ hoti.

In the case of rebirth-linking in the fine-material sphere, the object is a concept and is always a sign of kamma. So too, in the case of rebirth-linking in the immaterial sphere, the object—which may be a sublime state or a concept, whichever is appropriate—is always a sign of kamma.

Asaññasattānaṁ pana jīvitanavakam eva paṭisandhibhāvena patiṭṭhāti. Tasmā te rūpapaṭisandhikā nāma. Arūpā arūpapaṭisandhikā. Sesā rūpārūpapaṭisandhikā.

TABLE 5.6: DEATH AND REBIRTH

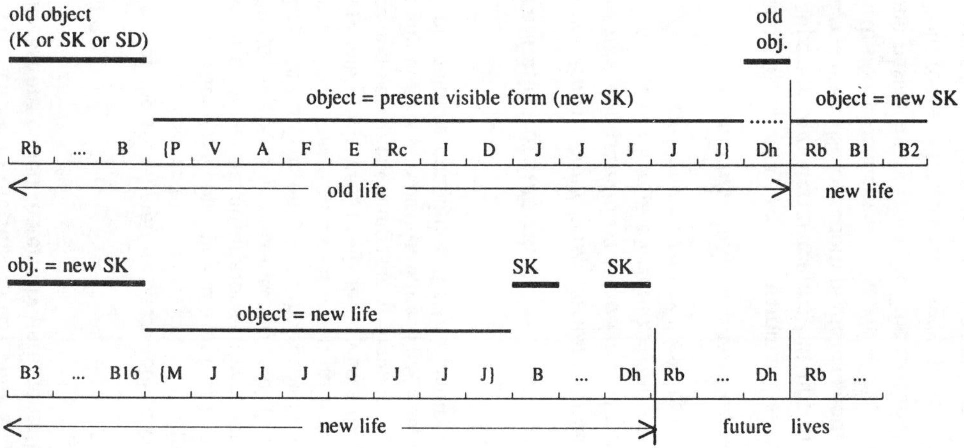

KEY: K = kamma; SK = sign of kamma; SD = sign of destiny; Rb = rebirth consciousness; Dh = death consciousness; rest as in Tables 4.2 and 4.3.

NOTE: The above diagram shows the rebirth process with a present visible form occurring as sign of kamma. With other objects the process would occur differently. Note that the visible form, with a duration of 17 mind-moments, is a present object for the 14 cittas of the last javana process of the old life and the first 3 cittas of the new life; from the third bhavanga on it becomes a past object.

In the case of non-percipient beings, only the vital nonad becomes established in the way of rebirth-linking. Hence they are called materially reborn. Those in the immaterial planes are called mentally reborn. The rest are called materially and mentally reborn.

Guide to §39

The object of the fine-material-sphere rebirth consciousness is the counterpart sign that served as the object of the jhāna generating rebirth. This is considered a concept and a sign of kamma. The objects of the first and third immaterial absorptions—the concepts of infinite space and of nothingness—become the objects of rebirth consciousness in the corresponding realms. The objects of the second and fourth immaterial absorptions are the cittas of the first and third immaterial absorptions, and these are sublime states. In all these cases the object is a sign of kamma. The non-percipient beings are without consciousness, and hence do not take any objects at rebirth-linking. The "vital nonad" is the group of material phenomena containing the life faculty, i.e. organic matter. See VI, §17.

§40 Determination of Rebirth

Āruppacutiyā honti heṭṭhimāruppavajjitā
Paramāruppasandhī ca tathā kāme tihetukā.
Rūpāvacaracutiyā aheturahitā siyuṁ
Sabbā kāmatihetumhā kāmesv' eva pan' etarā.

Ayam ettha cutipaṭisandhikkamo.

When one passes away from an immaterial realm, one may be reborn in superior immaterial realms but not in lower immaterial realms, and one may also be reborn in the sensuous plane with a three-rooted rebirth-consciousness.

When one passes away from the fine-material sphere, one is not reborn without roots. After passing away from a three-rooted existence in the sensuous plane, one may be reborn anywhere. The rest (i.e. those who pass away with two roots and no roots) are reborn only in the sense-sphere realms.

Herein, this is the procedure with regard
to death and rebirth.

Guide to §40

The determination of rebirth differs significantly for worldlings and noble disciples who have not yet reached Arahantship. The text above describes the procedure only in the case of worldlings. Here we will first explain the procedure for worldlings, then the procedure for noble disciples still in training.

Beings in the immaterial realms may develop the immaterial jhāna that corresponds to their level of rebirth or the higher jhānas, but not those that are lower. Thus when they pass away, they may be reborn on the same plane or on a higher plane, but not on a lower jhāna plane. If, however, they fall away from their jhāna attainment, they are reborn in the sensuous plane by the power of their access concentration (*upacārasamādhi*, see IX, §4) and thus take rebirth with one of the three-rooted sense-sphere resultants.

Those who pass away from the non-percipient realm are reborn in the sensuous plane with a sense-sphere resultant citta having either two or three roots. Passing away from elsewhere in the fine-material plane, one may be reborn either in an immaterial realm if one has possession of an immaterial jhāna, or in a fine-material realm if one has possession of a fine-material jhāna, or in the sensuous plane if one has generated strong kamma tending towards that plane. One who takes rebirth in the sensuous plane after passing away from the fine-material plane must do so with either a two-rooted or three-rooted rebirth consciousness.

Those who pass away with three roots in the sensuous plane may take rebirth in any plane, since a sense-sphere being with three roots can perform any type of kamma. Those who pass away within the sensuous plane with two roots or no roots are reborn only in the sensuous plane; they may take rebirth with either of the two rootless investigating cittas or with any of the sense-sphere resultant cittas possessing two or three roots.

In the case of noble disciples there can be no regression from a superior type of death consciousness to an inferior type of rebirth consciousness. All noble disciples pass away with a three-rooted death consciousness, since without three roots it is impossible to have attained the path and fruit. Noble disciples still in training (non-Arahants) re-arise either in the same plane or in a superior plane; they acquire either the same type of rebirth consciousness or a superior one. Of course, those who have reached the path and fruit of Arahantship do not take rebirth in any plane after death.

See Table 5.7 at the end of this chapter.

§41 The Continuity of Consciousness

Icc' evaṁ gahitapaṭisandhikānaṁ pana paṭisandhinirodhā-nantarato pabhuti tam ev' ālambanam ārabbha tad eva cittaṁ yāva cuticittuppādā asati vīthicittuppāde bhavass' angabhāvena bhavangasantatisankhātaṁ mānasaṁ abbocchinnaṁ nadīsoto viya pavattati. Pariyosāne ca cavanavasena cuticittaṁ hutvā nirujjhati. Tato parañ ca paṭisandhādayo rathacakkam iva yathākkamaṁ eva parivattantā pavattanti.

So, for those who have thus taken rebirth, from the moment immediately following the cessation of the rebirth-linking (consciousness), that same type of consciousness apprehending that same object flows on uninterruptedly like the stream of a river, and it does so until the arising of the death consciousness, so long as there is no occurrence of a cognitive process. Being an essential factor of existence (or life), this consciousness is called the life-continuum. At the end of life, having become the death consciousness on the occasion of passing away, it then ceases. Thereafter, the rebirth-linking consciousness and the others continue to occur, revolving in due sequence like the wheel of a cart.

Guide to §41

Immediately following ... the rebirth-linking: The rebirth-linking consciousness is followed by sixteen moments of the bhavanga citta. Thereafter a mind-door adverting consciousness arises, followed by a process of seven javanas in which an attachment develops to the new existence (*bhavanikanti-javana*). This cognitive process, the first in the new life, takes as object the rebirth-linking consciousness; the javanas consist in sense-sphere cittas rooted in greed, dissociated from wrong views, unprompted. When this process ends, the bhavanga again arises and perishes, and continues thus whenever there is no intervention of a cognitive process. In this way the stream of consciousness flows on from conception until death, and from death to new birth "revolving like the wheel of a cart."

§42 Conclusion

Paṭisandhibhavangavīthiyo
Cuti c'eha tathā bhavantare
Puna sandhibhavangam icc' ayaṁ
Parivattati cittasantati.

Paṭisankhāya pan' etam addhuvaṁ
Adhigantvā padam accutaṁ budhā
Susamucchinnasinehabandhanā
Samam essanti cirāya subbatā.

Just as here, so again in the next existence, there arise rebirth-linking consciousness, life-continuum, cognitive processes, and death consciousness. Again, with rebirth and life-continuum, this stream of consciousness turns round.

The wise, disciplining themselves long, understand the impermanence (of life), realize the deathless state, and completely cutting off the fetters of attachment, attain peace.

Iti Abhidhammatthasangahe
Vīthimuttasangahavibhāgo nāma
pañcamo paricchedo.

Thus ends the fifth chapter
in the Manual of Abhidhamma entitled
the Compendium of the Process-freed.

TABLE 5.7: DETERMINATION OF REBIRTH

A. Worldlings

	Old Realm	Death Consciousness	New Realm	Rebirth Consciousness
31	Neither perception nor non-perception	4th IS rst.	5-11, 31	4th IS rst.; 3-rtd. SS rst. 4
30	Nothingness	3rd IS rst.	5-11, 30, 31	3rd-4th IS rst.; 3-rtd. SS rst. 4
29	Infinite consness.	2nd IS rst.	5-11, 29-31	2nd-4th IS rst.; 3-rtd. SS rst. 4
28	Infinite space	1st IS rst.	5-11, 28-31	1st-4th IS rst.; 3-rtd. SS rst. 4
22	Non-percipient	None	5-11	Gt. SS rst. 8
21	Great Reward	5th FMS rst.	5-31	Gt. SS rst. 8; FMS rst. 5; IS rst. 4
20	Steady Aura	4th FMS rst.	"	"
19	Infinite Aura	"	"	"
18	Minor Aura	"	"	"
17	Radiant Lustre	2nd-3rd FMS rst.	"	"
16	Infinite Lustre	"	"	"
15	Minor Lustre	"	"	"

TABLE 5.7 — Continued

A. Worldlings

	Old Realm	Death Consciousness	New Realm	Rebirth Consciousness
14	Mahā Brahmā	1st FMS rst.	5-31	Gt.SS rst. 8; FMS rst. 5; IS rst. 4
13	Brahmā's Ministers	"	"	"
12	Brahmā's Retinue	"	"	"
11	Paranimmita- vasavatti	2-rtd. SS rst. 4; 3-rtd. SS rst. 4	1-11 1-31	Gt. SS rst. 8; invs. 2 All possibilities
10	Nimmānarati	Same as 11	Same as 11	Same as 11
9	Tusita	"	"	"
8	Yāma	"	"	"
7	Tāvatiṁsa	"	"	"
6	Cātummahārājika	Wh. rst. invs. 1 2-rtd. SS rst. 4 3-rtd. SS rst. 4	1-11 " 1-31	Gt. SS rst. 8; invs. 2 " All possibilities
5	Human	Same as 6	Same as 6	Same as 6
4	Asura	Unwh. rst. invs. 1	1-11	Gt. SS rst. 8; invs. 2
3	Peta	"	"	"
2	Animal	"	"	"
1	Hell	"	"	"

TABLE 5. 7: — Continued

B. Trainees

	Old Realm	Death Consciousness	New Realm	Rebirth Consciousness
31	Neither perception nor non-perception	4th IS rst.	31	4th IS rst.
30	Nothingness	3rd IS rst.	30, 31	3rd-4th IS rst.
29	Infinite consness.	2nd IS rst.	29-31	2nd-4th IS rst.
28	Infinite space	1st IS rst.	28-31	1st-4th IS rst.
27	Highest Pure Abode	5th FMS rst.	None	None
26	Clear-sighted " "	"	27	5th FMS rst.
25	Beautiful " "	"	26, 27	"
24	Serene " "	"	25-27	"
23	Durable " "	"	24-27	"
21	Great Reward	"	21, 23-31	"
20	Steady Aura	4th FMS rst.	20, 21, 23-31	4th-5th FMS rst.; IS rst.4
19	Infinite Aura	"	19-21, 23-31	"
18	Minor Aura	"	18-21, 23-31	"

TABLE 5.7 — Continued

B. Trainees

	Old Realm	Death Consciousness	New Realm	Rebirth Consciousness
17	Radiant Lustre	2nd-3rd FMS rst.	17-21, 23-31	2nd-5th FMS rst.; IS rst. 4
16	Infinite Lustre	"	16-21, 23-31	"
15	Minor Lustre	"	15-21, 23-31	"
14	Mahā Brahmā	1st FMS rst.	14-21, 23-31	1-5 FMS rst.; IS rst. 4
13	Brahmā's Ministers	"	13-21, 23-31	"
12	Brahmā's Retinue	"	12-21, 23-31	"
11	Paramimmita-vasavatti	3-rtd. SS rst. 4	5-21, 23-31	3-rtd. SS rst. 4; FMS rst. 5; IS rst. 4
10	Nimmānarati	Same as 11	Same as 11	Same as 11
6-9	Tusita, etc.	"	"	"
5	Human	"	"	"

CHAPTER VI
COMPENDIUM OF MATTER
(*Rūpasangahavibhāga*)

§1 Introductory Verse

Ettāvatā vibhattā hi sappabhedappavattikā
Cittacetasikā dhammā rūpaṁ dāni pavuccati.
Samuddesā vibhāgā ca samuṭṭhānā kalāpato
Pavattikkamato cā ti pañcadhā tattha sangaho.

Having thus far analyzed consciousness and mental factors in accordance with their classes and modes of occurrence, matter will now be dealt with.

The compendium of matter is fivefold: enumeration, classification, origination, groups, and the modes of occurrence.

Guide to §1

The first five chapters of the *Abhidhammattha Sangaha* form, in a way, a complete compendium dealing with various aspects of conscious experience—with the 89 or 121 types of consciousness, with the 52 mental factors and their permutations, with the occurrence of consciousness in cognitive processes and at rebirth, with the planes of existence, and with the classification of kamma and its result.

These first five chapters may be considered a detailed analysis of the first two ultimate realities—citta and cetasikas, consciousness and mental factors. In Chapter VI Ācariya Anuruddha will analyze in detail the third ultimate reality, matter (*rūpa*). He will first enumerate the kinds of material phenomena; then he will explain the principles by which they are classified, their causes or means of origination, their organization into groups, and their modes of occurrence. Finally he will conclude the chapter with a brief look at the fourth ultimate reality, the unconditioned element, Nibbāna.

The Pali word for matter, *rūpa*, is explained by derivation from the verb *ruppati*, which means "to be deformed, disturbed, knocked about, oppressed, broken."[1] The commentators maintain that "matter is so called because it undergoes and imposes alteration owing to adverse physical conditions such as cold and heat, etc."[2] The Buddha himself, in explanation of the term "matter" or "material form," declares: "And why, monks, do you say material form (*rūpa*)? It is deformed (*ruppati*), therefore it is called material form. Deformed by what? Deformed by cold, by heat, by hunger, by thirst, by flies, mosquitoes, wind, sunburn, and creeping things" (S.22:79/iii, 86).

Enumeration of Material Phenomena (*rūpasamuddesa*)

§2 In Brief: Great Essentials and Derived Matter

Cattāri mahābhūtāni, catunnañ ca mahābhūtānaṁ upādāya rūpan ti duvidham p' etaṁ rūpaṁ ekādasavidhena sangahaṁ gacchati.

Matter is twofold, namely: the four great essentials, and material phenomena derived from the four great essentials. These two constitute eleven categories.

Guide to §2

Matter is twofold: The Abhidhamma enumerates twenty-eight types of material phenomena, which are briefly comprised in two general categories: the four great essentials and material phenomena derived from the four great essentials. *The four great essentials* (*mahābhūta*) are the primary material elements—earth, water, fire, and air. These are the fundamental constituents of matter which are inseparable and which, in their various combinations, enter into the composition of all material substances, from the most minute particle to the most massive mountain. *Derived material phenomena* (*upādāya rūpa*) are material phenomena derived from, or dependent upon, the four great essentials. These are twenty-four in number. The great essentials may be compared to the earth, the derivative phenomena to trees and shrubs that grow in dependence on the earth.

All these twenty-eight types of material phenomena are distributed into eleven general classes. Seven of these are called concretely produced matter (*nipphannarūpa*), since they possess intrinsic natures and are thus suitable for contemplation and comprehension by insight. The other four classes, being more abstract in nature, are called non-concretely produced matter (*anipphannarūpa*). (See Table 6.1.)

TABLE 6.1:
THE 28 MATERIAL PHENOMENA AT A GLANCE

CONCRETELY PRODUCED MATTER (18)

I. *Great Essentials*

1. Earth element
2. Water element
3. Fire element
4. Air element

II. *Sensitive Phenomena*

5. Eye-sensitivity
6. Ear-sensitivity
7. Nose-sensitivity
8. Tongue-sensitivity
9. Body-sensitivity

III. *Objective Phenomena*

10. Visible form
11. Sound
12. Smell
13. Taste

*. Tangibility (= 3 elements: earth, fire, air)

IV. *Sexual Phenomena*

14. Femininity
15. Masculinity

V. *Heart Phenomenon*

16. Heart-base

VI. *Life Phenomenon*

17. Life faculty

VII. *Nutritional Phenomenon*

18. Nutriment

NON-CONCRETE MATTER (10)

VIII. *Limiting Phenomenon*

19. Space element

IX. *Communicating Phenomena*

20. Bodily intimation
21. Vocal intimation

X. *Mutable Phenomena*

22. Lightness
23. Malleability
24. Wieldiness
(plus two intimations)

XI. *Characteristics of Matter*

25. Production
26. Continuity
27. Decay
28. Impermanence

§3 In Detail: Concretely Produced Matter

Kathaṁ?

(1) *Paṭhavīdhātu, āpodhātu, tejodhātu, vāyodhātu bhūtarūpaṁ nāma.*

(2) *Cakkhu, sotaṁ, ghānaṁ, jivhā, kāyo pasādarūpaṁ nāma.*

(3) *Rūpaṁ, saddo, gandho, raso, āpodhātuvajjitaṁ bhūtattaya-sankhātaṁ phoṭṭhabbaṁ gocararūpaṁ nāma.*

(4) *Itthattaṁ purisattaṁ bhāvarūpaṁ nāma.*

(5) *Hadayavatthu hadayarūpaṁ nāma.*

(6) *Jīvitindriyaṁ jīvitarūpaṁ nāma.*

(7) *Kabaḷīkāro āhāro āhārarūpaṁ nāma.*

How?

(1) Essential material phenomena: the earth element, the water element, the fire element, and the air element.

(2) Sensitive material phenomena: eye, ear, nose, tongue, and body.

(3) Objective material phenomena: visible form, sound, smell, taste, and tangibility, the latter consisting in the three essentials excluding the water element.

(4) Material phenomena of sex: femininity and masculinity.

(5) Material phenomenon of the heart: the heart-base.

(6) Material phenomenon of life: the life faculty.

(7) Material phenomenon of nutriment: edible food.

Iti ca aṭṭhārasavidham p' etaṁ sabhāvarūpaṁ, salakkhaṇarūpaṁ, nipphannarūpaṁ, rūparūpaṁ, sammasanarūpan ti ca sangahaṁ gacchati.

Thus these eighteen kinds of material phenomena are grouped together as: matter possessing intrinsic nature, matter possessing real characteristics, concretely produced matter, material matter, and matter to be comprehended by insight.

Guide to §3

(1) **The earth element (*paṭhavīdhātu*)**: The great essentials are called elements (*dhātu*) in the sense that they bear their own intrinsic natures (*attano sabhāvaṁ dhārenti*). The earth element is so called because, like the earth, it serves as a support or foundation for the coexisting material phenomena. The word *paṭhavī* comes from a root meaning to ex-

pand or spread out, and thus the earth element represents the principle of extension. The earth element has the characteristic of hardness, the function of acting as a foundation (for the other primary elements and derived matter), and manifestation as receiving.[3] Its proximate cause is the other three great essentials. Both hardness and softness are modes in which the earth element is experienced by the sense of touch.

The water element (*āpodhātu*): The water element, or fluidity, is the material factor that makes different particles of matter cohere, thereby preventing them from being scattered about. Its characteristic is trickling or oozing, its function is to intensify the coexisting material states, and it is manifested as the holding together or cohesion of material phenomena. Its proximate cause is the other three great essentials. The Abhidhamma holds that unlike the other three great essentials, the water element cannot be physically sensed but must be known inferentially from the cohesion of observed matter.

The fire element (*tejodhātu*) has the characteristic of heat, its function is to mature or ripen other material phenomena, and it is manifested as a continuous supply of softness. Both heat and cold are modes in which the fire element is experienced.

The air element (*vāyodhātu*) is the principle of motion and pressure. Its characteristic is distension (*vitthambana*), its function is to cause motion in the other material phenomena, and it is manifested as conveyance to other places. Its proximate cause is the other three great essentials. It is experienced as tangible pressure.

Taken together, the four great essentials are founded upon the earth element, held together by the water element, maintained by the fire element, and distended by the air element.

(2) **Sensitive material phenomena (*pasādarūpa*)** are five types of matter located in each of the five sense organs.[4] The sensitivity is to be distinguished from the gross sense organ which functions as its support. What is conventionally called the eye is spoken of in the Abhidhamma as the composite eye (*sasambhāra-cakkhu*), a compound of various material phenomena. Among these is eye-sensitivity (*cakkhu-pasāda*), the sensitive substance in the retina that registers light and colour and serves as a physical base and door for eye-consciousness. Ear-sensitivity (*sota-pasāda*) is to be found inside the ear-hole, "in the place shaped like a finger-stall and surrounded by fine brown hairs"; it is the sensitive substance that registers sounds and serves as a physical base and door for ear-consciousness. Nose-sensitivity (*ghāna-pasāda*) is to be found inside the nasal orifice, as the substance that registers smells. Tongue-sensitivity (*jivhā-pasāda*) is to be found diffused over the tongue, serving to register tastes. And body-sensitivity (*kāya-pasāda*) extends

all over the organic body "like a liquid that soaks a layer of cotton," and serves to register tactile sensations.

The eye's characteristic is sensitivity of the primary elements that is ready for the impact of visible data; or its characteristic is sensitivity of the primary elements springing from a desire to see. Its function is to pick up a visible datum as object. It is manifested as the foundation of eye-consciousness. Its proximate cause is the primary elements born of kamma springing from a desire to see. Each of the other sensitive material phenomena—the ear, the nose, the tongue, and the body—should be similarly understood, with appropriate substitutions.

(3) **Objective material phenomena (*gocararūpa*)** are the five sense fields which serve as the objective supports for the corresponding types of sense consciousness. It should be noted that the tangible object is constituted by three of the great essentials: the earth element, experienced as hardness or softness; the fire element, experienced as heat or cold; and the air element, experienced as pressure. The water element, being the principle of cohesion, is not, according to the Abhidhamma, included in the tangible datum. The other four sense objects—visible forms, etc.—are types of derived matter.

Collectively, objective material phenomena have the characteristic of impinging on the sense bases. Their function is to be the objects of sense consciousness. They are manifested as the resort of the respective sense consciousness. Their proximate cause is the four great essentials.

(4) **Material phenomena of sex (*bhāvarūpa*)** are the two faculties of femininity and masculinity. These faculties have, respectively, the characteristic of the female sex and of the male sex. Their function is to show femininity and masculinity. They are manifested as the reason for the mark, sign, work, and ways of the female and of the male; that is, for the sexual structure of the body, for its feminine or masculine features, for the typical feminine or masculine occupations, and for the typical feminine or masculine deportment.

(5) **Material phenomenon of the heart (*hadayarūpa*)**: On the heart-base, see III, §20. The heart-base has the characteristic of being the material support for the mind element and the mind-consciousness element (see III, §21). Its function is to uphold them. It is manifested as the carrying of these elements. It is to be found in dependence on the blood inside the heart, and is assisted by the four great essentials and maintained by the life faculty.

(6) **The life faculty (*jīvitindriya*)** is the material counterpart of the mental life faculty, one of the seven universal cetasikas. Life, or vitality, is called a faculty because it has a dominating influence over its adjuncts. The life faculty has the characteristic of maintaining the coex-

istent kinds of matter at the moment of their presence. Its function is to make them occur. It is manifested as the establishment of their presence. Its proximate cause is the four great essentials that are to be maintained.

(7) **Edible food (*kabaḷīkārāhāra*)** has the characteristic of nutritive essence (*ojā*), that is, the nutritional substance contained in gross edible food. Its function is to sustain the physical body. It is manifested as the fortifying of the body. Its proximate cause is gross edible food, which is the base of nutritive essence.

These eighteen kinds of material phenomena: The eighteen material phenomena just enumerated are grouped together as *matter possessing intrinsic nature* (*sabhāvarūpa*) because each type has a distinct objective nature such as hardness in the case of the earth element, etc.; as *matter possessing real characteristics* (*salakkhaṇarūpa*) because they are marked by the three general characteristics of impermanence, suffering, and non-self; as *concretely produced matter* (*nipphannarūpa*) because they are directly produced by conditions such as kamma, etc.; as *material matter* (*rūparūpa*) because they possess matter's essential characteristic of undergoing deformation; and *as matter to be comprehended by insight* (*sammasanarūpa*) because they are to be made the objects of insight contemplation by way of the three characteristics.

§4 In Detail: Non-Concretely Produced Matter

(8) *Ākāsadhātu paricchedarūpaṁ nāma.*
(9) *Kāyaviññatti vacīviññatti viññattirūpaṁ nāma.*
(10) *Rūpassa lahutā, mudutā, kammaññatā, viññattidvayaṁ vikārarūpaṁ nāma.*
(11) *Rūpassa upacayo, santati, jaratā, aniccatā lakkhaṇarūpaṁ nāma. Jātirūpam eva pan' ettha upacayasantatināmena pavuccati.*

(8) Limiting material phenomenon: the element of space.
(9) Intimating material phenomena: bodily intimation and vocal intimation.
(10) Mutable material phenomena: material lightness, malleability, wieldiness, and the two forms of intimation.
(11) Characteristics of material phenomena: material production, continuity, decay, and impermanence. Here by production and continuity are meant the material phenomenon of birth.

Guide to §4

Non-concretely produced matter: The types of matter in groups (8)-(11) are designated non-concretely produced matter (*anipphannarūpa*) because they do not arise directly from the four main causes of matter (see §9) but exist as modalities or attributes of concretely produced matter. Thus they are not included among the ultimate realities (*paramattha dhamma*).

(8) **The space element (*ākāsadhātu*)**: Space, as understood in the Abhidhamma, is not bare geometric extension but the void region that delimits and separates objects and groups of material phenomena, enabling them to be perceived as distinct. The space element has the characteristic of delimiting matter. Its function is to display the boundaries of matter. It is manifested as the confines of matter, or as the state of gaps and apertures. Its proximate cause is the matter delimited.

(9) **Intimating material phenomena (*viññattirūpa*)**: *Viññatti*, intimation, is that by means of which one communicates one's ideas, feelings, and attitudes to another. There are two means of intimation, bodily and vocal. The former is a special modification in the consciousness-originated air element which causes the body to move in ways that reveal one's intentions. The latter is a special modification in the consciousness-originated earth element which issues in speech by which one reveals one's intentions. Both have the function of displaying intention. They are manifested, respectively, as a cause of bodily movement and of verbal expression. Their proximate causes are, respectively, the air element and the earth element born of consciousness.

(10) **Mutable material phenomena (*vikārarūpa*)**: This category comprises special modes or manifestations of concretely produced matter. It includes the two types of intimation and three other material phenomena: lightness, malleability, and wieldiness.

Among these, *lightness* (*lahutā*) has the characteristic of non-sluggishness. Its function is to dispel heaviness in matter. It is manifested as light transformability. Its proximate cause is light matter.

Malleability (*mudutā*) has the characteristic of non-rigidity. Its function is to dispel rigidity in matter. It is manifested as non-opposition to any kind of action. Its proximate cause is malleable matter.

Wieldiness (*kammaññatā*) has the characteristic of wieldiness that is favourable to bodily action. Its function is to dispel unwieldiness. It is manifested as non-weakness. Its proximate cause is wieldy matter.

(11) **Characteristics of material phenomena (*lakkhaṇarūpa*)**: This category includes four types of material phenomena. Of these, production (*upacaya*) and continuity (*santati*) are both terms for the genesis, arising, or birth (*jāti*) of matter. They differ in that production is the first

arising of a material process, the initial launching or setting up of the process, while continuity is the repeated genesis of material phenomena in the same material process. For example, the arising of the body, sex and heart groups at conception is production, while the subsequent arising of those same material groups throughout life is continuity.

Production of matter has the characteristic of setting up. Its function is to make material instances emerge for the first time. It is manifested as launching or as the completed state. Its proximate cause is the matter produced.

Continuity of matter has the characteristic of occurrence. Its function is to anchor. It is manifested as non-interruption. Its proximate cause is matter to be anchored.

Decay (*jaratā*) has the characteristic of the maturing or aging of material phenomena. Its function is to lead them on towards their termination. It is manifested as loss of newness without loss of being. Its proximate cause is matter that is decaying.

Impermanence (*aniccatā*) has the characteristic of the complete breaking up of material phenomena. Its function is to make them subside. It is manifested as destruction and falling away. Its proximate cause is matter that is completely breaking up.

§5 Twenty-eight Kinds of Matter

Iti ekādasavidham p'etaṁ rūpaṁ aṭṭhavīsatividhaṁ hoti sarūpavasena. Kathaṁ?

Bhūtappasādavisayā bhāvo hadayam icc' api
Jīvitāhārarūpehi aṭṭhārasavidhaṁ tathā.
Paricchedo ca viññatti vikāro lakkhaṇan ti ca
Anipphannā dasa cā ti aṭṭhavīsavidhaṁ bhave.

Ayam ettha rūpasamuddeso.

Thus the eleven kinds of material phenomena are treated as twenty-eight according to their specific properties. How (twenty-eight)?

Essentials, sensory organs, objects, sex, heart, life, and nutriment—thus concrete matter is eighteenfold.

Limitation (space), intimation, mutability, and characteristics—thus there are ten that are not concretely produced. In all there are twenty-eight.

Herein, this is the enumeration of matter.

Classification of Matter
(*rūpavibhāga*)

§6 As Singlefold

Sabbañ ca pan' etaṁ rūpaṁ ahetukaṁ, sappaccayaṁ, sāsavaṁ, sankhataṁ, lokiyaṁ, kāmāvacaraṁ, anārammaṇaṁ, appahātabbam evā ti ekavidham pi ajjhattikabāhirādivasena bahudhā bhedaṁ gacchati.

Now all this matter is singlefold in so far as it is all: rootless, with conditions, subject to taints, conditioned, mundane, pertaining to the sense-sphere, objectless, not to be abandoned. However, when conceived as internal and external, etc., matter becomes manifold.

Guide to §6

All this matter is singlefold: All matter is *rootless* because it does not associate with either the wholesome, unwholesome, or indeterminate roots, association with roots being restricted to mental phenomena. All matter is *with conditions* because it arises dependent on the four causes (see §9 below). It is *subject to taints* (*sāsava*) because it can be made an object of the four taints (see VII, §3).[5] It is all *conditioned* and *mundane* because there is no matter that transcends the world of the five clinging aggregates. All matter is of the *sense sphere*: though matter exists in the fine-material plane, it pertains by its nature to the sense sphere because it is the object of sensual craving. Matter is *objectless* because, unlike mental phenomena, it cannot know an object; and it is *not to be abandoned* because it cannot be abandoned, like the defilements, by the four supramundane paths.

§7 As Manifold

Kathaṁ?

Pasādasankhātaṁ pañcavidham pi ajjhattikarūpaṁ nāma; itaraṁ bāhirarūpaṁ.

Pasāda-hadayasankhātaṁ chabbidham pi vatthurūpaṁ nāma; itaraṁ avatthurūpaṁ.

Pasāda-viññattisankhātaṁ sattavidham pi dvārarūpaṁ nāma; itaraṁ advārarūpaṁ.

Pasāda-bhāva-jīvitasankhātaṁ aṭṭhavidham pi indriyarūpaṁ nāma; itaraṁ anindriyarūpaṁ.

How?

The five kinds of sensitive material phenomena are internal; the rest are external.

The six kinds, comprising the sensitive organs and the heart, are material phenomena that are bases; the rest are not bases.

The seven kinds, comprising the sensitive organs and (the two) media of intimation, are material phenomena that are doors; the rest are not doors.

The eight kinds, comprising the sensitive organs, sex states and life, are material phenomena that are faculties; the rest are not faculties.

Pasāda-visayasankhātaṁ dvādasavidham pi oḷārikarūpaṁ, santike rūpaṁ, sappaṭigharūpañ ca; itaraṁ sukhumarūpaṁ, dūre rūpaṁ, appaṭigharūpañ ca.

Kammajaṁ upādinnarūpaṁ; itaraṁ anupādinnarūpaṁ.
Rūpāyatanaṁ sanidassanarūpaṁ; itaraṁ anidassanarūpaṁ.

The twelve kinds, comprising the five sensitive organs and (seven) sense objects, are gross, proximate, and impinging material phenomena; the rest are subtle, distant, and non-impinging.

Material phenomena born of kamma are "clung-to"; the others are "not clung-to."

The visible form base is visible; the rest are non-visible.

Cakkhādidvayaṁ asampattavasena, ghānādittayaṁ sampattavasenā ti pañcavidham pi gocaraggāhikarūpaṁ; itaraṁ agocaraggāhikarūpaṁ.

Vaṇṇo, gandho, raso, ojā, bhūtacatukkañ cā ti aṭṭhavidham pi avinibbhogarūpaṁ; itaraṁ vinibbhogarūpaṁ.

Eye and ear, as not reaching (their object), and nose, tongue and body, as reaching (their object), are five kinds of material phenomena that take objects; the others are material phenomena that do not take objects.

Colour, odour, taste, nutritive essence, and the four essentials are the eight kinds of material phenomena that are inseparable; the rest are separable.

Guide to §7

Internal (*ajjhattika*): Here, the term "internal" is used in relation to matter in a technical sense applicable only to the five types of sensitive materiality which serve as the doors for the mental phenomena. Although other types of material phenomena occur within the physical body, only these five sensitive factors are referred to as internal.

Bases (*vatthu*): see III, §20.

Doors (*dvāra*): The five sensitive material phenomena are doors of cognition, that is, media for consciousness and mental factors to encounter their objects. Bodily and vocal intimation are doors of action, that is, channels for bodily and verbal deeds.

Faculties (*indriya*): The sensitivities are so called because they exercise a controlling power (*indra*) in their respective spheres. Each of these controls the coexistent material phenomena in exercising its specific function, such as seeing, hearing, etc. The sex faculty controls the manifestation of masculine or feminine features and traits. The life faculty controls the coexistent types of matter, as a pilot controls a ship.

Gross, proximate, and impinging material phenomena: These three terms are used here in a technical sense which should not be confused with their ordinary connotations. They are restricted in application to the material phenomena that are instrumental in the genesis of sense consciousness, and imply nothing about the relative size or nearness of the object. These phenomena are twelvefold—the five sensitive organs and the seven objective data—the tangible base being reckoned as threefold because it consists of three great essentials.

Those material phenomena which do not directly contribute to the arising of sense consciousness are called subtle, distant, and non-impinging, again, regardless of their size and distance.

Clung-to (*upādinna*): The eighteen kinds of matter born of kamma are known as "clung-to," because they have been acquired as the fruits of kamma motivated by craving and wrong view. Matter produced by causes other than kamma is known as "not clung-to." Generally, however, in a less technical sense, all organic matter in the body is referred to as "clung-to," while inorganic matter is spoken of as "not clung-to." It should be noted that, unlike the other pairs of terms used for the purpose of classification, the pair "clung-to" and "not clung-to" does not establish a mutually exclusive dichotomy, for nine kinds of material phenomena born of kamma can also originate from other causes (see below, §17).

Eye and ear, as not reaching (their object): According to the Abhidhamma, the eye and ear are regarded as sense organs that do not reach or touch (*asampatta*) their respective objects. For the eye or ear to serve as a base for consciousness, its objects must be non-contiguous. In contrast, the other three sense organs, it is held, directly touch (*sampatta*) their objects.

Material phenomena that take objects: The Pali expression *gocaraggāhika* is used figuratively to indicate that the five sense organs serve as the bases for the consciousnesses that arise with their support. But the sense organs, being matter, cannot literally apprehend objects. Rather, it is the sense consciousnesses based on them that actually cognize the objects.

Material phenomena that are inseparable: The four great essentials and four derivatives—colour, smell, taste, and nutritive essence—are known as inseparable matter (*avinibbhogarūpa*) because they are always bound together and are present in all material objects from the simplest to the most complex. The other types of material phenomena may be present or not, and are thus regarded as separable. A material group (*kalāpa*) that consists solely of these eight elements is known as a "pure octad" (*suddhaṭṭhaka*) or a "group with nutritive essence as eighth" (*ojaṭṭhamaka*).

§8 Summary

Icc' evam aṭṭhavīsati vidham pi ca vicakkhaṇā
Ajjhattikādibhedena vibhajanti yathārahaṁ .

Ayam ettha rūpavibhāgo.

Thus the wise analyze in a fitting way the twenty-eight kinds of matter with respect to such divisions as the internal and so forth.

Herein, this is the classification of matter.

Guide to §8

For a schematic representation of the classifications of material phenomena, also in regard to their modes of origin and formation into groups, see Table 6.3 at the end of this chapter.

The Origination of Matter (*rūpasamuṭṭhāna*)

§9 The Four Modes of Origin

Kammaṁ, cittaṁ, utu, āhāro cā ti cattāri rūpasamuṭṭhānāni nāma.

Material phenomena originate in four ways, from kamma, consciousness, temperature, and nutriment.

§10 Kamma as a Mode of Origin

Tattha kāmāvacaraṁ rūpāvacarañ cā ti pañcavīsatividham pi kusalākusalakammam abhisankhataṁ ajjhattikasantāne kammasamuṭṭhānarūpaṁ paṭisandhim upādāya khaṇe khaṇe samuṭṭhāpeti.

Therein, the twenty-five kinds of wholesome and unwholesome kamma pertaining to the sense sphere and the fine-material sphere produce, in one's internal continuum, volitionally conditioned material phenomena originating from kamma, moment by moment beginning with rebirth-linking.

Guide to §10

Material phenomena originating from kamma (*kammasamuṭṭhānarūpa*): Kamma here refers to volition (*cetanā*) in past wholesome and unwholesome states of consciousness. The twenty-five kinds of kamma that produce material phenomena are the volitions of the twelve unwholesome cittas, the eight great wholesome cittas, and the five fine-material wholesome cittas. The volitions of the wholesome immaterial-sphere cittas generate rebirth in the immaterial plane and thus cannot produce material phenomena originating from kamma.

Kamma produces material phenomena at each sub-moment among the three sub-moments of consciousness—arising, presence, and dissolution—starting with the arising sub-moment of the rebirth-linking consciousness; it continues to do so throughout the course of existence up to the seventeenth mind-moment preceding the death consciousness. Eighteen kinds of material phenomena are produced by kamma: the eight inseparables in the nine groups produced by kamma (see §17); the five sensitivities; the two sex faculties; the life faculty; the heart-base; and space. Of these, nine kinds—the eight faculties and the heart-base—arise exclusively from kamma. The other nine kinds arise from kamma only when they occur in the kamma-born groups; otherwise they originate from the other causes.

§11 Consciousness as a Mode of Origin

Arūpavipāka-dvipañcaviññāṇa-vajjitaṁ pañcasattatividham pi cittaṁ cittasamuṭṭhānarūpaṁ paṭhamabhavangam upādāya jāyantam eva samuṭṭhāpeti.

The seventy-five types of consciousness, excluding the immaterial-sphere resultants and the two sets of fivefold sense consciousness, produce material phenomena originating from consciousness beginning with the first moment of the life-continuum, but they do so only (at the moment of) arising.

Tattha appanājavanaṁ iriyāpatham pi sannāmeti. Votthapana-kāmāvacarajavan'-ābhiññā pana viññattim pi samuṭṭhāpenti. Somanassajavanāni pan' ettha terasa hasanam pi janenti.

Therein, the javanas of absorption also uphold the bodily postures. But the determining consciousness, javanas of the sense sphere, and direct-knowledge consciousness produce also (bodily and vocal) intimation. Herein, the thirteen javanas accompanied by joy produce smiling too.

Guide to §11

Material phenomena originating from consciousness (*cittasamuṭṭhāna-rūpa*): Material phenomena produced by consciousness spring up starting from the arising moment of the first bhavanga citta immediately after the rebirth consciousness. The rebirth consciousness does not produce consciousness-born matter, since at the moment of rebirth the matter that arises is born of kamma, and because this consciousness is a newcomer to the new existence. The tenfold sense consciousness lacks the power to produce matter, and the four immaterial resultants cannot do so since they arise only in the immaterial realms. According to the commentators mental phenomena are strongest at the moment of arising, material phenomena strongest at the moment of presence. Consciousness therefore produces matter only at its arising moment, when it is strongest, not at the moments of presence and dissolution.

The javanas of absorption, etc.: The maintenance or upholding of the bodily postures is a function of states of consciousness. The twenty-six javanas of absorption perform this function minimally, by maintaining the body in a sitting, standing, or lying position. The other thirty-two cittas mentioned—the determining consciousness, sense-sphere javanas, and direct-knowledge cittas—not only uphold the postures but also activate bodily and vocal intimation.

Thirteen ... produce smiling too: An ordinary worldling may smile or laugh with any of the four cittas rooted in greed and accompanied by joy, or with any of the four great wholesome cittas accompanied by joy. Trainees smile with six of these cittas, the two connected with wrong view being excluded. Arahants may smile with one of five cittas—the four joyful great functionals and the rootless smile-producing citta.

On how different types of consciousness produce various material phenomena, see Table 6.2.

TABLE 6.2: CONSCIOUSNESS AS A CAUSE OF MATERIAL PHENOMENA

CITTAS	No. of Cittas	Consness.-born Matter	Postures	Intimation	Smiling
Greed-rooted - joy	4	+	+	+	+
" " - equanimity	4	+	+	+	—
Hate-rooted	2	+	+	+	—
Delusion-rooted	2	+	+	+	—
Sense consciousness	10	—	—	—	—
Receiving	2	+	—	—	—
Investigating	3	+	—	—	—
Five-door adverting	1	+	—	—	—
Mind-door adverting	1	+	+	+	—
Smile-producing	1	+	+	+	+
SS wholesome - joy	4	+	+	+	+
SS wholesome - equanimity	4	+	+	+	—
SS resultant	8	+	—	—	—
SS functional - joy	4	+	+	+	+
" " - equanimity	4	+	+	+	—
FMS wholesome	5	+	+	—	—
" resultant	5	+	—	—	—
" functional	5	+	+	—	—
IS wholesome	4	+	+	—	—
" resultant	4	—	—	—	—
" functional	4	+	+	—	—
Supramundane	8	+	+	—	—
Direct knowledge	2	+	+	+	—

§12 Temperature as a Mode of Origin

Sītuṇhotu-samaññātā tejodhātu ṭhitipattā va utusamuṭṭhānarūpaṁ ajjhattañ ca bahiddhā ca yathārahaṁ samuṭṭhāpeti.

The fire element, which comprises both cold and heat, on reaching its stage of presence, produces, according to circumstances, both internal and external material phenomena originating from temperature.

Guide to §12

Material phenomena originating from temperature (*utusamuṭṭhānarūpa*): Beginning from the stage of presence at the moment of rebirth-linking, the internal fire element found in the material groups born of kamma combines with the external fire element and starts producing organic material phenomena originating from temperature. Thereafter the fire element in the material groups born of all four causes produces organic material phenomena born of temperature throughout the course of existence. Externally, temperature or the fire element also produces inorganic material phenomena, such as climatic and geological transformations.

§13 Nutriment as a Mode of Origin

Ojāsankhāto āhāro āhārasamuṭṭhānarūpaṁ ajjhoharaṇakāle ṭhānappatto va samuṭṭhāpeti.

Nutriment, known as nutritive essence, on reaching its stage of presence, produces material phenomena originating from nutriment at the time it is swallowed.

Guide to §13

Material phenomena originating from nutriment (*āhārasamuṭṭhānarūpa*): The internal nutritive essence, supported by the external, produces material phenomena at the moment of presence starting from the time it is swallowed. The nutritive essence that has reached presence in the material groups originating from nutriment produces a further pure octad, and the nutritive essence in that octad originates still a further octad; thus the occurrence of octads links up ten or twelve times. The nutriment taken by a pregnant mother, pervading the body of the embryo, originates materiality in the child. Even nutriment smeared on the body is said to originate materiality. The nutritive essence in the internal groups born of the other three causes also originates several occurrences of pure octads in succession. The nutriment taken on one day can support the body for as long as seven days.

§14 Analysis by way of Origins

Tattha hadaya-indriyarūpāni kammajān' eva, viññattidvayaṁ cittajam eva, saddo cittotujo, lahutādittayaṁ utucittāhārehi sambhoti. Avinibbhogarūpāni c'eva ākāsadhātu ca catūhi sambhūtāni. Lakkhaṇarūpāni na kutoci jāyanti.

Therein, the material phenomena of the heart and the (eight) faculties are born of kamma. The two media of intimation are born only of consciousness. Sound is born of consciousness and temperature. The triple qualities of lightness, (malleability, and wieldiness) arise from temperature, consciousness, and nutriment. The inseparable material phenomena and the element of space arise from four causes. Characteristic material phenomena do not arise from any cause.

Guide to §14

Articulate sounds are caused by consciousness, inarticulate sounds by temperature. The triple qualities of lightness, malleability, and wieldiness arise from favourable climatic conditions, a buoyant state of mind, and wholesome nutriment, while unfavourable climate, depressed states of mind, and unwholesome nutriment cause heaviness, rigidity, and unwieldiness in the physical body. The space element occurs as the interstices between the material groups born of the four causes, and therefore it is regarded as being derivatively born of the four causes. The reason why the characteristics do not arise from any cause is explained in the next section.

§15 Summary

Aṭṭhārasa paṇṇarasa terasa dvādasā ti ca
Kammacittotukāhārajāni honti yathākkamaṁ.
Jāyamānādirūpānaṁ sabhāvattā hi kevalaṁ
Lakkhaṇāni na jāyanti kehicī ti pakāsitaṁ.

Ayam ettha rūpasamuṭṭhānanayo.

Eighteen, fifteen, thirteen, and twelve arise respectively from kamma, consciousness, temperature, and nutriment.

It is explained that the characteristics (of material phenomena) are not produced by any (modes of origin) since their intrinsic nature consists solely in the qualities of being produced, etc.

Herein, this is the origination of matter.

Guide to §15

The eighteen that arise from kamma are: 8 inseparables + 8 faculties + heart-base + space.

The fifteen that arise from consciousness are: 8 inseparables + 5 mutables + sound + space.

The thirteen that arise from temperature are: 8 inseparables + lightness triad + sound + space.

The twelve that arise from nutriment are: 8 inseparables + lightness triad + space.

The twenty-eight material phenomena can be further classified according to their number of causes as follows:

one cause: 8 faculties + heart-base + 2 intimations = 11;
two causes: sound = 1;
three causes: lightness triad = 3;
four causes: 8 inseparables + space = 9;
causeless: characteristics = 4.

The Grouping of Material Phenomena (*kalāpayojana*)

§16 In Brief

Ekuppādā ekanirodhā ekanissayā sahavuttino ekavīsati rūpakalāpā nāma.

There are twenty-one material groups inasmuch as they arise together, cease together, have a common basis, and occur together.

Guide to §16

Material phenomena do not occur singly, but in combinations or groups known as *rūpakalāpas*, of which twenty-one are enumerated. Just as all the cetasikas possess four characteristics (see II, §1), so too do the material phenomena in a group. All the material phenomena in a group arise together and cease together. They have a common base, namely, the conascent great essentials, which are the proximate cause for the derivative phenomena as well as for each other. And they all occur together from their arising to their cessation.

§17 Groups Originating from Kamma

Tattha jīvitaṁ avinibbhogarūpañ ca cakkhunā saha cakkhudasakan ti pavuccati. Tathā sotādīhi saddhiṁ sotadasakaṁ, ghānadasakam, jivhādasakaṁ, kāyadasakaṁ, itthibhāvadasakaṁ, pumbhāvadasakaṁ, vatthudasakañ cā ti yathākkamaṁ yojetabbaṁ. Avinibbhogarūpam eva jīvitena saha jīvitanavakan ti pavuccati. Ime nava kamma-samuṭṭhānakalāpā.

Therein, life and the (eight) inseparable material phenomena together with the eye are called the eye decad. Similarly, (by joining the former nine) together with the ear and so forth, the ear decad, nose decad, tongue decad, body decad, female decad, male decad, (heart-)base decad, should respectively be formed. Inseparable material phenomena, together with life, are called the vital nonad. These nine groups originate from kamma.

§18 Groups Originating from Consciousness

Avinibbhogarūpaṁ pana suddhaṭṭhakaṁ. Tad eva kāyaviññattiyā saha kāyaviññattinavakaṁ; vacīviññatti saddehi saha vacīviññattidasakaṁ; lahutādīhi saddhiṁ lahutādi-ekādasakaṁ, kāyaviññatti-lahutādi-dvādasakaṁ, vacīviññatti-saddalahutādi-terasakañ cā ti cha cittasamuṭṭhānakalāpā.

The inseparable material phenomena constitute the "pure octad." They, together with bodily intimation, constitute the bodily intimation nonad; together with vocal intimation and sound, the vocal intimation decad; together with the material phenomena of the lightness triad, the un-decad of the lightness triad; the dodecad of bodily intimation and the lightness triad; and the tridecad of vocal intimation, sound, and the lightness triad. These six material groups originate from consciousness.

§19 Groups Originating from Temperature

Suddhaṭṭhakaṁ, saddanavakaṁ, lahutādi-ekādasakaṁ, sadda-lahutādi-dvādasakañ cā ti cattāro utusamuṭṭhānakalāpā.

The pure octad, the sound nonad, the un-decad of the lightness triad; the dodecad of sound and the lightness triad—these four originate from temperature.

§20 Groups Originating from Nutriment

Suddhaṭṭhakaṁ lahutādi-ekādasakañ cā ti dve āhārasamuṭṭhāna-kalāpā.

The pure octad and the un-decad of the lightness triad are the two material groups that originate from nutriment.

§21 The Internal and External

Tattha suddhaṭṭhakaṁ saddanavakañ cā ti dve utusamuṭṭhāna-kalāpā bahiddhā pi labbhanti. Avasesā pana sabbe pi ajjhattikam eva.

Of them, the two material groups produced by temperature—the pure octad and the sound nonad—are found externally too. All the rest are strictly internal.

§22 Summary

Kammacittotukāhārasamuṭṭhānā yathākkamaṁ
Nava cha caturo dve ti kalāpā ekavīsati.
Kalāpānaṁ paricchedalakkhaṇattā vicakkhaṇā
Na kalāpangam icc' āhu ākāsaṁ lakkhaṇāni ca.

Ayam ettha kalāpayojanā.

There are twenty-one material groups—nine, six, four, and two—produced in due order from kamma, consciousness, temperature, and nutriment.

As space demarcates, and the characteristic marks just indicate, the wise state that they are not constituents of material groups.

Herein, this is the grouping of material phenomena.

Guide to §22

The nine groups produced by kamma are: (1) the eye decad; (2) the ear decad; (3) the nose decad; (4) the tongue decad; (5) the body decad; (6) the female decad; (7) the male decad; (8) the heart-base decad; (9) the vital nonad.

The six groups produced by consciousness are: (1) the pure octad; (2) the bodily intimation nonad; (3) the vocal intimation nonad; (4) the lightness triad un-decad; (5) the bodily intimation and lightness triad dodecad; (6) the vocal intimation, sound, and lightness triad tridecad.

The four groups produced by temperature are: (1) the pure octad; (2) the sound nonad; (3) the lightness triad un-decad; (4) the sound and lightness triad dodecad.

The two groups produced by nutriment are: (1) the pure octad; (2) the lightness triad un-decad.

The Occurrence of Material Phenomena (*rūpappavattikkama*)

§23 In the Sensuous World

Sabbāni pan' etāni rūpāni kāmaloke yathārahaṁ anūnāni pavattiyaṁ upalabbhanti. Paṭisandhiyaṁ pana saṁsedajānañ c' eva opapātikānañ ca cakkhu-sota-ghāna-jivhā-kāya-bhāva-vatthu-dasaka-saṅkhātāni satta dasakāni pātubhavanti ukkaṭṭhavasena. Omaka-vasena pana cakkhu-sota-ghāna-bhāva-dasakāni kadāci pi na labbhanti. Tasmā tesaṁ vasena kalāpahāni veditabbā.

All these material phenomena are obtained with no deficiency, according to circumstances, during the course of existence in the sensuous world. But at rebirth-linking, to moisture-born beings and to those of spontaneous birth, there arise at most the seven decads—the decads of eye, ear, nose, tongue, body, sex, and the heart-base. As a minimum, sometimes the eye, ear, nose, and sex decads are not obtained. This is how deficiencies of material groups should be understood.

Gabbhaseyyakasattānam pana kāya-bhāva-vatthu-dasaka-saṅkhātāni tīṇi dasakāni pātubhavanti. Tatthā pi bhāvadasakaṁ kadāci na labbhati. Tato paraṁ pavattikāle kamena cakkhudasakādīni ca pātubhavanti.

To the womb-born creatures there arise (at rebirth) three decads—the decads of body, sex, and the heart-base. Sometimes, however, the sex decad is not obtained. Thereafter, during the course of existence, gradually there arise the eye decad and so forth.

Guide to §23

The present section deals with the manner in which these material groups come into being at the moment of conception, during the course of existence, and in different realms. According to Buddhism there are four kinds of birth, namely, egg-born beings (*aṇḍaja*), womb-born beings (*jalābuja*), moisture-born beings (*saṁsedaja*), and beings having spontaneous birth (*opapātika*). Moisture-born beings include certain lowly forms of animal life. Beings having a spontaneous birth are generally invisible to the physical eye. Petas and devas usually belong to this class. By the mention of "womb-born creatures" in the text, egg-born beings are also implicitly included.

§24 The Continuity of Occurrence

Icc' evaṁ paṭisandhim upādāya kammasamuṭṭhānā, dutiyacittam upādāya cittasamuṭṭhānā, ṭhitikālam upādāya utusamuṭṭhānā, ojāpharaṇam upādāya āhārasamuṭṭhānā cā ti catusamuṭṭhāna-rūpakalāpasantati kāmaloke dīpajālā viya nadīsoto viya ca yāvatāyukaṁ abbocchinnaṁ pavattati.

Thus the continuity of material groups produced in four ways—namely, kamma-born from the time of rebirth-linking, consciousness-born from the second moment of consciousness, temperature-born from the time of the stage of presence, nutriment-born from the time of the diffusion of nutritive essence—uninterruptedly flows on in the sense sphere till the end of life, like the flame of a lamp or the stream of a river.

§25 At the Time of Death

Maraṇakāle pana cuticitt' opari sattarasamacittassa ṭhitikālam upādāya kammajarūpāni na uppajjanti. Puretaraṁ uppannāni ca kammajarūpāni cuticittasamakālam eva pavattitvā nirujjhanti. Tato paraṁ cittajāhārajarūpañ ca vocchijjati. Tato paraṁ utusamuṭṭhāna-rūpaparamparā yāva matakalebarasankhātā pavattanti.

But at the time of death, kamma-born material phenomena no longer arise starting with the stage of presence of the seventeenth consciousness preceding the death consciousness. Kamma-born material phenomena that arose earlier occur till the death-moment and then cease. Following that, the consciousness-born and nutriment-born material phenomena come to cessation. Thereafter, a continuity of material qualities produced by temperature persists in the form of the corpse.

§26 Verse

Icc' evaṁ matasattānaṁ punad eva bhavantare
Paṭisandhim upādāya tathā rūpaṁ pavattati.

Thus to the deceased beings, again in a subsequent life, material phenomena arise, starting from rebirth-linking, in the same way.

§27 In the Fine-material World

Rūpaloke pana ghāna-jivhā-kāya-bhāva-dasakāni ca āhāraja-kalāpāni ca na labbhanti. Tasmā tesaṁ paṭisandhikāle cakkhu-sota-vatthuvasena tīṇi dasakāni jīvitanavakañ cā ti cattāro kamma-samuṭṭhānakalāpā, pavattiyaṁ cittotusamuṭṭhānā ca labbhanti.

In the fine-material world, the decads of nose, tongue, body, sex, and the material groups produced by nutriment are not found. Therefore, to those beings, at the time of rebirth-linking there arise four material groups produced by kamma—the three decads of eye, ear, and heart-base, and the vital nonad. During the course of existence, material phenomena produced by consciousness and by temperature are found.

Guide to §27

The beings in the fine-material realms, being asexual, lack the two decads of sex, and though they possess the physical forms of the nose, tongue and body, these organs are destitute of sense receptivity.

§28 Among Non-Percipient Beings

Asaññasattānaṁ pana cakkhu-sota-vatthu-saddāni pi na labbhanti. Tathā sabbāni pi cittajarūpāni. Tasmā tesaṁ paṭisandhikāle jīvitanavakam eva pavattiyañ ca saddavajjitaṁ utusamuṭṭhānarūpaṁ atiricchati.

Among the non-percipient beings, the eye, ear, heart-base, and sound are also not found. Similarly, no consciousness-born material phenomena are found. Therefore, at the moment of their rebirth-linking, only the vital nonad arises. During the course of existence, material phenomena produced by temperature, with the exception of sound, continue.

§29 Summary

Icc' evaṁ kāma-rūp'-āsaññisankhātesu tīsu ṭhānesu paṭisandhi-pavattivasena duvidhā rūpappavatti veditabbā.

Thus in the three cases of the sensuous world, the fine-material world, and non-percipient beings, the occurrence of material phenomena should be understood as twofold, by way of rebirth-linking and the course of existence.

Aṭṭhavīsati kāmesu honti tevīsa rūpisu
Sattaras' ev' asaññīnaṁ arūpe natthi kiñci pi.
Saddo vikāro jaratā maraṇañ c' opapattiyaṁ
Na labbhanti pavatte tu na kiñci pi na labbhati.

Ayam ettha rūpappavattikkamo.

In the sense planes, twenty-eight material phenomena are found; in the fine-material planes, twenty-three; among the non-percipients, seventeen; but none in the immaterial plane.

At the moment of conception, sound, mutability, decay, and death are not found. In the course of existence, there is nothing that is not obtained.

Herein, this is the procedure regarding the occurrence of material phenomena.

Nibbāna

§30 Definition

Nibbānaṁ pana lokuttarasankhātaṁ catumaggañāṇena sacchikātabbaṁ magga-phalānam ālambanabhūtaṁ vānasankhātāya taṇhāya nikkhantattā nibbānan ti pavuccati.

Nibbāna is termed supramundane, and is to be realized by the knowledge of the four paths. It becomes an object to the paths and fruits, and is called Nibbāna because it is a departure from craving, which is an entanglement.

Guide to §30

Nibbāna is termed supramundane: The concluding section of this chapter deals briefly with the fourth ultimate reality, Nibbāna. Etymologically, the word *nibbāna* —the Pali form of the better known Sanskrit *nirvāṇa*—is derived from a verb *nibbāti* meaning "to be blown out" or "to be extinguished." It thus signifies the extinguishing of the worldly "fires" of greed, hatred, and delusion. But the Pali commentators prefer to treat it as the negation of, or "departure from" (*nikkhantatta*), the entanglement (*vāna*) of craving, the derivation which is offered here. For as long as one is entangled by craving, one remains bound in *saṁsāra*, the cycle of birth and death; but when all craving has been extirpated, one attains Nibbāna, deliverance from the cycle of birth and death.

§31 Analysis

Tad etaṁ sabhāvato ekavidham pi sa-upādisesa-nibbānadhātu anupādisesa-nibbānadhātu cā ti duvidhaṁ hoti kāraṇapariyāyena. Tathā suññataṁ animittaṁ appaṇihitañ cā ti tividhaṁ hoti ākārabhedena.

Though Nibbāna is onefold according to its intrinsic nature, by reference to a basis (for distinction), it is twofold, namely, the element of Nibbāna with the residue remaining, and the element of Nibbāna without the residue remaining. It is threefold according to its different aspects, namely, void, signless, and desireless.

Guide to §31

Though Nibbāna is onefold according to its intrinsic nature, etc.: Nibbāna is a single undifferentiated ultimate reality. It is exclusively supramundane, and has one intrinsic nature (*sabhāva*), which is that of being the unconditioned deathless element totally transcendent to the conditioned world. Nevertheless, by reference to a basis for distinction, Nibbāna is said to be twofold. The basis for distinction is the presence or absence of the five aggregates. The element of Nibbāna as experienced by Arahants is called "with the residue remaining" (*sa-upādisesa*) because, though the defilements have all been extinguished, the "residue" of aggregates acquired by past clinging remains through the duration of the Arahant's life. The element of Nibbāna attained with the Arahant's demise is called that "without the residue remaining" (*anupādisesa*), because the five aggregates are discarded and are never acquired again.

The two elements of Nibbāna are also called, in the Commentaries, the extinguishment of the defilements (*kilesa-parinibbāna*) and the extinguishment of the aggregates (*khandha-parinibbāna*).

It is threefold according to its different aspects: Nibbāna is called the void (*suññata*) because it is devoid of greed, hatred, and delusion, and because it is devoid of all that is conditioned. It is called signless (*animitta*) because it is free from the signs of greed, etc., and free from the signs of all conditioned things. It is called desireless (*appaṇihita*) because it is free from the hankering of greed, etc., and because it is not desired by craving.

§32 Summary

Padam accutam accantam asankhatam anuttaraṁ
Nibbānam iti bhāsanti vānamuttā mahesayo.
Iti cittaṁ cetasikaṁ rūpaṁ nibbānam icc' api
Paramatthaṁ pakāsenti catudhā va tathāgatā.

Great seers who are free from craving declare that Nibbāna is an objective state which is deathless, absolutely endless, unconditioned, and unsurpassed.

Thus as fourfold the Tathāgatas reveal the ultimate realities—consciousness, mental factors, matter, and Nibbāna.

Iti Abhidhammatthasangahe
Rūpasangahavibhāgo nāma
chaṭṭho paricchedo.

Thus ends the sixth chapter
in the Manual of Abhidhamma entitled
the Compendium of Matter.

TABLE 6.3

COMPREHENSIVE CHART ON MATTER

28 Material Phenomena (§§ 2-5)		16 Classifications (§§ 7-8)																	
		Essentials	Derived	Internal	External	Base	Non-Base	Door	Non-Door	Faculty	Non-faculty	Gross, Etc.	Subtle, Etc.	Clung-to	Not Clung-to	Taking Objects	No Objects	Inseparable	Separable
1	Earth	■			■		■		■		■	■		■	■		■	■	
2	Water	■			■		■		■		■		■	■	■		■	■	
3	Fire	■			■		■		■		■	■		■	■		■	■	
4	Air	■			■		■		■		■	■		■	■		■	■	
5	Eye		■	■		■		■		■		■		■		■			■
6	Ear		■	■		■		■		■		■		■		■			■
7	Nose		■	■		■		■		■		■		■		■			■
8	Tongue		■	■		■		■		■		■		■		■			■
9	Body		■	■		■		■		■		■		■		■			■
10	Form		■		■		■		■		■	■		■	■		■	■	
11	Sound		■		■		■		■		■	■			■		■		■
12	Smell		■		■		■		■		■	■		■	■		■	■	
13	Taste		■		■		■		■		■	■		■	■		■	■	
*	Tangibility																		
14	Femininity		■		■		■		■	■			■	■			■		■
15	Masculinity		■		■		■		■	■			■	■			■		■
16	Heart-base		■		■	■			■		■		■	■			■		■
17	Life faculty		■		■		■		■	■			■	■			■		■
18	Nutriment		■		■		■		■		■		■	■	■		■	■	
19	Space		■		■		■		■		■		■	■	■		■		■
20	Bodily intim.		■		■		■	■			■		■		■		■		■
21	Vocal intim.		■		■		■	■			■		■		■		■		■
22	Lightness		■		■		■		■		■		■		■		■		■
23	Malleability		■		■		■		■		■		■		■		■		■
24	Wieldiness		■		■		■		■		■		■		■		■		■
25	Production		■		■		■		■		■		■		■		■		■
26	Continuity		■		■		■		■		■		■		■		■		■
27	Decay		■		■		■		■		■		■		■		■		■
28	Impermanence		■		■		■		■		■		■		■		■		■
		4	24	5	23	6	22	7	21	8	20	12	16	18	19	5	23	8	20

4 Causes (§§ 9-15)				21 Groupings (§§ 16-22)																				
				9 Kamma-Born									6 Cons. -Born						4 Temp-Born				2 Nutrim-Born	
Kamma-Born	Cons.-Born	Temp.-Born	Nutrim.-Born	Eye Decad	Ear Decad	Nose Decad	Tongue Decad	Body Decad	Female Decad	Male Decad	Base Decad	Vital Nonad	Pure Octad	Bod. Int. Nonad	Vocal Int. Decad	Undecad	Dodecad	Tridecad	Pure Octad	Sound Nonad	Undecad	Dodecad	Pure Octad	Undecad
(= 3 great essentials - earth, fire, and air)																								
18	15	13	12	10	10	10	10	10	10	10	10	9	8	9	10	11	12	13	8	9	11	12	8	11

CHAPTER VII
COMPENDIUM OF CATEGORIES
(*Samuccayasangahavibhāga*)

§1 Introductory Verse

Dvāsattatividhā vuttā vatthudhammā salakkhaṇā
Tesaṁ dāni yathāyogaṁ pavakkhāmi samuccayaṁ.

The seventy-two kinds of entities have (already) been described with their characteristics. Now I will speak of their categories in the ways that are applicable.

Guide to §1

The seventy-two kinds of entities: The four ultimate realities that have been described in the first six chapters can be analyzed into seventy-two distinct entities (*vatthudhammā*), that is, phenomena which exist with intrinsic natures (*sabhāva*—see I, §2).

1. Consciousness, though divided into eighty-nine types, is regarded as one entity because all cittas have the same intrinsic nature—the cognizing of an object.
2. The fifty-two cetasikas are viewed each as a distinct ultimate entity since each mental factor has its own individual intrinsic nature.
3. The eighteen concretely produced material phenomena are, for the same reason, each reckoned separately as individual entities.
4. Nibbāna, which is one in essence, counts as a single entity.

Although the ten kinds of non-concretely produced matter are expounded under the heading of the ultimate realities, they are not considered to be concrete entities because they lack intrinsic natures and thus do not enter into the range of insight contemplation.

I will speak of their categories: Having described the four ultimate realities with their seventy-two constituents, the author will now show how they are grouped into the various categories employed for classification in the Abhidhamma Piṭaka.

§2 Enumeration of Categories

Akusalasangaho, missakasangaho, bodhipakkhiyasangaho, sabbasangaho cā ti samuccayasangaho catubbidho veditabbo.

The compendium of categories should be understood as fourfold:

(i) the compendium of the unwholesome;
(ii) the compendium of mixed categories;
(iii) the compendium of requisites of enlightenment; and
(iv) the compendium of the whole.

Compendium of the Unwholesome (*akusalasangaha*)

§3 Taints

Kathaṁ? Akusalasangahe tāva cattāro āsavā: kāmāsavo, bhavāsavo, diṭṭhāsavo, avijjāsavo.

How? First, in the compendium of the unwholesome, there are four taints: (1) the taint of sensual desire, (2) the taint of (attachment to) existence, (3) the taint of wrong views, (4) the taint of ignorance.

Guide to §3

The word *āsava* means literally that which flows out. In the Pali language the word denotes both pus oozing from an abscess and intoxicants which have been fermented for a long time. The defilements classified as taints are called *āsavas* because they are similar to oozing pus and to fermented intoxicants. The Commentaries state that the *āsavas* are so called because they flow right up to the topmost plane of existence or because they flow up to change-of-lineage (*gotrabhū*—see IX, §34).

Of the four taints, the taint of sensual desire and the taint of (attachment to) existence are both modes of the cetasika greed (*lobha*), directed in the one case to sense pleasure, in the other to continued existence. The taint of wrong view is identified as the cetasika wrong view (*diṭṭhi*) and the taint of ignorance as the cetasika delusion (*moha*).

§4 Floods

Cattāro oghā: kāmogho, bhavogho, diṭṭhogho, avijjogho.

Four floods: (1) the flood of sensual desire, (2) the flood of (attachment to) existence, (3) the flood of wrong views, (4) the flood of ignorance.

§5 Bonds

Cattāro yogā: kāmayogo, bhavayogo, diṭṭhiyogo, avijjāyogo.

Four bonds: (1) the bond of sensual desire, (2) the bond of (attachment to) existence, (3) the bond of wrong views, (4) the bond of ignorance.

Guide to §§4-5

The same defilements that are called taints are also called floods (*ogha*) because they sweep beings away into the ocean of existence, and because they are hard to cross. They are further called bonds (*yoga*) because they yoke beings to suffering and do not allow them to escape.

§6 Bodily Knots

Cattāro ganthā: abhijjhā kāyagantho, vyāpādo kāyagantho, sīlabbataparāmāso kāyagantho idaṁsaccābhiniveso kāyagantho.

Four bodily knots: (1) the bodily knot of covetousness, (2) the bodily knot of ill will, (3) the bodily knot of adherence to rites and ceremonies, (4) the bodily knot of dogmatic belief that "This alone is the truth."

Guide to §6

The bodily knots are so called because they tie the mind to the body or the present body to bodies in future existences. Here the term "body" (*kāya*) applies to both the mental and physical body in the sense of an aggregation. Of the four knots, covetousness means craving or greed, which pulls beings towards desirable objects. Ill will is identical with the cetasika hatred, which is manifested as aversion towards undesirable objects. "Adherence to rites and ceremonies" is the belief that the performance of rituals constitutes the means to liberation. Dogmatic belief is the firm conviction that one's own view is the only truth and that all other views are false. These last two bodily knots are both aspects of the cetasika wrong view.

§7 Clingings

Cattāro upādānā: kāmupādānaṁ, diṭṭhupādānaṁ, sīlabbatupādānaṁ, attavādupādānaṁ.

Four clingings: (1) clinging to sense pleasures, (2) clinging to wrong views, (3) clinging to rites and ceremonies, (4) clinging to a doctrine of self.

Guide to §7

Of the four kinds of clinging, the first may be understood as intensified craving for sense pleasures, though the Commentaries point out that this kind of clinging can also be understood more broadly as craving for any of the things of the world. Clinging to wrong views is the adoption of any of the morally pernicious views such as nihilism, fatalism, etc., or any of the speculative views about the eternal or non-eternal existence of the world, etc.[1] Clinging to rites and ceremonies is the wrong view that the performance of rites and rituals or the undertaking of ascetic practices and related observances can lead to liberation. Clinging to a doctrine of self is the adoption of personality view (*sakkāyadiṭṭhi*), the identification of any of the five aggregates as a self or the accessories of a self. The Suttas mention twenty types of personality view. These are obtained by considering each of the five aggregates in four ways, thus: "One regards materiality as self, or self as possessing materiality, or materiality as in self, or self as in materiality." The same is repeated with respect to feeling, perception, mental formations, and consciousness. (See e.g. M. 44/i,300.) The clinging to sense pleasures is a manifestation of greed, the other three clingings are modes of the cetasika wrong view.

§8 Hindrances

Cha nīvaraṇāni: kāmacchandanīvaraṇaṁ, vyāpādanīvaraṇaṁ, thīnamiddhanīvaraṇaṁ, uddhaccakukkuccanīvaraṇaṁ, vicikicchānīvaraṇaṁ, avijjānīvaraṇaṁ.

Six hindrances: the hindrances of (1) sensual desire, (2) ill will, (3) sloth and torpor, (4) restlessness and worry, (5) doubt, (6) ignorance.

Guide to §8

The hindrances are so called because they obstruct the way to a heavenly rebirth and to the attainment of Nibbāna. According to the commentary the hindrances are mental factors which prevent unarisen wholesome states from arising and which do not allow arisen wholesome states to endure. The first five hindrances are the major obstacles to the attainment of the jhānas, the sixth hindrance is the major obstacle to the arising of wisdom.

Altogether eight cetasikas are included among the hindrances. In two cases, however, a pair of mental factors is counted as a single hindrance. The Abhidhamma commentaries explain that sloth and torpor, and restlessness and worry, are joined into compounds because of the similarities in their respective functions, conditions, and antidotes. Sloth and torpor both have the function of engendering mental sluggishness, they are conditioned by laziness and drowsiness, and they are countered by arousing energy. Restlessness and worry share the function of engendering disquietude, they are conditioned by disturbing thoughts, and they are countered by the development of calm.

§9 Latent Dispositions

Satt' ānusayā: kāmarāgānusayo, bhavarāgānusayo, paṭighānusayo, mānānusayo, diṭṭhānusayo, vicikicchānusayo, avijjānusayo.

Seven latent dispositions: the latent dispositions to (1) sensual lust, (2) attachment to existence, (3) aversion, (4) conceit, (5) wrong views, (6) doubt, (7) ignorance.

Guide to §9

The latent dispositions (*anusaya*) are defilements which "lie along with" (*anusenti*) the mental process to which they belong, rising to the surface as obsessions whenever they meet with suitable conditions. The term "latent dispositions" highlights the fact that the defilements are liable to arise so long as they have not been eradicated by the supramundane paths. Though all defilements are, in a sense, *anusayas*, the seven mentioned here are the most prominent. Both sensual lust and attachment to existence are modes of greed; the others are each distinct cetasikas. Thus altogether six cetasikas function as *anusayas*.

§10 Fetters (Suttanta Method)

Dasa saṁyojanāni: kāmarāgasaṁyojanaṁ, rūparāgasaṁyojanaṁ, arūparāgasaṁyojanaṁ, paṭighasaṁyojanaṁ, mānasaṁyojanaṁ, diṭṭhisaṁyojanaṁ, sīlabbataparāmāsasaṁyojanaṁ, vicikicchāsaṁyojanaṁ, uddhaccasaṁyojanaṁ, avijjāsaṁyojanaṁ, suttante.

Ten fetters, according to the Suttanta method: the fetters of (1) sensual lust, (2) attachment to fine-material existence, (3) attachment to immaterial existence, (4) aversion, (5) conceit, (6) wrong views, (7) adherence to rites and ceremonies, (8) doubt, (9) restlessness, (10) ignorance.

§11 Fetters (Abhidhamma Method)

Aparāni dasa saṁyojanāni: kāmarāgasaṁyojanaṁ, bhavarāgasaṁyojanaṁ, paṭighasaṁyojanaṁ, mānasaṁyojanaṁ, diṭṭhisaṁyojanaṁ, sīlabbataparāmāsasaṁyojanaṁ, vicikicchāsaṁyojanaṁ, issāsaṁyojanaṁ, macchariyasaṁyojanaṁ, avijjāsaṁyojanaṁ, abhidhamme.

Another ten fetters, according to the Abhidhamma method: the fetters of (1) sensual lust, (2) attachment to existence, (3) aversion, (4) conceit, (5) wrong views, (6) adherence to rites and ceremonies, (7) doubt, (8) envy, (9) avarice, (10) ignorance.

Guide to §§10-11

The fetters are unwholesome mental factors which bind beings to the round of existence. The first set of ten fetters is mentioned both in the Sutta Piṭaka and in the Abhidhamma Piṭaka, the second set only in the Abhidhamma Piṭaka. In the first set (1)-(3) are aspects of greed and (6)-(7) aspects of wrong view; the rest are distinct cetasikas. In the second set (1)-(2) are aspects of greed, (5)-(6) aspects of wrong view, and the rest distinct cetasikas.

§12 Defilements

Dasa kilesā: lobho, doso, moho, māno, diṭṭhi, vicikicchā, thīnaṁ, uddhaccaṁ, ahirikaṁ, anottappaṁ.

Ten defilements: (1) greed, (2) hatred, (3) delusion, (4) conceit, (5) wrong views, (6) doubt, (7) sloth, (8) restlessness, (9) shamelessness, (10) fearlessness of wrongdoing.

Guide to §12

The defilements (*kilesa*) are so called because they afflict (*kilissanti*) or torment the mind, or because they defile beings by dragging them down to a mentally soiled and depraved condition.

§13 A Clarification

Āsavādīsu pan' ettha kāmabhavanāmena tabbatthukā taṇhā adhippetā. Sīlabbataparāmāso idaṁsaccābhiniveso attavādupādānañ ca tathāpavattaṁ diṭṭhigatam eva pavuccati.

TABLE 7.1: THE DEFILEMENTS AS MENTAL FACTORS

	Mental Factors / Defilements	Taints	Floods	Bonds	Knots	Clingings	Hindrances	Dispositions	Fetters	Defilements	Total
1	Greed	■	■	■	■	■	■	■	■	■	9
2	Wrong View	■	■	■	■	■		■	■	■	8
3	Delusion	■	■	■			■	■	■	■	7
4	Hatred				■		■	■	■	■	5
5	Doubt						■	■	■	■	4
6	Conceit							■	■	■	3
7	Restlessness						■		■	■	3
8	Sloth						■			■	2
9	Worry						■				1
10	Torpor						■				1
11	Shamelessness									■	1
12	Fearlessness									■	1
13	Envy								■		1
14	Avarice								■		1
	No. of factors	3	3	3	3	2	8	6	9	10	

Herein, among the taints, etc., it is craving that is intended by the terms "sensual desire" and "(attachment to) existence," since it has them (i.e. sensuality and existence) as its basis. It is wrong view that is spoken of as "adherence to rites and ceremonies," "the dogmatic belief that 'This alone is the truth,'" and "clinging to a doctrine of self," because it occurs in such modes.

§14 Summary

Āsavoghā ca yogā ca tayo ganthā ca vatthuto
Upādānā duve vuttā aṭṭha nīvaraṇā siyuṁ.
Chaḷevānusayā honti nava saṁyojanā matā
Kilesā dasa vutto' yaṁ navadhā pāpasangaho.

By way of entity, the taints, floods, bonds, and knots are threefold. There are two kinds of clinging spoken of and eight hindrances.

The latent dispositions are only six, and the fetters can be understood as nine. The defilements are ten. Thus the compendium of evil is stated as ninefold.

Guide to §14

This section attempts to show how the different categories of defilements can be reduced to the fourteen unwholesome cetasikas. The results of this reduction can be seen in Table 7.1.

Compendium of Mixed Categories (*missakasangaha*)

§15 Roots

Missakasangahe cha hetū: lobho, doso, moho, alobho, adoso, amoho.

In the compendium of mixed categories there are six roots: (1) greed, (2) hatred, (3) delusion, (4) non-greed, (5) non-hatred, (6) non-delusion.

Guide to §15

The compendium of mixed categories is so called because it presents classificatory schemes which include wholesome, unwholesome, and morally indeterminate factors together. On the roots, see III, §5.

§16 Jhāna Factors

Satta jhānangāni: vitakko, vicāro, pīti, ekaggatā, somanassaṁ, domanassaṁ, upekkhā.

The seven jhāna factors: (1) initial application, (2) sustained application, (3) zest, (4) one-pointedness, (5) joy, (6) displeasure, (7) equanimity.

Guide to §16

The word *jhāna* is not used here in the usual sense of meditative absorption, but in the broader sense of close contemplation (*upanijjhāyana*) of an object. Therefore the states listed here are considered jhāna factors even when they occur outside a meditative framework. These seven cetasikas are called jhāna factors because they enable the mind to closely contemplate its object. Of them, displeasure is exclusively unwholesome and occurs only in the two cittas connected with aversion. The other six can be wholesome, unwholesome, or indeterminate, depending on the citta in which they occur.

§17 Path Factors

Dvādasa maggangāni: sammādiṭṭhi, sammāsankappo, sammāvācā, sammākammanto, sammā-ājivo, sammāvāyāmo, sammāsati, sammāsamādhi, micchādiṭṭhi, micchāsankappo, micchāvāyāmo, micchāsamādhi.

Twelve path factors: (1) right view, (2) right intention, (3) right speech, (4) right action, (5) right livelihood, (6) right effort, (7) right mindfulness, (8) right concentration, (9) wrong view, (10) wrong intention, (11) wrong effort, (12) wrong concentration.

Guide to §17

Here the word "path" is used in the sense of that which leads to a particular destination, that is, towards the blissful states of existence, the woeful states, and Nibbāna. Of the twelve factors, the first eight lead to the blissful states and Nibbāna, the last four lead to the woeful states.

These twelve path factors can be reduced to nine cetasikas. Right view is the cetasika of wisdom. Right intention, right effort, right mindfulness and right concentration are, respectively, the cetasikas of initial application, energy, mindfulness, and one-pointedness found in the wholesome and indeterminate cittas with roots. Right speech, right action, and right livelihood are the three abstinences (*virati*) found collectively in the supramundane cittas and separately on particular occasions in mundane wholesome cittas.

Of the four wrong path factors, wrong view is the cetasika of views, and is the only exclusively unwholesome cetasika among the path factors. The other three factors are, in order, the cetasikas of initial application, energy, and one-pointedness in the unwholesome cittas. There are no distinct path factors of wrong speech, wrong action, and wrong livelihood, since these are simply unwholesome modes of conduct motivated by defilements. There is no factor of wrong mindfulness, since mindfulness is an exclusively beautiful cetasika absent in the unwholesome cittas.

§18 Faculties

Bāvīsat' indriyāni: cakkhundriyaṁ, sotindriyaṁ, ghānindriyaṁ, jivhindriyaṁ, kāyindriyaṁ, itthindriyaṁ, purisindriyaṁ, jīvitindriyaṁ, manindriyaṁ, sukhindriyaṁ, dukkhindriyaṁ, somanassindriyaṁ, domanassindriyaṁ, upekkhindriyaṁ, saddhindriyaṁ, viriyindriyaṁ, satindriyaṁ, samādhindriyaṁ, paññindriyaṁ, anaññātaññassāmītindriyaṁ, aññindriyaṁ, aññātāvindriyaṁ.

Twenty-two faculties: (1) the eye faculty, (2) the ear faculty, (3) the nose faculty, (4) the tongue faculty, (5) the body faculty, (6) the femininity faculty, (7) the masculinity faculty, (8) the life faculty, (9) the mind faculty, (10) the pleasure faculty, (11) the pain faculty, (12) the joy faculty, (13) the displeasure faculty, (14) the equanimity faculty, (15) the faith faculty, (16) the energy faculty, (17) the mindfulness faculty, (18) the concentration faculty, (19) the wisdom faculty, (20) the faculty, "I will know the unknown," (21) the faculty of final knowledge, (22) the faculty of one who has final knowledge.

Guide to §18

The faculties are phenomena which exercise control in their respective domains over their associated states. The first five faculties are identified with the five physical sensitivities; the two sexual faculties (6-7) with the two material phenomena of sex; the life faculty (8) is twofold, as the mental life faculty and the physical life faculty. The mind faculty (9) is consciousness (*citta*) in its entirety, that is, all eighty-nine cittas. The five faculties of feeling were discussed above (III, §2). The five spiritual faculties (15-19) reappear below at §27, and the last three faculties are explained at §22.

§19 Powers

Nava balāni: saddhābalaṁ, viriyabalaṁ, satibalaṁ, samādhibalaṁ, paññābalaṁ, hiribalaṁ, ottappabalaṁ, ahirikabalaṁ, anottappabalaṁ.

Nine powers: (1) the power of faith, (2) the power of energy, (3) the power of mindfulness, (4) the power of concentration, (5) the power of wisdom, (6) the power of shame, (7) the power of fear of wrongdoing, (8) the power of shamelessness, (9) the power of fearlessness of wrongdoing.

Guide to §19

These nine powers are so called because they cannot be shaken by their opposites and because they strengthen their adjuncts. Powers (1), (3), (5), (6), and (7) may be either wholesome or indeterminate; (8) and (9) are exclusively unwholesome; (2) and (4) are of all three qualities.

§20 Predominants

Cattāro adhipatī: chandādhipati, viriyādhipati, cittādhipati, vīmaṁsādhipati.

Four predominants: (1) predominance of desire, (2) predominance of energy, (3) predominance of consciousness, (4) predominance of investigation.

Guide to §20

The predominants are factors which dominate the cittas to which they belong in undertaking and accomplishing difficult or important tasks. The difference between the predominants and the faculties lies in the degree and range of their control. A predominant exercises supreme control over the entire citta, while a faculty exercises control only in its respective sphere. Thus, whereas several faculties can be present in a single citta, only one predominant can be present at any given time. In this respect a predominant is compared to a king who, as the sole head of state, lords over all his ministers, while the faculties are compared to the ministers who can govern their own districts but cannot interfere with the others.

The four predominants are the cetasika desire (that is, desire-to-act, which should not be confused with *lobha*, desire as greed), the cetasika energy, citta, and the cetasika wisdom, here called investigation. Desire, energy, and citta become predominants only in fifty-two javana cittas, the two rooted in delusion and the Arahant's smiling consciousness being the exceptions; investigation becomes a predominant only in the thirty-four three-rooted javana cittas. Only one state can be a predominant at a time, and then only when it dominates the conascent states. The predominant investigation may be wholesome or indeterminate; the other predominants are of all three ethical qualities.

§21 Nutriments

Cattāro āhārā: kabaḷīkāro āhāro, phasso dutiyo, manosañcetanā tatiyā, viññāṇaṁ catutthaṁ.

Four nutriments: (1) edible food, (2) contact as the second, (3) mental volition as the third, (4) consciousness as the fourth.

Guide to §21

The word nutriment (*āhāra*) means that which sustains by acting as a strong supporting condition. According to the Suttanta method of explanation, edible food as nutriment sustains the physical body; contact sustains feeling; mental volition sustains rebirth in the three realms of existence, because volition is kamma and kamma generates rebirth; and consciousness sustains the compound of mind-and-body. According to the Abhidhamma method, edible food sustains the material phenomena of fourfold origination in the body, and the other three nutriments sustain all their conascent mental and material phenomena. Whereas edible food, as matter, is indeterminate, the three mental nutriments can be of all three ethical qualities.

§22 Clarifications

Indriyesu pan' ettha sotāpattimaggañāṇaṁ anaññātaññassāmītindriyaṁ; arahattaphalañāṇaṁ aññātāvindriyaṁ; majjhe cha ñāṇāni aññindriyānī ti pavuccanti. Jīvitindriyañ ca rūpārūpavasena duvidhaṁ hoti.

Herein, among the faculties it is explained that the faculty "I will know the unknown" is the knowledge of the path of stream-entry; the faculty of one who has final knowledge is the knowledge of the fruit of Arahantship; the faculty of final knowledge is the six intermediate kinds of (supramundane) knowledge. The life faculty is twofold—physical and mental.

Pañcaviññāṇesu jhānangāni, aviriyesu balāni, ahetukesu maggangāni na labbhanti. Tathā vicikicchācitte ekaggatā maggindriyabalabhāvaṁ na gacchati. Dvihetuka-tihetukajavanesv' eva yathāsambhavaṁ adhipati eko' va labbhati.

The jhāna factors are not found in the fivefold sense consciousness, the powers in those (kinds of consciousness) that are without energy, or the path factors in those that are rootless. So too, in the consciousness accompanied by doubt, one-pointedness does not attain to the stature of a path factor, a faculty, or a power. Only one predominant is obtained at a time, according to circumstances, and only in javanas with two roots or three roots.

Guide to §22

The five types of sense consciousness are merely simple confrontations with their respective objects. Because their function and physical base are weak, and they occupy an elementary place in the cognitive process, they cannot engage in a close contemplation of the object, and thus their concomitant feeling and one-pointedness do not acquire the stature of jhāna factors. Moreover, initial application (*vitakka*) is the foundation of the jhāna factors, and in the five types of sense consciousness initial application is absent, not because it has been transcended (as in the higher jhānas) but because they are too primitive in function to include it.

Similarly, energy is required in a citta for its constituents to acquire the stature of powers (*bala*). Therefore, in the sixteen cittas devoid of energy, the mental factor of one-pointedness cannot fulfill the function of the power of concentration.

The cittas devoid of roots cannot serve as a path leading to a particular destination; thus the path factors are not found in the eighteen rootless cittas.

In the consciousness accompanied by doubt, one-pointedness lacks reinforcement by decision (*adhimokkha*) and is overrun by doubt, with its vacillating nature; thus it cannot attain the status of a path factor, faculty, or power.

The predominants can occur only one at a time, for it is inherent in the nature of predominance that only one state can function as a pre-

TABLE 7.2: MIXED CATEGORIES

	Unwholesome Only	Wholesome Only	Indeterminate Only	Wholesome & Indeterminate	All Three Qualities
Roots 6	Greed, hate, delusion			Non-greed, non-hate, non-delusion	
Jhāna factors 7	Displeasure				In. appl., sus. appl., zest, one-ptns., joy, eqn.
Path factors 12	4 wrong factors			8 right factors	
Faculties 22	Displeasure	"I will know the unknown"	5 senses, 2 sexes, mat. life, pleasure, pain, one w. final knwl.	Faith, mindfulness, wisdom, final knwl.	Mental life, mind, joy, eqn., energy, concentration
Powers 9	Shamelessness, fearlessness			Faith, mindfulness, wisdom, shame, fear	Energy, concentration
Predominants 4				Investigation	Desire, energy, consciousness
Nutriments 4			Edible food		Contact, volition, consciousness

dominant in any given citta, and then only in javanas with two or three roots "according to circumstances," that is, when one of the four predominant factors is exercising the role of predominance.

§23 Summary

Cha hetū pañca jhānangā maggangā nava vatthuto
Soḷas' indriyadhammā ca baladhammā nav' eritā.
Cattāro' dhipatī vuttā tathāhārā ti sattadhā
Kusalādisamākiṇṇo vutto missakasangaho.

By way of entity, six roots, five jhāna factors, nine path factors, sixteen faculties, and nine powers have been described.

Likewise, four predominants have been stated and four nutriments. Thus the compendium of mixed categories, consisting of a combination of wholesome states and the rest, has been stated in seven ways.

Guide to §23

By way of entity, the jhāna factors are fivefold because joy, displeasure, and equanimity are all feelings, and feeling is a single cetasika. The reduction of the path factors to nine has been explained above. The faculties become sixteenfold because faculties (10)-(14) are all represented by one cetasika, feeling, while faculties (19)-(22) are all aspects of the cetasika wisdom; the life faculty becomes two entities—one material counted among the twenty-eight kinds of material phenomena, the other mental counted among the fifty-two cetasikas.

The distribution of the mixed categories among the various ethical classes is shown in Table 7.2.

Compendium of Requisites of Enlightenment (*bodhipakkhiyasangaha*)

§24 Four Foundations of Mindfulness

Bodhipakkhiyasangahe cattāro satipaṭṭhānā: kāyānupassanā-satipaṭṭhānaṁ, vedanānupassanā-satipaṭṭhānaṁ, cittānupassanā-satipaṭṭhānaṁ, dhammānupassanā-satipaṭṭhānaṁ.

In the compendium of requisites of enlightenment, there are four foundations of mindfulness: (1) the foundation of mindfulness in contemplation of the body; (2) the foundation of mindfulness in contemplation of feelings; (3) the foundation of mindfulness in contemplation of consciousness; (4) the foundation of mindfulness in contemplation of mental objects.

Guide to §24

Requisites of enlightenment: The Pali expression *bodhipakkhiya-dhammā* means literally "states on the side of enlightenment." Although the expression appears rarely in the Suttas, in later literature it comes to be used as a general term for the thirty-seven factors into which the Buddha compressed the practice of his teaching (see D.16/ii,120, M.77/ii,11-12). These factors are called "requisites of enlightenment" because they conduce to the attainment of enlightenment, which is the knowledge of the four supramundane paths. The thirty-seven requisites, as shown, fall into seven groups.[2]

Four foundations of mindfulness (*satipaṭṭhānā*): The word *paṭṭhāna* here is taken to have the dual meanings of "setting up" (or "application" = *upaṭṭhāna*) and "foundations," that is, of *sati* or mindfulness. The four foundations of mindfulness form a complete system of meditative practice for the development of mindfulness and insight. The method is expounded at length in two suttas, D.22 and M.10, and in a collection of short suttas, the Satipaṭṭhāna Saṁyutta (S.47).[3]

The four foundations of mindfulness have a single essence, which consists of mindful contemplation of phenomena. They are differentiated insofar as this mindful contemplation is to be applied to four objects—the body, feelings, states of consciousness, and mental objects. The latter comprises such factors as the five hindrances, the five aggregates, the six sense bases, the seven enlightenment factors, and the Four Noble Truths. The practice of the four foundations of mindfulness is identical with right mindfulness as the seventh factor of the Noble Eightfold Path.

§25 Four Supreme Efforts

Cattāro sammappadhānā: uppannānaṁ pāpakānaṁ dhammānaṁ pahānāya vāyāmo, anuppannānaṁ pāpakānaṁ dhammānaṁ anuppādāya vāyāmo, anuppannānaṁ kusalānaṁ dhammānaṁ uppādāya vāyāmo, uppannānaṁ kusalānaṁ dhammānaṁ bhiyyobhāvāya vāyāmo.

There are four supreme efforts: (1) the effort to discard evil states that have arisen, (2) the effort to prevent the arising of unarisen evil states, (3) the effort to develop unarisen wholesome states, (4) the effort to augment arisen wholesome states.

Guide to §25

Four supreme efforts (*sammappadhānā*): Here one mental factor, energy, performs four separate functions. This fourfold effort is identical with right effort, the sixth factor of the Noble Eightfold Path.

§26 Four Means to Accomplishment

Cattāro iddhipādā: chandiddhipādo, viriyiddhipādo, cittiddhipādo, vīmaṁsiddhipādo.

There are four means to accomplishment: the means to accomplishment consisting of (1) desire, (2) energy, (3) consciousness, (4) investigation.

Guide to §26

Four means to accomplishment (*iddhipādā*): The word *iddhi* here signifies all sublime and supramundane states to be accomplished by applying effort to the practice of the Buddha's teaching. The principal methods of achieving these are called the means of accomplishment. These are identical with the four predominants (see §20). However, while those states become predominants (*adhipati*) on any occasion when they are instrumental in accomplishing a goal, they become *iddhipādas* only when they are applied to achieving the goal of the Buddha's teaching. The expression *iddhipāda* extends to both mundane and supramundane states.[4]

§27 Five Faculties

Pañc' indriyāni: saddhindriyaṁ, viriyindriyaṁ, satindriyaṁ, samādhindriyaṁ, paññindriyaṁ.

There are five faculties: the faculties of (1) faith, (2) energy, (3) mindfulness, (4) concentration, (5) wisdom.

§28 Five Powers

Pañca balāni: saddhābalaṁ, viriyabalaṁ, satibalaṁ, samādhibalaṁ, paññābalaṁ.

There are five powers: the powers of (1) faith, (2) energy, (3) mindfulness, (4) concentration, (5) wisdom.

Guide to §§27-28

The faculties and powers comprise the same five factors, though different functions are attached to the two categories. The faculties are factors which *exercise control* in their respective domains, while the powers are these same factors considered as being *unshakable by their opposites*. Thus the five faculties exercise control in the respective spheres of resolution (*adhimokkha*), exertion (*paggaha*), awareness (*upaṭṭhāna*), non-distraction (*avikkhepa*), and discernment (*dassana*); in doing so they help to overcome their opposites—indecision, laziness, negligence, agitation, and delusion. The five powers are these same states considered as unwavering and as incapable of being overcome by their opposites. In the development of the faculties, faith and wisdom are to be balanced to avoid the extremes of blind credulity and intellectual cleverness; energy and concentration are to be balanced to avoid restless agitation and sluggish immobility of mind. But strong mindfulness is always necessary, for mindfulness oversees the development of the other faculties and ensures that they are kept in balance.

§29 Seven Factors of Enlightenment

Satta bojjhangā: satisambojjhango, dhammavicayasambojjhango, viriyasambojjhango, pītisambojjhango, passaddhisambojjhango, samādhisambojjhango, upekkhāsambojjhango.

There are seven factors of enlightenment: the enlightenment factors of (1) mindfulness, (2) investigation of states, (3) energy, (4) zest, (5) tranquillity, (6) concentration, (7) equanimity.

Guide to §29

Among the seven factors of enlightenment, investigation of states (*dhammavicaya*) is a designation for wisdom (*paññā*), insight into mental and material phenomena as they really are. Tranquillity (*passaddhi*) means tranquillity both of consciousness and of the mental body (see II, §5). Equanimity (*upekkhā*) here means mental neutrality (*tatramajjhattatā*), one of the universal beautiful cetasikas, not neutral feeling. The three factors of investigation, energy, and zest are opposed to mental sluggishness; the three factors of tranquillity, concentration, and equanimity counteract mental excitation. Mindfulness assures that the two groups occur in balance, neither exceeding the other.

§30 Eight Path Factors

Aṭṭha maggangāni: sammādiṭṭhi, sammāsankappo, sammāvācā, sammākammanto, sammā-ājīvo, sammāvāyāmo, sammāsati, sammāsamādhi.

There are eight path factors: (1) right view, (2) right intention, (3) right speech, (4) right action, (5) right livelihood, (6) right effort, (7) right mindfulness, (8) right concentration.

Guide to §30

Of the eight factors of the Noble Eightfold Path, right view (*sammādiṭṭhi*) is the cetasika of wisdom exercised in understanding the Four Noble Truths. Right intention (*sammāsankappa*) is the cetasika of initial application (*vitakka*) directed towards renunciation, good will, and harmlessness. Path factors (3)-(5) are identical with the three abstinences (see II, §6). Right effort is the same as the four supreme efforts (§25). Right mindfulness is the same as the four foundations of mindfulness (§24). Right concentration is defined in ṭerms of the four jhānas of the Suttanta system (see D. 22/ii,313).

§31 A Clarification

Ettha pana cattāro satipaṭṭhānā ti sammāsati ekā va pavuccati. Tathā cattāro sammappadhānā ti ca sammāvāyāmo.

Here, by the four foundations of mindfulness, right mindfulness alone is implied. Similarly, by the four supreme efforts, right effort is implied.

§32 By way of States

Chando cittam upekkhā ca saddhā-passaddhi-pītiyo
Sammādiṭṭhi ca sankappo vāyāmo viratittayaṁ
Sammāsati samādhī ti cuddas' ete sabhāvato
Sattatiṁsappabhedena sattadhā tattha sangaho.

The sevenfold compendium of the thirty-seven factors is composed of these fourteen states considered by way of their intrinsic nature: desire, consciousness, equanimity, faith, tranquillity, zest, right view, intention, effort, the three abstinences, right mindfulness, and concentration.

§33 By way of Occurrence

Sankappa-passaddhi ca pīt' upekkhā
Chando ca cittaṁ viratittayañ ca
Nav' ekaṭṭhānā viriyaṁ nav' aṭṭha
Satī samādhī catu pañca paññā
Saddhā duṭṭhān' uttamasattatiṁsa
Dhammānam eso pavaro vibhāgo.
Sabbe lokuttare honti na vā saṁkappapītiyo
Lokiye pi yathāyogaṁ chabbisuddhippavattiyaṁ.

The analysis of these thirty-seven excellent factors is as follows: nine—intention, tranquillity, zest, equanimity, desire, consciousness, and the three abstinences—each occur only once; energy occurs nine times; mindfulness eight times; concentration four times; wisdom five times; and faith two times.

All these occur in the supramundane, except at times intention and zest. In the mundane, too, they occur in the course of the sixfold purification, according to circumstances.

Guide to §§32-33

In §32 the thirty-seven requisites of enlightenment are reduced to fourteen entities, one being citta, the other thirteen cetasikas. In §33 the occurrence of these entities among the requisites is tabulated by collating synonyms. The results of this tabulation are seen in Table 7.3.

Energy occurs nine times as: four supreme efforts, means of accomplishment, faculty, power, enlightenment factor, and path factor.

Mindfulness occurs eight times as: four foundations of mindfulness, faculty, power, enlightenment factor, and path factor.

Concentration occurs four times as: faculty, power, enlightenment factor, and path factor.

Wisdom occurs five times as: means of accomplishment, faculty, power, enlightenment factor, and path factor.

Faith occurs twice as a faculty and power. The remaining states occur only once.

Intention is not found in supramundane cittas occurring at the level of the second jhāna and above. This is because right intention (*sammāsankappa*) is the cetasika of *vitakka* or initial application, and the supramundane paths and fruits conjoined with the second and higher jhānas are free from *vitakka*. Similarly, zest (*pīti*) is not found in supramundane cittas occurring at the level of the fourth and fifth jhānas.

TABLE 7.3: THE REQUISITES OF ENLIGHTENMENT AS MENTAL FACTORS

Mental Factors		4 Fnd. of Mindfulness	4 Supreme Efforts	4 Means to Accomp.	5 Faculties	5 Powers	7 Enlight. Factors	8 Path Factors	Total
1	Energy		4	■	■	■	■	■	9
2	Mindfulness	4			■	■	■	■	8
3	Wisdom			■	■	■	■	■	5
4	Concentration				■	■	■	■	4
5	Faith				■	■			2
6	Initial Application							■	1
7	Tranquillity						■		1
8	Zest						■		1
9	Equanimity						■		1
10	Desire			■					1
11	Consciousness			■					1
12	Right Speech							■	1
13	Right Action							■	1
14	Right Livelihood							■	1

The sixfold purification (***chabbisuddhi***): These are the six mundane stages of purification preceding and culminating in the seventh, supramundane, stage of purification (see IX, §22). These six stages are an expanded version of the more common threefold division of the preliminary path into virtue, concentration, and wisdom. The seventh stage is the attainment of the supramundane paths. In the six mundane stages of purification the thirty-seven requisites of enlightenment are found in various combinations, according to circumstances.

Compendium of the Whole (*sabbasangaha*)

§34 The Five Aggregates

Sabbasangahe pañcakkhandhā: rūpakkhandho, vedanākkhandho, saññākkhandho, sankhārakkhandho, viññāṇakkhandho.

In the compendium of the whole, the five aggregates are: (1) the materiality aggregate, (2) the feeling aggregate, (3) the perception aggregate, (4) the mental formations aggregate, (5) the consciousness aggregate.

Guide to §34

The compendium of the whole: In this section the author's purpose is to collect those schemata of the Abhidhamma philosophy that incorporate the totality of concrete entities. These schemata are set forth, not for the purpose of developing an abstract ontology, but to show the range of phenomena that are to be comprehended with insight. This accords with the Buddha's statement: "Without directly knowing the whole, without fully understanding the whole, one is incapable of destroying suffering" (S.35:26/iii,17).

The five aggregates: The word *khandha* is understood in the sense of group, mass, or aggregate (*rāsi*). The Buddha analyzes a living being into these five groups. In the Suttas he states: "Whatever kind of materiality there is, whether past, future or present, internal or external, gross or subtle, inferior or superior, far or near—this is called the materiality aggregate." The same method is applied to the other four aggregates (S.22:48/iii,47). The relationship between the five aggregates and the four ultimate realities has been explained above (see I, §2).

§35 The Five Aggregates of Clinging

Pañc' upādānakkhandhā: rūpupādānakkhandho, vedan-upādānakkhandho, saññupādānakkhandho, sankhārupādānak-khandho, viññāṇupādānakkhandho.

The five aggregates of clinging are: (1) the materiality aggregate of clinging, (2) the feeling aggregate of clinging, (3) the perception aggregate of clinging, (4) the mental formations aggregate of clinging, (5) the consciousness aggregate of clinging.

Guide to §35

The five aggregates of clinging: These are called *upādānakkhandha*, aggregates of clinging, because they constitute the objects of clinging. The Buddha states: "Whatever kind of materiality there is, whether past, future or present, etc., connected with taints and subject to clinging—this is called the materiality aggregate of clinging." Again, the same method of definition applies to the other four aggregates (S.22:48/iii,48). Here, all components of the five aggregates that enter into range of the four types of clinging (see §7) are called aggregates of clinging. This includes the entire aggregate of materiality and the four mental aggregates of the mundane plane. The four mental aggregates of the supramundane plane are not aggregates of clinging because they entirely transcend the range of clinging; that is, they cannot become objects of greed or wrong views.[5]

§36 The Twelve Sense Bases

Dvādas' āyatanāni: cakkhāyatanaṁ, sotāyatanaṁ, ghānāyatanaṁ, jivhāyatanaṁ, kāyāyatanaṁ, manāyatanaṁ, rūpāyatanaṁ, saddāyatanaṁ, gandhāyatanaṁ, rasāyatanaṁ, phoṭṭhabbāyatanaṁ, dhammāyatanaṁ.

The twelve sense bases are: (1) the eye base, (2) the ear base, (3) the nose base, (4) the tongue base, (5) the body base, (6) the mind base, (7) the visible form base, (8) the sound base, (9) the smell base, (10) the taste base, (11) the tangible base, (12) the mental-object base.

Guide to §36

The twelve sense bases offer another perspective on the whole. From this perspective the totality of concrete entities is viewed by way of the doors and objects of consciousness. Bases (1)-(5) are identical with the five kinds of sensitive material phenomena and bases (7)-(11) with the five kinds of objective material phenomena. The mind base (6), however, has a wider range than the mind door. It is identified with the aggregate of consciousness in its totality, comprising all eighty-nine types of citta. The mental-object base does not completely coincide with mental object (*dhammārammaṇa*), but includes only those entities not found among the other bases. Thus it excludes the first five objective bases, the five types of sensitive matter, and citta, which is identical with the mind base. It also excludes concepts (*paññatti*), since the notion of base (*āyatana*) extends only to ultimate realities, i.e. things existing by way of intrinsic nature (*sabhāva*), and does not extend to things that owe their existence to conceptual construction. The mental-object base comprises the fifty-two mental factors, the sixteen kinds of subtle matter, and Nibbāna (see §39 below).[6]

§37 The Eighteen Elements

Aṭṭhārasa dhātuyo: cakkhudhātu, sotadhātu, ghānadhātu, jivhādhātu, kāyadhātu, rūpadhātu, saddadhātu, gandhadhātu, rasadhātu, phoṭṭhabbadhātu, cakkhuviññāṇadhātu, sotaviññāṇadhātu, ghānaviññāṇadhātu, jivhāviññāṇadhātu, kāyaviññāṇadhātu, manodhātu, dhammadhātu, manoviññāṇadhātu.

The eighteen elements are: (1) the eye element, (2) the ear element, (3) the nose element, (4) the tongue element, (5) the body element, (6) the visible form element, (7) the sound element, (8) the smell element, (9) the taste element, (10) the tangible element, (11) the eye-consciousness element, (12) the ear-consciousness element, (13) the nose-consciousness element, (14) the tongue-consciousness element, (15) the body-consciousness element, (16) the mind element, (17) the mental-object element, (18) the mind-consciousness element.

Guide to §37

The elements are called *dhātu* because they bear (*dhārenti*) their own intrinsic natures. The eighteen elements are obtained from the twelve bases by dividing the mind base into the seven elements of consciousness (see III, §21). In all other respects the bases and the elements are identical. For a correlation of the aggregates, bases, and elements with the four ultimate realities, see Table 7.4.

TABLE 7.4: THE FOUR ULTIMATES AS AGGREGATES, SENSE BASES, AND ELEMENTS

ULTIMATE REALITIES 4	AGGREGATES 5	SENSE BASES 12	ELEMENTS 18
Matter 28	Materiality Aggregate	Eye base	Eye element
		Ear "	Ear "
		Nose "	Nose "
		Tongue "	Tongue "
		Body "	Body "
		Form "	Form "
		Sound "	Sound "
		Smell "	Smell "
		Taste "	Taste "
		Tangible "	Tangible "
		Mental-object base (subtle matter, mental factors, Nibbāna)	Mental-object element (same as above)
Mental factors 52	Feeling Aggr.		
	Perception "		
	Formations "		
Nibbāna	None		
Consciousness 89	Consciousness Aggregate	Mind base	Eye - cons. "
			Ear - cons. "
			Nose - cons. "
			Tongue-cons. "
			Body - cons. "
			Mind - element
			Mind - cons. "

§38 The Four Noble Truths

Cattāri ariyasaccāni: dukkhaṁ ariyasaccaṁ, dukkhasamudayaṁ ariyasaccaṁ, dukkhanirodhaṁ ariyasaccaṁ, dukkhanirodha-gāminīpaṭipadā ariyasaccaṁ.

The Four Noble Truths are: (1) the noble truth of suffering, (2) the noble truth of the origin of suffering, (3) the noble truth of the cessation of suffering, and (4) the noble truth of the path leading to the cessation of suffering.

Guide to §38

The Four Noble Truths are the fundamental teaching of the Buddha, discovered by him on the night of his Enlightenment and expounded by him repeatedly during his long ministry. These four truths are called noble (*ariya*) because they are penetrated by the noble ones; because they are the truths taught by the supreme Noble One, the Buddha; because their discovery leads to the state of a noble one; and because they are the real, unalterable, undeceptive truths about existence.

The noble truth of suffering is expounded as twelvefold: the suffering of birth, aging, death, sorrow, lamentation, pain, grief, despair, association with the unpleasant, separation from the pleasant, not to get what one wants, and the five aggregates of clinging. Concisely, the noble truth of suffering comprises all phenomena of the three mundane planes of existence except craving.

The noble truth of the origin of suffering is a single factor, namely, craving (*taṇhā*), which is identical with the cetasika of greed (*lobha*). Craving, however, has three aspects: craving for sense pleasures (*kāmataṇhā*), craving for continued existence (*bhavataṇhā*), and craving for annihilation (*vibhavataṇhā*).

The noble truth of the cessation of suffering is also singlefold: it is Nibbāna, which is to be realized by the eradication of craving.

The noble truth of the way to the cessation of suffering is the Noble Eightfold Path. In the teaching of the four truths, this is the collection of eight cetasikas corresponding to the eight path factors arisen in the cittas of the four supramundane paths. It should be noted that while in the section on the requisites of enlightenment, the eight path factors may be either mundane or supramundane, in the teaching of the Four Noble Truths they are exclusively supramundane.[7]

§39 A Clarification

Ettha pana cetasika-sukhumarūpa-nibbānavasena ekūnasattati dhammā dhammāyatanaṁ dhammadhātū ti sankhaṁ gacchanti. Manāyatanam eva sattaviññāṇadhātuvasena bhijjati.

Herein, sixty-nine states comprising (fifty-two) mental factors, (sixteen kinds of) subtle matter, and Nibbāna, are regarded as the mental-object base and the mental-object element. The mind base itself is divided into the seven elements of consciousness.

§40 Summary

Rūpañ ca vedanā saññā sesā cetasikā tathā
Viññāṇam iti pañc' ete pañcakkhandhā ti bhāsitā.

Pañc' upādānakkhandhā ti tathā tebhūmakā matā
Bhedābhāvena nibbānaṁ khandhasangahanissaṭaṁ.

Dvārālambanabhedena bhavant' āyatanāni ca
Dvārālambataduppannapariyāyena dhātuyo.

Dukkhaṁ tebhūmakaṁ vaṭṭaṁ taṇhāsamudayo bhave
Nirodho nāma nibbānaṁ maggo lokuttaro mato.

Maggayuttā phalā c' eva catusaccavinissaṭā
Iti pañcappabhedena pavutto sabbasaṅgaho.

Matter, feeling, perception, the remaining mental factors, and consciousness—these five are called the five aggregates.

The same states that pertain to the three (mundane) planes are regarded as the five aggregates of clinging.

As Nibbāna lacks differentiation (such as past, present, future), it is excluded from the category of aggregates.

Owing to the difference between doors and objects, there are (twelve) sense bases. In accordance with doors, objects, and their corresponding consciousness, arise the (eighteen) elements.

The round of existence in the three planes is suffering. Craving is its origin. Cessation is Nibbāna. The path is regarded as supramundane.

Mental states associated with the paths and the fruits are excluded from the four truths.

Thus the compendium of the whole has been explained in five ways.

Guide to §40

Mental states associated with the paths: Apart from the eight cetasikas corresponding to the eight path factors, the other constituents of the supramundane path consciousness—the citta itself and the associated cetasikas—are not strictly speaking part of the eightfold path, and thus are not comprehended by the Four Noble Truths. The four fruits as well are excluded from the framework of the Four Noble Truths.

Iti Abhidhammatthasangahe
Samuccayasangahavibhāgo nāma
sattamo paricchedo.

Thus ends the seventh chapter
in the Manual of Abhidhamma entitled
the Compendium of Categories.

CHAPTER VIII
COMPENDIUM OF CONDITIONALITY
(*Paccayasangahavibhāga*)

§1 Introductory Verse

Yesaṁ sankhatadhammānaṁ ye dhammā paccayā yathā
Taṁ vibhāgam ih' edāni pavakkhāmi yathārahaṁ.

I shall now explain here, in a fitting manner, the detailed analysis of the conditioned states, and of those states which are their conditions, and of how (they are related).

Guide to §1

I shall now explain here: Having thus far explained the four types of ultimate realities and their categories, Ācariya Anuruddha now proceeds to explain, in this compendium of conditionality, the analysis of their relations as conditioning states (*paccayadhammā*) and conditionally arisen states (*paccayuppannadhammā*), linked by the conditioning forces (*paccayasatti*).

Of the conditioned states (*yesaṁ sankhatadhammānaṁ*): Conditioned states are phenomena (*dhammā*) that arise in dependence on conditions, that is, all cittas, cetasikas, and material phenomena (except the four material characteristics—see VI, §15).

Those states which are their conditions (*ye dhammā paccayā*): A condition is a state which is efficacious (*upakāraka*) in the arising or persistence of other states. This means that a condition, when operative, will cause other states connected to it to arise if they have not already arisen, or, if they have arisen, will maintain them in existence. All conditioned phenomena, as well as Nibbāna and concepts, are included in the category of conditioning states.

And of how (they are related) (*yathā*): This refers to the twenty-four kinds of conditioning forces that operate between the conditioning states and the conditioned states. These too will be analyzed.

§2 In Brief: The Two Methods

Paṭiccasamuppādanayo paṭṭhānanayo cā ti paccayasangaho duvidho veditabbo.

Tattha tabbhāvabhāvībhāvākāramattopalakkhito paṭiccasamuppādanayo. Paṭṭhānanayo pana āhaccapaccayaṭṭhitim ārabbha pavuccati. Ubhayaṁ pana vomissitvā papañcenti ācariyā.

The compendium of conditionality is twofold:

(1) the method of dependent arising; and
(2) the method of conditional relations.

Of these, the method of dependent arising is marked by the simple happening of a state in dependence on some other state. The method of conditional relations is discussed with reference to the specific causal efficacy of the conditions. Teachers explain them by mixing both methods.

Guide to §2

The method of dependent arising: The term "dependent arising" is a compound of *paṭicca*, dependent on, and *samuppāda*, arising, origination. The expression is generally applied to the twelve-term formula expounded in §3, commonly met with in the Suttas.

Abstractly stated, the principle of dependent arising is expressed by the oft-occurring dictum: "When this exists, that comes to be; with the arising of this, that arises" (*imasmiṁ sati idaṁ hoti, imass' uppādā idaṁ uppajjati*). In the present text this same principle of dependent arising is characterized as "the simple happening of a state in dependence on some other state" (*tabbhāvabhāvībhāvākāramatta*). Here *tabbhāva*, "some other state," refers to the occurrence of the condition; *bhāvī* means the conditioned state; and *bhāvākāramatta*, "the simple happening," means the mere occurrence of the conditioned state.

As applied to the twelve terms of the Sutta formula, this principle means that when any of the conditions, such as ignorance, etc., exist, then in dependence on those conditions the conditionally arisen states, such as kammic formations, etc., come to be.

The method of conditional relations: This is the method set forth in the *Paṭṭhāna*, the Book of Conditional Relations, the seventh and last part of the Abhidhamma Piṭaka. In contrast to the method of dependent arising, which deals only with the conditioning states and conditioned states and the structure of their arising, the method of the *Paṭṭhāna* also deals with the conditioning forces (*paccayasatti*). A force (*satti*) is that which has the power to bring about or accomplish an effect. Just as the hotness of chillis is inherent in the chillis and cannot exist without them, so too the conditioning forces are inherent in the conditioning states and cannot exist without them. All conditioning states have their particular force, and this force enables them to cause the arising of the conditioned states.

The specific causal efficacy of the conditions: This is a free rendering of the cryptic Pali expression *āhacca paccayaṭṭhiti.* Ledi Sayadaw explains the phrase to mean "the special force of the conditions, that is, their efficacy in various ways," and he states that unlike the method of dependent arising, where the mere conditioning state is exhibited, the method of conditional relations is taught in full by exhibiting the special force of the conditions.

Teachers explain them by mixing both methods: A mixed treatment of the methods is found in the *Visuddhimagga,* Chapter XVII, where the twenty-four conditional relations are used to elucidate the relationship between each pair of factors in the twelvefold formula of dependent arising.

The Method of Dependent Arising (*paṭiccasamuppādanaya*)

§3 The Basic Formula

Tattha (1) avijjāpaccayā sankhārā, (2) sankhārapaccayā viññāṇaṁ, (3) viññāṇapaccayā nāmarūpaṁ, (4) nāmarūpapaccayā saḷāyatanaṁ, (5) saḷāyatanapaccayā phasso, (6) phassapaccayā vedanā, (7) vedanāpaccayā taṇhā, (8) taṇhāpaccayā upādānaṁ, (9) upādānapaccayā bhavo, (10) bhavapaccayā jāti, (11) jātipaccayā jarāmaraṇa-soka-parideva-dukkha-domass'-upāyāsā sambhavanti. Evam etassa kevalassa dukkhakkhandhassa samudayo hotī ti. Ayam ettha paṭiccasamuppādanayo.

Therein:

(1) Dependent on ignorance arise kammic formations.
(2) Dependent on kammic formations arises consciousness.
(3) Dependent on consciousness arises mind-and-matter.
(4) Dependent on mind-and-matter arise the six sense bases.
(5) Dependent on the six sense bases arises contact.
(6) Dependent on contact arises feeling.
(7) Dependent on feeling arises craving.

(8) Dependent on craving arises clinging.
(9) Dependent on clinging arises existence.
(10) Dependent on existence arises birth.
(11) Dependent on birth arise decay-and-death, sorrow, lamentation, pain, grief, and despair.

Thus arises this whole mass of suffering.

Herein, this is the method of dependent arising.

Guide to §3

The method of dependent arising: Dependent arising is essentially an account of the causal structure of the round of existence (*vaṭṭa*), disclosing the conditions that sustain the wheel of birth and death and make it revolve from one existence to another. In the Commentaries dependent arising is defined as the arising of effects evenly in dependence on a conjunction of conditions (*paccaya-sāmaggiṁ paṭicca samaṁ phalānaṁ uppādo*). This implies that no single cause can produce an effect, nor does only one effect arise from a given cause. Rather, there is always a collection of conditions giving rise to a collection of effects. When, in the familiar formula, one state is declared to be the condition for another, this is said in order to single out the chief condition among a collection of conditions and relate it to the most important effect among a collection of effects.[1]

(1) **Dependent on ignorance arise the kammic formations**: Ignorance (*avijjā*) is the cetasika delusion, which obscures perception of the true nature of things just as a cataract obscures perception of visible objects. According to the Suttanta method of explanation, ignorance is non-knowledge of the Four Noble Truths. According to the Abhidhamma method, ignorance is non-knowledge of eight things: the Four Noble Truths, the pre-natal past, the post-mortem future, the past and the future together, and dependent arising.

Kammic formations (*sankhārā*) are the twenty-nine volitions associated with mundane wholesome and unwholesome cittas. The volitions in the eight great wholesome cittas and in the five wholesome fine- material jhāna cittas are collectively called meritorious volitional formations (*puññābhisankhāra*). The volitions in the twelve unwholesome cittas are called demeritorious volitional formations (*apuññābhisankhāra*). And the volitions in the four wholesome immaterial jhāna cittas are called imperturbable volitional formations (*āneñjābhisankhāra*).

When the mental continuum of a living being is imbued with ignorance, then his volitional activity generates kamma with the potency to produce results in the future. Hence ignorance is called the chief condition for kammic formations. Ignorance is predominant in unwholesome activities, while it is latent in mundane wholesome activities. Hence both mundane wholesome and unwholesome kammic formations are said to be conditioned by ignorance.

(2) **Dependent on kammic formations arises consciousness:** That is, the kammic formations—the twenty-nine wholesome and unwholesome volitions—condition the arising of the thirty-two kinds of resultant consciousness. At the moment of conception one especially potent kammic formation accumulated in the mental continuum of the deceased being generates one of the nineteen types of rebirth consciousness in the realm appropriate for that kamma to mature. Thereafter, during the course of existence, other accumulated kammas generate other resultant types of consciousness according to circumstances, as explained at V, §§27-33.

(3) **Dependent on consciousness arises mind-and-matter**: Whereas in step (2) *viññāṇa* refers exclusively to resultant consciousness, here it signifies both resultant consciousness and the kammic consciousness of previous lives. The term "mind" (*nāma*) denotes the cetasikas associated with resultant consciousness, the term "matter" (*rūpa*) denotes material phenomena produced by kamma. In five-constituent existence (*pañcavokārabhava*)—that is, those realms where all five aggregates are found—consciousness conditions both mind and matter together. But in four-constituent existence (*catuvokārabhava*), the immaterial realms, it conditions mind alone. And in one-constituent existence (*ekavokārabhava*), the realm of non-percipient beings, it conditions matter alone. In the event of a five-constituent rebirth, when the rebirth consciousness arises at the moment of rebirth-linking there arise simultaneously the other three mental aggregates of feeling, perception, and mental formations, along with a particular conglomeration of material phenomena—in the case of human beings, the material decads of the body, sex, and the heart-base. Because consciousness is the chief of these coexistent mental and material elements, it is said that consciousness conditions mind-and-matter.

(4) **Dependent on mind-and-matter arise the six sense bases**: Here, "mind-and-matter" has the same denotation as in step (3). Of the six sense bases, the first five bases are the sensitive matter of the eye, ear, nose, tongue, and body, while the mind base denotes the thirty-two kinds of resultant consciousness. When the kamma-born material phenomena arise, they condition the arising of the five sense organs, which are also types of kamma-born matter. When the associated cetasikas arise, they condition the arising of the resultant consciousness, here called the mind base. In other words, the resultant consciousness conditions mind (*nāma*),

and mind conditions the resultant consciousness: they relate to each other as mutuality condition (*aññamaññapaccaya*). In the sensuous plane mind-and-matter conditions the arising of all six sense bases; in the fine-material plane only three bases arise—the eye, ear, and mind bases; in the immaterial plane mind alone conditions the arising of the mind base alone, the only sense base in that plane as the five material sense bases are necessarily absent.

(5) **Dependent on the six sense bases arises contact**: Contact (*phassa*) here denotes the contact associated with resultant consciousness. Contact is the "coming together" (*sangati*) of consciousness and the mental factors with an object at one or another of the six sense bases. The contact which arises at the sensitive eye base is called eye-contact. It marks the coming together of the eye, a visible form, and eye-consciousness. The other kinds of contact—ear-contact, etc.—likewise arise in dependence on their respective sense bases. Mind-contact is the contact associated with the twenty-two kinds of resultant consciousness, excluding the two sets of fivefold sense consciousness. As contact can occur only when the sense bases exist, it is said that contact is dependent on the six sense bases.

(6) **Dependent on contact arises feeling:** Whenever contact occurs, feeling (*vedanā*) arises simultaneously, conditioned by that same contact. Contact is the encounter of consciousness with the object, and that encounter is necessarily accompanied by a particular affective tone, the feeling produced by the contact. There are six classes of feeling: feeling born of eye-contact, feeling born of ear-contact, etc., to feeling born of mind-contact. In terms of its affective quality, feeling may be pleasant, painful, or neutral, according to the base and object.

(7) **Dependent on feeling arises craving**: Feeling conditions the arising of craving (*taṇhā*). There are six kinds of craving: craving for forms, for sounds, for smells, for tastes, for tangibles, and for mental objects. Each of these again becomes threefold according to whether it is simply craving for sensual pleasure; or craving for existence, i.e. craving conjoined with an eternalist view (*sassatadiṭṭhi*); or craving for annihilation, i.e. craving conjoined with an annihilationist view (*ucchedadiṭṭhi*). In all its varieties, craving is ultimately reducible to the cetasika greed (*lobha*). See VII, §38.

Although craving is distinguished by way of its object, the craving itself actually depends on the feeling that arises through contact with that object. If one experiences a pleasant feeling, one relishes that pleasant feeling and desires the object only insofar as it arouses the pleasant feeling. On the other hand, when one experiences a painful feeling, one has a craving to be free from the pain and one longs for a pleasurable feeling to replace it. Neutral feeling has a peaceful nature, and this too becomes an object of craving. Thus the three kinds of feeling condition the arising of various types of craving.

(8) **Dependent on craving arises clinging:** Here clinging (*upādāna*) is of the four kinds explained above (VII, §7). Clinging to sense pleasures is intensified craving, a mode of the cetasika greed; the other three kinds of clinging are modes of the cetasika wrong view. Each of these types of clinging is conditioned by craving. In the first case, weak or initial greed for an object is called craving, while the intensified greed is called clinging. In the other three cases, the greed that conditions wrong views is called craving, while the views that are accepted under the influence of that greed are called clinging.

(9) **Dependent on clinging arises existence**: There are two kinds of existence—the kammically active process of existence (*kammabhava*) and the passive or resultant process of existence (*upapattibhava*). Active existence denotes the twenty-nine types of wholesome and unwholesome volition, or all wholesome and unwholesome kamma that leads to new existence. Resultant existence denotes the thirty-two kinds of resultant cittas, their associated cetasikas, and material phenomena born of kamma.

Clinging is a condition for active existence because, under the influence of clinging, one engages in action that is accumulated as kamma. Clinging is a condition for resultant existence because that same clinging leads one back into the round of rebirth in a state determined by one's kamma.

(10) **Dependent on existence arises birth**: Here birth (*jāti*) means the arising of the mundane resultant cittas, their cetasikas, and kamma-born matter in a new life in one or another realm of existence. The essential condition for the occurrence of a future birth lies in wholesome and unwholesome kamma, that is, in present kammically active existence.

(11) **Dependent on birth arise decay-and-death, etc.**: Once birth has occurred, there inevitably follow decay-and-death and all the other kinds of suffering between birth and death, such as sorrow, lamentation, pain, grief, and despair. All of this suffering is rooted in birth, thus birth is singled out as their principal condition.

Thus arises the whole mass of suffering: The whole mass of suffering mentioned in step (11) arises through the concatenation of interdependent conditioning and conditioned states described in the formula.

§4 Categories of Analysis

Tattha tayo addhā, dvādas' angāni, vīsat' ākārā, tisandhi, catusankhepā, tīṇi vaṭṭāni, dve mūlāni ca veditabbāni.

It should be understood that there are three periods, twelve factors, twenty modes, three connections, four groups, three rounds, and two roots.

§5 The Three Periods

Kathaṁ? Avijjā, sankhārā atīto addhā; jāti, jarāmaraṇaṁ anāgato addhā; majjhe aṭṭha paccuppanno addhā ti tayo addhā.

How? Ignorance and kammic formations belong to the past; birth and decay-and-death belong to the future; the intermediate eight factors belong to the present. Thus there are three periods.

Guide to §5

When the twelve factors are divided into three periods of time, this should be seen as a mere expository device for exhibiting the causal structure of the round of existence. It should not be taken to imply that the factors assigned to a particular temporal period operate only in that period and not on other occasions. In fact, the twelve factors are always present together in any single life, mutually implicative and interpenetrating, as §7 below will demonstrate.

§6 The Twelve Factors

Avijjā, sankhārā, viññāṇaṁ, nāmarūpaṁ, saḷāyatanaṁ, phasso, vedanā, taṇhā, upādānaṁ, bhavo, jāti, jarāmaraṇan ti dvādas' angāni. Sokādivacanam pan' ettha nissandaphalanidassanaṁ.

(1) Ignorance, (2) kammic formations, (3) consciousness, (4) mind-and-matter, (5) the six sense bases, (6) contact, (7) feeling, (8) craving, (9) clinging, (10) existence, (11) birth, (12) decay-and-death are the twelve factors. The terms sorrow and so on are shown as incidental consequences (of birth).

§7 The Four Groups

Avijjā-sankhāraggahaṇena pan' ettha taṇh'-ūpādāna-bhavā pi gahitā bhavanti. Tathā taṇh'-ūpādāna-bhavaggahaṇena ca avijjā-

sankhārā; jāti-jarāmaraṇaggahaṇena ca viññāṇādiphalapañcakam eva gahitan ti katvā:

Atīte hetavo pañca idāni phalapañcakaṁ
Idāni hetavo pañca āyatiṁ phalapañcakan ti.

Vīsat' ākārā, tisandhi, catusankhepā ca bhavanti.

Here, by taking ignorance and kammic formations, craving, clinging, and existence are also taken. Likewise, by taking craving, clinging, and existence, ignorance and kammic formations are also taken. By taking birth and decay-and-death, the five effects—consciousness and so on—are also taken.

Thus there are:

(1) Five causes pertaining to the past,
(2) And five effects to the present;
(3) Five causes pertaining to the present,
(4) And five effects to the future.

There are twenty modes, three connections, and four groups.

Guide to §7

When ignorance remains unabandoned in the mind, then craving and clinging are bound to arise; and whenever craving and clinging occur, they are rooted in and accompanied by ignorance. Further, the terms "kammic formations" and "existence" both refer to the same reality—kammically active volition. Therefore, when one set of terms is mentioned, the other is implied, and when the other is mentioned, the former is implied. Birth and decay-and-death are not enumerated separately among the twenty modes because they are characteristics of mind and matter, not ultimate realities. The ultimates which they qualify are the five factors from consciousness through feeling (3-7).

The three connections obtain between past causes and present results (2-3), between present results and present causes (7-8), and between present causes and future results (10-11). The classifications proposed in this passage are shown schematically in Table 8.1.

§8 The Three Rounds

Avijjā-taṇh'-ūpādānā ca kilesavaṭṭaṁ; kammabhavasankhāto bhav' ekadeso sankhārā ca kammavaṭṭaṁ; upapattibhavasankhāto bhav' ekadeso avasesā ca vipākavaṭṭan ti tīṇi vaṭṭāni.

The three rounds :

(1) Ignorance, craving, and clinging belong to the round of defilements.

(2) One part of existence known as kammic existence and kammic formations belong to the round of kamma.

(3) One part of existence known as rebirth existence and the rest belong to the round of results.

Guide to §8

The three rounds exhibit the cyclic pattern of existence in *saṁsāra.* The most fundamental round is the round of defilements. Blinded by ignorance and driven by craving, a person engages in various unwholesome and mundane wholesome activities. Thus the round of defilements

TABLE 8.1: DEPENDENT ARISING

3 Periods	12 Factors	20 Modes & 4 Groups
Past	1. Ignorance 2. Formations	Past causes 5: 1, 2, 8, 9, 10
Present	3. Consciousness 4. Mind - & - matter 5. Six sense bases 6. Contact 7. Feeling	Present effects 5: 3 –7
	8. Craving 9. Clinging 10. Existence	Present causes 5: 8, 9, 10, 1, 2
Future	11. Birth 12. Decay - & - death	Future effects 5: 3 –7

Three Connections

1. Past causes with present effects (between 2 & 3)
2. Present effects with present causes (between 7 & 8)
3. Present causes with future effects (between 10 & 11)

Three Rounds

1. Round of defilements: 1, 8, 9
2. Round of kamma: 2, 10 (part)
3. Round of results: 3–7, 10 (part), 11, 12

Two Roots

1. Ignorance: from past to present
2. Craving: from present to future

gives rise to the round of kamma. When this kamma matures it ripens in the resultants, and thus the round of kamma gives rise to the round of resultants. In response to these resultants—the pleasant and painful fruits of his own actions—the person still immersed in ignorance is overcome by craving to enjoy more pleasant experiences, clings to those he already has, and tries to avoid the painful ones. Thus the round of resultants generates another round of defilements. In this way the threefold round turns incessantly until the ignorance at its base is removed by the wisdom of insight and the supramundane paths.

§9 The Two Roots

Avijjātaṇhāvasena dve mūlāni ca veditabbāni.

Ignorance and craving should be understood as the two roots.

Guide to §9

Ignorance is called the root from the past extending into the present, which reaches its culmination in feeling. Craving is called the root from the present extending into the future, which reaches its culmination in decay-and-death.

§10 Summary

Tesam eva ca mūlānaṁ nirodhena nirujjhati
Jarāmaraṇamucchāya pīḷitānam abhiṇhaso
Āsavānaṁ samuppādā avijjā ca pavattati.
Vaṭṭam abandham icc' evaṁ tebhūmakam anādikaṁ
Paṭiccasamuppādo ti paṭṭhapesi mahāmuni.

By the destruction of these roots the round ceases. With the arising of the taints in those who are constantly oppressed by infatuation with decay and death, ignorance again occurs.

The Great Sage has thus expounded this entangled, beginningless round of becoming with its three planes as "dependent arising."

Guide to §10

In the Sammādiṭṭhi Sutta (M.9/i,54-55) the Venerable Sāriputta is asked to explain the cause of ignorance and he replies that ignorance arises from the taints (*āsavasamudayā avijjāsamudayo*). When he is asked to state the cause of the taints, he replies that the taints arise from ignorance (*avijjāsamudayā āsavasamudayo*). Since the most fundamental of the taints is the taint of ignorance (*avijjāsava*), the Venerable Sāriputta's statement implies that the ignorance in any given existence arises from the ignorance in the preceding existence. This, in effect, establishes the round of becoming as beginningless (*anādikaṁ*) since any instance of ignorance always depends on a preceding life in which ignorance was present, entailing an infinite regression. On the taints, see VII, §3.

The Method of Conditional Relations (*paṭṭhānanaya*)

§11 The Twenty-four Conditions

(1) Hetupaccayo, (2) ārammaṇapaccayo, (3) adhipatipaccayo, (4) anantarapaccayo, (5) samanantarapaccayo, (6) sahajātapaccayo, (7) aññamaññapaccayo, (8) nissayapaccayo, (9) upanissayapaccayo, (10) purejātapaccayo, (11) pacchājātapaccayo, (12) āsevanapaccayo, (13) kammapaccayo, (14) vipākapaccayo, (15) āhārapaccayo, (16) indriyapaccayo, (17) jhānapaccayo, (18) maggapaccayo, (19) sampayuttapaccayo, (20) vippayuttapaccayo, (21) atthipaccayo, (22) natthipaccayo, (23) vigatapaccayo, (24) avigatapaccayo ti ayam ettha paṭṭhānanayo.

The following is the method of conditional relations: (1) root condition, (2) object condition, (3) predominance condition, (4) proximity condition, (5) contiguity condition, (6) conascence condition, (7) mutuality condition, (8) support condition, (9) decisive support condition, (10) prenascence condition, (11) postnascence condition, (12) repetition condition, (13) kamma condition, (14) result condition, (15) nutriment condition, (16) faculty condition, (17) jhāna condition, (18) path condition, (19) association condition, (20) dissociation condition, (21) presence condition, (22) absence condition, (23) disappearance condition, (24) non-disappearance condition.

Guide to §11

The twenty-four conditions listed above form the subject matter of the *Paṭṭhāna*, which presents a detailed exposition of the various ways in which they inter-relate the mental and material phenomena enumerated in the *Dhammasaṅgaṇī*, the first book of the Abhidhamma Piṭaka. In order to properly comprehend the Abhidhamma teaching on conditional relations, it is essential to understand the three factors involved

TABLE 8.2: THE TWENTY-FOUR CONDITIONS AND THEIR VARIETIES

1. Root condition
2. Object condition
3. Predominance condition
   (1) Object predominance
   (2) Conascence predominance
4. Proximity condition
5. Contiguity condition
6. Conascence condition
7. Mutuality condition
8. Support condition
   (1) Conascence support
   (2) Prenascence support
      (a) Base-prenascence support
      (b) Base-object-prenascence support
9. Decisive support condition
   (1) Object decisive support
   (2) Proximity decisive support
   (3) Natural decisive support
10. Prenascence condition
   (1) Base prenascence
   (2) Object prenascence
11. Postnascence condition
12. Repetition condition
13. Kamma condition
   (1) Conascent kamma
   (2) Asynchronous kamma
14. Result condition
15. Nutriment condition
   (1) Material nutriment
   (2) Mental nutriment
16. Faculty condition
   (1) Prenascence faculty
   (2) Material life faculty
   (3) Conascence faculty
17. Jhāna condition
18. Path condition
19. Association condition
20. Dissociation condition
   (1) Conascence dissociation
   (2) Prenascence dissociation
   (3) Postnascence dissociation
21. Presence condition
   (1) Conascence presence
   (2) Prenascence presence
   (3) Postnascence presence
   (4) Nutriment presence
   (5) Faculty presence
22. Absence condition
23. Disappearance condition
24. Non-disappearance condition

in any particular relation: (1) the conditioning states (*paccayadhammā*), the phenomena that function as conditions for other phenomena either by producing them, by supporting them, or by maintaining them; (2) the conditionally arisen states (*paccayuppannadhammā*), the states conditioned by the conditioning states, the phenomena that arise and persist in being through the assistance provided by the conditioning states; and (3) the conditioning force of the condition (*paccayasatti*), the particular way in which the conditioning states function as conditions for the conditioned states.

In the following sections (§§13-27) Ācariya Anuruddha will explain how the twenty-four conditions structure the relations betwen the different classes of phenomena. Instead of proceeding to explicate each condition in the original order, he classifies the conditioning states and the conditioned states as mind, matter, and mind-and-matter conjoined, and then introduces the conditions pertinent to the relations between these classes in their six permutations. In elaborating upon these sections we will call attention to the three factors involved in each condition when they are not immediately clear from the text.[2] In Table 8.3 the conditioning and conditioned states for each condition are listed following the traditional order.

§12 Application in Brief

Chadhā nāman tu nāmassa pañcadhā nāmarūpinaṁ
Ekadhā puna rūpassa rūpaṁ nāmassa c'ekadhā.
Paññattināmarūpāni nāmassa duvidhā dvayaṁ
Dvayassa navadhā cā ti chabbidhā paccayā—kathaṁ?

In six ways mind is a condition for mind. In five ways mind is a condition for mind-and-matter. Again, mind is a condition in one way for matter, and matter in one way for mind. In two ways concepts and mind-and-matter are a condition for mind. In nine ways the dyad—mind-and-matter—is a condition for mind-and-matter. Thus the relations are sixfold. How?

§13 Mind for Mind

Anantaraniruddhā cittacetasikā dhammā paccuppannānaṁ cittacetasikānaṁ anantara-samanantara-natthi-vigatavasena; purimāni javanāni pacchimānaṁ javanānaṁ āsevanavasena; sahajātā cittacetasikā dhammā aññamaññaṁ sampayuttavasenā ti chadhā nāmaṁ nāmassa paccayo hoti.

In six ways mind is a condition for mind:

Consciousness and mental factors that immediately cease are a condition for present consciousness and mental factors by way of proximity, contiguity, absence and disappearance.

Preceding javanas are a condition for subsequent javanas by way of repetition.

Conascent consciousness and mental factors are a condition for one another by way of association.

Guide to §13

Proximity condition (4), contiguity condition (5): These two conditions are identical in meaning; they differ only in the letter, which highlights the same relation from slightly different angles. Formally defined, proximity condition is a condition where one mental state, the conditioning state, causes another mental state, the conditioned state, to arise immediately after it has ceased, so that no other mental state can intervene between them. Contiguity condition is a condition where the conditioning mental state causes the conditioned mental state to arise immediately after it has ceased, in accordance with the fixed order of the mental process. These two conditions apply to the relationship between the citta and cetasikas ceasing at any given moment and the citta and cetasikas that arise in immediate succession. The citta and cetasikas that have just ceased are the conditioning states; the citta and cetasikas that arise immediately afterwards are the conditioned states. The death consciousness of an Arahant, however, does not function as proximity or contiguity condition, since it is not followed by any other citta.

Absence condition (22), disappearance condition (23): These two conditions are another pair which are identical in substance but differ merely in the letter. Absence condition is a condition where a mental state in ceasing gives the opportunity to another mental state to arise immediately next to itself. Disappearance condition is a condition where a mental state, by its own disappearance, gives the opportunity to the next mental state to arise. The conditioning and conditioned states in these two relations are identical with those of the proximity and contiguity conditions.

Repetition condition (12) is a condition where the conditioning mental state causes the conditioned states, mental phenomena similar to itself, to arise with increased power and efficiency after it has ceased. Just as a student, by repeated study, becomes more proficient in his lessons, so the conditioning states, by causing states similar to themselves to arise in succession, impart greater proficiency and strength to them. The conditioning states in this relation are solely mundane wholesome, unwholesome, and functional mental phenomena at any given moment in the javana process except the last javana, insofar as they serve as a condition for mental phenomena having the same kammic quality (wholesome, unwholesome, or functional) in the following javana moment. The latter are the conditioned states in this relation.

Although the four supramundane path cittas are wholesome javanas, they do not become the conditioning states of repetition condition because they are followed by fruition cittas, which are resultants, and thus the repetition essential to this relation is lacking. And though fruition cittas can occur in succession in a javana process, because they are resultants they do not meet the full definition of the conditioning states in repetition condition. However, the triple-rooted sense-sphere wholesome cittas which immediately precede the path cittas are conditioning states and the latter are conditioned states in the repetition condition.

Association condition (19) is a condition where a mental state, the conditioning state, causes other mental states, the conditioned states, to arise and be associated in an inseparable group characterized by its members having a common arising and cessation, a common object, and a common physical base (see II, §1). This condition obtains between any citta or cetasika as the conditioning state and all the other mental phenomena in the same unit of consciousness as the conditioned states.

§14 Mind for Mind-and-Matter

Hetu-jhānanga-maggangāni sahajātānaṁ nāmarūpānaṁ hetādivasena; sahajātā cetanā sahajātānaṁ nāmarūpānaṁ; nānākkhaṇikā cetanā kammābhinibbattānaṁ nāmarūpānaṁ kammavasena; vipākakkhandhā aññamaññaṁ sahajātānaṁ rūpānaṁ vipākavasenā ti ca pañcadhā nāmaṁ nāmarūpānaṁ paccayo hoti.

In five ways mind is a condition for mind-and-matter:

Roots, jhāna factors, and path factors are a condition for conascent mind-and-matter by way of root, etc.

Conascent volition is a condition for conascent mind-and-matter, and asynchronous volition for mind-and-matter born of kamma, by way of kamma.

The (mental) resultant aggregates are a condition for one another and for conascent matter by way of result.

Guide to §14

Root condition (1) is a condition where a conditioning state functions like a root by imparting firmness and fixity to the conditioned states. The conditioning states in this relation are the six mental factors known as roots (see III, §5): the three unwholesome roots—greed, hatred, and delusion; and the three beautiful roots—non-greed, non-hatred, and non-delusion—which may be either wholesome or indeterminate. The conditioned states are the mental states associated with each root and the conascent material phenomena. Conascent material phenomena are those born of kamma at the moment of rebirth-linking, and those born of consciousness during the course of existence. Just as the roots of a tree

TABLE 8.3: CONDITIONING AND CONDITIONED STATES OF THE TWENTY-FOUR CONDITIONS

Condition	Conditioning States	Conditioned States
1. Root	6 roots	71 rtd. cittas, 52 cetas. exc. delusion conas. w. 2 delus.-rtd. cittas, mat. born of rtd. cittas, kamma-born mat. at rtd. reb.
2. Object	89 cittas, 52 cetas., 28 mat., Nibbāna, concepts	89 cittas, 52 cetas.
3. Predominance		
(1) Object "	18 concrete mat., 84 cittas (exc. 2 hate-rtd., 2 delus.-rtd., body-cons. w. pain), 47 cetas. (exc. hate, envy, avarice, worry, doubt), Nibbāna	8 greed-rtd. cittas, 8 gt. wh. cittas, 4 gt. fnc. cittas w. knwl., 8 spm. cittas, 45 cetas. (exc. hate, etc., 2 illimitables)
(2) Conascence "	One of 3 predom. factors (desire, energy, wisdom) conas. w. 52 predom. javs., citta of those 52 javs.	52 predom. javs., 51 cetas. (exc. doubt) other than predom. factor, mat. born of predom. citta
4. Proximity	Preceding 89 cittas (exc. Arh.'s death cons.), 52 cetas.	Succeeding 89 cittas, 52 cetas.
5. Contiguity	Same as 4	Same as 4
6. Conascence	(a) Both at reb. and exs.: 89 cittas, 52 cetas. which support each other and conascent mat.	89 cittas, 52 cetas. supported by each other, conascent mat.
	(b) 4 gt. ess. which support each other and derived mat.	4 gt. ess. supported by each other, derived conascent mat.

TABLE 8.3 – Continued

CONDITION	CONDITIONING STATES	CONDITIONED STATES
	(c) At reb. in 5-aggr. planes: 4 mental aggrs. and heart-base	Heart-base supported by mental aggrs.; mental aggrs. supported by heart-base
7. Mutuality	(a) Both at reb. and exs.: 89 cittas, 52 cetas.	89 cittas, 52 cetas. (mutually)
	(b) 4 gt. ess.	4 gt. ess. (mutually)
	(c) Same as 6(c)	Same as 6(c)
8. Support		
(1) Conascence "	Same as 6	Same as 6
(2) Prenascence "		
(a) Base- " "	During exs.: 6 mat. bases	In 5-aggr. planes: 85 cittas (exc. 4 IS rsts.), 52 cetas.
(b) Base-object- " "	The heart-base taken as object of the same citta and cetas. it supports as base	M-d-advt., 29 SS javs., 11 regs., 44 cetas. (exc. envy, avarice, worry, 3 abstinences, 2 illimitables) taking their heart-base as object
9. Decisive support		
(1) Object " "	Same as 3(1)	Same as 3(1)
(2) Proxim. " "	Same as 4	Same as 4
(3) Natural " "	Strong past 89 cittas, 52 cetas., 28 mat., some concepts	Later 89 cittas, 52 cetas.
10. Prenascence		
(1) Base "	Same as 8(2)(a)	Same as 8(2)(a)
(2) Object "	Present 18 concrete mat.	54 SS cittas, 2 dir-knwl., 50 cetas. (exc. 2 illimitables)

TABLE 8.3 – Continued

CONDITION	CONDITIONING STATES	CONDITIONED STATES
11. Postnascence	In 5-aggr. planes: later 85 cittas starting from first bhv., 52 cetas.	In 5-aggr. planes; mat. of body arisen along with preceding citta, from reb. on, at phase of presence
12. Repetition	47 mun. javs. exc. last jav. of same kind, 52 cetas.	Following 51 javs. exc. first jav. and fruit jav.
13. Kamma		
(1) Conascent "	Volition in 89 cittas	89 cittas, 51 cetas. (exc. volition), conascent mat.
(2) Asynchronous "	33 past wh. and unwh. volitions	36 rst. cittas, 38 cetas., kamma-born mat.
14. Result	Both at reb. and exs.: 36 rst. cittas, 38 cetas. which support each other and conascent mat.	36 rst. cittas, 38 cetas. (mutually), conas. mat. exc. 2 intimations
15. Nutriment		
(1) Material "	(a) Nutr. essence in food	Mat. born of nutriment
	(b) Internal nutr. essence in groups born of 4 causes	Mat. of same group (exc. nutr. essence), all mat. of other groups
(2) Mental "	Contact, volition, citta	89 cittas, 52 cetas., mat. conas. w. each nutriment
16. Faculty		
(1) Prenascence "	5 mat. sensitivities	10 sense cons., 7 univ. cetas.
(2) Material life "	Mat. life faculty at reb. and during exs.	9 kamma-born mat. conas. w. life faculty
(3) Conascence "	8 mental faculties: life, citta, feeling, faith, energy, mindfulness, one-ptns., wisdom	89 cittas, 52 cetas., mat. conas. w. faculties

TABLE 8.3 – Continued

Condition	Conditioning States	Conditioned States
17. Jhāna	In. applic., sus. applic., zest, feeling, one-ptns. conas. w. 79 cittas (exc. 10 sense cons.)	79 cittas (exc. 10 sense cons.), 52 cetas., conascent mat.
18. Path	9 cetas. conas. w. 71 rtd. cittas; wisdom, in. applic. 3 abstinences, energy, mindfulness, one-ptns, view	71 rtd. cittas, 52 cetas., mat. conas. w. rtd. cittas
19. Association	Same as 7(a)	Same as 7(a)
20. Dissociation		
(1) Conascence "	(a) In 5-aggr. planes: at reb. and exs., 75 cittas (exc. 4 IS rsts., 10 sense cons., Arh.'s death cons.), 52 cetas.	Conascent mat.
	(b) Same as 6(c)	Same as 6(c)
(2) Prenascence "	Same as 8(2)(a) and (b)	Same as 8(2)(a) and (b)
(3) Postnascence "	Same as 11	Same as 11
21. Presence		
(1) Conascence "	Same as 6	Same as 6
(2) Prenascence "	Same as 10	Same as 10
(3) Postnascence "	Same as 11	Same as 11
(4) Nutriment "	Same as 15(1)	Same as 15(1)
(5) Faculty "	Same as 16(2)	Same as 16(2)
22. Absence	Same as 4	Same as 4
23. Disappearance	Same as 4	Same as 4
24. Non-disappearance	Same as 2	Same as 2

are the basis for a tree's existence, growth, and stability, so these roots give rise to the conditioned states and make them firm and steady.

Jhāna condition (17) is a condition where a conditioning state causes the conditioned states to participate in the close contemplation of an object. The conditioning states are the seven jhāna factors, which reduce to five cetasikas (see VII, §16, §23). The conditioned states are the cittas and cetasikas associated with the jhāna factors—that is, all cittas except the ten types of sense consciousness—and the conascent material phenomena. Although the conascent material phenomena cannot contemplate the object themselves, because they are produced by the close contemplation accomplished by the jhāna factors they are included among the conditioned states.

Path condition (18) is a condition where a conditioning state relates to the conditioned states by causing them to function as a means for reaching a particular destination. The conditioning states in this relation are the twelve path factors, which reduce to nine cetasikas (see VII, §17, §23). The four wrong path factors are the means for reaching the woeful destinations; the eight right path factors are the means for reaching the blissful destinations and Nibbāna. The conditioned states are all cittas except the eighteen that are rootless, the associated cetasikas, and the conascent material phenomena. While the path factors in the resultant and functional cittas do not lead to any destinations, they are still classed as path factors because, considered abstractly in their own nature, they are identical with those capable of leading to different destinations.

Kamma condition (13): This condition is of two kinds: (i) conascent kamma condition (*sahajāta-kammapaccaya*), and (ii) asynchronous kamma condition (*nānākkhaṇika-kammapaccaya*).

(i) In the conascent kamma condition, the conditioning states are the volitions (*cetanā*) in the eighty-nine cittas. The conditioned states are the citta and cetasikas associated with those volitions and the conascent material phenomena. Volition here functions as a conascent kamma condition by causing its concomitants to perform their respective tasks and by arousing the appropriate kinds of material phenomena simultaneously with its own arising.

(ii) In the asynchronous kamma condition there is a temporal gap between the conditioning state and the conditioned states. The conditioning state in this relation is a past wholesome or an unwholesome volition. The conditioned states are the resultant cittas, their cetasikas, and material phenomena born of kamma, both at rebirth-linking and in the course of existence. The conditioning force here is the ability of such volition to generate the appropriate resultant mental states and kamma-born materiality. This conditional relation also obtains between a path consciousness and its fruition.

Result condition (14) is a condition where a conditioning state makes the conditioned states that arise together with it be as passive, effortless, and quiescent as itself. The conditioning states in this relation are the resultant cittas and cetasikas. The conditioned states are those same resultants with respect to each other and the conascent material phenomena. Since resultants are produced from the maturing of kamma, they are not active but passive and quiescent. Thus in the mind of a person in deep sleep, the resultant bhavanga consciousness arises and passes away in constant succession, yet during this time no efforts are made for action by body, speech, or mind, and there is not even distinct awareness of an object. Similarly, in the five-door cognitive process, the resultant cittas do not make an exertion to know their object. It is only in the javana phase that effort is made to clearly cognize the object, and again it is only in the javana phase that actions are performed.

§15 Mind for Matter

Pacchājātā cittacetasikā dhammā purejātassa imassa kāyassa pacchājātavasenā ti ekadhā va nāmaṁ rūpassa paccayo hoti.

Only in one way is mind a condition for matter: Subsequent consciousness and mental factors are a condition for this preceding (material) body by way of postnascence.

Guide to §15

Postnascence condition (11) is a condition where a conditioning state assists conditioned states that had arisen prior to itself by supporting and strengthening them. The conditioning states in this relation are subsequently arisen cittas and cetasikas, the conditioned states are the material phenomena of the body born of all four causes, which material phenomena had arisen along with preceding cittas. This condition begins with the first bhavanga in relation to the material phenomena born of kamma at the moment of rebirth-linking. Just as the rainwater that falls later promotes the growth and development of the already existing vegetation, so the subsequently arisen mental states support the pre-arisen material phenomena so that they continue to produce similar material phenomena in succession.

§16 Matter for Mind

Cha vatthūni pavattiyaṁ sattannaṁ viññāṇadhātūnaṁ; pañc' ālambanāni ca pañcaviññāṇavīthiyā purejātavasenā ti ekadhā va rūpaṁ nāmassa paccayo hoti.

Only in one way is matter a condition for mind: The six bases during the course of existence are a condition for the seven elements of consciousness, and the five objects for the five processes of sense consciousness, by way of prenascence.

Guide to §16

Prenascence condition (10) is a condition where a conditioning state—a material state which has already arisen and reached the stage of presence (*ṭhiti*)—causes mental states, the conditioned states, to arise after it. This is like the sun, which arises first in the world and gives light to people who appear after it has arisen. There are two main types of prenascence condition, (i) base prenascence (*vatthu-purejāta*) and (ii) object prenascence (*ārammaṇa-purejāta*).

(i) Each of the six physical bases during the course of existence is a conditioning state by way of base prenascence for the citta and cetasikas—the conditioned states—that take it as the material support for their arising (see III, §§20-22). The heart-base is not a prenascence condition for the mental states at the moment of rebirth-linking, since on that occasion the heart-base and mental states arise simultaneously as conascence and mutuality conditions. But the heart-base arisen at the rebirth moment becomes a prenascence condition for the first bhavanga citta immediately following the rebirth consciousness, and thereafter it becomes a prenascence condition for all mind element and mind-consciousness element cittas during the course of life.

(ii) Each of the five sense objects is a conditioning state by way of object prenascence for the citta and cetasikas in a sense door cognitive process that take it as object. In addition, all eighteen types of concretely produced matter (see VI, §2) that have reached the stage of presence can become object prenascence condition for the cittas and cetasikas in a mind-door process.

§17 Mind-and-Matter for Mind

Ārammaṇavasena upanissayavasenā ti ca duvidhā paññatti nāmarūpāni nāmass' eva paccayā honti.

Tattha rūpādivasena chabbidhaṁ hoti ārammaṇaṁ.

Upanissayo pana tividho hoti: ārammaṇūpanissayo, anantarūpanissayo, pakatūpanissayo cā ti. Tatth' ālambanam eva garukataṁ ārammaṇūpanissayo. Anantaraniruddhā cittacetasikā dhammā anantarūpanissayo. Rāgādayo pana dhammā saddhādayo ca sukhaṁ dukkhaṁ puggalo bhojanaṁ utu senāsanañ ca yathārahaṁ ajjhattañ ca bahiddhā ca kusalādidhammānaṁ kammaṁ vipākānan ti ca bahudhā hoti pakatūpanissayo.

In two ways concepts and mind-and-matter are conditions for mind—namely, by way of object and decisive support.

Therein, object is sixfold as visible form, etc. But decisive support is threefold, namely, object decisive support, proximity decisive support, and natural decisive support.

Of them, the object itself when it becomes prominent serves as object decisive support. Consciousness and mental factors that immediately cease, act as the proximity decisive support. The natural decisive support is of many kinds: states of lust, etc., states of faith, etc., pleasure, pain, individuals, food, season, lodgings—(all such things) internal and external, as the case may be, are conditions for wholesome states, etc. Kamma, too, is similarly a condition for its results.

Guide to §17

Object condition (2) is a condition where a conditioning state, as object, causes other states, the conditioned states, to arise taking it as their object. The six classes of objects (see III, §16) are the conditioning states in this relation, the corresponding cittas and cetasikas are the conditioned states.

Decisive support condition (9): Of the three types of this condition:

(i) Object decisive support (*ārammaṇūpanissaya*) is a condition where the conditioning state is an exceptionally desirable or important object which causes the conditioned states, the mental phenomena that apprehend it, to arise in strong dependence on it.

(ii) Proximity decisive support (*anantarūpanissaya*) is identical with proximity condition with respect to the conditioning and conditioned states, but differs from it slightly in the forces of the conditions. Proximity is the force which causes the succeeding mental states to arise immediately after the preceding states have ceased; proximity decisive support is the force which causes the succeeding states to arise because they are strongly dependent on the ceasing of the preceding states.

(iii) Natural decisive support (*pakatūpanissaya*) is a wide relation that includes as the conditioning states all past mental or material phenomena that become strongly efficacious for the arising, at a subsequent time, of the conditioned states, which are subsequent cittas and cetasikas. For example, prior lust may be a natural decisive support condition for the volitions of killing, stealing, sexual misconduct, etc.; prior faith for the volitions of giving alms, undertaking precepts, and practising meditation; the gaining of health for happiness and energy, the onset of sickness for sorrow and torpor, etc.

§18 Mind-and-Matter for Mind-and-Matter

Adhipati-sahajāta-aññamañña-nissaya-āhāra-indriya-vippayutta-atthi-avigatavasenā ti yathārahaṁ navadhā nāmarūpāni nāmarūpānaṁ paccayā bhavanti.

Mind-and-matter is a condition for mind-and-matter in nine ways according to circumstances, namely, by way of predominance, conascence, mutuality, support, nutriment, faculty, dissociation, presence, and non-disappearance.

Guide to §18

These conditions will be elaborated upon in the following sections.

§19 The Predominance Condition

Tattha garukataṁ ālambanaṁ ālambanādhipativasena nāmānaṁ sahajātādhipati catubbidho pi sahajātavasena sahajātānaṁ nāmarūpānan ti ca duvidho hoti adhipatipaccayo.

Therein, the predominance condition is twofold:
(i) The object to which weight is attached is a condition for states of mind by way of object predominance.
(ii) The fourfold conascent predominance is a condition for conascent mind-and-matter by way of conascence.

Guide to §19

Predominance condition (3): Of the two types of this condition:
(i) Object predominance (*ārammaṇādhipati*) is a condition where the conditioning state, as object, dominates over the mental states which take it as their object. Only those objects which are esteemed, cherished, or strongly desired can become the conditioning states in this relation. This condition is virtually identical with the object decisive support condition, differing from it only slightly in the conditioning forces: while the latter has the force of being a strongly efficacious cause for the arising of the citta and cetasikas, the former has the force of strongly attracting and dominating those states.

(ii) Conascence predominance (*sahajātādhipati*) is a condition where a conditioning state dominates conditioned states conascent with itself. The conditioning states in this relation are the four predominants—desire, energy, consciousness, and investigation (see VII, §20). Only one of these can take on the role of predominance condition on a given occasion, and then only in javana cittas. The conascent mental and material phenomena are the conditioned states.

§20 The Conascence Condition

Cittacetasikā dhammā aññamaññaṁ sahajātarūpānañ ca, mahābhūtā aññamaññaṁ upādārūpānañ ca, paṭisandhikkhaṇe vatthu-vipākā aññamaññan ti ca tividho hoti sahajātapaccayo.

The conascence condition is threefold: consciousness and mental factors are a condition for one another and for the conascent material phenomena; the four great essentials mutually and for the derived material phenomena; the heart-base and the resultant (mental aggregates) for one another at the moment of rebirth-linking.

Guide to §20

Conascence condition (6) is a condition where a conditioning state, on arising, causes the conditioned states to arise simultaneously with itself. This is compared to the flame of a lamp which, on arising, causes the light, colour, and heat to arise along with it. This condition may be divided into three types, as is done in the above text, or it may be more finely divided into five types: (i) each mental state—citta or cetasika—for the associated mental states; (ii) each mental state for the conascent material phenomena; (iii) each of the four great essentials for the other three great essentials; (iv) each of the four great essentials for derived material phenomena; and (v) at the moment of rebirth-linking, the heart-base for the resultant mental states, and the latter in turn for the heart-base.

§21 The Mutuality Condition

Cittacetasikā dhammā aññamaññaṁ, mahābhūtā aññamaññaṁ paṭisandhikkhaṇe vatthu-vipākā aññamaññan ti ca tividho hoti aññamaññapaccayo.

The mutuality condition is threefold: consciousness and mental factors are a condition for one another; the four great essentials for one another; the heart-base and the resultant (mental aggregates) for one another at the moment of rebirth-linking.

Guide to §21

Mutuality condition (7) is actually a subordinate type of conascence condition. In the general conascence condition, the conditioning state simply causes the conditioned states to arise together with itself, but no reciprocity in the conditioning force is required. However, in the mutuality condition each of the conditioning states is, at the same time and in the same way, a conditioned state in relation to the very states that it conditions. Thus a conditioning state in the relation of mutuality gives its force to the conditioned state and also receives the force of the conditioned state, which is a conditioning state relative to itself. This is compared to a tripod, each leg of which assists the other two legs reciprocally in enabling the tripod to stand upright.

§22 The Support Condition

Cittacetasikā dhammā aññamaññaṁ sahajātarūpānañ ca mahābhūtā aññamaññaṁ upādārūpānañ ca cha vatthūni sattannaṁ viññāṇadhātūnan ti ca tividho hoti nissayapaccayo.

The support condition is threefold: consciousness and mental factors are a condition for one another and conascent material phenomena; the four great essentials for one another and derived material phenomena; and the six bases for the seven consciousness elements.

Guide to §22

Support condition (8) is a condition where the conditioning state causes the conditioned states to arise by serving as the support or foundation on which they depend. The conditioning state is said to be related to the conditioned state in a manner similar to the way the earth supports trees and vegetation or a canvas supports a painting.

Two main categories of support condition are recognized: (i) conascence support (*sahajāta-nissaya*) and (ii) prenascence support (*purejāta-nissaya*). Conascence support condition is identical in all respects with the conascence condition. Prenascence support condition includes two subsidiary types. One is simple base-prenascence support (*vatthu-purejāta-nissaya*), which is identical with base prenascence, discussed under the prenascence condition. The other is called base-object-prenascence support (*vatthārammaṇa-purejāta-nissaya*). This refers to the special case when a citta arises supported by the heart-base and at the same time makes that heart-base its object. Thus on such an occasion the heart-base is simultaneously a support and an object for a single citta. Referring to this condition, the *Paṭṭhāna* states: "One contemplates with insight that internal base as impermanent, suffering, non-self; one enjoys it and delights in it; making it an object, lust arises, wrong view arises, doubt arises, restlessness arises, displeasure arises."[3]

§23 The Nutriment Condition

Kabaḷīkāro āhāro imassa kāyassa, arūpino āhārā sahajātānaṁ nāmarūpānan ti ca duvidho hoti āhārapaccayo.

The nutriment condition is twofold: edible food is a condition for this body; and immaterial nutriment, for the conascent mind-and-matter.

Guide to §23

Nutriment condition (15) is a condition where a conditioning state relates to the conditioned states by maintaining them in existence and supporting their growth and development. This is compared to a prop which supports an old house and prevents it from collapsing. Thus the essential function of nutriment is supporting or reinforcing (*upatthambana*).

The nutriment condition is twofold: (i) material nutriment (*rūpāhāra*) and mental nutriment (*nāmāhāra*).

(i) Material nutriment is the nutritive essense found in edible food, which is a conditioning state for this physical body. When food is ingested its nutritive essence produces new matter born of nutriment, and it also reinforces the material groups born of all four causes, keeping them strong and fresh so that they can continue to arise in succession. The internal nutriment contained in the material groups born of all four causes also serves as a condition by reinforcing the internal material phenomena coexisting with it in its own group and the material phenomena in the other groups situated in the body.

(ii) Mental nutriment is threefold: the nutriments contact, mental volition, and consciousness. These are conditions for the conascent mental and material phenomena.

§24 The Faculty Condition

Pañcapasādā pañcannaṁ viññāṇānaṁ, rūpajīvitindriyaṁ upādinnarūpānaṁ, arūpino indriyā sahajātānaṁ nāmarūpānan ti ca tividho hoti indriyapaccayo.

The faculty condition is threefold: the five sensitive organs are a condition for the five kinds of consciousness; the material life faculty, for the material phenomena born of kamma; the immaterial faculties, for conascent mind-and-matter.

Guide to §24

Faculty condition (16) is a condition where a conditioning state relates to the conditioned states by exercising control in a particular department or function. This condition is compared to a panel of ministers, each of whom has freedom of control in governing his particular region of the country and does not attempt to govern the other regions. As stated in the text, there are three types of faculty condition: (i) prenascence faculty, (ii) material life faculty, and (iii) conascence faculty.

(i) In prenascence faculty, each of the five sensitivities (arisen at the static phase of the past bhavanga citta) is a faculty condition for its respective type of sense consciousness along with its cetasikas. This is so because the sensitive organ controls the efficiency of the consciousness that takes it as a base. For example, good eyes produce acute vision while weak eyes result in poor vision.

(ii) The material life faculty in the material groups born of kamma is a faculty condition for the other nine material phenomena in the same groups, for it controls them by maintaining their vitality.

(iii) The fifteen immaterial faculties (see VII, §18) are each a conascence faculty condition for the associated mental states and the conascent material phenomena.

Of the faculties, the two sex faculties of femininity and masculinity do not become conditioning states in the faculty condition. They are excluded because they do not have the functions of a condition. A condition has three functions—producing, supporting and maintaining—but the sex faculties do not execute any of these functions. Nevertheless, they are still classed as faculties because they control the sexual structure, appearance, character, and disposition of the body, so that the whole personality tends towards either femininity or masculinity.[4]

§25 The Dissociation Condition

Okkantikkhaṇe vatthu vipākānaṁ, cittacetasikā dhammā sahajātarūpānaṁ sahajātavasena, pacchājātā cittacetasikā dhammā purejātassa imassa kāyassa pacchājātavasena, cha vatthūni pavattiyaṁ sattannaṁ viññāṇadhātūnaṁ purejātavasenā ti ca tividho hoti vippayuttapaccayo.

The dissociation condition is threefold: at the moment of rebirth-linking the heart-base is a condition for resultant (mental aggregates), and consciousness and mental factors for conascent matter, by way of conascence; the postnascent consciousness and mental factors for this prenascent material body by way of postnascence; the six bases, in the course of life, for the seven consciousness elements by way of prenascence.

Guide to §25

Dissociation condition (20) is a condition where the conditioning state is either a mental phenomenon that assists present material phenomena, or a material phenomenon that assists present mental phenomena. In this relationship the two components—the conditioning state and the conditioned states—are necessarily of different types: if one is matter the other must be mind; if one is mind the other must be matter. This is like a mixture of water and oil, which remain separate though placed together.

Thus at the moment of rebirth the heart-base and the mental aggregates arise simultaneously, each a dissociation condition for the other by reason of the particular characteristics that distinguish them as material and mental phenomena. At the moment of rebirth, again, the mental aggregates are a condition for the other kinds of kamma-born matter, and during the course of existence for mind-born matter, by way of dissociation condition. Dissociation also comprises prenascent and postnascent types: the former obtains between matter as the conditioning state and mind as the conditioned state; the latter obtains between mind as the conditioning state and matter as the conditioned state. These are identical with prenascence support condition and postnascence condition, respectively.

§26 Presence and Non-Disappearance

Sahajātaṁ purejātaṁ pacchājātaṁ ca sabbathā
Kabaḷīkāro āhāro rūpajīvitam icc' ayan ti.

Pañcavidho hoti atthipaccayo avigatapaccayo ca.

The presence and non-disappearance conditions are altogether of five kinds: conascence, prenascence, postnascence, edible food, and material life.

Guide to §26

Presence condition (21), non-disappearance condition (24): These are two conditions identical in meaning and differing only in the letter. In this relationship a conditioning state helps the conditioned states to arise or persist in being during a time when it exists alongside the conditioned states. It is not necessary, however, for the conditioning state and the conditioned states to be conascent; all that is required is for the two to temporally overlap, and for the conditioning state to support in some way the conditioned states during the time they overlap. Thus presence condition includes prenascence and postnascence as well as conascence. While the text mentions only five types of presence condition, since these five in turn include additional subsidiary types, presence condition comprises a wide variety of other conditions. This will become clear in the next section, which deals with the subsumption of all conditional relations under four master conditions.

§27 The Synthesis of Conditions

Āramman'-ūpanissaya-kamma-atthipaccayesu ca sabbe pi paccayā samodhānaṁ gacchanti.

Sahajātarūpan ti pan' ettha sabbatthā pi pavatte cittasamuṭṭhānānaṁ paṭisandhiyaṁ kaṭattā rūpānañ ca vasena duvidho hoti veditabbaṁ.

All conditions are included in the conditions of object, decisive support, kamma, and presence.

Herein, in all cases conascent material phenomena should be understood as twofold: throughout the course of existence they should be understood as those born of consciousness, and at rebirth-linking, as those born of kamma.

Guide to §27

The way in which all conditions are included in these four conditions is explained by Ledi Sayadaw in his commentary as follows:

The predominance condition being twofold, object predominance is always comprised by the object and decisive support conditions, and

TABLE 8.4: THE SYNTHESIS OF CONDITIONS

OBJECT	DECISIVE SUPPORT	KAMMA	PRESENCE
Object predominance Base-object-prenascence support Object prenascence Dissociation*	Object predominance Base-object prenascence support* Object prenascence* Asynchronous kamma* Dissociation* Proximity Contiguity Repetition Absence Disappearance	Asynchronous kamma	Object predominance* Conascence predominance* Conascence support Base-prenascence support Base-object-prenascence support Base prenascence Conascent kamma Dissociation Root Conascence Mutuality Result Nutriment Faculty Jhāna Path Association Non-disapearance Postnascence

* = sometimes only

sometimes by the presence condition as well; while conascence predominance is comprised by the presence condition.

The main types of support condition—conascence support and base-prenascence support—both come within the scope of the presence condition. The special case of base-object-prenascence support, in which the heart-base becomes an object of the same mind-door cittas it supports as a base, is included in both object and presence conditions, and in decisive support as well if the heart-base is given special importance as object.

Of the two main types of prenascence condition, base prenascence is included in presence condition while object prenascence is included in both object and presence and possibly in decisive support too.

Of the two types of kamma condition, conascent kamma is included in presence condition, while asynchronous kamma is included in kamma condition and, if strong, in decisive support as well.

Dissociation condition is included in presence condition, but if the heart-base becomes simultaneously base and object, it is included in presence, object, and possibly decisive support.

Of the remaining conditions, the following eleven are always included within presence condition: root, conascence, mutuality, resultant, nutriment, faculty, jhāna, path, association, non-disappearance, and postnascence. The following five are always included in decisive support condition: proximity, contiguity, repetition, absence, and disappearance.

The manner in which the various conditions are subsumed under the main types of conditions is shown schematically in Table 8.4.

§28 Summary

Iti tekālikā dhammā kālamuttā ca sambhavā
Ajjhattañ ca bahiddhā ca sankhatāsankhatā tathā.
Paññattināmarūpānaṁ vasena tividhā ṭhitā
Paccayā nāma paṭṭhāne catuvīsati sabbathā ti.

Thus the things pertaining to the three periods of time and timeless, internal and external, conditioned and unconditioned, are threefold by way of concepts, mind, and matter.

In all, the conditions in the scheme of conditional relations are twenty-four.

Analysis of Concepts
(*paññattibheda*)

§29 In Brief

Tattha rūpadhammā rūpakkhandho va; cittacetasikasankhātā cattāro arūpino khandhā nibbānañ cā ti pañcavidham pi arūpan ti ca nāman ti ca pavuccati.

Tato avasesā paññatti pana paññāpiyattā paññatti, paññāpanato paññattī ti ca duvidhā hoti.

Therein, the material phenomena are just the aggregate of matter. Consciousness and mental factors, which comprise the four immaterial aggregates, and Nibbāna, are the five kinds that are immaterial. They are also called "name."

What remains are concepts, which are twofold: concept as that which is made known, and concept as that which makes known.

Guide to §29

At this point Ācariya Anuruddha has completed his exposition of the four ultimate realities, their classification in various schemata, and their treatment according to the principles of conditionality. However, he has not yet discussed concepts (*paññatti*). Although concepts pertain to conventional reality and not to ultimate reality, they are still included in the Abhidhamma by the treatise *Puggalapaññatti*. Therefore in the last part of Chapter VIII he will briefly discuss concepts.

They are also called "name": The four immaterial aggregates are called *nāma*, "name," in the sense of bending (*namana*) because they bend towards the object in the act of cognizing it. They are also called *nāma* in the sense of causing to bend (*nāmana*) since they cause one another to bend on to the object. Nibbāna is called *nāma* solely in the sense of causing to bend. For Nibbāna causes faultless states—that is, the supramundane cittas and cetasikas—to bend on to itself by acting as an objective predominance condition.[5]

What remains are concepts: There are two kinds of concepts, *atthapaññatti* or concepts-as-meanings, and *nāmapaññatti* or concepts-as-names. The former are the meanings conveyed by the concepts, the latter the names or designations which convey that meaning. For example, the notion of a four-legged furry domestic animal with certain physical features and traits is the concept-as-meaning of the term "dog"; the designation and idea "dog" is the corresponding concept-as-name.

The meaning-concept is the concept as that which is made known; the name-concept is the concept as that which makes known.

§30 Concept as What is Made Known

Kathaṁ? Taṁtaṁ bhūtapariṇāmākāram upādāya tathā tathā paññattā bhūmipabbatādikā, sasambhārasannivesākāram upādāya geharathasakaṭādikā, khandhapañcakam upādāya purisapuggalādikā, candāvattanādikam upādāya disākālādikā, asamphuṭṭhākāram upādāya kūpaguhādikā, taṁtaṁ bhūtanimittaṁ bhāvanāvisesañ ca upādāya kasiṇanimittādikā cā ti evam ādippabhedā pana paramatthato avijjamānā pi atthacchāyākārena cittuppādānam ālambanabhūtā taṁtaṁ upādāya upanidhāya kāraṇaṁ katvā tathā tathā parikappiyamānā sankhāyati, samaññāyati, vohariyati, paññāpīyatī ti paññattī ti pavuccati. Ayaṁ paññatti paññāpiyattā paññatti nāma.

How? There are such terms as "land," "mountain," and the like, so designated on account of the mode of transition of the respective elements; such terms as "house," "chariot," "cart," and the like, so named on account of the mode of formation of materials; such terms as "person," "individual," and the like, so named on account of the five aggregates; such terms as "direction," "time," and the like, named according to the revolution of the moon and so forth; such terms as "well," "cave," and the like, so named on account of the mode of non-impact and so forth; such terms as kasiṇa signs and the like, so named on account of respective elements and distinguished mental development.

All such different things, though they do not exist in the ultimate sense, become objects of consciousness in the form of shadows of (ultimate) things.

They are called concepts because they are thought of, reckoned, understood, expressed, and made known on account of, in consideration of, with respect to, this or that mode. This kind of concept is so called because it is made known.

Guide to §30

"Concept as what is made known" is the same as meaning-concept (*atthapaññatti*). Here the author enumerates different types of meaning-concepts.

Land, mountain, etc., are called in Pali *saṇṭhānapaññatti*, formal concepts, since they correspond to the form or configuration of things.

House, chariot, village, etc., are called *samūhapaññatti*, collective concepts, since they correspond to a collection or group of things.

East, west, etc., are called *disāpaññatti*, local concepts, since they correspond to a locality or direction.

Morning, noon, week, month, etc., are called *kālapaññatti*, temporal concepts, since they correspond to periods or units of time.

Well, cave, etc., are called *ākāsapaññatti*, spatial concepts, since they correspond to spatial regions void of perceptible matter.

The kasina signs are called *nimittapaññatti*, sign concepts, since they correspond to mental signs gained by meditative development.

§31 Concept as What Makes Known

Paññāpanato paññatti pana nāma-nāmakammādināmena paridīpitā. Sā vijjamānapaññatti, avijjamānapaññatti, vijjamānena avijjamānapaññatti, avijjamānena vijjamānapaññatti, vijjamānena vijjamānapaññatti, avijjamānena avijjamānapaññatti cā ti chabbidhā hoti.

Tattha yadā pana paramatthato vijjamānaṁ rūpavedanādiṁ etāya paññāpenti tadā'yaṁ vijjamānapaññatti. Yadā pana paramatthato avijjamānaṁ bhūmipabbatādiṁ etāya paññāpenti, tadā'yaṁ avijjamānapaññattī ti pavuccati. Ubhinnaṁ pana vomissakavasena sesā yathākkamaṁ chaḷabhiñño, itthisaddo, cakkhuviññāṇaṁ, rājaputto ti ca veditabbā.

Then, as it makes known, it is called concept. It is described as name, nomenclature, etc.

It is sixfold: (1) a (direct) concept of the real; (2) a (direct) concept of the unreal; (3) a concept of the unreal by means of the real; (4) a concept of the real by means of the unreal; (5) a concept of the real by means of the real; and (6) a concept of the unreal by means of the unreal.

As, for instance, when it makes known what really exists in the ultimate sense by a term such as "matter," "feeling," and so forth, it is called a (direct) concept of the real.

When it makes known what does not really exist in the ultimate sense by a term, such as "land," "mountain," and so forth, it is called a (direct) concept of the unreal.

The rest should be respectively understood by combining both as, for instance, "possessor of sixfold direct knowledge," "woman's voice," "eye-consciousness," and "king's son."

Guide to §31

"Concept as what makes known" is the same as name concept (*nāmapaññatti*). Again, the author provides an enumeration of instances.

A (direct) concept of the real: Matter, feeling, etc., are ultimate realities; therefore the concepts that designate them are direct concepts of the real.

A (direct) concept of the unreal: "Land" and "mountain," etc., are not ultimate realities but conventional entities established conceptually through mental construction. Though these concepts are based on ultimate entities, the meanings they convey are not things that are themselves ultimate entities since they do not correspond to things that exist by way of their own intrinsic nature (*sabhāvato*).

The rest should be respectively understood: Here, "possessor of sixfold direct knowledge" is a concept of the unreal by means of the real, since the direct knowledges are ultimately real but the "possessor" is a mental construction. "Woman's voice" is a concept of the real by means of the unreal, since the sound of the voice ultimately exists but not the woman. "Eye-consciousness" is a concept of the real by means of the real, since both eye-sensitivity and the consciousness dependent on it exist in an ultimate sense. "King's son" is a concept of the unreal by way of the unreal, since neither the king nor the son ultimately exists. [6]

§32 Summary

Vacīghosānusārena sotaviññāṇavīthiyā
Pavattānantaruppannā manodvārassa gocarā
Atthā yassānusārena viññāyanti tato paraṁ
Sāyaṁ paññatti viññeyyā lokasanketanimmitā ti.

By following the sound of speech through the process of ear-consciousness, and then by means of the concept conceived by (the process in the) mind-door that subsequently arises, meanings are understood. These concepts should be understood as fashioned by worldly convention.

Iti Abhidhammatthasangahe
Paccayasangahavibhāgo nāma
aṭṭhamo paricchedo.

Thus ends the eighth chapter
in the Manual of Abhidhamma entitled
the Compendium of Conditionality.

CHAPTER IX
COMPENDIUM OF MEDITATION SUBJECTS
(*Kammaṭṭhānasaṅgahavibhāga*)

§1 Introductory Verse

Samathavipassanānaṁ bhāvanānam ito paraṁ
Kammaṭṭhānaṁ pavakkhāmi duvidham pi yathākkamaṁ.

From here on I will explain in order the two types of meditation subject for the respective development of calm and insight.

Guide to §1

Two types of meditation subject: The Pali term *kammaṭṭhāna* means literally "field of action" or "workplace." The term is used to designate a subject of meditation, the workplace for the meditator to develop the special attainments in the field of contemplation. In Buddhism two approaches to meditative development are recognized, calm and insight. Of the two, the development of insight is the distinctively Buddhistic form of meditation. This system of meditation is unique to the Buddha's Teaching and is intended to generate direct personal realization of the truths discovered and enunciated by the Buddha. The development of calm is also found in non-Buddhist schools of meditation. However, in the Buddha's Teaching calming meditation is taught because the serenity and concentration which it engenders provide a firm foundation for the practice of insight meditation. Each of the two types of meditation has its own methodology and range of meditation subjects, to be explained in the course of this chapter.

Calm and insight: The word *samatha*, rendered "calm," denotes quietude of mind. The word is almost synonymous with concentration (*samādhi*), though it derives from a different root, *sam*, meaning to become peaceful. Technically, *samatha* is defined as the one-pointedness of mind (*cittass' ekaggatā*) in the eight meditative attainments—the four fine-material-sphere jhānas of the Suttanta system (five in the Abhidhamma system) and the four immaterial-sphere jhānas. These attainments are called calm because, owing to the one-pointedness of mind, the wavering or trepidation of the mind is subdued and brought to an end.[1]

The word *vipassanā*, rendered "insight," is explained as seeing in diverse ways (*vividhākārato dassana*). Insight is the direct meditative perception of phenomena in terms of the three characteristics—impermanence, suffering, and non-self. It is a function of the cetasika of wisdom (*paññā*) directed towards uncovering the true nature of things.

The explanation of calm and insight meditation in this chapter of the *Abhidhammattha Sangaha* is a summary of the entire *Visuddhimagga*, to which the reader is referred for an elaborate treatment of these topics.

Compendium of Calm
(*samathasangaha*)

Basic Categories

§2 Meditation Subjects

Tattha samathasangahe tāva dasa kasiṇāni, dasa asubhā, dasa anussatiyo, catasso appamaññāyo, ekā saññā, ekaṁ vavatthānaṁ, cattāro āruppā cā ti sattavidhena samathakammaṭṭhānasangaho.

Therein, in the compendium of calm, first the compendium of meditation subjects for developing calm is sevenfold: (1) ten kasinas, (2) ten kinds of foulness, (3) ten recollections, (4) four illimitables, (5) one perception, (6) one analysis, and (7) four immaterial states.

Guide to §2

These seven categories amount to forty separate meditation subjects, to be enumerated in §§6-12. See Table 9.1.

§3 Temperaments

Rāgacaritā, dosacaritā, mohacaritā, saddhācaritā, buddhicaritā, vitakkacaritā cā ti chabbidhena caritasangaho.

The compendium of temperaments is sixfold: (1) the lustful, (2) the hateful, (3) the deluded, (4) the faithful, (5) the intellectual, and (6) the discursive.

Guide to §3

"Temperament" (*carita*) means personal nature, the character of a person as revealed by his or her natural attitudes and conduct. The temperaments of people differ owing to the diversity of their past kammas.

The commentators state that the temperament is determined by the kamma productive of the rebirth-linking consciousness.

Of the six temperaments, the lustful and the faithful types form a parallel pair since both involve a favourable attitude towards the object, one unwholesome, the other wholesome. So too, the hateful and the intellectual temperaments form a parallel pair, since in an unwholesome way hate turns away from its object, while intelligence does so through the discovery of genuine faults. The deluded and the discursive temperaments also form a pair, since a deluded person vacillates owing to superficiality, while a discursive one does so due to facile speculation. For more on the temperaments, see Vism. III, 74-102.

§4 Development

Parikammabhāvanā, upacārabhāvanā, appanābhāvanā cā ti tisso bhāvanā.

The three stages of mental development are: preliminary development, access development, and absorption development.

Guide to §4

Preliminary development occurs from the time one begins the practice of meditation up to the time the five hindrances are suppressed and the counterpart sign emerges. *Access development* occurs when the five hindrances become suppressed and the counterpart sign emerges. It endures from the moment the counterpart sign arises up to the change-of-lineage citta (*gotrabhū*) in the cognitive process culminating in jhāna. The citta that immediately follows change-of-lineage is called absorption. This marks the beginning of *absorption development*, which occurs at the level of the fine-material-sphere jhānas or the immaterial-sphere jhānas.

§5 Signs

Parikammanimittaṁ, uggahanimittaṁ, paṭibhāganimittañ cā ti tīṇi nimittāni ca veditabbāni.

The three signs should be understood as: the preliminary sign, the learning sign, and the counterpart sign.

Guide to §5

The *preliminary sign* is the original object of concentration used during the preliminary stage of practice. The *learning sign* is a mental replica of the object perceived in the mind exactly as it appears to the physical eyes. The mentally visualized image freed of all defects is the *counterpart sign*. The counterpart sign, it is said, "appears as if breaking out from the learning sign, and a hundred times or a thousand times more purified, ... like the moon's disk coming out from behind a cloud" (Vism. IV, 31). See too §17 below.

The Forty Meditation Subjects (*kammaṭṭhānasamuddesa*)

§6 The Kasinas

Kathaṁ? Paṭhavīkasiṇaṁ, āpokasiṇaṁ, tejokasiṇaṁ, vāyokasiṇaṁ, nīlakasiṇaṁ, pītakasiṇaṁ, lohitakasiṇaṁ, odātakasiṇaṁ, ākāsakasiṇaṁ, ālokakasiṇañ cā ti imāni dasa kasiṇāni nāma.

How? The ten kasinas are: the earth kasina, the water kasina, the fire kasina, the air kasina, the blue kasina, the yellow kasina, the red kasina, the white kasina, the space kasina, and the light kasina.

Guide to §6

The ten kasinas: The word *kasiṇa* means "whole" or "totality." It is so called because the counterpart sign is to be expanded and extended everywhere without limitation.

The earth kasina, etc.: In the case of the *earth kasina* one prepares a disk of about thirty centimeters in diameter, covers it with clay the colour of the dawn, and smoothens it well. This is the kasina-disk, which serves as the preliminary sign for developing the earth kasina. One then places the disk about a meter away and concentrates on it with the eyes partly opened, contemplating it as "earth, earth."

To develop the *water kasina* one may use a vessel full of clear water and contemplate it as "water, water." To develop the *fire kasina* one may kindle a fire and view it through a hole in a piece of leather or a piece of cloth, thinking "fire, fire." One who develops the *air kasina* concentrates on the wind that enters through a window or an opening in the wall, thinking "air, air."

To develop the *colour kasinas* one may prepare a disk of the prescribed size and colour it blue, yellow, red or white. Then one should concentrate upon it by mentally repeating the name of the colour. One may even prepare an object from flowers of the required colour.

The *light kasina* may be developed by concentrating on the moon or on an unflickering lamplight, or on a circle of light cast on the ground, or on a beam of sunlight or moonlight entering through a wall-crevice or hole and cast on a wall.

The *space kasina* can be developed by concentrating on a hole about thirty centimeters in diameter, contemplating it as "space, space."

For a full treatment of the kasinas, see Vism. IV and V.

§7 Foulness

Uddhumātakaṁ, vinīlakaṁ, vipubbakaṁ, vicchiddakaṁ, vikkhāyitakaṁ, vikkhittakaṁ, hatavikkhittakaṁ, lohitakaṁ, puḷavakaṁ, aṭṭhikañ cā ti ime dasa asubhā nāma.

The ten kinds of foulness are: a bloated corpse, a livid corpse, a festering corpse, a dismembered corpse, an eaten corpse, a scattered-in-pieces corpse, a mutilated and scattered-in-pieces corpse, a bloody corpse, a worm-infested corpse, and a skeleton.

Guide to §7

The ten kinds of foulness are corpses in different stages of decay. This set of meditation subjects is especially recommended for removing sensual lust. See Vism. VI.

§8 The Recollections

Buddhānussati, dhammānussati, saṅghānussati, sīlānussati, cāgānussati, devatānussati, upasamānussati, maraṇānussati, kāyagatāsati, ānāpānasati cā ti imā dasa anussatiyo nāma.

The ten recollections are: the recollection of the Buddha, the recollection of the Dhamma, the recollection of the Sangha, the recollection of morality, the recollection of generosity, the recollection of the devas, the recollection of peace, the recollection of death, mindfulness occupied with the body, and mindfulness of breathing.

Guide to §8

The recollection of the Buddha, etc.: The first three recollections are practised by calling to mind the virtues of the Buddha, the Dhamma, or the Sangha, as enumerated in the traditional formulas.[2]

The recollection of morality is the practice of mindfully recollecting the special qualities of virtuous conduct, considered as untorn and free from breach and blemish.

TABLE 9.1:
THE FORTY MEDITATION SUBJECTS AT A GLANCE

Subject	Temperament	Development			Sign			Jhāna		
		Pr	Ac	Ab	Pr	Ln	Cp	1st	to	5th
Kasina (10)										
Earth kasina	All	Pr	Ac	Ab	Pr	Ln	Cp	1st	to	5th
Water "	"	"	"	"	"	"	"	"		"
Fire "	"	"	"	"	"	"	"	"		"
Air "	"	"	"	"	"	"	"	"		"
Blue "	Hateful	"	"	"	"	"	"	"		"
Yellow "	"	"	"	"	"	"	"	"		"
Red "	"	"	"	"	"	"	"	"		"
White "	"	"	"	"	"	"	"	"		"
Space "	All	"	"	"	"	"	"	"		"
Light "	"	"	"	"	"	"	"	"		"
Foulness (10)										
Bloated corpse	Lustful	"	"	"	"	"	"		1st only	
Discoloured "	"	"	"	"	"	"	"		"	
Festering "	"	"	"	"	"	"	"		"	
Dismembered "	"	"	"	"	"	"	"		"	
Eaten "	"	"	"	"	"	"	"		"	
Scattered "	"	"	"	"	"	"	"		"	
Mutilated "	"	"	"	"	"	"	"		"	
Bloody "	"	"	"	"	"	"	"		"	
Worm-infested "	"	"	"	"	"	"	"		"	
Skeleton "	"	"	"	"	"	"	"		"	
Recollections (10)										
Buddha	Faithful	"	"	...	"	"	...		None	
Dhamma	"	"	"	...	"	"	...		"	
Sangha	"	"	"	...	"	"	...		"	

TABLE 9.1 – Continued

SUBJECT	TEMPERAMENT	DEVELOPMENT			SIGN			JHĀNA
Generosity	Faithful	Pr	Ac	...	Pr	Ln	...	None
Devas	"	"	"	...	"	"	...	"
Peace	Intellectual	"	"	...	"	"	...	"
Death	"	"	"	...	"	"	...	"
Body	Lustful	"	"	Ab	"	"	Cp	1st
Breathing	Deluded, discursive	"	"	"	"	"	"	1st to 5th
Illimitables (4)								
Lovingkindness	Hateful	"	"	"	"	"	...	1st to 4th
Compassion	"	"	"	"	"	"	...	" "
Appreciative joy	"	"	"	"	"	"	...	" "
Equanimity	"	"	"	"	"	"	...	5th only
Perception (1)								
Food as loathsome	Intellectual	"	"	...	"	"	...	None
Analysis (1)								
Four elements	Intellectual	"	"	...	"	"	...	None
Immaterial States								
Infinite space	All	"	"	"	"	"	...	1st IS jhāna
Infinite consness.	"	"	"	"	"	"	...	2nd IS jhāna
Nothingness	"	"	"	"	"	"	...	3rd IS jhāna
Neither-perc.-nor-non-perc.	"	"	"	"	"	"	...	4th IS jhāna

KEY: Pr = preliminary; Ac = access; Ab = absorption; Ln = learning; Cp = counterpart.

The recollection of generosity involves mindful reflection on the special qualities of generosity.

The recollection of the devas is practised by mindfully considering: "The deities are born in such exalted states on account of their faith, morality, learning, generosity, and wisdom. I too possess these same qualities." This meditation subject is a term for mindfulness with the special qualities of one's own faith, etc., as its object and with the devas standing as witnesses.

The recollection of peace is contemplation on the peaceful attributes of Nibbāna.

The recollection of death is contemplation of the fact that one's own death is absolutely certain, that the arrival of death is utterly uncertain, and that when death comes one must relinquish everything.

Mindfulness occupied with the body is contemplation of the thirty-two repulsive parts of the body—hairs of the head, hairs of the body, nails, teeth, skin, flesh, sinews, bones, marrow, etc.

Mindfulness of breathing is attentiveness to the touch sensation of the in-breath and out-breath in the vicinity of the nostrils or upper lip, wherever the air is felt striking as one breathes in and out.

On the ten recollections, see Vism. VII and VIII.

§9 The Illimitables

Mettā, karuṇā, muditā, upekkhā cā ti imā catasso appamaññāyo nāma, brahmavihārā ti pi pavuccanti.

The four illimitables, also called divine abodes, are: loving-kindness, compassion, appreciative joy, and equanimity.

Guide to §9

The four illimitables: These states are called illimitables (*appamaññā*) because they are to be radiated towards all living beings without limit or obstruction. They are also called *brahmavihāras*, "divine abodes" or sublime states, because they are the mental dwellings of the Brahmā divinities in the Brahma-world.

Loving-kindness (*mettā*) is the wish for the welfare and happiness of all living beings. It helps to eliminate ill will.

Compassion (*karuṇā*) is that which makes the heart quiver when others are subject to suffering. It is the wish to remove the suffering of others, and it is opposed to cruelty.

Appreciative joy (*muditā*) is the quality of rejoicing at the success and prosperity of others. It is the congratulatory attitude, and helps to eliminate envy and discontent over the success of others.

Equanimity (***upekkhā***), as a divine abode, is the state of mind that regards others with impartiality, free from attachment and aversion. An impartial attitude is its chief characteristic, and it is opposed to favouritism and resentment.

For a full explanation of the divine abidings, see Vism. IX.

§10 One Perception

Āhāre paṭikkūlasaññā ekā saññā nāma.

The one perception is the perception of loathsomeness in food.

Guide to §10

The perception of the loathsomeness of food is the perception which arises through reflection upon the repulsive aspects of nutriment, such as the difficulty of searching for food, the repulsiveness of using it, the digestive process, excretion, etc. See Vism. XI, 1-26.

§11 One Analysis

Catudhātuvavatthānaṁ ekaṁ vavatthānaṁ nāma.

The one analysis is the analysis of the four elements.

Guide to §11

The analysis into the four elements involves contemplation of the body as compounded out of the four great essentials—the earth element as manifested in the solid parts of the body, the water element in the bodily fluids, the fire element in the body's heat, and the air element in the breath and vital currents. See Vism. XI, 27-117.

§12 The Immaterial States

Ākāsānañcāyatanādayo cattāro āruppā nāmā ti sabbathā pi samathaniddese cattāḷīsa kammaṭṭhānāni bhavanti.

The four immaterial states are the base of infinite space, and so forth. Thus in the exposition of calm there are altogether forty subjects of meditation.

Guide to §12

These are the objects of the four immaterial jhānas: (1) the base of infinite space; (2) the base of infinite consciousness; (3) the base of nothingness; and (4) the base of neither-perception-nor-non-perception. See Vism. X.

§13 Analysis of Suitability (*sappāyabheda*)

Caritāsu pana dasa asubhā kāyagatāsatisankhātā koṭṭhāsabhāvanā ca rāgacaritassa sappāyā.

Catasso appamaññāyo nīlādīni ca cattāri kasiṇāni dosacaritassa.

Ānāpānaṁ mohacaritassa vitakkacaritassa ca.

Buddhānussati ādayo cha saddhācaritassa.

Maraṇa-upasama-saññā-vavatthānāni buddhicaritassa.

Sesāni pana sabbāni pi kammaṭṭhānāni sabbesam pi sappāyāni.

Tatthā pi kasiṇesu puthulaṁ mohacaritassa, khuddakaṁ vitakkacaritass' evā ti.

Ayam ettha sappāyabhedo.

With respect to temperaments, the ten kinds of foulness and mindfulness occupied with the body, i.e. meditation on the thirty-two parts, are suitable for those of a lustful temperament.

The four illimitables and the four coloured kasinas are suitable for those of a hateful temperament.

Mindfulness of breathing is suitable for those of a deluded and discursive temperament.

The six recollections of the Buddha, and so forth, are suitable for those of a faithful temperament; recollection of death, of peace, the perception of loathsomeness in food, and the analysis of the four elements, are suitable for those of an intellectual temperament.

All of the remaining subjects of meditation are suitable for all temperaments.

Of the kasinas, a wide one is suitable for one of deluded temperament, and a small one for one of discursive temperament.

Herein, this is the analysis by way of suitability.

Analysis of Development (*bhāvanābheda*)

§14 By way of the Three Stages

Bhāvanāsu pana sabbatthā pi parikammabhāvanā labbhat' eva.

Buddhānussati ādisu aṭṭhasu saññā-vavatthānesu cā ti dasasu kammaṭṭhānesu upacārabhāvanā va sampajjati, natthi appanā.

Sesesu pana samatiṁsa kammaṭṭhānesu appanābhāvanā pi sampajjati.

The preliminary stage of development is attainable in all these forty subjects of meditation. In ten subjects of meditation—the eight recollections of the Buddha and so forth, the one perception, and the one analysis—only access development is attained but not absorption. In the thirty remaining subjects of meditation, the absorption stage of development is also attained.

Guide to §14

In the ten subjects beginning with the recollection of the Buddha, the mind is engaged in reflecting upon many different qualities and themes, and this involves an intense application of thought (*vitakka*) which prevents one-pointedness from gaining the fixity needed to attain absorption.

§15 By way of Jhāna

Tatthā pi dasa kasiṇāni ānāpānañ ca pañcakajjhānikāni. Dasa asubhā kāyagatāsati ca paṭhamajjhānikā. Mettādayo tayo catukkajjhānikā. Upekkhā pañcamajjhānikā. Iti chabbīsati rūpāvacarajjhānikāni kammaṭṭhānāni. Cattāro pana āruppā arūpajjhānikā.

Ayam ettha bhāvanābhedo.

Therein, the ten kasinas and mindfulness of breathing produce five jhānas; the ten foulnesses and mindfulness occupied with the body (only) the first jhāna; the first three illimitables, such as loving-kindness, four jhānas; equanimity, the fifth jhāna (only).

Thus these twenty-six subjects of meditation produce fine-material-sphere jhānas.

The four immaterial states produce immaterial jhānas.

Herein, this is the analysis by way of development.

Guide to §15

The ten kinds of foulness and mindfulness occupied with the body both require the exercise of *vitakka*, and thus they are incapable of inducing the jhānas higher than the first, which are free from *vitakka*. The first three illimitables necessarily arise in association with joyful feeling (*somanassa*) and thus can lead only to the four lower jhānas, which are accompanied by joyful feeling. The illimitable of equanimity arises in association with neutral feeling, and thus can occur only at the level of the fifth jhāna, which is accompanied by equanimous feeling.

Analysis of the Terrain (*gocarabheda*)

§16 The Signs

Nimittesu pana parikammanimittaṁ uggahanimittañ ca sabbatthā pi yathārahaṁ pariyāyena labbhant' eva. Paṭibhāganimittaṁ pana kasiṇ'-āsubha-koṭṭhāsa-ānāpānesv' eva labbhati. Tattha hi paṭibhāganimittam ārabbha upacārasamādhi appanāsamādhi ca pavattanti.

Of the three signs, the preliminary sign and the learning sign are generally found in relation to every object, in the appropriate way. But the counterpart sign is found only in the kasinas, foulness, the parts of the body, and mindfulness of breathing. It is by means of the counterpart sign that access concentration and absorption concentration occur.

§17 Appearance of the Signs in Meditation

Kathaṁ? Ādikammikassa hi paṭhavīmaṇḍalādisu nimittaṁ uggaṇhantassa tam ālambanaṁ parikammanimittan ti pavuccati. Sā ca bhāvanā parikammabhāvanā nāma.

How? When a beginner apprehends a particular sign from the earth disk, etc., that object is called the preliminary sign, and that meditation is called preliminary development.

Yadā pana taṁ nimittaṁ cittena samuggahitaṁ hoti, cakkhunā passantass' eva manodvārassa āpātham āgataṁ tadā tam ev' ālambanaṁ uggahanimittaṁ nāma. Sā ca bhāvanā samādhiyati.

When that sign has been thoroughly apprehended and enters into range of the mind door just as if it were seen by the eye, then it is called the learning sign, and that meditation becomes concentrated.

Tathāsamāhitassa pan' etassa tato paraṁ tasmiṁ uggahanimitte parikammasamādhinā bhāvanam anuyuñjantassa yadā tappaṭibhāgaṁ vatthudhammavimuccitaṁ paññattisankhātaṁ bhāvanāmayam ālambanaṁ citte sannisinnaṁ samappitaṁ hoti, tadā taṁ paṭibhāganimittaṁ samuppannan ti pavuccati.

When one is thus concentrated, one then applies oneself to meditation by means of that preliminary concentration based on that learning sign. As one does so, an object which is the counterpart of that (learning sign) becomes well established and fixed in the mind—(an object) which is freed of the flaws of the original object, reckoned as a concept, born of meditation. Then it is said that the counterpart sign has arisen.

§18 Attainment of Jhāna

Tato paṭṭhāya paripanthavippahīnā kāmāvacarasamādhisankhātā upacārabhāvanā nipphannā nāma hoti. Tato paraṁ tam eva paṭibhāganimittaṁ upacārasamādhinā samāsevantassa rūpāvacarapaṭhamajjhānam appeti.

Thereafter, access development is accomplished, consisting in concentration of the sense sphere in which the obstacles have been abandoned. Following this, as one cultivates the counterpart sign by means of access concentration, one enters the first jhāna of the fine-material sphere.

Tato paraṁ tam eva paṭhamajjhānaṁ āvajjanaṁ, samāpajjanaṁ, adhiṭṭhānaṁ, vuṭṭhānaṁ, paccavekkhaṇā cā ti imāhi pañcahi vasitāhi vasībhūtaṁ katvā vitakkādikam oḷārikangaṁ pahānāya vicārādisukhumang'uppattiyā padahato yathākkamaṁ dutiyajjhānādayo yathāraham appenti.

Following this, one masters the first jhāna by means of the five kinds of mastery—in adverting, attainment, resolution, emergence, and reviewing. Then, by striving to abandon the successive gross factors such as initial application, etc., and to arouse the successive subtle factors, such as sustained application, etc., one enters the second jhāna, etc., in due sequence according to one's ability.

Icc' evaṁ paṭhavīkasiṇādīsu dvāvīsatikammaṭṭhānesu paṭibhāganimittam upalabbhati. Avasesesu pana appamaññā sattapaññattiyaṁ pavattanti.

Thus the counterpart sign is found in twenty-two meditation subjects—the earth kasina, etc.—but of the remaining (eighteen) subjects, the illimitables occur with the concept of beings (as their object).

Guide to §18

The five kinds of mastery: Of these, mastery in adverting (*āvajjanavasitā*) is the ability to advert to the different jhāna factors such as *vitakka, vicāra*, etc., quickly and easily in accordance with one's wish. Mastery in attainment (*samāpajjanavasitā*) is the ability to attain the different jhānas quickly and easily, without many bhavangas arising in the process of their attainment. Mastery in resolution (*adhiṭṭhānavasitā*) is the ability to remain in the jhāna for a length of time determined by one's prior resolution. Mastery in emergence (*vuṭṭhānavasitā*) is the ability to emerge from the jhānas quickly and easily. And mastery in reviewing (*paccavekkhaṇāvasitā*) is the ability to review the jhāna from which one has just emerged. Besides these five masteries, the meditator is also encouraged to develop skill in extending the visualized counterpart sign by gradually increasing its size until it appears as if encompassing the entire world.

§19 The Immaterial Attainments

Ākāsavajjitakasiṇesu pana yaṁ kiñci kasiṇaṁ ugghāṭetvā laddham ākāsaṁ anantavasena parikammaṁ karontassa paṭhamāruppam appeti. Tam eva paṭhamāruppaviññāṇaṁ anantavasena parikammaṁ karontassa dutiyāruppam appeti. Tam eva paṭhamāruppaviññāṇābhāvaṁ pana natthi kiñcī ti parikammaṁ karontassa tatiyāruppam appeti. Tatiyāruppaṁ santam etaṁ paṇītam etan ti parikammaṁ karontassa catutthāruppam appeti.

Next one withdraws any kasina except the space kasina, and does the preliminary work by contemplating the space that remains as infinite. By doing so, one enters the first immaterial attainment. When one does the preliminary work by contemplating the first immaterial-sphere consciousness as infinite, one enters the second immaterial attainment. When one does the preliminary work by contemplating the absence of the first immaterial-sphere consciousness thus, "There is nothing," one enters the third immaterial attainment. When one does the preliminary work by contemplating the third immaterial attainment thus, "This is peaceful, this is sublime," one enters the fourth immaterial attainment.

§20 Other Meditation Subjects

Avasesesu ca dasasu kammaṭṭhānesu buddhaguṇādikam ālambanam ārabbha parikammaṁ katvā tasmiṁ nimitte sādhukam uggahite tatth' eva parikammañ ca samādhiyati, upacāro ca sampajjati.

With the other ten meditation subjects, when one does the preliminary work by taking the virtues of the Buddha, etc., as one's object, when that sign has been thoroughly acquired, one becomes concentrated upon it by means of preliminary development and access concentration is also accomplished.

§21 Direct Knowledge

Abhiññāvasena pavattamānaṁ pana rūpāvacarapañcamajjhānaṁ abhiññāpādakā pañcamajjhānā vuṭṭhahitvā adhiṭṭheyyādikam āvajjetvā parikammaṁ karontassa rūpādisu ālambanesu yathāraham appeti.

Abhiññā ca nāma:

Iddhividhaṁ dibbasotaṁ paracittavijānanā
Pubbenivāsānussati dibbacakkhū ti pañcadhā.

Ayam ettha gocarabhedo.

Niṭṭhito ca samathakammaṭṭhānanayo.

Having emerged from the fifth jhāna taken as a basis for direct knowledge, having adverted to the resolution, etc., when one does the preliminary work, one enters into the fifth fine-material-sphere jhāna occurring by way of direct knowledge with respect to such objects as visible forms, etc.

The direct knowledges are fivefold: the supernormal powers, the divine ear, knowledge of others' minds, recollection of past lives, and the divine eye.

Herein, this is the analysis of the terrain.

The method of meditation
for developing calm is finished.

Guide to §21

Having emerged from the fifth jhāna, etc.: *The Visuddhimagga* explains the procedure for exercising the direct knowledges thus: "(After accomplishing the preliminaries) he attains jhāna as the basis for direct knowledge and emerges from it. Then if he wants to become a hundred,[3] he does the preliminary work thus, 'Let me become a hundred,' after which he again attains jhāna as the basis for direct knowledge, emerges, and resolves. He becomes a hundred simultaneously with the resolving consciousness" (XII,57).

The direct knowledges are fivefold:

(1) *Supernormal powers* include the ability to display multiple forms of one's body, to appear and vanish at will, to pass through walls unhindered, to dive in and out of the earth, to walk on water, to travel through the air, to touch and stroke the sun and moon, and to exercise mastery over the body as far as the Brahma-world.

(2) *The divine ear* enables one to hear subtle and coarse sounds, both far and near.

(3) *The knowledge of others' minds* is the ability to read the thoughts of others and to know directly their states of mind.

(4) *The recollection of past lives* is the ability to know one's past births and to discover various details about those births.

(5) *The divine eye* is the capacity for clairvoyance, which enables one to see heavenly or earthly events, both far or near. Included in the divine eye is the knowledge of the passing away and rebirth of beings (*cutūpapātañāṇa*), that is, direct perception of how beings pass away and re-arise in accordance with their kamma.

These kinds of direct knowledge are all mundane and are dependent on mastery over the fifth jhāna. The texts also mention a sixth direct knowledge. This is the knowledge of the destruction of the taints (*āsavakkhayañāṇa*), which is supramundane and arises through insight.

Compendium of Insight
(*vipassanāsangaha*)

Basic Categories

§22 Stages of Purification

Vipassanākammaṭṭhāne pana sīlavisuddhi, cittavisuddhi, diṭṭhivisuddhi, kankhāvitaraṇavisuddhi, maggāmaggañāṇadassanavisuddhi, paṭipadāñāṇadassanavisuddhi, ñāṇadassanavisuddhi cā ti sattavidhena visuddhisangaho.

TABLE 9.2: THE SEVEN STAGES OF PURIFICATION

PURIFICATION	PRACTICE
I. Of virtue	Four kinds of purified virtue
II. Of mind	Access and absorption concentration
III. Of view	Understanding characteristics, etc., of mental and material phenomena
IV. By overcoming doubt	Discernment of conditions for mental and material phenomena
V. By knowledge and vision of path and not path	1. Knowledge of comprehension 2. Knowledge of rise and fall (tender phase) Distinguishing wrong path from right path of contemplation
VI. By knowledge and vision of the way	2. Knowledge of rise and fall (mature phase) 3. Knowledge of dissolution 4. Knowledge of fearfulness 5. Knowledge of danger 6. Knowledge of disenchantment 7. Knowledge of desire for deliverance 8. Knowledge of reflection 9. Knowledge of equanimity towards formations 10. Knowledge of conformity
Between VI and VII	11. Change-of-lineage
VII. By knowledge and vision	Knowledge of four supramundane paths

NOTE: The insight knowledges are enumerated in the right-hand column using arabic numbers.

In insight meditation, the compendium of purifications is sevenfold: (1) purification of virtue, (2) purification of mind, (3) purification of view, (4) purification by overcoming doubt, (5) purification by knowledge and vision as to what is the path and what is not the path, (6) purification by knowledge and vision of the way, and (7) purification by knowledge and vision.

Guide to §22

These seven stages of purification are to be attained in sequence, each being the support for the one that follows. The first purification corresponds to the morality aspect of the path, the second to the concentration aspect, the last five to the wisdom aspect. The first six stages are mundane, the last is the supramundane paths. See Table 9.2.

§23 The Three Characteristics

Aniccalakkhaṇaṁ, dukkhalakkhaṇaṁ, anattalakkhaṇañ cā ti tīṇi lakkhaṇāni.

There are three characteristics: the characteristic of impermanence, the characteristic of suffering, and the characteristic of non-self.

Guide to §23

The characteristic of impermanence is the mode of rise and fall and change, that is, reaching non-existence after having come to be.

The characteristic of suffering is the mode of being continuously oppressed by rise and fall.

The characteristic of non-self is the mode of being insusceptible to the exercise of mastery, that is, the fact that one cannot exercise complete control over the phenomena of mind and matter.

§24 The Three Contemplations

Aniccānupassanā, dukkhānupassanā, anattānupassanā cā ti tisso anupassanā.

There are three contemplations: the contemplation of impermanence, the contemplation of suffering, and the contemplation of non-self.

§25 The Ten Insight Knowledges

(1) Sammasanañāṇaṁ, (2) udayabbayañāṇaṁ, (3) bhangañāṇaṁ, (4) bhayañāṇaṁ, (5) ādīnavañāṇaṁ, (6) nibbidāñāṇaṁ, (7) muñcitukamyatāñāṇaṁ, (8) paṭisankhāñāṇaṁ, (9) sankhār'upekkhāñāṇaṁ, (10) anulomañāṇañ cā ti dasa vipassanāñāṇāni.

There are ten kinds of insight knowledge: (1) knowledge of comprehension, (2) knowledge of rise and fall (of formations), (3) knowledge of the dissolution (of formations), (4) knowledge (of dissolving things) as fearful, (5) knowledge of (fearful) things as dangerous, (6) knowledge of disenchantment (with all formations), (7) knowledge of desire for deliverance (8) knowledge of reflecting contemplation, (9) knowledge of equanimity towards formations, and (10) knowledge of conformity.

§26 The Three Emancipations

Suññato vimokkho, animitto vimokkho, appaṇihito vimokkho cā ti tayo vimokkhā.

There are three emancipations: the void emancipation, the signless emancipation, and the desireless emancipation.

§27 The Three Doors to Emancipation

Suññatānupassanā, animittānupassanā, appaṇihitānupassanā cā ti tīṇi vimokkhamukhāni ca veditabbāni.

There are three doors to emancipation: contemplation of the void, contemplation of the signless, and contemplation of the desireless.

Guide to §§26-27

These categories will be explained in the course of the following exposition.

Analysis of Purification
(*visuddhibheda*)

§28 Purification of Virtue

Kathaṁ? Pātimokkhasaṁvarasīlaṁ, indriyasaṁvarasīlaṁ, ājīvapārisuddhisīlaṁ, paccayasannissitasīlañ cā ti catupārisuddhisīlaṁ sīlavisuddhi nāma.

Purification of virtue consists of the four kinds of purified virtue, namely:

(1) virtue regarding restraint according to the Pātimokkha;
(2) virtue regarding restraint of the sense faculties;
(3) virtue consisting in purity of livelihood; and
(4) virtue connected with the use of the requisites.

Guide to §28

These four kinds of purified virtue are explained with reference to the life of a bhikkhu, a Buddhist monk.

Virtue regarding restraint according to the Pātimokkha: The Pātimokkha is the code of fundamental disciplinary rules binding upon a Buddhist monk. This code consists of 227 rules of varying degrees of gravity. Perfect adherence to the rules laid down in the Pātimokkha is called "virtue regarding restraint according to the Pātimokkha."

Virtue regarding restraint of the sense faculties means the exercise of mindfulness in one's encounter with sense objects, not allowing the mind to come under the sway of attraction towards pleasant objects and repulsion towards unpleasant objects.

Virtue consisting in purity of livelihood deals with the manner in which a bhikkhu acquires the necessities of life. He should not acquire his requisites in a manner unbecoming for a monk, who is dedicated to purity and honesty.

Virtue connected with the use of the requisites means that the bhikkhu should use the four requisites—robes, almsfood, lodging, and medicines—after reflecting upon their proper purpose.

§29 Purification of Mind

Upacārasamādhi, appanāsamādhi cā ti duvidho pi samādhi cittavisuddhi nāma.

Purification of mind consists of two kinds of concentration, namely: access concentration and absorption concentration.

Guide to §29

The Pali Buddhist tradition recognizes two different approaches to the development of insight. One approach, called the vehicle of calm (*samathayāna*), involves the prior development of calm meditation to the level of access concentration or absorption concentration as a basis for developing insight. One who adopts this approach, the *samathayānika* meditator, first attains access concentration or one of the fine-material or immaterial-sphere jhānas. Then he turns to the development of insight by defining the mental and physical phenomena occurring in the jhāna as mentality-materiality and seeking their conditions (see §§30-31), after which he contemplates these factors in terms of the three characteristics (see §32). For this meditator, his prior attainment of access or absorption concentration is reckoned as his purification of mind.

The other approach, called the vehicle of pure insight (*suddhavipassanāyāna*), does not employ the development of calm as a foundation for developing insight. Instead the meditator, after purifying his morality, enters directly into the mindful contemplation of the changing mental and material processes in his own experience. As this contemplation gains in strength and precision, the mind becomes naturally concentrated upon the ever-changing stream of experience with a degree of concentration equal to that of access concentration. This moment-by-moment fixing of the mind on the material and mental processes in their present immediacy is known as momentary concentration (*khaṇika-samādhi*). Because it involves a degree of mental stabilization equal to that of access concentration, this momentary concentration is reckoned as purification of mind for the *vipassanāyānika* meditator, the meditator who adopts the vehicle of pure insight. Such a meditator is also called a "dry insight worker" (*sukkhavipassaka*) because he develops insight without the "moisture" of the jhānas.[4]

§30 Purification of View

Lakkhaṇa-rasa-paccupaṭṭhāna-padaṭṭhāna-vasena nāma-rūpapariggaho diṭṭhivisuddhi nāma.

Purification of view is the discernment of mind and matter with respect to their characteristics, functions, manifestations, and proximate causes.

Guide to §30

Purification of view is so called because it helps to purify one of the wrong view of a permanent self. This purification is arrived at in the course of meditation by discerning the personality as a compound of mental and material factors which occur interdependently, without any controlling self within or behind them. This stage is also called the analytical knowledge of mind-and-matter (*nāmarūpavavatthānañāṇa*) because the mental and material phenomena are distinguished by way of their characteristics, etc.

§31 Purification by Overcoming Doubt

Tesam eva ca nāmarūpānaṁ paccayapariggaho kankhāvitaraṇavisuddhi nāma.

Purification by overcoming doubt is the discernment of the conditions of that same mind and matter.

Guide to §31

Purification by overcoming doubt is so called because it develops the knowledge which removes doubts about the conditions for mind-and-matter during the three periods of time—past, present, and future. It is achieved by applying, during the contemplative process, one's knowledge of dependent arising in order to understand that the present compound of mind-and-matter has not arisen by chance or through a hypothetical cause such as a creator god or primordial soul, but has come into being from previous ignorance, craving, clinging and kamma. One then applies this same principle to the past and future as well. This stage is also called the knowledge of discerning conditions (*paccaya-pariggahañāṇa*).

§32 Purification of Path and Not-Path

Tato paraṁ pana tathāpariggahitesu sappaccayesu tebhūmaka-saṅkhāresu atītādibhedabhinnesu khandhādinayam ārabbha kalāpavasena saṅkhipitvā aniccaṁ khayaṭṭhena, dukkhaṁ bhayaṭṭhena, anattā asārakaṭṭhenā ti addhānavasena santativasena khaṇavasena vā sammasanañāṇena lakkhaṇattayaṁ sammasantassa tesv' eva paccayavasena khaṇavasena ca udayabbayañāṇena udayabbayaṁ samanupassantassa ca.

When he has thus discerned the formations of the three planes together with their conditions, the meditator collects them into groups by way of such categories as the aggregates, etc., divided into the past (present, and future).

He next comprehends, with the knowledge of comprehension, those formations in terms of the three characteristics—impermanence in the sense of destruction, suffering in the sense of fearfulness, and non-self in the sense of corelessness—by way of duration, continuity, and moment. Then he contemplates with the knowledge of rise and fall the rising and falling (of those formations) by way of condition and by way of moment.

Obhāso pīti passaddhi adhimokkho ca paggaho
Sukhaṁ ñāṇam upaṭṭhānam upekkhā ca nikanti cā ti.

Obhāsādi-vipassan' upakkilese paripanthapariggahavasena maggāmaggalakkhaṇavavatthānaṁ maggāmaggañāṇadassana-visuddhi nāma.

As he does so, there arise: an aura, zest, tranquillity, resolution, exertion, happiness, knowledge, mindfulness, equanimity, and attachment.

Purification by knowledge and vision of what is the path and what is not the path is the discrimination of the characteristics of what is the path and what is not the path by discerning that those imperfections of insight—the aura, etc.—are obstacles to progress.

Guide to §32

Collects them into groups: This shows the preparation for knowledge of comprehension (*sammasanañāṇa*), the phase in the development of insight wherein the mental and material phenomena are explored in terms of the three characteristics. The meditator first considers all materiality—whether past, future, or present, internal or external, gross or subtle, inferior or superior, far or near—as comprised by the materiality aggregate. Similarly, he considers all feelings, perceptions, mental formations, and acts of consciousness to be comprised by their respective aggregates—the feeling aggregate, the perception aggregate, the formations aggregate, and the consciousness aggregate.

He next comprehends, with the knowledge of comprehension: This shows the actual ascription of the three characteristics to the formations collected into the five aggregates. All those formations are characterized by "impermanence in the sense of destruction" (*khayaṭṭhena*) because they undergo destruction exactly where they arise, and do not pass on to some other state retaining their identity; they are "suffering in the sense of fearfulness" (*bhayaṭṭhena*) because whatever is impermanent provides no stable security and thus is to be feared; and they are "non-self in the sense of corelessness" (*asārakaṭṭhena*) because they lack any core of self or substance or any inner controller.

By way of duration, continuity, and moment: "By way of duration" (*addhāna*) means in terms of an extended period of time. One begins by considering that the formations in each single lifetime are all impermanent, suffering, and non-self, then one progressively reduces the periods: to the three stages of a single life, to the ten decades, to each year, month, fortnight, day, hour, etc., until one recognizes that even in a single step formations are impermanent, painful, and non-self. (See Vism. XX, 46-65.) "By way of continuity" (*santati*) means by way of a continuous series of similar mental or material phenomena. "By way of moment" (*khaṇa*) means by way of momentary mental and material phenomena.

The knowledge of rise and fall (*udayabbayañāṇa*) is the knowledge in contemplating the arising and cessation of formations. By "rise" is meant the generation, production, or arising of states; by "fall" is meant their change, destruction, dissolution. The knowledge of rise and fall is exercised "by way of condition" (*paccayavasena*) when one sees how formations arise through the arising of their conditions and cease through the cessation of their conditions. It is exercised "by way of moment" (*khaṇavasena*) when one contemplates the actual generation and dissolution of the momentary phenomena in the present moment as they arise and pass away. (See Vism. XX, 93-99.)

As he does so: The knowledge of rise and fall occurs in two phases. During the first phase, "tender" knowledge of rise and fall, as the process of contemplation gains momentum, ten "imperfections of insight" (*vipassan'upakkilesā*) arise in the meditator. He may witness an aura of light (*obhāsa*) emanating from his body. He experiences unprecedented zest (*pīti*), tranquillity (*passaddhi*), and happiness (*sukha*). His resolution (*adhimokkha*) increases, he makes a great exertion (*paggaha*), his knowledge (*ñāṇa*) ripens, his mindful awareness (*upaṭṭhāna*) becomes steady, and he develops unshaken equanimity (*upekkhā*). And underlying these experiences there is a subtle attachment (*nikanti*)—an enjoyment of these experiences and a clinging to them.

The discrimination of the characteristics of what is the path, etc.: When such elevated experiences occur to a meditator, if he lacks discrimination he will give rise to the misconception that he has reached the supramundane path and fruit. He will then drop his insight meditation and sit enjoying these experiences, unaware that he is clinging to them. But if he possesses discrimination, he will recognize these states as mere natural by-products of maturing insight. He will contemplate them as impermanent, suffering, and non-self and proceed with his insight contemplation, without becoming attached to them. This discrimination between the ten imperfections as not being the path, and the practice of insight contemplation as being the correct path, is called purification by knowledge and vision of what is the path and what is not the path.

§33 Purification of the Way

Tathā paripanthavimuttassa pana tassa udayabbayañāṇato paṭṭhāya yāvānulomā tilakkhaṇaṁ vipassanāparamparāya paṭipajjantassa nava vipassanāñāṇāni paṭipadāñāṇadassanavisuddhi nāma.

When he is thus free from those obstacles to progress, as he practises he passes through a succession of insights in regard to the three characteristics, beginning with knowledge of rise and fall and culminating in conformity. These nine insight knowledges are called purification by knowledge and vision of the way.

Guide to §33

These nine insight knowledges: The nine insight knowledges that constitute purification by knowledge and vision of the way are as follows (see §25):

(1) *Knowledge of rise and fall*: This is the same knowledge as that which preceded the imperfections of insight, but when the imperfections have been overcome, it now matures and develops with increased strength and clarity.

(2) *Knowledge of dissolution (bhangañāṇa)*: When the meditator's knowledge becomes keen, he no longer extends his mindfulness to the arising or presence of formations, but brings it to bear only on their cessation, destruction, fall, and breakup. This is knowledge of dissolution.

(3) *Knowledge of the fearful (bhayañāṇa)*: As the meditator contemplates the dissolution of formations in all three periods of time, he recognizes that all such dissolving things in all realms of existence are necessarily fearful.

(4) *Knowledge of danger (ādīnavañāṇa)*: By recognizing that all formations are fearful, the meditator sees them as utterly destitute of any core or any satisfaction and as nothing but danger. He also understands that only in the unconditioned, free from arising and destruction, is there any security.

(5) *Knowledge of disenchantment (nibbidāñāṇa)*: When he sees all formations as danger, he becomes disenchanted with them, and takes no delight in the field of formations belonging to any realm of existence.

(6) *Knowledge of desire for deliverance (muñcitukamyatāñāṇa)* is the desire, arisen in the course of contemplation, of being delivered from the whole field of formations and escaping from it.

(7) *Knowledge of reflective contemplation (paṭisankhāñāṇa)*: In order to be delivered from the whole field of formations, the meditator again re-examines those same formations, attributing the three characteristics to them in various ways. When he clearly reviews those formations as marked by the three characteristics, this is knowledge of reflective contemplation.

(8) *Knowledge of equanimity towards formations (sankhār'upekkhāñāṇa)*: After he has passed through the reflective contemplation, the meditator sees nothing in formations to be taken as "I" and "mine," so he abandons both terror and delight and becomes indifferent and neutral towards all formations. Thus there arises in him knowledge of equanimity towards formations.

(9) *Knowledge of conformity (anulomañāṇa)*: This knowledge (also rendered "adaptation") is the knowledge in the sense-sphere cittas that

arise preceding the change-of-lineage citta in the cognitive process of the supramundane path (dealt with in the following section). This phase of insight is called conformity because it conforms to the functions of truth both in the preceding eight kinds of insight knowledge and in the path attainment to follow.

§34 Purification by Knowledge and Vision

Tass' evaṁ paṭipajjantassa pana vipassanāparipākam āgamma idāni appanā uppajjissatī ti bhavangaṁ vocchinditvā uppanna-manodvārāvajjanānantaraṁ dve tīṇī vipassanācittāni yaṁ kiñci aniccādilakkhaṇam ārabbha parikamm'-opacār'-ānulomanāmena pavattanti. Yā sikhāppattā sā sānulomasankhārupekkhā vuṭṭhāna-gāminīvipassanā ti ca pavuccati.

When he thus practises contemplation, owing to the ripening of insight (he feels), "Now the absorption (of the path) will arise." Thereupon, arresting the life-continuum, there arises mind-door adverting, followed by two or three (moments of) insight consciousness having for their object any of the characteristics such as impermanence, etc. They are termed preparation, access, and conformity (moments). That knowledge of equanimity towards formations together with knowledge that conforms (to the truths), when perfected, is also termed "insight leading to emergence."

Tato paraṁ gotrabhūcittaṁ nibbānam ālambitvā puthujjanagottam abhibhavantaṁ ariyagottam abhisambhontañ ca pavattati. Tass' ānantaram eva maggo dukkhasaccaṁ parijānanto samudayasaccaṁ pajahanto nirodhasaccaṁ sacchikaronto maggasaccaṁ bhāv-anāvasena appanāvīthim otarati. Tato paraṁ dve tīṇi phalacittāni pavattitvā nirujjhanti. Tato paraṁ bhavangapāto va hoti.

Thereafter, the change-of-lineage consciousness, having Nibbāna as its object, occurs, overcoming the lineage of the worldlings and evolving the lineage of the noble ones. Immediately after this, the path (of stream-entry), fully understanding the truth of suffering, abandoning the truth of its origin, realizing the truth of its cessation, and developing the truth of the path to its cessation, enters upon the (supramundane) cognitive process of absorption. After that, two or three moments of fruition consciousness arise and cease. Then there is subsidence into the life-continuum.

Puna bhavangaṁ vocchinditvā paccavekkhaṇañāṇāni pavattanti.

Maggaṁ phalañ ca nibbānaṁ paccavekkhati paṇḍito
Hīne kilese sese ca paccavekkhati vā na vā.
Chabbisuddhikkamen' evaṁ bhāvetabbo catubbidho
Ñāṇadassanavisuddhi nāma maggo pavuccati.

Ayam ettha visuddhibhedo.

Then, arresting the life-continuum, reviewing knowledge occurs.

The wise person reviews the path, fruit, Nibbāna, and he either reviews or does not review the defilements destroyed and the remaining defilements.

Thus the fourfold path which has to be developed in sequence by means of the sixfold purity is called purification by knowledge and vision.

Herein, this is the section on purification.

Guide to §34

There arises mind-door adverting: On the cognitive process of the path, see IV, §14. Three moments of insight consciousness occur in an individual with normal faculties, two moments (omitting the moment of preparation) in one with unusually acute faculties.

Insight leading to emergence (*vuṭṭhānagāminīvipassanā*): This is the culminating phase of insight preceding the arising of the supramundane path. The path is called emergence because, objectively, it emerges from formations and takes Nibbāna as object, and because subjectively it emerges from defilements.

The change-of-lineage consciousness (*gotrabhūcitta*): This citta is the first advertence to Nibbāna and the proximity condition for the supramundane path. It is called change-of-lineage because it marks the transition from the "lineage" or family of the worldlings (*puthujjanagotra*) to the lineage or family of the noble ones (*ariyagotra*). However, while this knowledge is like the path in that it cognizes Nibbāna, unlike the path it cannot dispel the murk of defilements that conceals the Four Noble Truths. In the approach to the second and higher paths this mind-moment is called *vodāna*, cleansing, instead of change-of-lineage because the practitioner already belongs to the lineage of the noble ones.

The path: The path consciousness (*maggacitta*) simultaneously performs four functions, one with respect to each of the four truths. These four functions, mentioned here, are the full understanding (*pariññā*) of suffering; the abandoning (*pahāna*) of craving, its origin; the realization (*sacchikiriya*) of Nibbāna, its cessation; and the development (*bhāvanā*) of the Noble Eightfold Path. For one of sharp faculties who has skipped the preparatory moment three fruition cittas occur following the path; for others, who have gone through the preparatory moment, two fruition cittas occur.

Reviewing knowledge (*paccavekkhaṇañāṇa*): After each of the four supramundane path attainments, the disciple reviews the path, fruition, and Nibbāna; usually, but not invariably, he reviews as well the defilements abandoned and the defilements remaining. Thus there are a maximum of nineteen kinds of reviewing knowledge: five each for each of the first three paths, and four for the final path. This is because an Arahant, who is fully liberated, has no more defilements remaining to be reviewed.

Analysis of Emancipation (*vimokkhabheda*)

§35 The Three Doors to Emancipation

Tattha anattānupassanā attābhinivesaṁ muñcantī suññatānupassanā nāma vimokkhamukhaṁ hoti. Aniccānupassanā vipallāsanimittaṁ muñcantī animittānupassanā nāma. Dukkhānupassanā taṇhāpaṇidhiṁ muñcantī appaṇihitānupassanā nāma.

Therein, the contemplation of non-self, which discards the clinging to a self, becomes the door to emancipation termed contemplation of the void. The contemplation of impermanence, which discards the sign of perversion, becomes the door to emancipation termed contemplation of the signless. The contemplation of suffering, which discards desire through craving, becomes the door to emancipation termed contemplation of the desireless.

Guide to §35

When insight reaches its culmination, it settles upon one of the three contemplations—of impermanence, or suffering, or non-self—as determined by the inclination of the meditator. According to the Commentaries, one in whom faith is the dominant faculty settles upon the contemplation of impermanence; one in whom concentration is the dominant faculty settles upon the contemplation of suffering; and one in whom wisdom is the dominant faculty settles upon the contemplation of non-self. This final phase of contemplation, being the meditator's immediate access to the emancipating experience of the supramundane path, is thus called his "door to emancipation" (*vimokkhamukha*). Here, it is the noble path that is called emancipation, and the contemplation leading to the path that is called the door to emancipation.

The contemplation of non-self is termed contemplation of the void because it sees formations as being void of a self, a living being, a person. The contemplation of impermanence is termed contemplation of the signless because it abandons "the sign of perversion" (*vipallāsanimitta*), that is, the deceptive appearance of permanence, stability, and durability which lingers over formations owing to the perversion of perception. And the contemplation of suffering is termed contemplation of the desireless because it terminates desire by abandoning the false perception of pleasure in formations.

§36 Emancipation in the Path and Fruit

Tasmā yadi vuṭṭhānagāminīvipassanā anattato vipassati, suññato vimokkho nāma hoti maggo; yadi aniccato vipassati, animitto vimokkho nāma; yadi dukkhato vipassati, appaṇihito vimokkho nāmā ti ca. Maggo vipassanāgamanavasena tīṇi nāmāni labhati. Tathā phalañ ca maggāgamanavasena maggavīthiyaṁ.

Hence, if with the insight leading to emergence one contemplates on non-self, then the path is known as the void emancipation; if one contemplates on impermanence, then the path is known as the signless emancipation; if one contemplates on suffering, then the path is known as the desireless emancipation. Thus the path receives three names according to the way of insight. Likewise, the fruit (occurring) in the cognitive process of the path receives these three names according to the way of the path.

Guide to §36

When the meditator attains the path through the contemplation of non-self, the path makes Nibbāna its object through the aspect of voidness as devoid of self and it is thus known as the void emancipation. When he attains the path through the contemplation of impermanence, the path makes Nibbāna its object through the signless aspect—as devoid of the sign of formations—and it is thus known as the signless emancipation. When he attains the path through the contemplation of suffering, the path makes Nibbāna its object through the desireless aspect—as being free from the desire of craving—and it is thus known as the desireless emancipation. The fruit too receives the same designation as the path that preceded it.

§37 Emancipation in Fruition Attainment

Phalasamāpattivīthiyaṁ pana yathāvuttanayena vipassantānaṁ yathāsakaṁ phalam uppajjamānam pi vipassanāgamanavasen' eva suññatādivimokkho ti ca pavuccati. Ālambanavasena pana sarasavasena ca nāmattayaṁ sabbattha sabbesam pi samam eva.

Ayam ettha vimokkhabhedo.

However, in the cognitive process of the attainment of fruition, to those who contemplate in the foregoing manner, the fruits that arise respectively in each case are termed the void emancipation, etc., only in accordance with the way of insight. But as regards objects and respective qualities, the three names are applied equally to all (paths and fruits) everywhere.

Herein, this is the analysis of emancipation.

Guide to §37

When a noble disciple enters his respective fruition attainment, the fruition experience is named after the type of insight that led immediately to its attainment, not after the original path attainment in the cognitive process of the path. That is, if he enters the fruition attainment by the contemplation of non-self, the fruition is called the void emancipation; if by the contemplation of impermanence, the signless emancipation; and if by the contemplation of suffering, the desireless emancipation. But loosely speaking all paths and fruits can receive all three names because they all take as object Nibbāna—which is signless, desireless, and void—and they all share the qualities of being signless, desireless, and void.

Analysis of Individuals
(*puggalabheda*)

§38 The Stream-Enterer

Ettha pana sotāpattimaggaṁ bhāvetvā diṭṭhivicikicchāpahānena pahīnāpāyagamano sattakkhattuparamo sotāpanno nāma hoti.

Herein, having developed the path of stream-entry, by abandoning wrong views and doubt one becomes a stream-enterer, one who has escaped from rebirth in woeful states and will be reborn at most seven more times.

Guide to §38

A stream-enterer is one who has entered the stream that leads irreversibly to Nibbāna, that is, the Noble Eightfold Path. A stream-enterer has cut off the coarsest three fetters—personality view, doubt, and adherence to rules and rituals; he has unshakable confidence in the Buddha, Dhamma, and Sangha; and he is free from the prospect of rebirth in any of the woeful realms. Of the four taints (*āsava*), he has eliminated the taint of wrong views, and of the fourteen unwholesome cetasikas he has eliminated wrong view and doubt, and according to the Commentaries, also envy and avarice. He has freed himself as well from all degrees of defilements strong enough to lead to rebirth in the woeful planes. His conduct is marked by scrupulous observance of the Five Precepts: abstinence from taking life, stealing, sexual misconduct, false speech, and use of intoxicants.

There are three types of stream-enterer:

(1) One who will be reborn seven times at most in the human and celestial worlds (*sattakkhattuparama*).

(2) One who takes birth in good families two or three times before attaining Arahantship (*kolankola*).

(3) One who will be reborn only once more before attaining the goal (*ekabījī*).

§39 The Once-Returner

Sakadāgāmimaggaṁ bhāvetvā rāgadosamohānaṁ tanukarattā sakadāgāmī nāma hoti, sakid eva imaṁ lokaṁ āgantā.

Having developed the path of once-returning, with the attenuation of lust, hatred, and delusion, one becomes a once-returner, one who returns to this world only one more time.

Guide to §39

The once-returner has eliminated the grosser forms of lust, hate, and delusion. Thus, although attenuated forms of these defilements can still arise in him, they do not occur often and their obsessive force is weak.

TABLE 9.3: ERADICATION OF DEFILEMENTS BY THE PATHS

		Stream-entry	Once-returning	Non-returning	Arahantship
1	Delusion				■
2	Shamelessness				■
3	Fearlessness of wrong				■
4	Restlessness				■
5	Greed (sensual)			■	
	Greed (other)				■
6	Wrong view	■			
7	Conceit				■
8	Hatred			■	
9	Envy	■			
10	Avarice	■			
11	Worry			■	
12	Sloth				■
13	Torpor				■
14	Doubt	■			
	Total	4	0	3	8

Ledi Sayadaw points out that the Commentaries offer two conflicting interpretations of the expression "this world" (*imaṁ lokaṁ*), to which the once-returner may return one more time. On one interpretation it is the human world, to which he may return from a heavenly world; on the other it is the sense-sphere world, to which he may return from a Brahma-world. Ledi Sayadaw maintains that in spite of commentarial support for the former interpretation, the second seems better supported by the canonical texts.

According to the commentary to the *Puggalapaññatti* there are five kinds of once-returner:

(1) One attains the fruit of once-returning in the human world, takes rebirth in the human world, and attains final Nibbāna here.

(2) One attains the fruit of once-returning in the human world, takes rebirth in a heavenly world, and attains final Nibbāna there.

(3) One attains the fruit in a heavenly world, takes rebirth in a heavenly world, and attains final Nibbāna there.

(4) One attains the fruit in a heavenly world, takes rebirth in the human world, and attains final Nibbāna here.

(5) One attains the fruit in the human world, takes rebirth in a heavenly world and passes the full life-span there, and then takes rebirth again in the human world, where one attains final Nibbāna.

It should be noted that whereas the *ekabījī* stream-enterer has only one more rebirth, the fifth type of once-returner has two. Nevertheless, he is still called "once-returner" because he returns only once more to the human world.

§40 The Non-Returner

Anāgāmimaggaṁ bhāvetvā kāmarāgavyāpādānaṁ anavasesappahānena anāgāmī nāma hoti, anāgantā itthattaṁ.

Having developed the path of non-returning, by totally abandoning sensual lust and ill will, one becomes a non-returner, one who does not return to this (sensuous) state.

Guide to §40

A non-returner has fully eradicated sensual lust and ill will, the fetters that bind to the sensuous world. He has also eradicated the taint of sensual desire and the unwholesome cetasikas, hatred and worry, as well as all greed taking a sensuous object. Thus he will be spontaneously reborn in a fine-material realm and there attain final Nibbāna. It should be noted that while only non-returners are reborn in the Pure Abodes, there is no fixed determination that all non-returners are reborn there.

The texts mention five types of non-returner:

(1) One who, having been reborn spontaneously in a higher world, generates the final path before he has reached the midpoint of the life-span (*antarā-parinibbāyī*).

(2) One who generates the final path after passing the midpoint of the life-span, even when on the verge of death (*upahacca-parinibbāyī*).

(3) One who attains the final path without exertion (*asankhāra-parinibbāyī*).

(4) One who attains the final path with exertion (*sasankhāra-parinibbāyī*).

(5) One who passes from one higher realm to another until he reaches the Akaniṭṭha realm, the Highest Pure Abode, and there attains the final path (*uddhaṁsoto akaniṭṭhagāmī*).

§41 The Arahant

Arahattamaggaṁ bhāvetvā anavasesakilesappahānena arahā nāma hoti khīṇāsavo loke aggadakkhiṇeyyo.

Ayam ettha puggalabhedo.

Having developed the path of Arahantship, with the total abandonment of defilements one becomes an Arahant, a destroyer of the taints, a supreme recipient of offerings in the world.

Herein, this is the analysis of individuals.

Guide to §41

The five fetters abandoned by the first three paths are called the lower fetters (*orambhāgiya-saṁyojana*) because they bind beings to the lower world, the sensuous plane of existence. One who has eradicated them, the non-returner, no longer returns to the sensuous plane, but he is still bound to the round of existence by the five higher fetters (*uddhambhagiya-saṁyojana*). With the attainment of the path of Arahantship, these five higher fetters are also eradicated: desire for fine-material existence, desire for immaterial existence, conceit, restlesness, and ignorance. The fourth path also destroys the remaining two taints—the taint of attachment to existence and the taint of ignorance—for which reason the Arahant is called a "destroyer of the taints" (*khīnāsava*). The path of Arahantship eradicates, too, the remaining unwholesome cetasikas left unabandoned by the earlier paths: delusion, shamelessness, fearlessness of wrongdoing, restlessness, conceit, sloth, and torpor.

Analysis of Attainments
(*samāpattibheda*)

§42 Accessibility

Phalasamāpattiyo pan' ettha sabbesam pi yathāsakaphalavasena sādhāraṇā' va. Nirodhasamāpattisamāpajjanaṁ pana anāgāmīnañ c'eva arahantānañ ca labbhati.

Herein, the attainment of fruition is common to all, each being able to attain their respective fruition. But the attainment of cessation is accessible only to non-returners and Arahants.

Guide to §42

The attainment of fruition (*phalasamāpatti*) is a meditative attainment by which a noble disciple enters into supramundane absorption with Nibbāna as object. It is attained for the purpose of experiencing the bliss of Nibbāna here and now. The cittas that occur in this attainment are the fruition cittas corresponding to the disciple's level of realization. Thus each of the four grades of noble individuals can enter their own proper fruition attainment—the stream-enterer attaining the fruition attainment of stream-entry, etc. The attainment is reached by first making the resolution to attain fruition and then developing in sequence the insight knowledges beginning with knowledge of rise and fall. (See Vism. XXIII, 6-15.)

§43 The Attainment of Cessation

Tattha yathākkamaṁ paṭhamajjhānādimahaggatasamāpattiṁ samāpajjitvā vuṭṭhāya tattha gate sankhāradhamme tattha tatth'eva vipassanto yāva ākiñcaññāyatanaṁ gantvā tato paraṁ adhiṭṭheyyādikaṁ pubbakiccaṁ katvā n'evasaññānāsaññāyatanaṁ samāpajjati. Tassa dvinnaṁ appanājavanānaṁ parato vocchijjati cittasantati. Tato nirodhasamāpanno nāma hoti.

In this case, one enters successively upon the sublime attainments beginning with the first jhāna, and then after emerging from them, one contemplates with insight the conditioned states within each of those attainments.

Having proceeded thus up to the base of nothingness, one then attends to the preliminary duties such as the resolution, etc., and enters the base of neither-perception-nor-non-perception. After two occasions of javana in absorption, the continuum of consciousness is suspended. Then one is said to have attained cessation.

Guide to §43

The attainment of cessation is a meditative attainment in which the stream of consciousness and mental factors is completely cut off temporarily. It can be obtained only by non-returners and Arahants who have mastery over all the fine-material and immaterial jhānas. Further, it can be obtained only within the sensuous plane or the fine-material plane of existence. It cannot be obtained within the immaterial plane, for there is no attaining of the four fine-material jhanas there, which are the prerequisites for entering cessation.

To enter cessation the meditator must attain each jhāna in proper sequence. After emerging from each one, he contemplates its factors as impermanent, suffering, and non-self. In this manner the procedure is carried as far as the base of nothingness. After emerging from the base of nothingness the meditator then makes four resolutions: (1) that his requisites should not be destroyed; (2) that he should emerge if his services are needed by the Sangha; (3) that he should emerge if he is summoned by the Buddha (during the Buddha's lifetime); and (4) that he is not bound to die within seven days.

After making these resolutions, he enters the fourth immaterial jhāna, which occurs for two moments of javana. Immediately after, he attains cessation, wherein the stream of consciousness is temporarily suspended.

§44 Emergence from Cessation

Vuṭṭhānakāle pana anāgāmino anāgāmiphalacittaṁ arahato arahattaphalacittaṁ ekavāram eva pavattitvā bhavangapāto hoti. Tato paraṁ paccavekkhaṇañāṇaṁ pavattati.

Ayam ettha samāpattibhedo.

Niṭṭhito ca vipassanākammaṭṭhānanayo.

At the time of emergence (from cessation), in the case of a non-returner the fruit of non-returning consciousness occurs one time—in the case of an Arahant, the fruit of Arahantship consciousness (occurs one time)—and then there is subsidence into the life-continuum. Following this, reviewing knowledge occurs.

Herein, this is the analysis of attainments.

The method of meditation
for developing insight is finished.

§45 Conclusion

Bhāvetabbaṁ pan' icc' evaṁ bhāvanādvayam uttamaṁ
Paṭipattirasassādaṁ patthayantena sāsane.

One who aspires to enjoy the taste
Of practice in the Buddha's Dispensation
Should develop this twofold meditation
So excellent in the way explained.

Guide to §45

The "twofold meditation" is calm and insight.

Iti Abhidhammatthasangahe
Kammaṭṭhānasangahavibhāgo nāma
navamo paricchedo.

Thus ends the ninth chapter
in the Manual of Abhidhamma entitled
the Compendium of Meditation Subjects.

COLOPHON

Cārittasobhitavisālakulodayena
Saddhābhivuddhaparisuddhaguṇodayena
Nambavhayena paṇidhāya parānukampaṁ
Yaṁ patthitaṁ pakaraṇaṁ pariniṭṭhitaṁ taṁ

Puññena tena vipulena tu mūlasomaṁ
Dhaññādhivāsamuditoditamāyugantaṁ
Paññāvadātaguṇasobhitalajjibhikkhū
Maññantu puññavibhavodayamangalāya.

This treatise—composed out of compassion for others at the request of Namba, a person of refined manners, belonging to a respectable family, full of faith, and replete with sterling virtues—has been completed.

By this great merit may the modest monks, who are purified by wisdom and who shine with virtues, remember till the end of the world the most famous Mūlasoma Monastery, the fortunate abode, for the acquisition of merit and for their happiness.

Guide to Colophon

The teachers of Abhidhamma hold two different opinions about the name of the monastery where Ācariya Anuruddha composed the *Abhidhammattha Sangaha*. One school of thought takes the name to be Tumūlasoma Vihāra, holding *tumūla* to be synonymous with *mahā*, meaning great. No such word as *tumūla*, however, exists in Pali or Sanskrit. Both languages contain a word *tumula*, which does not mean great but uproar or "tumult," a word to which it is etymologically related. This word is generally used in connection with warfare; it occurs in the Vessantara Jātaka in the line, *Ath' ettha vattatī saddo tumulo bheravo mahā*: "Then sounded forth a mighty sound, a terrible great roar" (Mahānipāta, v. 1809; PTS ed. vi, 504).

The other line of interpretation holds that the name of the monastery is Mūlasoma Vihāra. The syllable *tu* is taken to be an indeclinable conjunctive particle here used for the sake of euphony. Since Ācariya Anuruddha has used *tu* in a similar way elsewhere in his treatise (see I, §32; VIII, §12), it seems probable that he is using it here as well. Thus we should regard the name of the monastery as the Mūlasoma Vihāra. In the Sri Lankan tradition it is generally believed that this monastery was situated in the district of Chilaw and that present Munnessaram Kovil stands on its site.[1]

The phrase *dhaññādhivāsa*, which the author uses to describe this monastery, does not mean "the abode of grain," as earlier translations have rendered it. The word *dhañña* here bears the derivative meaning of fortunate or meritorious. Ledi Sayadaw explains that the monastery is so described because it was the residence of meritorious elders beginning with its founder, an elder named Mahinda.

Iti Anuruddhācariyena racitaṁ
Abhidhammatthasangahaṁ nāma
pakaraṇaṁ niṭṭhitaṁ.

Thus ends the treatise called
the Manual of Abhidhamma composed
by Ācariya Anuruddha.

Notes
Appendices
Bibliography

NOTES

INTRODUCTION

1. Asl. 2; *Expos.*, p. 3.
2. Asl. 2-3; *Expos.*, pp. 3-4.
3. The *Dhammasaṅgaṇī* also includes a Suttanta matrix consisting of forty-two dyads taken from the Suttas. However, this is ancillary to the Abhidhamma proper and serves more as an appendix for providing succinct definitions of key Suttanta terms. Moreover, the definitions themselves are not framed in terms of Abhidhamma categories and the Suttanta matrix is not employed in any subsequent books of the Abhidhamma Piṭaka.
4. See, for example, the following: A.K. Warder, *Indian Buddhism*, 2nd rev. ed. (Delhi: Motilal Banarsidass, 1980), pp. 218-24; Fumimaro Watanabe, *Philosophy and its Development in the Nikāyas and Abhidhamma* (Delhi: Motilal Banarsidass, 1983), pp. 18-67; and the article "Abhidharma Literature" by Kogen Mizuno in *Encyclopaedia of Buddhism*, Fasc. 1 (Govt. of Ceylon, 1961).
5. Asl. 410; *Expos.*, p. 519.
6. Asl. 13; *Expos.*, p. 16-17.
7. Asl. 16; *Expos.*, p. 20.
8. The first book of the Sarvāstivādin Abhidharma, the *Saṅgītiparyāya*, is ascribed to Sāriputta by Chinese sources (but not by Sanskrit and Tibetan sources), while the second book, the *Dharmaskandha*, is ascribed to him by Sanskrit and Tibetan sources (but not by Chinese sources). The Chinese canon also contains a work entitled the *Shāriputra Abhidharma-Shāstra*, the school of which is not known.
9. These are reduced to the familar eighty-nine cittas by grouping together the five cittas into which each path and fruition consciousness is divided by association with each of the five jhānas.
10. The *Yamaka*, in its chapter "Citta-yamaka," uses the term *khaṇa* to refer to the subdivisions of a moment and also introduces the *uppāda-khaṇa* and *bhanga-khaṇa*, the sub-moments of arising and dissolution. However, the threefold scheme of sub-moments seems to appear first in the Commentaries.
11. Ven. A. Devananda Adhikarana Nayaka Thero, in Preface to *Paramattha-vinicchaya and Paramattha-vibhāvinī-vyākhyā* (Colombo: Vidyā Sāgara Press, 1926), p. iii.
12. G.P. Malalasekera, *The Pali Literature of Ceylon* (Colombo: M.D. Guna-

sena, repr. 1958), pp. 168-70. Malalasekera points out that James Gray, in his edition of the *Buddhaghosuppatti*, gives a chronological list of saintly and learned men of Southern India, taken from the Talaing records, and there we find Anuruddha mentioned after authors who are supposed to have lived later than the seventh or eighth century. Since Bhadanta Sāriputta Mahāsāmi compiled a Sinhala paraphrase of the *Abhidhammattha Sangaha* during the reign of Parākrama-Bāhu the Great (1164-97), this places Anuruddha earlier than the middle of the twelfth century.

13. See the article "Anuruddha (5)" in *Encyclopaedia of Buddhism*, Fasc. 4 (Govt. of Ceylon, 1965). Ven. Buddhadatta's view is also accepted by Warder, *Indian Buddhism*, pp. 533-34.
14. This author is commonly confused with another Burmese monk called Chapada who came to Sri Lanka during the twelfth century and studied under Bhadanta Sāriputta. The case for two Chapadas is cogently argued by Ven. A.P. Buddhadatta, *Corrections of Geiger's Mahāvaṁsa, Etc.* (Ambalangoda: Ananda Book Co., 1957), pp.198-209.

CHAPTER I

1. *Paramassa uttamassa ñāṇassa attho gocaro*. Vibhv.
2. According to Vibhv. *diṭṭhigata* denotes just wrong view, the suffix *gata* having no particular meaning here.
3. (i) *Vici* (*vicinanto*) = inquiring + *kicch*, to be vexed; (ii) *vi* = devoid of + *cikicchā* = remedy.
4. Sometimes also called *rūpajjhānas*, "fine-material absorptions," to distinguish them from the *arūpajjhānas* which follow.
5. *Ārammaṇ'upanijjhānato paccanīkajjhāpanato jhānaṁ*. Vism. IV,119.
6. *So hi ārammaṇe cittaṁ āropeti*. Asl.114.
7. Vism. IV, 89-91.
8. In *The Path of Purification*, his translation of the *Visuddhimagga*, Bhikkhu Ñāṇamoli has translated it as happiness. This rendering is often used for *sukha*, the next factor, and thus may lead to a confusion of the two.
9. Vism. IV,94-100.
10. For a detailed elaboration of this simile, see Asl. 117-18; *Expos*., pp. 155-56.
11. This qualification is made in regard to the path of once-returning; see p. 67.
12. For details, see Henepola Gunaratana, *The Jhānas in Theravada Buddhist Meditation* (BPS Wheel No. 351/353, 1988), pp. 60-62.

CHAPTER II

1. Asl. 67; *Expos*., p. 90.
2. *Kāyaviññatti, vacīviññatti*. See VI, §3.

3. On the bases, see III, §§20-22.
4. See above, p. 29.
5. The following explanations of the characteristics, etc., of the different cetasikas have been collected from Vism. IV, 88-100; IX, 93-96; XIV,134-77; and Asl. 107-33, 247-60. See *Expos.*, pp. 142-80, 330-46.
6. So say the Commentaries, but it seems that tranquillity as proximate cause applies solely to the pleasant feeling arisen when developing concentration. A more general proximate cause for feeling would be contact, in accordance with the principle "with contact as condition, feeling comes to be" (*phassapaccayā vedanā*). In fact, the entire treatment of feeling here is limited to a particular kind of feeling. For a fuller treatment of feeling in all its variety, see III, §§2-4, and Guide.
7. Again, these last two commentarial statements seem fitting only for one-pointedness that has reached the level of profound concentration.
8. See above, pp. 56-57.
9. Or: the mounting of the mind onto the object (*ārammaṇe cittassa abhiniropana*).
10. Or: continued stroking of the object (*ārammaṇ'ānumajjana*).
11. In the Suttas *chanda* is often used as a synonym for *lobha* and *rāga*, thus as meaning desire in the reprehensible sense as well. But the Suttas also recognize *chanda* as a potentially beneficial factor, as when they speak about the arousing of desire for the abandoning of unwholesome states and for the acquisition of wholesome states. See for example the definition of right effort at D.22/ii,312 (= M.141/iii, 251-52).
12. As these two factors are the opposites of shame and fear of wrongdoing, their meaning can be more fully understood by contrast with these beautiful cetasikas. See below, p. 86.
13. Since seeing the noble ones leads to hearing the true Dhamma, which can prevent wrong view from getting a grip on the mind.
14. *Ketukamyatā*, lit. a desire to fly the banner (to advertise oneself).
15. Because conceit arises only in greed-rooted cittas dissociated from views.
16. For the nine grounds for annoyance (or causes of malice, *aghātavatthu*), see D.33/iii, 262.
17. The complete version of these similes is found in the Milindapañha, cited at Asl. 119-20. See *Expos.*, pp. 157-58.
18. *Apilāpana*, also rendered "not wobbling." The commentators explain that *sati* keeps the mind as steady as a stone instead of letting it bob about like a pumpkin in water.
19. Asl. 103-104; *Expos.*, pp. 136-37.
20. It should be noted that while compassion involves empathy with those

beset by suffering, it is never accompanied by sadness or sorrow, which is a feeling pertaining only to unwholesome cittas.

21. While non-hatred and mental neutrality are found in the supramundane cittas, they do not occur there as the illimitables of loving-kindness and equanimity towards beings.

CHAPTER III

1. Tranquillity (*passaddhi*), it seems, is the proximate cause only for the joyful feeling that arises in meditative development.
2. On the heart-base, see below §20.
3. These definitions of the five feelings are found at Vism.XIV,128.
4. Asl. 263; *Expos.*, pp. 349-50. The five types of sensitivity are considered species of derived matter, as are the first four sense objects. The tangible object, however, consists of three primary elements. See VI, §3.
5. See the explanation of javana in §8 below. Mental pleasure does precede the javana phase in the joyful investigating consciousness that arises in the case of an exceptionally pleasant object, but this too follows the bare sense consciousness.
6. *Suppatiṭṭhitabhāvasādhanasankhāto mūlabhāvo*. Vibhv.
7. Vism. XVII, 70.
8. That is, in a five-door process. In a mind-door process the javana phase follows the mind-door adverting consciousness.
9. This is so in the case of non-Arahants. For Arahants the javanas are ethically indeterminate. Javana is treated more fully in Chapter IV.
10. That is, the four cittas rooted in greed and accompanied by wrong view and the citta accompanied by doubt will be absent in the stream-enterer and once-returner, while the two cittas rooted in hatred will be absent in the non-returner.
11. The word *rūpa* has two primary meanings: (1) matter, or materiality; and (2) visible form. The former is a generic category within which the latter is included as a species.
12. The distinction between primary matter and derived matter will be dealt with more fully at VI, §2.
13. See Vism. VIII, 111.

CHAPTER IV

1. For the mind-door process the heart-base is only required in those realms where matter is found. While a mind-door process can also take any of the five sense data as object, mental object is listed to show its distinctive datum.
2. An exception, however, is made for bodily and verbal intimation and for the four material characteristics (see VI, §4). The two types of intima-

tion have the temporal duration of one mind-moment. Of the four characteristics, production and continuity are equal in duration to the arising moment, impermanence to the dissolution moment, and decay to forty-nine sub-moments of mind.

3. The simile is introduced in Asl. 271-72, *Expos.*, pp. 359-60, however without continuation beyond the eating of the mango. Later tradition (as in Vibhv.) adds the swallowing of the fruit and going back to sleep as counterparts of registration and the lapse back into the bhavanga.
4. See Vism. XXII, 23, note 7.
5. Smv. 10-11. *Dispeller of Delusion*, 1:10-11.
6. From this stipulation it seems that if aversion arises towards an extremely desirable object, the registration cittas will not be accompanied by joy (as stated in §17); instead they will be wholesome-resultants accompanied by equanimity.

Chapter V

1. Though the logic of the temporal sequence seems to imply that in the case of the Brahmā realms, too, the *mahākappa* is intended, the commentators base their interpretation upon another tradition (derived from the Suttas) which holds that the periodic destruction of the world by fire extends through the realm of Mahā Brahmās. Since this destruction takes place at the end of one *asankheyyakappa* within the *mahākappa*, the conclusion follows that the Mahā Brahmās cannot live longer than a single *asankheyyakappa*. The sources for this other tradition are D.1/i,17-18 and D.27/iii,84-85.
2. For a detailed analysis of the ten courses of action, see Asl. 97-102; *Expos.*, pp. 128-35.
3. These three views are found at D.2, M.60, M.76, and elsewhere. For the commentarial analysis, see Bhikkhu Bodhi, *The Discourse on the Fruits of Recluseship* (BPS 1989), pp. 69-83.
4. See Asl. 267-88; *Expos.*, pp. 354-79.

Chapter VI

1. According to the Mahāniddesa: *ruppati, kuppati, ghaṭṭīyati, pīḷīyati, bhijjati.*
2. *Sītoṇhādi-virodhippaccayehi vikāraṁ āpajjati āpādiyati.* Vibhv.
3. This explanation of the characteristics, etc., of the great essentials is taken from Vism. XI, 93 and 109.
4. A detailed exposition of derived matter is found at Vism. XIV, 36-70, on which the account given here is based.
5. Here the prefix *sa*, "with," does not imply association (*sampayutta*) but the ability to be made an object of the taints.

CHAPTER VII

1. The Brahmajāla Sutta (D.1) enumerates 62 species of wrong views concerning the nature of the self and the world. These all fall into the two extreme views of eternalism, which affirms their eternal existence, and annihilationism, which posits their eventual destruction.
2. For a detailed account, see Ledi Sayadaw, *The Requisites of Enlightenment* (BPS Wheel No. 171/174, 1971).
3. For the sutta and its commentaries, see Soma Thera, *The Way of Mindfulness* (Kandy: BPS, 1981). The best modern expositions are Nyanaponika Thera, *The Heart of Buddhist Meditation* (London: Rider, 1962), and U Silananda, *The Four Foundation of Mindfulness* (Boston: Wisdom, 1990).
4. The explanation given here is derived from Ledi Sayadaw. The view expressed by Ven. Nārada in the previous editions of the Manual, that the *iddhipādas* are solely supramundane, appears to be mistaken.
5. For a detailed analysis of the aggregates, see Vism. XIV.
6. The sense bases and elements are dealt with in detail in Vism. XV.
7. The Four Noble Truths are explained in detail in Vism. XVI.

CHAPTER VIII

1. The explanations to follow are based on Vism. XVII and Smv. VI.
2. The sources for these explanations are: Vism. XVII, 66-100; U Nārada, *Guide to Conditional Relations*, 1:8-79; and Ledi Sayadaw, *The Buddhist Philosophy of Relations*, pp. 1-57.
3. One line of Abhidhamma interpretation adopted by the teachers would restrict the base-object-prenascence support condition to the heart-base arisen at the seventeenth mind-moment preceding the death consciousness, on an occasion when the last javana process takes the heart-base as object. Ledi Sayadaw argues at length in the *Paramatthadīpanī* against this narrow interpretation, and his position is accepted here.
4. Ledi Sayadaw, *Buddhist Philosophy of Relations*, pp. 50-51.
5. Asl. 392; *Expos.*, p. 501. There is a word-play here that cannot be reproduced in English: the word *nāma*, "name" or "mind," is derived from a verbal root *nam* meaning "to bend."
6. For more on the developed theory of concepts in the Abhidhamma, see Vism. VIII, note 11.

CHAPTER IX

1. Asl. 144; *Expos.*, p.191.
2. See *The Mirror of the Dhamma* (BPS Wheel No. 54 A/B, 1984), pp. 5-8.
3. That is, to exercise the supernormal power of manifesting a hundred replicas of one's physical body.

4. For a fuller discussion of the differences between the *samathayāna* and *vipassanāyāna* approaches, see Gunaratana, *The Jhānas*, pp. 51-55.

COLOPHON

1. Ven. A. Devananda Adhikarana Nayaka Thero, in Preface to *Paramattha vinicchaya*, p. ii. Some scholars identify the Mūlasoma Vihāra with a monastery mentioned in the *Mahāvaṁsa* (xxxiii, 84) that was built by King Vaṭṭagāmaṇi (88-76 B.C.) for his queen Somā. The monastery is referred to thus: "When he had sent for Somadevī he raised her again to her rank and built, in her honour, the Somārāma, bearing her name." The translator, Geiger, has a note to this verse stating that the monastery must be sought for near the Abhayagiri Vihāra, perhaps in the place of the building popularly called "the Queen's Pavilion." Ven. Saddhātissa, however, in his introduction to his edition of the *Abhidhammattha Saṅgaha* (p. xvi), states that stone inscriptions dating back to the tenth century record that the Mūlasoma Vihāra was built by King Vaṭṭagāmaṇi and his minister Mūla at Polonnaruwa, in honour of Somadevī the queen. Ven. Saddhātissa also mentions the popular Sri Lankan tradition which holds that the Munnessaram Hindu temple was the original Mūlasoma Vihāra where Anuruddha used to reside.

APPENDIX I
TEXTUAL SOURCES FOR THE 89 AND 121 CITTAS

		Dhs.	Vism.	Asl.
UNWHOLESOME CITTAS—12				
Greed-rooted	1st	365	90-91	336
"	2nd	399		339-40
"	3rd	400	"	340
"	4th	402	"	341
"	5th	403	"	"
"	6th	409	"	"
"	7th	410	"	"
"	8th	412	"	"
Hatred-rooted	1st	413	92	341-44
"	2nd	421	"	344
Delusion-rooted	1st	422	93	344-45
"	2nd	427	"	346
ROOTLESS CITTAS—18				
Unwholesome·resultant				
Eye-consciousness		556	101	384-85
Ear-consciousness, etc.		"	"	"
Receiving		562	"	"
Investigating		564	"	"
Wholesome·resultant				
Eye-consciousness		431	96	348-49
Ear-consciousness, etc.		443	"	349-50
Receiving		455	97	350
Investigating (joy)		469	97-98	351-52
Investigating (equanimity)		484	97-98	351-52
Functional				
Five-door adverting		566	107	385-86
Mind-door adverting		574	108	388
Smile-producing		568	108	386-88

		Dhs.	Vism.	Asl.
SENSE-SPHERE BEAUTIFUL—24				
Wholesome	1st	1	83-85	141-207
"	2nd	146	"	207
"	3rd	147	"	208
"	4th	149	"	"
"	5th	150	"	"
"	6th	156	"	"
"	7th	157	"	"
"	8th	159	"	"
Resultant	1st-8th	498	100	353-79
Functional	1st-8th	576	109	388
FINE-MATERIAL SPHERE—15				
Wholesome	1st jhāna	160,167	86	216-25
"	2nd jhāna	161,168	"	239-43
"	3rd jhāna	163,170	"	225
"	4th jhāna	165,172	"	228-34
"	5th jhāna	174	"	235-39
Resultant	1st jhāna	499	103	379-80
"	2nd-5th jhāna	500	"	"
Functional	1st jhāna	577	109	388-89
"	2nd-5th jhāna	578	"	"
IMMATERIAL SPHERE—12				
Wholesome	1st	265	87	270
"	2nd	266	"	275
"	3rd	267	"	276
"	4th	268	"	277-83
Resultant	1st	501	104	379-80
"	2nd	502	"	"
"	3rd	503	"	"
"	4th	504	"	"
Functional	1st	579	109	388-89
"	2nd	580	"	"
"	3rd	581	"	"
"	4th	582	"	"
SUPRAMUNDANE—8 or 40				
Wholesome				
Stream-entry path		277	88	289-319
"	1st jhāna	277	...	307-10

		Dhs.	Vism.	Asl.
Stream-entry path	2nd-5th jhāna	342	...	307-10
Once-return path		361	88	319-20
Non-return path		362	"	320
Arahant path		363	"	320-29
Resultant				
Stream-entry fruit		505	105	380-84
"	1st jhāna	505	...	...
"	2nd-5th jhāna	508	...	...
Higher three fruits		553	105	380-84

NOTE: References to the *Dhammasanganī* are by paragraph number; to the *Visuddhimagga*, by paragraph number of Chapter XIV in *The Path of Purification*; to the *Atthasālinī*, by page number of *The Expositor*.

APPENDIX II
TEXTUAL SOURCES FOR THE 52 MENTAL FACTORS

		Dhs.	Vism.	Asl.
ETHICALLY VARIABLES—13				
Universals—7				
(1)	Contact	2	134	144
(2)	Feeling	3	125-28	145
(3)	Perception	4	129-30	146
(4)	Volition	5	135	147
(5)	One-pointedness	11	139	156
(6)	Life faculty	19	138	163
(7)	Attention	...	152	175
Occasionals—6				
(8)	Initial application	7	88-98*	151
(9)	Sustained application	8	"	152
(10)	Decision	...	151	175
(11)	Energy	13	137	158
(12)	Zest	9	94-100*	153
(13)	Desire	...	150	175
UNWHOLESOME FACTORS—14				
(14)	Delusion	390	163	332
(15)	Shamelessness	387	160	331
(16)	Fearlessness of wrong	388	160	331
(17)	Restlessness	429	165	346
(18)	Greed	389	162	332
(19)	Wrong view	381	164	331
(20)	Conceit	1116	168	340
(21)	Hatred	418	171	342
(22)	Envy	1121	172	342
(23)	Avarice	1122	173	343
(24)	Worry	1161	174	343
(25)	Sloth	1156	167	340
(26)	Torpor	1157	167	340
(27)	Doubt	425	177	344

	Dhs.	Vism.	Asl.
BEAUTIFUL FACTORS—25			
Beautiful Universals—19			
(28) Faith	12	140	157
(29) Mindfulness	14	141	159
(30) Shame	30	142	164
(31) Fear of wrongdoing	31	142	164
(32) Non-greed	32	143	167
(33) Non-hatred	33	143	167
(34) Neutrality of mind	153	153	176
(35) Tranquillity of mental body	40	144	171
(36) Tranquillity of consness.	41	144	171
(37) Lightness of mental body	42	145	172
(38) Lightness of consness.	43	145	172
(39) Malleability of mental body	44	146	172
(40) Malleability of consness.	45	146	172
(41) Wieldiness of mental body	46	147	172
(42) Wieldiness of consness.	47	147	172
(43) Proficiency of mental body	48	148	172
(44) Proficiency of consness.	49	148	172
(45) Rectitude of mental body	50	149	173
(46) Rectitude of consness.	51	149	173
Abstinences—3			
(47) Right speech	299	155	296
(48) Right action	300	155	297
(49) Right livelihood	301	155	298
Illimitables—2			
(50) Compassion	...	154	176
(51) Appreciative joy	...	154	176
Non·Delusion—1			
(52) Wisdom faculty	16	143	161

NOTE: References to the three sources are by the method explained in the Note to Appendix I. References to the *Visuddhimagga* marked by an asterisk are to paragraph number of Chapter IV rather than Chapter XIV.

BIBLIOGRAPHY

A. EDITIONS OF THE ABHIDHAMMATTHA SANGAHA CONSULTED

Kosambi, Dhammānanda. *Abhidhammatthasangaha and Navanīta-Ṭikā* Colombo: Mangala Traders, n.d. (Pali in Sinhala script.)

Nārada Mahāthera. *A Manual of Abhidhamma*. 4th ed. Kandy: BPS, 1980. (Pali in Roman script with English translation.)

Rewata Dhamma, Bhadanta. *Abhidhammattha Sangaha with Vibhāvinī-Ṭīkā*. Varanasi: Bauddhaswadhyaya Satra, 1965. (Pali in Devanagari script.)

Saddhātissa, Hammalawa. *The Abhidhammatthasangaha and the Abhidhammatthavibhāvinī-Ṭīkā*. Oxford: PTS, 1989. (Pali in Roman script.)

B. COMMENTARIES ON THE SANGAHA CONSULTED

(1) Abhidhammatthavibhāvinī-Ṭīkā by Acariya Sumangalasāmi:

Paññānanda, Rev. Welitara, ed. *Abhidharmārtha Sangraha Prakaraṇa, containing the Abhidharmārtha Vibhāvini-Ṭīkā*. Colombo 1898. (Pali in Sinhala script.)

Rewata Dhamma, Bhadanta, ed. See entry under "Editions of the *Abhidhammattha Sangaha* consulted" above.

Saddhātissa, Hammalawa, ed. See entry under "Editions of the *Abhidhammattha Sangaha* consulted" above.

(2) *Paramatthadīpanī-Ṭīkā* by Ledi Sayadaw:

Ledi Sayadaw. *Paramatthadīpanī Sangaha Mahā-Ṭīkā*. Rangoon, 1907.

(3) Other Commentaries Consulted:

Kosambi, Dhammānanda. *Navanīta-Ṭīkā*. See entry under "Editions of the *Abhidhammattha Sangaha* consulted" above.

Rewata Dhamma, Bhadanta. *Abhidharma Prakāsinī*. 2 vols. Varanasi: Varanaseya Sanskrit University, 1967. (Hindi commentary.)

C. The Abhidhamma Piṭaka in Translation

Dhammasaṅgaṇī: C.A.F. Rhys Davids, trans. *A Buddhist Manual of Psychological Ethics*. 1900. Reprint. London: PTS, 1974.

Vibhanga: U Thittila, trans. *The Book of Analysis*. London: PTS, 1969.

Dhātukathā: U Nārada, trans. *Discourse on Elements*. London: PTS, 1962.

Puggalapaññatti: B.C. Law, trans. *A Designation of Human Types*. London: PTS, 1922, 1979.

Kathāvatthu: Shwe Zan Aung and C.A.F. Rhys Davids, trans. *Points of Controversy*. London: PTS, 1915, 1979.

Paṭṭhāna: U Nārada, trans. *Conditional Relations*. London: PTS, Vol. 1, 1969; Vol. 2, 1981.

D. Abhidhamma Commentaries in Translation

Atthasālinī (Commentary on the *Dhammasaṅgaṇī*): Pe Maung Tin, trans. *The Expositor*. 2 vols. London: PTS, 1920-21, 1976.

Sammohavinodanī (Commentary on the *Vibhanga*): Bhikkhu Ñāṇamoli, trans. *The Dispeller of Delusion*. Vol. 1. London: PTS, 1987; Vol. 2. Oxford: PTS, 1991.

Kathāvatthu Commentary: B.C. Law, trans. *The Debates Commentary*. London: PTS 1940, 1988.

E. Other Works Consulted

Aung, Shwe Zan Aung and Rhys Davids, C.A.F. *Compendium of Philosophy*. London: PTS, 1910, 1979. Pioneering English translation of the *Abhidhammattha Sangaha*, with interesting Introduction and Appendix.

Devananda, Ven. A., Adhikarana Nayaka Thero. *Paramattha-vinicchaya and Paramattha-vibhāvinī-vyākhyā*. Colombo: Vidyā Sāgara Press, 1926.

Ledi Sayadaw. *Buddhist Philosophy of Relations* (*Paṭṭhānuddesa Dīpanī*). 1935. Reprint. Kandy: BPS, 1986.

Malalasekera, G.P. *The Pali Literature of Ceylon*. 1928. Reprint. Colombo: M.D. Gunasena, 1958.

Mizuno, Kogen. "Abhidharma Literature." *Encyclopaedia of Buddhism*. Fasc. 1. Government of Ceylon, 1961.

Ñāṇamoli, Bhikkhu, trans. *The Path of Purification* (*Visuddhimagga*). Kandy: BPS, 1975.

Nārada, U. *Guide to Conditional Relations*. Part 1. London: PTS, 1979.

Nyanaponika Thera. *Abhidhamma Studies*. Kandy: BPS, 1965. Essays focused mainly on the *Dhammasaṅgaṇī*.

Nyanatiloka Thera. *Guide through the Abhidhamma Piṭaka*. Kandy: BPS, 1971.

Perera, H.R. "Anuruddha (5)." *Encyclopaedia of Buddhism*. Fasc. 4. Government of Ceylon, 1965.

Van Gorkom, Nina. *Abhidhamma in Daily Life*. Bangkok: Dhamma Study Group, 1975.

Warder, A.K. *Indian Buddhism*. 2nd rev. ed. Delhi: Motilal Banarsidass, 1980.

Watanabe, Fumimaro. *Philosophy and its Development in the Nikāyas and Abhidhamma*. Delhi: Motilal Banarsidass, 1983.

Glossary
&
Index

PALI-ENGLISH GLOSSARY

akusala—unwholesome
anga—factor
ajjhatta—internal
ajjhattika—internal
aññamañña—mutuality (condition)
aññasamāna—ethically variable (mental factor)
aññātāvindriya—faculty of one who has final knowledge
aññindriya—faculty of final knowledge
ati-iṭṭha—extremely desirable
atiparitta—very slight (object)
atimahanta—very great (object)
atīta—past
attavāda—doctrine of self
atthapaññatti—concept-as-meaning
atthi—presence (condition)
adukkhamasukha—neither-painful-nor-pleasant (feeling)
adosa—non-hatred
addha—period (of time)
addhāna—duration
adhiṭṭhāna—(1) locus, foundation; (2) resolution
adhipati—predominant; predominance (condition)
adhimokkha—decision
anaññātaññassāmītindriya—faculty "I will know the unknown"
anattā—non-self
anantara—proximity (condition)
anāgata—future
anāgāmī—non-returner
anicca—impermanent
aniccatā—impermanence
aniṭṭha—undesirable
anipphanna—non-concretely produced (matter)
animitta—signless
aniyatayogī—unfixed adjunct
anupassanā—contemplation
anupādisesa—without residue remaining (Nibbāna element)
anuloma—conformity
anusaya—latent disposition
anussati—recollection
anottappa—fearlessness of wrongdoing
aparāpariyavedanīya—indefinitely effective (kamma)
apāyabhūmi—woeful plane
appaṭigharūpa—non-impinging matter
appaṇihita—desireless
appanā—absorption
appamaññā—illimitable
abyākata—(kammically) indeterminate
abhijjhā—covetousness
abhiññā—direct knowledge
amoha—non-delusion
arahatta—Arahantship
arahant—Arahant (liberated one)
ariya—noble, noble one
ariyasacca—noble truth
arūpa—immaterial
arūpāvacara—immaterial sphere
alobha—non-greed
avacara—sphere
avigata—non-disappearance (condition)

avijjā—ignorance
avinibbhogarūpa—inseparable material phenomena
avibhūta—obscure (object)
asankhata—unconditioned
asankhārika—unprompted (consciousness)
asaññasatta—non-percipient being
asāraka—coreless
asubha—foulness
asura—asura ("titan")
asekkha—one beyond training (i.e. an Arahant)
ahirika—shamelessness
ahetuka—rootless
ahosi—defunct (kamma)

ākāra—mode
ākāsa—space
ākāsānañcāyatana—base of infinite space
ākiñcaññāyatana—base of nothingness
āciṇṇa—habitual (kamma)
ādīnava—danger
āpātha—avenue (of sense)
āpo—water
āyatana—base
āyu, āyuppamāṇa—life-span
ārammaṇa—object
āruppa—immaterial (sphere or state)
ālambana—object
āloka—light
āvajjana—adverting
āsanna—death-proximate (kamma)
āsava—taint
āsevana—repetition (condition)

iṭṭha—desirable
iṭṭhamajjhatta—desirable-neutral
itthatta—femininity
idaṁsaccābhinivesa—dogmatic belief that "This alone is the truth"
iddhipāda—means to accomplishment
iddhividha—supernormal powers
indriya—faculty
iriyāpatha—bodily posture
issā—envy

ukkaṭṭha—superior (kamma)
uggaha—learning (sign)
ujjukatā—rectitude
utu—temperature
udayabbaya—rise and fall
uddhacca—restlessness
upakkilesa—imperfection (of insight)
upaghātaka—destructive (kamma)
upacaya—production
upacāra—access
upacchedaka—destructive (kamma)
upaṭṭhāna—awareness
upatthambaka—supportive (kamma)
upanissaya—decisive support (condition)
upapajjavedanīya—subsequently effective (kamma)
upapīḷaka—obstructive (kamma)
upādāna—clinging
upādārūpa—derivative matter
upādinnarūpa—clung-to matter
upekkhā—equanimity
uppāda—(1) arising; (2) arising (submoment)

ekaggatā—one-pointedness

ogha—flood
ojā—nutritive essence
ottappa—fear of wrongdoing
obhāsa—aura
omaka—inferior (kamma)
oḷārikarūpa—gross matter

kaṭattā—reserve (kamma)
kappa—aeon
kabaḷīkāra āhāra—edible food
kamma—kamma, action, deed

kammaññatā—wieldiness
kammaṭṭhāna—meditation subject
kammanimitta—sign of kamma
kammapatha—course of kamma
karuṇā—compassion
kalāpa—group
kasiṇa—kasina (meditation device)
kāma—(1) sense (sphere), sensuous (plane); (2) sensual (desire or pleasure)
kāmāvacara—sense sphere
kāya—body (physical or mental)
kāyaviññatti—bodily intimation
kāla—time
kālavimutta—independent of time
kicca—function
kiriya, kriyā—functional
kilesa—defilement
kukkucca—worry
kusala—wholesome

khaṇa—moment; sub-moment
khandha—aggregate
khaya—destruction

gati—destiny
gatinimitta—sign of destiny
gantha—knot
gandha—smell
garuka—weighty (kamma)
gocara—object
gocaraggāhika—taking objects
gocararūpa—objective matter
gotrabhū—change-of-lineage

ghāna—nose
ghāyana—smelling

cakkhu—eye
carita—temperament
citta—consciousness
cittavīthi—cognitive process
cittasantāna—stream of consciousness
cittuppāda—consciousness, act or state of consciousness
cuti—death
cetanā—volition
cetasika—mental factor

chanda—desire (to do or to attain)

janaka—productive (kamma)
jaratā—decay
jarāmaraṇa—decay-and-death
javana—javana (i.e. active phase of cognitive process)
jāti—birth
jivhā—tongue
jīvitarūpa—material phenomenon of life
jīvitindriya—life faculty
jhāna—jhāna (i.e. meditative absorption)
jhānanga—jhāna factor

ñāṇa—knowledge

ṭhāna—(1) stage; (2) presence (sub-moment)
ṭhiti—presence (sub-moment)

taṇhā—craving
tatramajjhattatā—neutrality of mind
tadārammaṇa—registration
tiracchānayoni—animal kingdom
tihetuka—triple rooted
tejo—fire

thīna—sloth

dasaka—decad
dassana— (1) seeing; (2) vision (as knowledge)
dāna—giving
diṭṭhadhammavedanīya—immediately effective (kamma)
diṭṭhi—view, wrong view
diṭṭhigata—wrong view
dibbacakkhu—divine eye
dibbasota—divine ear

dukkha—(1) suffering; (2) pain, painful (feeling)
deva—god
domanassa—displeasure
dosa—hatred
dvāra—door
dvāravimutta—door-freed
dvipañcaviññāṇa—two sets of five-fold sense consciousness

dhamma— (1) Dhamma (i.e. Buddha's teaching); (2) phenomenon, state; (3) mental object
dhammavicaya—investigation of states (enlightenment factor)
dhātu—element

natthi—absence (condition)
navaka—nonad
nānakkhaṇika—asynchronous (kamma condition)
nāma— (1) mind, mental; (2) name
nāmapaññatti—concept-as-name
nāmarūpa—mind-and-matter
nikanti—attachment
nipphanna—concretely produced (matter)
nibbāna—Nibbāna
nibbidā—disenchantment
nimitta—sign
niyatayogī—fixed adjunct
niyama—procedure
niraya—hell
nirodha—cessation
nirodhasamāpatti—attainment of cessation
nissaya—support (condition)
nīvaraṇa—hindrance
n'evasaññānāsaññāyatana—base of neither-perception-nor-non-perception

pakatūpanissaya—natural decisive support (condition)
pakiṇṇaka—(1) occasional (mental factor); (2) miscellaneous
paggaha—exertion
paccaya—condition
paccayasatti—conditioning force
paccayuppanna—conditionally arisen
paccavekkhaṇa—reviewing
paccupaṭṭhāna—manifestation
paccuppanna—present
pacchājāta—postnascence (condition)
pañcadvāra—five sense doors
pañcadvārāvajjana—five-sense-door adverting (consciousness)
paññatti—concept
paññā—wisdom
paññindriya—wisdom faculty
paṭigha—(1) aversion; (2) (sensory) impingement
paṭiccasamuppāda—dependent arising
paṭipadā—way
paṭibhāga—counterpart (sign)
paṭisankhā—reflective contemplation
paṭisandhi—rebirth-linking
paṭṭhāna—conditional relations
paṭhavī—earth
padaṭṭhāna—proximate cause
paracittavijānanā—knowledge of others' minds
paramattha—ultimate reality
parikamma—preliminary
pariggaha—discernment
paricchedarūpa—limiting material phenomenon (i.e. space)
pariññā—full understanding
paritta—(1) limited (i.e. sense sphere); (2) slight (object)
pavatta, pavatti—course of existence
pasādarūpa—sensitive matter
passaddhi—tranquillity
pahāna—abandoning
pāka—resultant

pāguññatā—proficiency
pīti—zest
puggala—individual
puñña—merit, meritorious
puthujjana—worldling
pubbenivāsānussati—recollection of past lives
purisatta—masculinity
purejāta—prenascence (condition)
peta—peta ("hungry ghost")
pettivisaya—sphere of petas

phala—fruit, fruition
phassa—contact
phusana—touching
phoṭṭhabba—tangible (object)

bala—power
bahiddhā—external
bāhira—external
bojjhanga—factor of enlightenment
bodhipakkhiyadhamma—requisite of enlightenment

bhanga—dissolution; dissolution (sub-moment)
bhaya—fear, fearful
bhava—existence
bhavanga—life-continuum
bhāvanā—meditation, development (of the eightfold path, or of calm and insight)
bhāvarūpa—sexual material phenomena
bhūtarūpa—essential matter
bhūmi—plane (of existence or of consciousness)

magga—path
magganga—path factor
macchariya—avarice
manasikāra—attention
manussa—human being
mano—mind
manodvāra—mind door
manodvārāvajjana—mind-door adverting (consciousness)
manodhātu—mind element
manoviññāṇadhātu—mind-consciousness element
manosañcetanā—mental volition
maraṇa—death
mahaggata—sublime
mahanta—great (object)
mahākiriya—great functional (consciousness)
mahākusala—great wholesome (consciousness)
mahābhūta—great essential (matter)
mahāvipāka—great resultant (consciousness)
māna—conceit
mānasa—consciousness
micchādiṭṭhi—wrong view
middha—torpor
muñcitukamyatā—desire for deliverance
muditā—appreciative joy
mudutā—malleability
mūla—root
mettā—loving-kindness
mogha—futile (cognitive process)
momūha—sheer delusion
moha—delusion

yoga—bond

rasa—(1) function; (2) taste
rāga—lust, attachment
rūpa—(1) matter, material phenomenon; (2) fine-material (sphere or plane); (3) visible form
rūpakalāpa—material group
rūpāvacara—fine-material sphere

lakkhaṇa—characteristic
lakkhaṇarūpa—characteristic of matter
lahutā—lightness

loka—world
lokiya—mundane
lokuttara—supramundane
lobha—greed

vacī—speech
vacīviññatti—vocal intimation
vaṭṭa—round of existence
vaṇṇa—colour
vatthu—(1) base; (2) entity
vavatthāna—analysis
vasitā—mastery
vāyāma—effort
vāyo—air
vikārarūpa—mutable matter
vigata—disappearance (condition)
vicāra—sustained application
vicikicchā—doubt
viññatti—intimation
viññāṇa—consciousness
viññāṇañcāyatana—base of infinite consciousness
vitakka—initial application
vinibbhogarūpa—separable material phenomena
vipassanā—insight
vipāka—result, resultant
vippayutta—dissociated from; dissociation (condition)
vibhūta—clear (object)
vimokkha—emancipation
vimokkhamukha—door to emancipation
virati—abstinence
viriya—energy
visaya—object
visuddhi—purification
vīthi—process
vīthicitta—consciousness belonging to a cognitive process
vīthimutta—process-freed (i.e. outside the cognitive process)
vīmaṁsā—investigation
vuṭṭhāna—emergence
vedanā—feeling
votthapana—determining
vohāra—conventional expression
vyāpāda—ill will

sa-upādisesa—with residue remaining (Nibbāna element)
saṁyojana—fetter
sakadāgāmī—once-returner
sankappa—intention
sankhata—conditioned
sankhāra—(1) formation; (2) mental formation (4th aggregate); (3) kammic formation; (4) prompting
sankhepa—group
sangaha—(1) compendium; (2) combination, inclusion
sacca—truth
sacchikiriya—realization
saññā—perception
sati—mindfulness
satipaṭṭhāna—foundation of mindfulness
sadda—sound
saddhā—faith
sanidassanarūpa—visible matter
santati—continuity
santīraṇa—investigating (consciousness), investigation
sandhi—connection
sappaccaya—with conditions
sappaṭigharūpa—impinging matter
sabhāva—intrinsic nature
samatha—calm
samanantara—contiguity (condition)
samādhi—concentration
samāpajjana—(act of) attainment
samāpatti—(meditative) attainment
samuṭṭhāna—origination; mode of origin

samudaya—origin (as noble truth)
sampaṭicchana—receiving
sampayutta—associated with; association (condition)
sampayoga—association
sammappadhāna—supreme effort
sammasana—comprehension (knowledge)
sammā-ājīva—right livelihood
sammākammanta—right action
sammādiṭṭhi—right view
sammāvācā—right speech
sammāvāyāma—right effort
sammāsankappa—right intention
sammāsati—right mindfulness
sammāsamādhi—right concentration
sammuti—conventional (reality or truth)
saḷāyatana—six sense bases
savana—hearing
sasankhārika—prompted (consciousness)
sahagata—accompanied by
sahajāta—conascence (condition)
sahita—together with
sahetuka—rooted, with roots
sādhāraṇa—universal, common
sāyana—tasting
sāsava—subject to taints
sīla—virtue
sīlabbataparāmāsa—adherence to rites and ceremonies
sukha—happiness, pleasure, pleasant (feeling)
sukhumarūpa—subtle matter
sugati—blissful (plane)
suññata—void
suddhāvāsa—Pure Abode
sekkha—trainee (i.e. three lower grades of noble disciples)
sota—ear
sota—stream
sotāpatti—stream-entry
sotāpanna—stream-enterer
sobhana—beautiful
somanassa—joy

hadayavatthu—heart-base
hasana—smiling
hasituppāda—smile-producing (consciousness)
hiri—shame
hetu—root

INDEX

All technical terms, except the few left untranslated, have been indexed under their English renderings, which will be found in the Pali-English Glossary preceding the Index. References are to chapter and section number, inclusive of both translation and explanatory guide. Numbers in parenthesis following the section number signify the number of the item in the numerical list found within the section referred to.

VI 9, 10, 14, 15, 17, 22; condition VIII 14, 27; functions V 18; order of ripening V 19; place of ripening V 21-26; round of VIII 8; time of ripening V 20. *See also* resultant; sign: of rebirth

kammic formation (*sankhāra*) V 37; VIII 3 (1, 2), 7, 8

kasina I 18-20, 22-24; VIII 30; IX 6, 19

knowledge (*ñāṇa*) I 13-17; II 25; and vision, purification by IX 34; insight IX 25, 32-33; of others' minds III 18; IX 21. *See also* wisdom

latent disposition (*anusaya*) VIII 9, 14

Ledi Sayadaw I 6, 21; III 13; IV 6, 12, 17; V 10-11, 18, 38; VIII 2, 27; IX 39

life-continuum (*bhavanga*) III 8 (2), 12, 13, 17, 18; IV 6, 12; V 10, 11, 13, 15, 17, 38, 40, 41; adventitious IV 18; function of III 8 (2), 9, 10

life faculty (*jīvitindriya*): mental II 2 (6); VII 18; physical V 34; VI 3; VII 18; VIII 24

life span (*āyuppamāṇa*) V 12, 14, 16, 34

lightness (*lahutā*): mental II 5 (10, 11); physical VI 4 (10), 14

loving-kindness (*mettā*) II 5, 7; IX 9

Mahā Dhammarakkhita Thera V 30

malleability (*mudutā*): mental II 5 (12, 13); physical VI 4 (10)

mango simile IV 6

masculinity (*purisatta*) VI 3 (4); VIII 24

matter (*rūpa*) I 2; II 1; IV 6; VI 1-29 *passim*; VII 1; VIII 3, 15, 16; classifications VI 6-8; enumeration VI 2-5; groups VI 16-22; origins VI 9-15; occurrence VI 23-29. *See also* mind (*nāma*): -and-matter

means to accomplishment (*iddhipāda*) VII 26

meditation (*bhāvanā*) I 18-20, 22-24, 26-28; V 23, 25, 26: IX 1-45 *passim*; subjects of (*kammaṭṭhāna*) IX 1, 2, 6-15

mental body (*nāmakāya*) II 5

mental factor (*cetasika*) I 2; II 1-30 *passim*; III 12, 16, 20; VII 1, 14, 23, 32-33; associations of II 10-17, 30; beautiful II 5-8, 15-16; combinations of II 18-29, 30; definition II 1; ethically variable II 2-3, 11-12; fixed and unfixed II 17; unwholesome II 4, 13-14

mental object (*dhammārammaṇa*) III 16, 17; VII 39

merit (*puñña*) V 24

mind (*nāma*) VIII 3 (3, 4), 13, 14, 15, 16, 17; -and-matter (°*rūpa*) I 3; VIII 3 (3, 4), 14, 17, 18; IX 30-31

mind (*mano*): base (°*āyatana*) VII 39; VIII 3 (4); door (°*dvāra*) I 10; III 12, 13; IV 4, 12; V 22, 24, 38; element (°*dhātu*) II 28; III 10, 14, 18, 21

mind, purification of (*cittavisuddhi*) IX 29

mindfulness (*sati*) II 5 (2); VII 27-28, 29, 31, 33; foundations of (°*paṭṭhāna*) VII 24, 31

moment (*khaṇa*) IV 6; VI 10, 11

mundane (*lokiya*) I 3, 25; II 15; VI 6

mutuality condition (*aññamaññapaccaya*) VIII 21

name (*nāma*) VIII 29

neither-perception-nor-non-perception, base of (*n'evasaññānāsaññāyatana*) I 22-24; V 7; IX 19

neutrality of mind (*tatramajjhattatā*) II 5 (7)

Nibbāna I 2, 3, 26-28; III 16, 17, 18; VI 30-32; VII 1, 39, 40; VIII 29; IX 34, 36, 37, 42

Noble Eightfold Path I 26-28; II 15; VII 30, 38, 40; IX 34

noble one (*ariya*) I 1, 26-28; IV 25; V 8, 40; IX 34, 38-41, 42

noble truth (*ariyasacca*) VII 38, 40; IX 34

non-concrete matter (*anipphannarūpa*) VI 2, 4

non-delusion (*amoha*) II 8; III 5-7. *See also* knowledge; wisdom

non-disappearance condition (*avigatapaccaya*) VIII 26

non-greed (*alobha*) II 5 (5); III 5-7

non-hatred (*adosa*) II 5 (6); III 5-7

non-percipient beings (*asaññasattā*) III 17; IV 28; V 8, 13, 31, 39, 40; VI 28; 29

non-returner (*anāgāmī*) I 26-28, 31; IV 22, 25, 26; V 6, 31; IX 40

non-self (*anattā*) IX 23, 32, 35, 36

nose (*ghāna*) VI 3 (2)

nothingness, base of (*ākiñcaññāyatana*) I 22-24; V 7; IX 19

nutriment (*āhāra*) VI 3 (7), 9, 13, 14, 15, 21, 22; VII 21; VIII 23

object (*ārammaṇa*) I 25; II 1; III 13, 16-19; IV 17; V 17; V 35-39, 41; VI 3; VIII 16, 17, 19; condition VIII 17, 27

SPECIAL ACKNOWLEDGEMENT

The publisher wishes to acknowledge the generous contributions of the following towards the publication of this book:

Sushila & Ranjan Jayasuriya of Canada
in loving memory of Dr. & Mrs. W.F. Jayasuriya
who encouraged the study and application
of the Abhidhamma in daily life

Ms. Hiranthi Jayasinghe of Canada
in loving memory of Mrs. Ransiri Menike Jayasinghe

Ms. Sandra Jeneliunas of U.S.A.
in memory of her teacher
Ven. Mahāthera Nārada

A group of Sri Lankan Buddhists
resident in Ontario, Canada

THE BUDDHIST PUBLICATION SOCIETY

The BPS is an approved charity dedicated to making known the Teaching of the Buddha, which has a vital message for people of all creeds. Founded in 1958, the BPS has published a wide variety of books and booklets covering a great range of topics. Its publications include accurate annotated translations of the Buddha's discourses, standard reference works, as well as original contemporary expositions of Buddhist thought and practice. These works present Buddhism as it truly is—a dynamic force which has influenced receptive minds for the past 2500 years and is still as relevant today as it was when it first arose. A full list of our publications will be sent upon request with an enclosure of U.S. $1.00 or its equivalent to cover air mail postage. Write to:

The Hony. Secretary
BUDDHIST PUBLICATION SOCIETY
P.O. Box 61
54, Sangharaja Mawatha
Kandy Sri Lanka